The Pocket Instructor

· ·

Literature

The Pocket Instructor

Literature

101 EXERCISES

FOR THE COLLEGE CLASSROOM

Edited by Diana Fuss and William A. Gleason

Princeton University Press

Princeton and Oxford

Published by Princeton University Press, 41 William Street, Princeton, New Jersey 08540
In the United Kingdom: Princeton University Press, 6 Oxford Street, Woodstock,
    Oxfordshire OX20 1TW

press.princeton.edu
    Cover image courtesy of Shutterstock.

"August 1968," copyright © 1968 by W.H. Auden; from *W. H. Auden Collected Poems*
by W. H. Auden. Used by permission of Random House, an imprint and division of
Penguin Random House LLC, and of Curtis Brown, Ltd. All rights reserved.

"Simile" from *In the Presence of the Sun* by N. Scott Momaday. Copyright © 2009
University of New Mexico Press.

Library of Congress Cataloging-in-Publication Data
The pocket instructor, literature : 101 exercises for the college classroom / edited by Diana Fuss,
William A. Gleason.
            pages cm
        Includes index.
        ISBN 978-0-691-15713-9 (hardback) — ISBN 978-0-691-15714-6 (paperback)
        1. Literature—Study and teaching (Higher). 2. Lesson planning. 3. Education—Curricula. I. Fuss,
Diana, 1960—
PN59.P57 2015
        807.1'1—dc23   2015001785

British Library Cataloging-in-Publication Data is available

This book has been composed in Garamond and Archer

Printed on acid-free paper. ∞

Printed in the United States of America

10 9 8 7 6 5 4 3 2

Contents

· ·

Introduction

. . . .

This book is a collection of undergraduate teaching activities in the field of literary studies. We offer here 101 exercises for the college classroom, solicited from scholars and teachers around the United States (and beyond). Our contributors come from small private colleges, local community colleges, and large state or private universities. All have contributed a favorite literature exercise—one that has been tested and refined in the college classroom and proven a hit with undergraduates. As our volume title suggests, *The Pocket Instructor* offers an array of successful classroom activities: activities you can pull out of your back pocket whenever you may be in need of new teaching ideas or general inspiration.

Every exercise in these pages is designed to get students talking, thinking, and learning and affirms the central philosophy behind the volume: active learning pedagogy. Compared to traditional pedagogy, active learning pedagogy places greater emphasis on student communication and collaboration. This student-centered approach to teaching promotes more decentralized learning, often in the form of small-group work (discussion pods, warm-up activities, class debates, role-playing, problem sets, teamwork, group presentations). Active learning classrooms favor exercises that develop critical thinking skills, like brainstorming ideas, formulating questions, or solving problems. Such approaches can involve activities on a small scale (students listing items on a blackboard) or on a large scale (students collectively working on a case study). What active learning exercises all have in common is a core commitment to students working side by side, under the guidance of an instructor, not simply to receive knowledge but to discover, create, analyze, or apply it. The main purpose of this collection is to bring together, in one accessible volume, exercises that honor the importance of active learning in the college literature classroom.

THE ACTIVE LEARNER

Teaching practices and philosophies have changed dramatically in the decades since we began teaching. Most strikingly, teaching has become a far more interactive enterprise. While active learning emerged long before the World Wide Web and social media, the availability of new technologies in particular has fundamentally altered how students learn. Today's college students, members of the "Net generation," who have come of age in a multimedia and multitasking era, expect a more stimulating and engaged learning environment, and rightly so.[1] Teachers are now faced with the challenge of creating not just more dynamic teaching exercises but more meaningful ones, exercises that do more than convey facts and figures already easily accessed with the tap of a finger.

Behind the current movement from teacher-centered to student-centered pedagogy is a much larger historical shift from an industrial economy to an information economy. Whereas an industrial economy required a hierarchical transmission of information from teacher to student, an information economy ushers in a world where information is already readily available. Students now must negotiate a learning environment of complex networks and relationships, a world in which knowledge is no longer discrete but embedded, no longer revealed but discovered.[2] This larger historical shift from producing market goods to manipulating informational networks is changing not just what we teach but how we teach. These days the work environment is frequently an extension of the learning environment. Our capacities for social interaction, group problem-solving, and intellectual play, along with a willingness to keep on learning, innovating, and implementing, have become core conditions for success in a rapidly evolving and increasingly networked global economy.[3]

Active learning pedagogy prepares students to work more creatively, and frequently more collaboratively, to tackle and solve problems while negotiating differing opinions and diverse worldviews. Educators have understood this teaching practice in both general and specific terms. In perhaps its simplest definition, active learning "involves students in doing things and thinking about the things they are doing."[4] In its fuller definition, active learning provides "opportunities for students to meaningfully *talk* and *listen*, *write*, *read*, and *reflect* on the content, ideas, issues, and concerns of an academic subject."[5] Whether broadly or narrowly defined, a vast body of research has revealed that active learning exercises work significantly better than traditional teaching methods—methods based on the old industrial knowledge-transmission model that relies heavily on the conventional lecture format. Since the late twentieth century, extensive research on pedagogy (nearly six hundred studies by 1990 alone) has consistently shown that students at all levels not only learn more from active learning exercises but also retain what they learn longer.[6]

Studies have also demonstrated that active learning exercises create more comfortable learning spaces for many different types of students, including unacknowledged or alienated students who feel more welcome in peer learning environments, women and minority students who perform better in collaborative rather than competitive classrooms, and shy students who feel more at ease talking in small groups.[7] Enhanced experience and understanding of diversity is one particularly significant side benefit of active learning classrooms. Another important bonus: students and teachers alike are reminded that honing and improving oral skills, and not just writing skills, is a vital component of critical thinking. Rather than remain largely silent or passive, students exposed to active learning exercises have regular opportunities to practice and develop their oral proficiency.

Designing and incorporating into our teaching more interactive activities, in which students learn not just from us but from each other, requires a conceptual shift in how we understand the classroom itself. The classroom becomes less a lecture space and more a learning studio or workshop, a place for students to actively practice their reading, writing, reasoning, and other abilities and to do so not in isolation but in groups. Anyone who has spent time in the college classroom already knows that students working together bring a different kind of energy and focus to the classroom. Undergraduates often learn best when they learn from each other. But as the exercises in this volume attest, such learning activities need to be carefully set up and closely supervised. Active learning holds both teachers and students accountable for the open-ended intellectual activities that take place in an organized and supportive environment. Striking this important balance—between too much freedom, on the one hand, and too much regimentation, on the other hand—is the key to a successful active learning exercise. The aim is to promote intellectually adventurous critical thinking guided from the start by a clearly stated learning goal.

"Active learning," which sometimes also goes under the names "engaged learning," "collaborative learning," or "deep learning," has been around for much longer than its name. The assumption that educators have only recently discovered the many benefits of interactive learning may not tell the whole story.[8] It has never been quite the case that college teachers have concentrated solely on conveying information to students; in discussion sections, seminars, and assignments, faculty have long experimented with creative learning exercises even beyond the familiar student oral presentation. Diana remembers from college a small-group assignment to prepare, present, and revise a contemporary poetry syllabus. And Bill recalls one of his college classes being asked to insert themselves imaginatively into individual lines from Shakespeare plays in order to understand the impact of character on tone and diction. Significantly, these are the classroom exercises that we have never forgotten (and that may well have decided our future careers).

It is important to recognize that while the exercises featured in this volume include new ideas for interactive teaching and learning, they also represent the collective wisdom of generations of teachers dedicated to engaging their students in fresh and inventive ways. Some of these favorite literature exercises have been handed down from teacher to teacher over decades. Some are much newer and reflect changes in classroom technology (the availability of Blackboard or the use of laptops) or recent evolutions in literature itself (the emergence of graphic novels or the popularity of slam poetry). Our goal has been to gather together in one place the best of these literary exercises and make them available to a wide audience.

THE LITERATURE CLASSROOM

New teachers can find a number of useful teaching handbooks to ease their way into the classroom. The most popular of these guides—Wilbert Mc-Keachie's *Teaching Tips: Strategies, Research, and Theory for College and University Teachers*, 14th edition (2014), Anne Curzan and Lisa Damour's *First Day to Final Grade: A Graduate Student's Guide to Teaching*, 3rd edition (2011), and Barbara Gross Davis's *Tools for Teaching*, 2nd edition (2009), all periodically revised and reissued since their original dates of publication—have excellent pieces of general advice, including tips for leading discussion and ideas for organizing lesson plans.[9] None, however, focus on what new teachers often need most: a comprehensive set of discipline-specific exercises to use in the classroom.

Within the field of literary studies, *Teaching Literature* (2003), by our former colleague Elaine Showalter, is especially helpful for its reflections on many important aspects of teaching that too often go undiscussed: "the anxiety dreams, the students who won't talk or can't talk, the days when we can't talk ourselves."[10] Our volume differs in focus by offering not general teaching anecdotes but detailed teaching recipes. This volume also departs from the Modern Language Association's Approaches to Teaching World Literature, a series that focuses primarily on individual literary texts (for example, *Approaches to Teaching Dickens's "David Copperfield"*). Containing essays rather than exercises, the MLA volumes usefully identify structures and themes within the text, review available editions and works of criticism, and provide biographies and chronologies. While some of the ideas in the "Approaches" section of this long-standing series might be convertible into specific classroom activities, they are not presented in the user-friendly format we offer here, nor are they broadly conceived as active learning exercises.

The following pages present specific interactive exercises pitched directly to the literature classroom. With a focus on dialogue and reflection, conversation and cooperation, these exercises demonstrate a variety of ways teachers of literature might both cover course content and help students actively formulate questions and develop skills. The opposition between old "content-based" teaching and new "skill-based" teaching is, in our minds, largely a specious one. It is impossible to do one without the other. In the words of cognitive psychologist Daniel Willingham, "deep knowledge" may be our goal but "shallow knowledge" will always come first. Thanks to the new brain research on how we learn, we now know that the things we value most in active learning, skills like problem solving and complex reasoning, are actually closely linked to the information retained in our long-term memories.[11]

For this reason we have sought to offer exercises that are both content rich and adjustable—exercises with enough options to satisfy any literature instructor teaching across a range of genres and periods, to majors or non-majors. If you are in the market for a good exercise on how to teach poetic scansion, or narrative voice, or dramatic situation; if you are wondering how to get students excited about *The Canterbury Tales*, *Paradise Lost*, or *The Waste Land*; or if you are searching for ways to integrate noncanonical, interdisciplinary, or cross-cultural materials into your literature classroom, then this book is specifically for you.

This is the book, in other words, that we wish we had had when we first started our own teaching careers. Our goal in assembling it—from soliciting the individual exercises to deciding how to organize them into useful, discrete sections—has been to capture, collate, and codify those unique disciplinary strategies that make teaching literature a distinct enterprise, not at all the same as leading a discussion on labor economics, running a lab on chemical synthesis, or conducting a workshop on language instruction. While different academic departments teach some of the same skills—critical thinking chief among them—the strategies for teaching both content and method can vary widely across disciplines. Equally important, they can vary considerably across fields within the same discipline. In literary studies a Socratic dialogue approach that might work brilliantly in a fiction class on characterization can fail miserably in a poetry lesson on ekphrasis.

This volume suggests ways to teach literature *as* literature more effectively. The exercises featured here have all been selected for their adaptability—their usefulness for teaching more than a single author or a single text. But you will also find among them useful approaches for teaching the idiosyncrasies of Geoffrey Chaucer's language or Alexander Pope's couplets, William Shakespeare's soliloquies or Robert Browning's dramatic monologues, Jane Austen's beginnings or Nella Larsen's endings, Oscar Wilde's aphorisms or N. Scott Momaday's metaphors. Although most of the textual examples are drawn from literature in English or in translation, almost all of the exercises are appropriate for teaching literature in other languages as well. Several of the exercises are also designed to help students engage with critical and literary theory, or can be adapted to theoretical texts.

Good teachers know that, in the classroom, process is as important as content, which is why you'll also find here a variety of methods and approaches, everything from exercises that deploy classic close-reading aids (circle, underline, annotate, imitate) to exercises that invite creative visualization techniques (write, draw, map, design). You'll even find exercises that get students on their feet (debate, declaim, stage, perform), a process that truly brings out the "active" in active learning.

All of the exercises are also compatible with many of the classroom assessment techniques you may currently be incorporating into your lesson plans. Students who have already written short response papers or one-sentence summaries, for example, will be more than ready to dive into the active and practical exercises that populate this volume. You can also use common assessment techniques at the end of a lesson or a unit to gauge the success of these exercises at promoting better learning, or simply to get student feedback on the exercises.[12] One of the most immediate and useful forms of assessment is to ask students directly, in the class time remaining, what they thought of the exercise itself: What did they learn or not learn from this activity? What was its greatest benefit or limitation? What are some changes they might recommend for repeating the lesson in the future? Can they imagine a useful follow-up exercise? Inviting students as a group to assess critically what you have just asked them to do constitutes an active learning exercise in its own right and is illustrated by many of the exercises in this volume.

Whether you are a new teacher finding your footing in the college classroom or a veteran faculty member on the lookout for new ideas, we hope *The Pocket Instructor* will be a useful resource at any moment you might need it. Designed for classes, seminars, and discussion sections, most of these classroom exercises take fifty minutes or less (nearly half can be completed in thirty minutes) and are versatile and flexible enough to be adjusted for different class sizes and for students with different skill sets. For example, a small-class exercise designed as a full-group discussion might, for a larger class, be reconfigured into a pair or small-group activity. (We define "small group" as three to five students working collaboratively.) Or an exercise designed for beginners might be combined with a second exercise of moderate difficulty to fashion a more challenging lesson plan. The best classroom learning activities tend to lend themselves readily to creative revision and resourceful repurposing. These are the exercises we have been most interested in showcasing.

The Pocket Instructor is not a guide to lecturing in the classroom. Though many of these active learning exercises require that the instructor introduce or model the activity at the beginning, summarize or clarify what the class has learned at the end, or provide some necessary orientation or information along the way, they do not rely on the traditional lecture format. We still believe in the large lecture format, for reasons both pedagogical and practical. There is a case to be made for the power of lectures to model for students the learning skills they seek to acquire.[13] And few schools, in any case, have the money, space, or resources to dispense entirely with traditional lecture courses. That said, it is worth remembering that lecturing and active learning strategies are not in fact mutually exclusive and that the two can even work in tandem. Spot writing, pair conversations, polls, clickers, and smart phones are all popular strategies for involving students more actively in even the largest of lecture halls.[14]

For nonlecture classes (the focus of this volume) we suspect that many teachers of literature conduct their lessons in the same eclectic way we often do. For example, we might begin a class with some formal remarks to set things up or cover a bit of ground, then segue into a small-group or other collaborative exercise, next reconvene the class for a full-group discussion, and finally bring things to a close with a quick summary, a final question, or a brief look at what's to come. Variety and pacing are the keys to holding student attention and making the most of classroom time. Yet while there may be more effective ways to teach, there is still no single correct way to teach. So much depends on our learning objectives, our class sizes, and even our physical classrooms, which are not always friendly environments for student dialogue and group activities.

At our own institution, the classrooms—many with heavy tables, bolted chairs, or tiered floors—are not properly set up for active learning exercises. And yet (perhaps like you) we try the exercises anyway, inevitably teaching not so much with the room as against it. Ideally, a classroom environment that encourages engaged student learning contains movable, reconfigurable furniture that can be instantly arranged and rearranged to accommodate small-group work. But in the absence of such popular "flex" rooms, nearly all of the exercises offered here can still be successfully executed by having students turn to the person next to them, reposition themselves, stand at the board, or move around the room. While most classroom designs have not caught up with the new pedagogy, we have found that exercises that involve students actively talking and learning from each other can still be pulled off, even in the most traditional of classrooms, with a little patience and creativity.

THE CLASSROOM EXERCISES

The Pocket Instructor is composed of eleven sections, each preceded by a short introduction that describes the general approach of that section and also explains how the exercises are organized within it. (We recommend that you read these section introductions before picking out a specific exercise to try.) We begin with a section called "Discussions," since getting students talking is often the primary goal of active learning exercises. We follow up with another foundational section, "Essentials," which identifies a handful of exercises that seem to work well in any literature classroom, whether the focus is genre, period, or theme. That said, because genre so often organizes literature courses—and in many cases determines which type of classroom activities are likely to succeed—we have allotted the largest sections of the volume to the three most frequently taught literary genres: stories, poems, and plays. These sections form the core of the volume, with fifteen exercises each, ranging from lessons appropriate for introductory survey courses to activities suitable for advanced courses. The six remaining sections focus attention on a range of other important topics, scales, and approaches. "Genres" and "Canons" explore the boundaries and conventions of literary forms and literary histories. "Words" and "Styles" tackle the nuances and subtleties of authorial expression. "Pictures" and "Objects" probe the rich visual and material contexts of imaginative literature. If it happens in a literary text, one of the exercises in these eleven sections will help your students understand it.

Each of the 101 entries assumes a two-part structure: precise step-by-step directions ("Exercise") followed by more general ruminations ("Reflections"). Combining practical details with experiential advice, authors first share specific instructions for how to execute the actual lesson plans and then provide a peek into how things went in their classrooms. In concise, readable format, entries offer additional guideposts: clear rationales for the exercise itself, useful tips on what to do or what to avoid, helpful recommendations on what texts might work best, and thoughtful reflections on what students learned. Some entries even suggest variations on the main exercise—alternative approaches that, with a slight shift in method, might also work well for a different student group or pedagogical purpose.

All entries begin with a tagline that briefly describes the nature and purpose of the exercise: a collaborative exercise for finding the keywords in a novel ("Word Clouds"), an introductory exercise for listening to the distinctive sound of poetry ("Close Listening"), a slowing-down exercise for teaching the importance of style ("The One-Liner"). Immediately after the opening taglines, you will find the following nine navigational keys:

Genre (any, fiction, poetry, drama, prose)
Course Level (any, introductory, intermediate, advanced)
Student Difficulty (easy, moderate, hard)
Teacher Preparation (low, medium, high)
Class Size (any, small, medium, large)
Semester Time (any, first day, early, midterm, late, last day, exam review, all semester)
Writing Component (none, before class, in class, after class, optional)
Close Reading (none, low, medium, high)
Estimated Time (minutes, hours, full class)

These keys help identify the practical requirements of each exercise, and help you efficiently locate the type of exercise for which you may be searching.

For class size we have calculated a small class as one to fifteen students, a medium class as sixteen to thirty students, and a large class as more than thirty students. Roughly half the exercises are suitable for any class size; the rest work best with classes that are small or medium sized. The Estimated Time key denotes classroom time only and does not include the time it might take for students to complete homework or for groups to meet outside of class. Along with the Student Difficulty key, the Estimated Time key should also be considered more an estimate than a promise. Only you know your group, and only you can anticipate how long your students might need for the exercise and how easy or difficult it might be for them. These keys are intended to make that estimate easier.

Along with the keys that begin each exercise, cross-indexes at the end of each of the last nine sections offer additional pathways for exploring the volume. We have placed each of the exercises in the section where it most comfortably belongs, but many exercises are versatile enough to be cross-listed in multiple sections. For instance, not all the fiction exercises are in the "Stories" section; you will find many additional suitable options spread throughout the volume, in places like "Words," "Styles," or "Pictures." These cross-indexes guide you to exercises that offer further activities for any section that sparks your interest. After the last section, four more cross-indexes are designed to help instructors plan ahead, highlighting exercises where timing matters (full semester, first day, last day) or exercises that require students to prepare writing before class. At the end of the volume you will also find a general index that includes literary authors, works, and related topics mentioned in the exercises.

TEACHING CLOSE READING

If there is a dominant theme across this collection of exercises, it is the many different and creative ways to teach close reading. Close reading is the art of attending to the details of a text (its structure, diction, tone, syntax, sound, imagery, theme), often as a way to identify or understand its larger cultural, historical, or literary contexts. This approach, first developed as a practice in the 1920s by Cambridge scholars I. A. Richards and William Empson before making its way across the Atlantic, remains central to the literature classroom of the twenty-first century.[15] Indeed, the skill of close reading is uniquely suited to a postindustrial world defined by networks, connections, and relationships. Finding patterns and identifying themes is the very work of close reading, for which students of literature have a special affinity and training. One might assume that teaching the art of close reading always happens in the same fashion, but in fact there are many approaches to scanning a line, mapping a structure, or identifying a theme. The exercises in this volume capture just some of the imaginative ways that close reading might be deployed as a constructive critical practice.

The practice of reading closely is so pervasive across literary genres, and so common a thread in active learning exercises, that at first we wondered if we even needed a separate key for it. In the end we decided in favor of a Close Reading key to recognize and highlight, across exercises, the great diversity and varying degrees of close reading deployed in the literature classroom, techniques that might extend anywhere from registering the significance of a text's general external appearance ("Judge a Book by Its Cover") to attending to its every internal punctuation mark ("Punctuation Matters"). Some exercises in this volume are entirely close reading activities that lean heavily on "micro" analysis of single texts ("The Blow Up" or "The Cut Up"), while others widen out to encompass more "macro" strategies for understanding the formal intricacies and patterns across texts and periods ("First Paragraphs" or "Moving Scenes"). Still others seek to complement or counterbalance formalist reading practices by inviting students to contextualize either historically ("Digital Literacy") or culturally ("Spin the Globe, Shakespeare"). There are even some exercises in this collection that require no close reading at all, focusing instead on what happens either before ("Reading without Reading") or after ("Build-A-Canon") engagement with the text proper. In the final analysis, however, few exercises in the literature classroom are very far from the details of language, style, or voice that mark a text as "literary." Judging from the sheer volume of exercises in this collection that rely on the technique of annotation or other forms of explication, literary studies continue to put a high premium on close reading as a core foundational skill for the understanding and interpretation of texts.

Whichever activities you use, you will find in these entries not hard-and-fast rules but creative and crafty inspiration—prompts for pedagogical experimentation and innovation in your own classroom. We invite you to try these exercises as they are, to reimagine them for your own audience, or to use them as incentives to pilot something new. No one owns a good teaching exercise; favorite classroom activities are not copyrighted but shared. As teaching seminars and teaching centers continue to crop up in colleges and universities around the country, and as the profession rededicates itself to the fundamentals of good teaching, now seems the appropriate time for all of us to share favorite lesson plans on a larger scale.

NOTES

1. Scott Carlson, "The Net Generation Goes to College," *Chronicle of Higher Education* 52.7 (October 7, 2005), A34–A37.

2. On the movement from an industrial economy to an information economy and its particular influence on the classroom, see Paul Cornell's "The Impact of Changes in Teach-

ing and Learning on Furniture and the Learning Environment," *New Directions for Teaching and Learning* 2002.92 (2002), 33–42. As he marks this important historical change, Cornell identifies additional pedagogical shifts—from directed learning to facilitated learning, passive learning to active learning, learning content only to learning content and process, and working alone to working alone and together.

3. For more on the new learning paradigms emerging in the Information Age, see Daniel Araya and Michael A. Peters, eds., *Education in the Creative Economy: Knowledge and Learning in the Age of Innovation* (New York: Peter Lang, 2010). Of particular note: Greg Hearn and Ruth Bridgstock, "Education for the Creative Economy: Innovation, Transdisciplinarity, and Networks" (93–116), and Patrick Whitney, "Learning in the Creative Economy" (447–68).

4. Charles C. Bonwell and James A. Eison, *Active Learning: Creating Excitement in the Classroom*. ASHE-ERIC Higher Education Report No. 1 (Washington, DC: George Washington University, School of Education and Human Development, 1991), 2.

5. Chet Meyers and Thomas B. Jones, *Promoting Active Learning: Strategies for the College Classroom* (San Francisco: Jossey-Bass, 1993), 6.

6. As Meyers and Jones rightly note, "we know that unless students actually use and appropriate ideas and information, they will not retain them" (34). For a useful survey of the early research on active learning, see R. T. Johnson and D. W. Johnson, "An Overview of Cooperative Learning," in *Creativity and Collaborative Learning*, ed. J. Thousand, A. Villa, and A. Nevin (Baltimore: Brookes Press, 1994), 31–44. More recent endorsements of active learning pedagogy include S. D. Brookfield and S. Preskill, *Discussion as a Way of Teaching: Tools and Techniques for Democratic Classrooms* (San Francisco: Jossey-Bass, 1999); L. D. Fink, *Creating Significant Learning Experiences: An Integrated Approach to Designing College Courses* (San Francisco: Jossey-Bass, 2003); Ken Bain, *What the Best College Teachers Do* (Cambridge, MA: Harvard University Press, 2004); Elizabeth F. Barkley, K. Patricia Cross, and Claire Howell Major, *Collaborative Learning Techniques: A Handbook for College Faculty* (San Francisco: Jossey-Bass, 2004); J. C. Bean, *Engaging Ideas: A Professor's Guide to Integrating Writing, Critical Thinking, and Active Learning in the Classroom*, 2nd ed. (San Francisco: Jossey-Bass, 2011); and Maryellen Weimer, *Learner-Centered Teaching: Five Key Changes to Practice*, 2nd ed. (San Francisco: Jossey-Bass, 2013).

7. See Barbara Gross Davis, "Diversity and Complexity in the Classroom: Considerations of Race, Ethnicity, and Gender," in her *Tools for Teaching*, 2nd ed. (San Francisco: Jossey-Bass, 2009), 39–51.

8. For an excellent review of the most influential scientific research on cognition, learning, and teaching, see James G. Greeno, Allan M. Collins, and Lauren B. Resnick, "Cognition and Learning," in *Handbook of Educational Psychology*, ed. David C. Berliner and Robert C. Calfee (New York: Macmillan, 1996), 15–46. And for a more recent study of learning techniques based on this research (techniques like summarizing, highlighting, rereading, and identifying keywords), see John Dunlosky, Katherine A. Rawson, Elizabeth J. Marsh, Mitchell J. Nathan, and Daniel T. Willingham, "Improving Students' Learning with Effective Learning Techniques: Promising Directions from Cognitive and Educational Psychology," *Association for Psychological Science* 14.1 (2013), 4–58.

9. Wilbert J. McKeachie and Marilla Svinicki, *McKeachie's Teaching Tips: Strategies, Research, and Theory for College and University Teachers*, 14th ed. (Belmont, CA: Wadsworth, Cengage Learning, 2014; orig. pub. 1950); Anne Curzan and Lisa Damour, *First Day to Final*

Grade: A Graduate Student's Guide to Teaching, 3rd ed. (Ann Arbor: University of Michigan Press, 2011; orig. pub. 2000); and Barbara Gross Davis's *Tools for Teaching*, 2nd ed. (San Francisco: Jossey-Bass Publishers, 2009; orig. pub. 2001).

10. Elaine Showalter, *Teaching Literature* (Oxford: Blackwell, 2003), vii.

11. Daniel T. Willingham, *Why Don't Students Like School? A Cognitive Scientist Answers Questions about How the Mind Works and What It Means for the Classroom* (San Francisco: Jossey-Bass, 2009), 95–97.

12. For a thorough discussion of the philosophy and practice of classroom assessment technique (CAT), including fifty sample CATs, see Thomas A. Angelo and K. Patricia Cross, *Classroom Assessment Techniques: A Handbook for College Teachers*, 2nd ed. (San Francisco: Jossey-Bass, 1993). And for a more recent discussion of how rubrics might be used in classroom assessment, see Dannell D. Stevens and Antonia J. Levi, *Introduction to Rubrics: An Assessment Tool to Save Grading Time, Convey Effective Feedback, and Promote Student Learning*, 2nd ed. (Sterling, VA: Stylus Publishing, 2012).

13. Abigail Walthausen, "Don't Give Up on the Lecture," *Atlantic Monthly* (November 21, 2013), available in the archives of the *Atlantic*, http://theatlantic.com/education, last accessed February 23, 2015.

14. For additional ideas on making lectures more interactive, see Frank Heppner, *Teaching the Large College Class: A Guidebook for Instructors with Multitudes* (San Francisco: Jossey-Bass, 2007), especially chapters 5 ("Using Media Effectively") and 6 ("Auditorium Classroom Activities"), 67–98, and Linda B. Nilson, "Making the Lecture a Learning Experience," in her *Teaching at Its Best: A Research-Based Resource for College Instructors*, 3rd ed. (San Francisco: Jossey-Bass, 2010), 113–25.

15. See I. A. Richards, *Principles of Literary Criticism* (New York: Harcourt, Brace, 1924), and *Practical Criticism: A Study of Literary Judgment* (New York: Harcourt, Brace, & World, 1929), and William Empson, *Seven Types of Ambiguity* (London: Chatto and Windus, 1930), three founding texts in the history of close reading. A recent reconsideration of the discontinuous evolution of close reading in the British and American traditions reminds us that we may know much less about the early philosophies of close reading practices than we think we do. It was not the case that literary critics like I. A. Richards or William Empson idolized the text at the expense of authors, readers, and contexts; on the contrary, their experiments in textual close reading sought to shed light on these very subjects. See Joseph North's interesting "What's 'New Critical' about 'Close Reading'?: I. A. Richards and His New Critical Reception," *New Literary History* 44.1 (Winter 2013), 141–57.

DISCUSSIONS

Active learning almost always starts with getting students talking. The exercises in this opening section—which include several classic activities with time-honored track records—are designed to do just that. Ranging from a simple around-the-room discussion starter (with a twist) that will work in any classroom, to more complex and in some cases multistage group activities, these exercises are designed to train students in the critical skills that make for effective, even transformative, classroom conversation: how to enter a discussion, how to listen to your peers, how to frame a useful question, how to develop a supportable argument, and how to work together to create an illuminating analytical synthesis.

The section begins with three general, easily adaptable exercises. "The Sixty Second Game" and "Fishbowl" involve everyone quickly and help normalize a discussion-based classroom in which all are counted on to contribute, while "Read, Reread, Close Read" creates a community of careful readers through close listening. All three exercises model discussion as a collaborative activity rather than a sequence of loosely related comments funneled through the instructor. The next three activities use the students' own questions to organize discussion, whether those questions are prepared ahead of time, as in "Put the Question" and "It's Time We Talked," or generated during class itself, as in "Reverse Entropy." Each exercise in this set also helps students recognize what makes a good question in the first place. The final two activities, "Debate" and "Leader, Skeptic, Scribe," turn from pointed questions to arguable answers, asking students to produce and defend interpretive claims about literary texts. Adaptable to any genre and almost any class size, these eight exercises will help turn even the quietest students into lively, engaged participants.

The Sixty Second Game

Vanessa L. Ryan

A classic around-the-room discussion starter with a twist.

Genre: *any*
Course Level: *any*
Student Difficulty: *easy*
Teacher Preparation: *low*
Class Size: *small*
Semester Time: *any, especially midterm*
Writing Component: *optional*
Close Reading: *none to low*
Estimated Time: *20 minutes*

EXERCISE

Bring a timer to class—a kitchen timer with a bell, or a phone or tablet with a timer application—and introduce your students to "The Sixty Second Game." In this classic "one minute around the table" discussion starter, each student has exactly sixty seconds to comment on the day's reading: no more, no less. The twist is the timer: even if a student is in the middle of a sentence when the bell rings, move on to the next person. Students who complete their comments before the clock is up can recite the alphabet to finish the time (though students usually find they have another thought to share instead).

After you explain the ground rules, invite the students to use their sixty seconds to discuss their favorite or most challenging moment, make a connection to another reading in the course, or comment on a previous student's reflection. Go around the room in order, so that everyone knows when he or she is next. As each student speaks, write a keyword or phrase on the board that captures a salient aspect of each contribution. Group the comments as you record them, underlining observations that are made multiple times, but do not interject your own responses: let the students do all the talking until everyone has had a chance to speak.

Once all the contributions are on the board, open discussion for follow-up comments. Now your own voice can emerge as well. If you like, continue to use the board to track the discussion. At the end of class, return to the board to show students how their insights took shape: pull out the most valuable shared interests, highlighting the larger claims that emerged from their original comments.

REFLECTIONS

This exercise adds a gamelike element to the classroom, and shifts the energy from the instructor to the students. The buzzer makes the exercise fun and leads to a fair amount of laughter; I find that students feel a shared camaraderie as they fight the clock and are "saved by the bell." The key is for the instructor to refrain from speaking for the first twenty minutes or so of class. (The length will vary depending on how many students you have; for larger classes, you can shorten the time for each initial comment to forty-five or even thirty seconds.) Putting keywords and phrases on the board as each student speaks validates and reinforces each student's comment. (For beginning students, it also models the process of note taking.) It is essential to write something on the board for each student.

This exercise is particularly successful when you anticipate a set of groupings in which the initial comments might fall, and then use different quadrants of the board to record those groupings. (For example, you might reserve one quadrant for observations about form, another for comments about themes, another for connections to other works, and so on.) This will also allow you to add any topic you think the discussion has missed, or to dedicate one area of the board to an aspect of the text you want to concentrate on for the rest of the class hour. Anticipating these groupings helps you not only to organize the comments but also to demonstrate later to students how their larger claims took shape. Students are always surprised when you show them that what looks like a messy board actually has an underlying structure, which helps them see that even a freewheeling discussion leads to broader insights.

For example, in a discussion of Sigmund Freud's *Dora: A Case of Hysteria* in a senior seminar, "The Sixty Second Game" allowed students to voice their initial reactions to the work—some impassioned—and begin the complex work of understanding and analyzing together, without my intervention. As we went around the room, students began with their first responses, particularly what they saw as Freud's coercive interpretations of Dora. Students quickly turned the discussion to consider questions of method, interpretation, and narrative technique, especially Freud's storytelling. Each time a student echoed a thought already on the board, I underlined the original comment. When a student mentioned a central term of psychoanalysis, I put a box around it to mark it as a key term ("case study," "transference," "unconscious"). After allowing additional time for follow-up comments, I began by reviewing the key terms in boxes, adding one ("dream work"): the board showed that as a group, the students had together identified the central concepts that structured Freud's text.

During the exercise, I had written comments on Freud's interpretations of Dora on one side of the board, and comments capturing our interpretations of Freud and his method on the other. On both sides, I put more negative comments on the top and more positive comments on the bottom. I was then able to "reveal" the parallels between Freud's dream work and our interpretive reading process simply by drawing arrows connecting both sides of the board. The top and bottom halves of the board also showed us that Freud's reading of Dora and our readings of Freud were both—not unlike Dora herself—participating in a process of identification and resistance. Students left class with ownership over a key insight into the way analysis, whether psychoanalytic or literary, is a constructive process.

"The Sixty Second Game" achieves a number of important goals: all students participate, long-winded students learn to be concise, and reserved students learn to expand on their comments. It can be used at any time in the course but often works best at midsemester or after, when students feel confident about the nature and direction of the course. For a particularly reserved group of students, you could add a sixty-second prewriting component before starting the exercise. "The Sixty Second Game" can be a great way to clear the air, before heading into more structured discussion, for texts that students have strong opinions about (for example, George Orwell's *Nineteen Eighty-Four* or the conclusion to George Eliot's *Middlemarch*). It also works particularly well with capacious and challenging works: one of my best experiences using "The Sixty Second Game" was in a class on Samuel Beckett's *Waiting for Godot* in a first-year seminar. I have found that students often take pictures of the board at the end of class, amazed and excited by what they have come up with.

Fishbowl √

Ellen M. Bayer

A small-group exercise in which students take turns at the center—literally—of the conversation.

Genre: *any*
Course Level: *any*
Student Difficulty: *easy*

Teacher Preparation: *low*
Class Size: *any*
Semester Time: *any*
Writing Component: *none*
Close Reading: *medium*
Estimated Time: *variable, 30 to 60 minutes*

EXERCISE

This classic retreat exercise and popular teaching strategy adapts particularly well to the literature classroom. To prepare, develop a series of questions related to the text you will cover during the next class meeting. Questions that are open to a range of possible interpretations will lead to more productive conversations: Who would you identify as the protagonist in "Bartleby"? What is Sethe's motivation for killing her daughter in *Beloved*? How do you account for the changes in tone and diction between the indented and nonindented stanzas of "Do not weep, maiden, for war is kind"? How might gender, place of origin, age, or some other factor influence the characters' relationships to the natural world in "A White Heron"? You might pose questions about key passages or the function of literary techniques, or broader questions related to theme. You could also offer a few potential interpretations of a specific aspect of a text and ask students to defend one or offer an alternative reading of their own. Typically, five or six solid questions will carry you through a one-hour class period.

In class, begin by placing four or five desks in the center of the room, and arrange the remaining desks in a circle around them. (If you don't have a classroom with movable desks, set up four or five chairs in front of the room. In a fixed-seat or seminar-style room, you could reframe the activity as a panel discussion, in which the "panelists" sit together along one side of the table or stand at the front of the classroom.) You will now need four or five volunteers to jump into the "fishbowl." Inform the volunteers that you will pose a question, and they should have a conversation with each other in response to the question, drawing from the text to cite supportive evidence as necessary. Encourage them to speak with each other and *not* to direct their comments to you. In fact, you should avoid eye contact with students in the fishbowl, to remove the temptation for them to converse with you instead of their peers. Transcribing key points raised by the fishbowl on the board can validate students' ideas and keep you engaged without directing the conversation.

Students outside the fishbowl may not join the conversation, but they should listen closely. After roughly five minutes, once the initial group has had the opportunity to express their ideas, students outside the fishbowl can "tag in," gently tapping a participant on the shoulder and taking that student's place in the fishbowl. After this first rotation, you can invite students to enter the fishbowl as they feel compelled, but be sure to instruct them to tag a person who has already had the opportunity to speak.

Continue to pose your prepared questions, and feel free to add a new question if the conversation takes a track you did not anticipate. You can adjust the pace based on the quality and quantity of responses. If the conversation feels productive and many students seem eager to join in, you might allow students to explore a question for up to ten minutes. Students outside the circle will tag in throughout the process, but you can also pause the discussion after the fishbowl has exhausted a topic and ask for a fresh set of volunteers. Repeat the process until everyone has participated. While you could extend this activity through a full class period, consider saving five to ten minutes for reflection at the end of class. This gives students the opportunity to pose any additional thoughts about the material that were not raised by the discussion questions.

REFLECTIONS

"Fishbowl" pushes students to go beyond directing an answer to the instructor and teaches them to become active participants in the learning process. The physical positioning of the microgroup encourages the students in the fishbowl to look at each other as they speak; they are on the spot, so they must pay careful attention to their peers and be prepared to respond to them. They can agree with and expand a peer's idea, constructively challenge it, or examine the question from a different angle. Students outside the fishbowl must remain equally engaged, because either they will tag in voluntarily or you will ask them to enter the fishbowl.

Students might seem hesitant during the initial attempt, but I like to introduce the fishbowl during the first week of class to encourage active participation in class discussion. You can then weave the exercise into your lesson plans periodically throughout the semester, and the interaction will be much more energized once students are comfortable with you and their classmates. "Fishbowl" works particularly well in an introductory literature course, as many students enter with a sense that there is one correct interpretation of a text and that the instructor is there to provide it. The fishbowl demonstrates that literary texts are open to a variety of readings and that each student brings a unique perspective to the conversation. At the same time, it also challenges students to ground those readings in concrete textual evidence in order to present a compelling case to their peers.

My students tend to enjoy "Fishbowl." Even in the quieter classes, this activity draws them into the conversation, as students who typically shy away from standard class discussion will often take part in heated debates once inside the fishbowl. My sense is that students like to debate ideas, and by providing a structured, conversational forum, this exercise makes them feel more comfortable sharing their thoughts. There's something about the idea of tagging in that appeals to them as well, and the physical activity of getting up and moving helps keep them engaged.

While I pair "Fishbowl" with all genres, and at all course levels, I have found it especially effective during the poetry unit of my introductory course. My students tend to believe that there is only one correct reading of a poem. To unsettle this view, I pose an intentionally polarizing question to initiate a conversation about possible interpretations. This worked particularly well, for example, during a discussion of Edgar Allan Poe's "Annabel Lee." After seating the fishbowl participants, I led off the conversation by asking if the speaker were in need of serious grief counseling, if he should be inducted into the romance hall of fame, or if the situation appears more complicated than that. A lively discussion followed, with students taking all sides—including creating their own alternatives—and pointing to the text in defense of their readings. The first respondent argued that the speaker was incredibly romantic, and two additional students chimed in to agree. The remaining two students listened to the supporting evidence, and then they voiced their objections. They described the speaker as "creepy" and pointed to elements of the poem to reinforce this reading. With the debate opened, other students soon tagged in and argued in favor of one of these two interpretations.

After nearly ten minutes, one student offered a new perspective: that the poem represents "puppy love," and the speaker is simply a naive youth. This first-year student explained that in making sense of the poem, he drew from his own experience with romantic relationships in high school. This reading gained traction, and soon other students either rethought their interpretations or joined in to support this line of thought. As often happens in "Fishbowl," the trajectory of this opening discussion led naturally toward some of the other questions I had prepared, and soon the class was exploring a series of related matters, such as the reliability of the narrator, his rationale for understanding the cause of Annabel Lee's death, and the tone of the poem. At the end of class, to return the discussion to our starting point, I used the "puppy love" interpretation to open a brief reflection on the ways in which personal experiences can shape our understanding of literary texts.

Read, Reread, Close Read ✓

Kerry Hasler-Brooks

An oral-reading exercise that sharpens close-reading skills through careful listening.

Genre: *any*
Course Level: *any*
Student Difficulty: *moderate*
Teacher Preparation: *medium*
Class Size: *small to medium*
Semester Time: *early*
Writing Component: *in class*
Close Reading: *medium*
Estimated Time: *40 to 45 minutes*

EXERCISE

Reading out loud can be a surprisingly effective way for students to sharpen their interpretive skills. This three-part exercise blends reading aloud with group discussion and individual reflection to help students see how meaning is shaped by intellectual exchange.

Because reading aloud can create anxiety for some students, introduce the practice as a group activity in which everyone, including the instructor, will contribute to an oral reading. Choose a one- to two-page excerpt from a course text that your students have read for class, preferably one that invites many voices to participate. Ideally, the excerpt should have as many sentences or lines as there are students in your class, plus yourself, so that everyone will have one sentence or line to read. For example, I often use a passage from Tim O'Brien's short story "On the Rainy River," in which the recently drafted narrator imagines a massive crowd—including family, friends, cheerleaders, Abraham Lincoln, Lyndon Baines Johnson, Huck Finn, Jane Fonda, an unborn daughter, and a nameless Vietnamese soldier—shouting for him to fight or to flee. But excerpts from poems and plays work equally well. What you're looking for is a passage that offers layers of voice, perspective, sound, or emotion.

Direct students to the selected excerpt, and tell them you will read it aloud together. Assign a simple reading order, including yourself; instruct each participant to read a single sentence or line, in order; and begin reading without any further "performance" directions. When the excerpt has been read aloud in its entirety, ask the class to reflect on the effect of the exercise: How did reading the passage *aloud* and as a *group* affect your sense of the passage? Did it reinforce your initial interpretation or revise it? What about your sense of the text as a whole?

After exploring students' initial responses to the group reading, ask each student to return to the single sentence or line he or she read aloud, write it out on a piece of paper, and annotate a new, *planned* oral reading. To guide the annotations, ask students to consider these questions: How will you read the line, and where will your emphasis fall? Will you read it loudly, quietly, quickly, slowly, smoothly, choppily, sarcastically, seriously, angrily, joyfully? Why? This part of the exercise may invite quick online research (if, for example, the sentence names a specific person like Jane Fonda) or deeply personal introspection (if, for example, the sentence names an abstraction like a daughter, which might be only vaguely imaginable to a young man). Complete this brainstorming work for your own sentence or line, too. Tell students to spend about five minutes on their annotations.

When everyone is ready, reread the entire passage aloud as a group following the new annotations, and direct students this time to pay particular attention to the readers on either side of them. Once again, discuss the effect of the exercise as a group: How did a *planned* reading revise or reinforce your ideas about the passage and/or text as a whole? How did *individual* attention to words and sentences affect the collective reading?

Finally, complete the activity one more time. Direct students back to the text for another five minutes to plan and justify a *third* oral reading of their sentences or lines. Tell them that this third reading should reflect a possible interpretation informed by the choices made by readers around them. Reread the entire passage aloud once more, and discuss the implications for making meaning: How did a planned *rereading* revise or reinforce your interpretation of the passage and/or the text as a whole? How did the readers around you influence your rereading choices?

REFLECTIONS

Although oral reading is typically reserved for new readers learning to translate characters into sounds, words, sentences, and paragraphs, "Read, Reread, Close Read" shows that reading out loud, when taught, practiced, and applied, can be an interpretive exercise that makes any student of literature a better close reader. Students also learn that close reading can be more than the self-contained textual analysis they often find so mysterious; it can instead be a synthesis of textual scrutiny, personal response, and experimentation. When students read and reread a text aloud as a group, they experience literary interpretation as a trying out and weaving together of many possible readings, not a restrictive hunt for a single "correct" meaning. Students appreciate this activity because it models the possibilities of cooperative literary study, unites the class as a community of close readers, and demonstrates the value of intellectual exchange in literary study.

You can use different genres to guide students toward different kinds of literary analysis. Group readings of fiction (or dramatic monologues) work particularly well in helping students discuss tone, characterization, and point of view. Oral readings of lyric poetry can help students focus on sound and rhythm, while scenes from plays might foreground questions of stage direction and blocking.

In my class discussions of "On the Rainy River," for example, the close-reading exercise helps students come to terms with the perplexing character of the narrator. After reading the story on their own, students are often baffled by the narrator, who is obscured by seemingly nonsensical statements like "I was a coward. I went to the war." Through the oral reading and rereading of the selected passage, the scrutiny of individual words, phrases, and sentences, and the insights of other readers, students become intimately involved in the emotional turmoil captured in the overwhelming list of onlookers screaming and urging the narrator toward one side of the river or the other. As a result, students can better parse the startling logic of a soldier who describes the quintessential act of bravery—going to war—as an act of cowardice.

"Read, Reread, Close Read" works best as an introductory activity followed by other oral-reading exercises that sharpen textual interpretation. These might include a comparative oral-reading assignment in which several small groups present the same text to the class; a poetry project in which each student uses oral reading to present his or her interpretation of a single poem; or a culminating research paper for which each student completes an individual oral-reading exercise to develop close-reading evidence for his or her argument. Oral-reading activities do require significant class time, and this group activity specifically demands careful attention to pacing and execution. A commitment to oral reading, however, trains students to use their ears, rather than just their eyes, to become more accomplished close readers.

Put the Question

Chris Baratta

An analytic exercise that helps students produce effective discussion questions.

Genre: *any*
Course Level: *introductory or intermediate*
Student Difficulty: *easy or moderate*
Teacher Preparation: *medium*
Class Size: *any*
Semester Time: *any*
Writing Component: *before class*
Close Reading: *medium to high*
Estimated Time: *full class*

EXERCISE

One of the most important skills literature students can develop is the ability to generate effective discussion questions. Not only do such questions stimulate class discussion, but also they help train students in the core elements of literary analysis: formulating a claim, developing an idea, and evaluating evidence.

"Put the Question" helps students generate effective discussion questions and also gives them the opportunity to guide part of an in-class discussion. To prepare students for this exercise, spend part of the previous class session discussing the characteristics of effective questions. In addition to asking the students themselves ("What makes a good discussion question?"), I do this with the help of a handout, which includes this overview:

> Ultimately, good discussion questions should accomplish three goals. First, they should be specific enough to indicate that you have read the literature for the week. Second, they should be a true reflection of topics that you would find interesting to have the class discuss. Third, they should represent questions that you honestly have about the author or the literature. Whenever possible, you should ask questions to which you really want to find or hear the answers. Effective questions will
>
> - stimulate conversation;
> - focus on something specific (avoid summary);
> - be understood easily by everyone (craft them well!);

- solicit answers beyond yes or no, or answers that can be easily answered by looking back to the text (that is, ask open-ended questions that provoke thought and/or a personal response or interpretation);
- excite, interest, challenge your fellow students

Model a few sample discussion questions for the students as well, or ask them to generate a few together. (I include several examples on the handout.) It's up to you whether to place a word limit on the questions (in my classes, I make the word-count requirement roughly two hundred words) or to leave the length of the questions completely open ended.

For homework, ask each student to develop a discussion question on the reading for the next class session. If you have a large class, instead of asking every student to generate a question on the same day, you can designate a subset of the class to develop questions—perhaps ten students at a time—until each student has had an opportunity to participate. You can also ask students to work in pairs outside of class to arrive at a set of questions. However you proceed, ask students to send you the questions in advance. (I set a deadline of 11:59 p.m. the night before.) If your class uses a curriculum management website such as Blackboard, students can submit their questions online. Collate the questions, organizing them by themes or topics according to the lesson plan you have in mind for the next day, and bring the questions to class.

In class, project the questions on the board, via PowerPoint or an overhead projector, for all the students to see. (Writing questions on the board or reading them aloud will work, too. If the class is small, you can give each student a copy of the questions.) Introduce each question at the appropriate point in your lesson plan, making sure to credit the student contributor ("Alice asks. . ."). Inviting students to elaborate on their question if they wish not only gives them ownership of the question but also gives them a leadership role in the discussion.

REFLECTIONS

This is my favorite active learning exercise for literature courses, no matter what the genre under discussion. It works well at any level of difficulty, and it can be done on a daily or weekly basis, depending on your needs, the class size, and schedule. "Put the Question" allows the instructor to shift from a lecture to a discussion in which students can consider a variety of ideas and viewpoints.

One of the main benefits of this exercise is that it involves students more directly in the classroom conversation. If ten students present questions for a given day, it is almost certain that you will have ten different perspectives on a work's key themes, scenes, characters, or passages. Even the shyer students often appreciate the opportunity to guide discussion on a certain topic or passage that resonates with them. Some might not like to be put on the spot, but overall, students report that they like the chance to have their work showcased and to express and further expand on their ideas.

The other considerable benefit of this exercise is the hands-on practice it gives students in formulating good questions. For example, in the course Postmodern American Literature and Culture, one of my students posed the following substantive question about Hunter S. Thompson's *Fear and Loathing in Las Vegas* (1971):

> The structure of Part 2, Chapter 9, caught my attention. Instead of a first-person narrative by Duke, it is an audio recording transcribed verbatim, detailing Duke and Gonzo's trip to the outskirts of Las Vegas to find a place called the American Dream. They ask for directions at a diner, but the waitresses who are trying to help them are having a hard time figuring out exactly where it is. They're not even sure if the place exists. What is Thompson saying about the nature of the American Dream? Has it always been so inaccessible or has it gradually become more difficult to find? Maybe the Dream that Duke and Gonzo seek no longer exists in a system that feeds off the weak and wounded in order for a few to be successful. After hours of searching, they eventually find the American Dream, only to discover that it is burned down, abandoned, and overrun with weeds. According to the editor's note, it is at this point in their journey that Duke "appears to have broken down completely" (161). If the search for the American Dream is "sort of a wild goose chase, more or less" (165), why has this moment affected Duke so much? In comparison, why does his attorney seem relatively unaffected by the disappointing result of their search?

Meeting all the criteria of a successful question—specific, well crafted, open ended, and interesting—this student prompt generated a productive class discussion. Believing that Thompson was speaking to *their* generation, particularly to the predicament many face with unemployment and income inequality, many in the class argued that this was not simply a contemporary issue but an institutional one. This eminently discussable question also prompted students to dissect Las Vegas as a setting—an analysis that helped the class see how Thompson uses "Sin City" to represent the new culture he sees emerging from the ashes of the 1960s counterculture. Students then connected the ideas in this discussion question to one of the most important passages of the novel, in which Duke reminisces about the disappearance of the ideals and values of that counterculture.

The discussion then took an interesting turn: students began to analyze the ideals—and labels—of their own generation, expressing how they feel about being called the "9/11 generation" and the "Millennials," connecting

Thompson's ideas (and his prose) to their own lives. As a teacher who stresses the need for critical awareness and analytical thinking, I am always pleased to see such an outcome arise from a single well-formulated student question: a common result of this discussion exercise.

. . . .

It's Time We Talked

Hannah Stark and Guinevere Narraway

A question-building exercise that offers an array of options for starting discussion.

Genre: *any*
Course Level: *intermediate or advanced*
Student Difficulty: *moderate*
Teacher Preparation: *low*
Class Size: *any*
Semester Time: *any*
Writing Component: *before class*
Close Reading: *low to medium*
Estimated Time: *variable, 10 minutes to full class*

EXERCISE

We developed this exercise as a semester-long activity, but it can also be used for individual class sessions, or as often as you like.

Ask each student to bring a discussion question to your next class meeting. Each question should relate to the text or topic of focus and should be written on a sheet of paper. The questions should be considered and informed and demonstrate a significant level of engagement with the material. The strongest questions will also be succinct and may even make use of secondary research. As the instructor, you should prepare a question as well.

To help students generate strong questions, spend time preparing for the activity in the class period *before* you give this assignment. Divide the class into small groups, provide each group with a selection of sample questions, and give the students seven to ten minutes to evaluate the effectiveness of each question in promoting productive discussion. (You can give each group the same sample questions, or you can vary them.) After each group has had time to evaluate its samples, let the groups report back to the class as a whole to share their findings. Providing and discussing sample questions before asking students to generate their own improves the standard not only of the questions the students themselves will produce but also of class discussion in general.

At the beginning of the next class meeting, collect the student-generated questions and quickly review them. You can now use the questions in several different ways:

- Select the most insightful questions for the whole class to discuss. Ask the class to explain what makes them productive discussion questions.
- Divide the class into small groups and give each group a few questions. Ask the students to select one question to discuss in their group and one that they would like the whole class to consider. As the instructor you can join one of the groups, move among the groups, or extricate yourself from the discussion.
- Select a pair of students to decide which questions will be discussed in the class. Ask the pair to make an evaluative statement justifying their choice.
- Let chance play a role. Fold the questions up and put them in a box. Get individual students to pull out a question either for class discussion or for small-group discussion.
- Set up a "speed-dating" structure. If you have movable chairs, arrange the students in two circles, with one circle inside the other. Have each student face his or her "date" in the other ring, and give every pair a question. Time the discussion for two minutes. After this time has elapsed, move the students to the left and the questions to the right so that every student has a new discussion partner and a new question. (If you don't have movable chairs, you can ask every other row to turn and face the row behind it.) If you have an odd number of students in the class, you can join the circle that has one fewer student, in order to even out the groups.
- With smaller classes, ask each student to read out his or her question, discussing each question in turn. Invite students to explain why they have posed their particular question. Encourage the class to identify patterns that are emerging.

REFLECTIONS

Student-generated discussion questions cultivate a vibrant classroom culture and respect the unique contribution that each participant can make. Because everyone, including the teacher, contributes a single question, this activity also creates a democratic structure by which all participants express their ideas and contribute to shaping the content of each class. It therefore works particularly well in groups in which some students tend to dominate the discussion and other students seem to lack confidence. Moreover, through this activity, focus shifts from the teacher as the arbiter of knowledge to the students as critical contributors. That's why we like to make this activity a structuring device for every class session: we find that it creates a dynamic classroom culture in which students take responsibility for, and ownership of, their learning environment. It has also proven effective for increasing student attendance and ensuring that everyone comes to class well prepared and with a contribution to make.

When using discussion questions weekly, it is best to start the semester with versions of the activity that require students to evaluate which questions are the most productive and to consider how and why they are posing particular questions. As the semester progresses and students become more relaxed sharing ideas, most sessions can sustain full-group discussions with little intervention from the instructor.

In one particularly fruitful class session early in the semester, for example, we asked students to generate questions for J. M. Coetzee's novel *Disgrace*, which we were studying in the context of the nonhuman as examined in recent theories of posthumanism. At the beginning of class, we selected the questions that we thought would lead to broad-ranging discussion and would encourage students to think directly about intersectionality (how multiple cultural identities interrelate). For example:

- In *Disgrace*, animals play a central role. What is the significance of David's relationship to Driepoot, a disabled dog?
- Why does Coetzee obscure the race of most of his characters?
- How and where do gender and sexuality intersect in the text in relation to both Lucy and David?

By grouping together these particular student questions, we were able, first, to draw attention to the connections in the novel among animals, race, disability, gender, and sexuality, and, second, to help students arrive at an intersectional reading of their own.

We divided the class into three groups and gave each group one of the above questions. After ten minutes we then brought the whole class together to discuss their findings. The discussion of disability was particularly significant: some of the students had not even observed that the dog is disabled. On noting that David and the dog can be read as doubles of each other, many students questioned how Coetzee uses language to privilege the human over the nonhuman, raising this issue: for which beings do we use the terms "disabled," "crippled," or "maimed"? Because this discussion emerged spontaneously out of the students' own questions, we found that they were more willing to reflect on structures of power, both in the text and in their own lived experience.

Reverse Entropy

Benjamin Widiss

An exercise that turns chaos into order to help students grapple with difficult texts.

Genre: *any*
Course Level: *any*
Student Difficulty: *moderate*
Teacher Preparation: *low*
Class Size: *any*
Semester Time: *any*
Writing Component: *in class*
Close Reading: *none*
Estimated Time: *45 to 50 minutes*

EXERCISE

This exercise works best for a particularly vexing text, one that excites in students the fear of simply "not getting it" in various ways. Before the students arrive, place a small box (or clean trash can or recycling bin) inconspicuously by the classroom door. When class begins, ask each student to write on a piece of scratch paper his or her single biggest, most nagging, or most embarrassing question about the text you are reading, assuring them that they will not have to take responsibility for their queries. (I set no limits on the questions beyond these, but you can add any further instructions as you see fit.) Direct the students to crumple their papers into balls and, on the count of three, to fling them about the room.

Ask each student to retrieve and uncrumple a ball of paper, to study the question on it briefly, and then—through a process of trial and error—to find another student holding a question that might enter into productive dialogue with the one he or she is already holding. For this to work, students must be relatively stringent about finding matches; encourage them to try several times in pursuit of a tight connection. (For example, an individual with a question about plot should find someone with another question about structure or sequence, or alternatively another question concerning the same character, institution, and so on. Students with questions about certain metaphors might search out questions about the same or analogous metaphors, or about the nature of metaphor in the work more generally.) Then, ask students to repeat this process as a twosome. Have the resulting groups of four spend some time considering whether one of their questions could serve as an umbrella for the other three, and, if not, ask them to create an umbrella question together.

Next, depending on the size of the class, mood in the room, or time on the clock, either repeat the last two steps again, to create groups of eight, or move on to the last stage of the exercise. Here, the groups report on their results to the rest of the class while you take notes on the board and talk them through what has emerged, with an eye to arriving jointly at further analytic syntheses and modes of corralling the book's details into mutually revealing assemblies. At the end of class, ask the students to deposit their questions in the receptacle you've provided as they leave the room, making it possible for you to read them over and thus to pick up on unreported nuances (or entire questions) in the next meeting.

REFLECTIONS

I use "Reverse Entropy" primarily with fiction. It is especially well suited to any novel that frustrates easy modes of reader identification: Gertrude Stein's *The Making of Americans*, Clarice Lispector's *The Hour of the Star*, Samuel Beckett's *Nohow On* trilogy, or Ishmael Reed's *Mumbo Jumbo*. But it can also work with difficult pieces in any genre, including multigenre texts, such as James Agee and Walker Evans's *Let Us Now Praise Famous Men*, Theresa Cha's *Dictée*, Christian Bök's *Eunoia*, or Harriet Mullen's *S*PeRM**K*T*.

As the title of this exercise hints, it was invented to deal with the extreme perplexity that Thomas Pynchon's *The Crying of Lot 49* occasions in many students, and it replicates in the classroom one of the novel's props: a small box putatively containing a literal "Maxwell's Demon" able to convert entropy to energy on the strength of information (by sorting fast molecules from slow ones). The students likewise generate interpretive order—and energy—out of an initial theatricalized moment of chaos. As they attempt to conjoin their growing portfolios of questions with those held by various groups of their peers, students must experiment with one abstract organizational schema after another, evaluating the character and the reach of analytical purchase offered by each. Over time, the students arrive not just at diverse and unforeseen collations of the questions before them but also at multiple methods and categories of inquiry to bring to bear on the rest of the book.

When I first created this exercise, I simply had students harvest one another's questions from the floor and then read them aloud, more or less randomly, while I drew all the connections. This alone yielded a singular experience—my teaching assistant that day said, "They will never forget the sight of sixty questions flying through the air at once," and she has confirmed the lasting impression it made on her many times since. But a longer and more collaborative format produces even better and more memorable results. If I allow at least forty-five minutes for the full exercise, we can reflect together on what a strange novel *The Crying of Lot 49* is, decked out in the trappings of California noir but replacing even that genre's diminished moral and epistemological satisfactions with an exponentially ramifying series of questions. We can approach our own myriad uncertainties constructively, finding points of confluence or analogy between our questions as we collectively map the novel's difficult territory.

My most recent use of "Reverse Entropy" yielded especially exciting results. We connected the closed system of Pynchon's Nefastis box to the "anarchist miracle" of the ballroom packed with deaf dancers but free of collisions, Randolph Driblette's planetarium, Remedios Varo's imprisoned maidens at the start of the novel and the locked auction hall at the end, all of these riffing on the traditional whodunit's locked room. But that generic locus classicus functioned in turn, we decided, as a figure for the book's central ambiguity: whether Oedipa's own head is effectively enclosed upon itself, paranoid ideation bouncing around ever more frantically within, or whether she has in fact stumbled upon a vast conspiracy. Thus, we considered whether the novel's many communicating networks—W.A.S.T.E., the highway system, the manifold puns, the careening circles of the plot—should read as metaphors of the internal or the external world. We extended this difficulty with establishing boundaries to the book's gender dynamics: the recurrent incest thematic that Oedipa inherits with her name, the challenges she faces as a private investigator who strikes most of her subjects as a sexual object, the metaphors of pregnancy and fertilization that dot the later pages. Finally, we asked whether the novel itself could confidently be treated as a locked room, or if the many impingements of verifiable history on its plot implied that events and individuals less easily documented could not safely be presumed entirely fictional.

In addition to providing a fresh protocol for students to engage with one another (early in the term, it helps break the ice) and a form of discussion that is initially more kaleidoscopic than sequential, this exercise also helps validate the teacherly claim that the only bad question is the one that doesn't get asked. Muscular abstractions and bewildered grasping at particulars can cohabit productively, and queries that students might be afraid to pose on their own are ushered into the debate by proxies. Still, sometimes the most telling questions—profoundly embarrassed or openly hostile to the book—don't get voiced aloud when groups report back to the class, which is where the wastepaper basket comes in handy. These responses can be the most revealing of all; explicitly modeling in the next class how even apparently "throwaway" questions can be harnessed to exciting interpretive ends makes for an especially effective lesson.

Debate

Melissa J. Ganz

An interactive exercise that teaches students to formulate and defend interpretive arguments.

Genre: *any*
Course Level: *any*
Student Difficulty: *easy or moderate*
Teacher Preparation: *low*
Class Size: *any*
Semester Time: *any*
Writing Component: *in class*
Close Reading: *high*
Estimated Time: *25 to 35 minutes*

EXERCISE

Choose a richly ambiguous or controversial passage from a novel, short story, poem, or play, and ask for a volunteer to read the passage aloud. (If the passage contains more than one speaker, assign different students to read the different parts so that everyone hears the multiple voices and perspectives in the text.) Next, present students with two opposing interpretations of the passage. For example, in a class on Wordsworth's "We Are Seven," you could ask whether the final two stanzas of the ballad support the perspective of the literal-minded speaker or that of the seemingly "simple" child. In a discussion of Shakespeare's *The Taming of the Shrew*, you could ask whether the play endorses or undermines the views about marriage that Kate articulates in her final speech. Or, after reading a passage from *Moll Flanders* recounting the narrator's dizzying but exciting adventures as a thief, you might ask whether Defoe celebrates or criticizes Moll's illicit behavior. The question you ask should contain two strikingly different but plausible interpretations of the text.

After you pose your question, ask students to jot down as many pieces of evidence as they can to support the first interpretation. ("Let's first make the case that Defoe celebrates Moll's career as a thief," you might say.) Give students at least five minutes to consider the passage (and perhaps look at surrounding passages) and write down their ideas. You might remind students to look for specific literary devices that could help support this interpretation—imagery, tone, or point of view, for example, or alliteration, rhyme, or enjambment—as these may be key pieces of evidence to support their claims. Now ask students to share their ideas with the larger group. Write these ideas on the board (in the first of two columns) to help everyone keep track of the evidence.

When the class finishes marshaling evidence to support the first claim, ask them to consider the opposing position. ("Now, let's make the case that Defoe *undermines* Moll's illicit behavior.") As before, you can ask students to jot down their ideas on a piece of paper before sharing them with the larger group. (Alternatively, you can skip this step and simply ask students to share their ideas with the class.) After you assemble the evidence for this second claim in the other column on the board, ask students to take sides: "Which interpretation is the most persuasive? Why?" At this point, the activity should become a true debate. You may find that a third (or even a fourth) possible interpretation emerges. For example, a student may suggest a reading that reconciles the two positions under consideration; another student may argue that the text is itself ambivalent about this point. (If no one raises these possibilities, you can introduce them yourself or attempt to elicit them from students by asking further questions.) At the end of the class, recap the different arguments and then ask for a show of hands to see which interpretation students find the most convincing. This last question requires students who have remained quiet thus far to take a position in the debate.

REFLECTIONS

Debates result in lively, engaged classrooms that help students gain crucial analytical skills. Especially in introductory courses, but often in upper-level classes as well, students tend to summarize rather than analyze texts. By modeling how to articulate and defend strong interpretive claims, this exercise shows students how to move from a descriptive mode ("What happens in the text?") to an analytical one ("What does it mean"?). Equally important, the exercise teaches students to formulate multiple arguments about the same work. It thus undermines the myth that there is a single "right" way to interpret a text, while refuting the idea that literary analysis is entirely subjective. Debates work especially well with endings of novels and plays and with crucial or ambiguous moments, which you can use as jumping-off points to develop claims about texts as a whole.

When I teach *Moll Flanders*, for example, the pace of the discussion invariably quickens after I ask students to consider the novel's stance toward criminality. Students immediately note that Moll gains a sense of agency and pride as well as a much-needed livelihood from her career as a thief. They point as well to the first-person narration, which works to align readers with Moll's perspective, implicitly celebrating her ingenuity. Students, however, find it hard to ignore the costs of Moll's transgressive behavior—the isolation and alienation that she experiences and the eagerness with which she takes advantage of those around her. The class becomes intrigued, too, when I prompt them to consider how the form of the text—its series of short, choppy episodes—evokes Moll's sense of disorientation. Students generally agree that, while Moll's illicit career brings her a degree of autonomy, the benefits come at a considerable price. The debate thus helps us understand the novel's complex portrait of criminality at the same time that it sheds light on the tension between sympathy and irony that runs through the work.

The ultimate payoff of such debates is that they teach students to construct nuanced arguments while attending to a range of possible interpretations. The exercise reminds students that there are lively and legitimate disagreements about the meaning of literary texts. And it shows students that they can join the conversation by taking a stand.

. . . .

Leader, Skeptic, Scribe

Andrew Logemann

An exercise that teaches evidence-based argumentation and clear communication.

Genre: *any*
Course Level: *introductory or intermediate*
Student Difficulty: *moderate*
Teacher Preparation: *low*
Class Size: *any*
Semester Time: *any*
Writing Component: *in class*
Close Reading: *medium to high*
Estimated Time: *40 to 50 minutes*

EXERCISE

Divide the class into groups of three. Within the small groups, assign each student one of three roles: the Leader, the Scribe, or the Skeptic. The Leader directs the group's conversation by supplying ideas, sketching out an initial argument, and locating evidence in the text. The Skeptic asks critical questions and tries to poke holes in the Leader's claim, ideally by citing other passages and ideas from the text. (A good Skeptic will be productive rather than destructive, keeping the group honest by preventing anyone from getting away with sloppy thinking or neglecting important textual evidence.) The Scribe is the only member of the group who is allowed to write anything down. Beyond taking notes, the Scribe prompts the Leader and the Skeptic to clarify the points they make during the discussion. Clear communication within the group is the Scribe's responsibility. (If your class doesn't divide neatly into groups of three, introduce a second Skeptic to a group as necessary.)

Once the groups have formed and the students understand their roles, give the class an interpretive question that asks them to make an argument about the day's assigned reading. The prompt should direct them to support their arguments with evidence drawn from the text. Some of the prompts I have used in my classes for this exercise include the following:

1. In her "Modern Fiction" essay, Virginia Woolf argues that fiction should "attempt to come closer to life" by examining "an ordinary mind on an ordinary day." Select a particular technique from *To the Lighthouse* and make an argument about the extent to which it succeeds at bringing this novel "closer to life" than the other fiction we've read so far.
2. What is the effect of Michael Frayn's metaphorical use of Heisenberg's Uncertainty Principle and Bohr's Complementarity in his play *Copenhagen*?
3. How do these short stories by Gabriel García Márquez make use of magical realist elements?

The goal of the exercise is for each group to work together to produce a strong analytical claim that addresses the prompt. Be sure to provide students with plenty of time—at least thirty minutes—to develop this claim. As the small-group discussions begin, the Leader and the Skeptic should skim back through the text and identify passages that may be relevant to the question. The Scribe writes these down. Next, the Leader should propose an initial claim and sketch out the particulars of his or her argument. The Skeptic responds by posing questions and/or offering an alternative claim. Meanwhile, the Scribe writes each claim down and encourages the others to clarify their ideas and support them, as necessary, with evidence. The process continues until the group has settled on a claim.

When the small-group conversations begin to wind down, reassemble the class and ask each group to share its analytical claim and explain the reasoning behind it. Ask the class as a whole which claims they find most persuasive, and why. Finally, ask the students to reflect on the exercise itself. Which role was the most challenging? Which seemed easiest? Point out that every critic must play all three roles during various stages of the interpretive process and that being one's own skeptic is often the most difficult role of all.

REFLECTIONS

"Leader, Skeptic, Scribe" directly addresses several pedagogical goals in an introductory or intermediate literature class. First, the exercise builds on an interpretive question you supply, which provides an excellent opportunity for you to model the kinds of questions the discipline of literary studies asks of texts. (Students often struggle with this.) Second, the exercise asks students to practice making good arguments about literary texts and to develop attentiveness to their audience. And third, the exercise identifies three essential habits of mind for a critic and allows students to practice them in isolation.

In a recent class session on Mary Shelley's novel, *Frankenstein*, for example, I asked students to develop arguments in response to the following prompt:

> The novel offers several frameworks for understanding Victor Frankenstein. He is presented variously as a successful inventor, as a godlike creator, and as the father of a new race. Considering the novel as a whole, which of these options is the most compelling way to understand Victor, his actions, and his creature?

One of the groups, picking up on a pattern of father/son imagery in the text, proposed that considering Victor as a father highlighted the humanity of the Creature and brought the novel into conversation with bildungsroman tropes familiar from other texts. Another group's discussion also centered on Victor as the Creature's father but emphasized instead the way in which Victor's asexual reproduction cuts women out of the biological process and therefore privileges maleness. The majority of the groups, however, selected the framework of Victor as a godlike creator as the most compelling interpretive option.

As evidence for their claims, these latter groups cited the frequent references to Milton's *Paradise Lost* and the Creature's accusation that violating the compact between a creation and its creator was Victor's primary transgression. While this view compelled the largest number of students, the minority reports supporting other positions added depth to our class conversation and allowed us to raise issues of gender that might not have surfaced had the discussion centered solely on Milton's influence in the novel. In their reflections on the exercise itself, students observed that none of the three roles was easy, and each presented its own challenges. The Leaders had to figure out how to guide their group's conversation, the Skeptics had to think quickly on their feet and remain attentive to weaknesses in their group's ideas, and the Scribes had to pull everything together.

Students typically respond enthusiastically to this exercise. The constraints of each assigned role break them out of familiar habits of thinking, and each one has its strengths and weaknesses. Some students are reluctant to be the Leader, for example, but love playing the Skeptic or the Scribe. If you do this exercise more than once in a semester, vary the roles students play so that they have the opportunity to try out more than one.

ESSENTIALS

This section features essential exercises that work well with almost any literary work. Of easy or moderate difficulty, they can serve as key building blocks for training students to look carefully at the meaning of words and passages, lines and titles, or definitions and themes. Because the exercises work with more than one genre, they can also be used and reused across courses, whether your focus is on literary formalism, literary periods, or literary history. Arranged in order from the small to the large, and the specific to the general, these are classic exercises that everyone should try.

"The Blow Up" and "The Cut Up" each teach the essentials of close reading, but from two different directions: the first works through deduction (taking a text apart), while the second operates through induction (putting a text back together). In both cases, students learn to produce a coherent and cohesive literary interpretation.

The next pair of exercises, "The One-Liner" and "The New Title," shows students how to multiply a text's meaning and how to widen the interpretive frame. These exercises emphasize both the way literary texts contain many meanings and the way readers actively participate in the construction of those meanings.

The final set of exercises, "The Descriptive Word" and "The Common Thread," continue to move from a close-up view to a long view. Ideal for the start or end of a course, such overview exercises are perfect for taking stock, particularly of big-picture subjects like genre or period. Whether these six essential exercises aim to teach patient close reading or to demonstrate careful consideration of larger themes, they all show students the importance of slowing down.

The Blow Up

Wendy Lee

A classic exercise in the closeness of close reading.

Genre: *any, especially fiction*
Course Level: *any*
Student Difficulty: *easy*
Teacher Preparation: *low*
Class Size: *any*
Semester Time: *any*
Writing Component: *none*
Close Reading: *high*
Estimated Time: *25 to 35 minutes*

EXERCISE

Choose a passage of no more than two hundred words from the text that your class is reading. It may help to choose a particularly idiosyncratic passage that can stand apart from the rest of the book, like a dream sequence in *Jane Eyre* or a single conversation in *Pride and Prejudice* that reads more like a film script than a novel. Format the passage on a handout so that it looks like a page from a children's book: 14-point font and at least half-inch margins all around the text. Feel free to experiment with the way the passage looks on the page. (Get creative with that Microsoft Word toolbox!)

After distributing the handout, instruct your students to take advantage of all the white space to mark up the passage with any observations or associations that come to them during the exercise. Then call on a student to read the passage aloud. Direct the student to read "very slowly and very loudly." Immediately after she or he is finished, call on a second student (preferably with a very different voice) to read the same passage, also very slowly and loudly. After the second reading, give students a few minutes to respond by marking up their passages. (You might show them a sample of a heavily marked-up handout that looks like graffiti so that they are not afraid of the page.)

When students have finished circling words and jotting down comments on the page, go in a circle around the room and invite each student to make a comment about something they noticed (an interesting word, a curious turn of phrase, a notable repetition, an arresting metaphor). If the class is large or time is short, you can instead move straight to framing the discussion according to your needs. For students who need practice close reading, you might begin with purely formal observations: Who is speaking? To whom? How do you know? Do any words repeat? What kinds of sentences are being used? When you are ready to conclude the exercise, have students find the passage in their books. Does resituating the text yield any surprises?

REFLECTIONS

The point of this exercise is to get students to see and hear the text in a new and focused way. It allows students first to forget what they know about the book and then revisit it from the angle of a carefully examined and *spoken* snippet of text. Changing the actual form of the passage—by enlarging the letters and creating ample white space around them—can transform an otherwise recondite text into an accessible and inviting piece of language.

The exercise works equally well to reframe an all-too-familiar passage. For example, students who devotedly recite the first line of *Pride and Prejudice* by heart ("It is a truth universally acknowledged, that a single man in possession of a good fortune, must be in want of a wife") are often surprised and discomfited to see the succeeding sentence blown up so starkly on the page: "However little known the feelings or views of such a man may be on his first entering a neighborhood, this truth is so well fixed in the minds of the surrounding families, that he is considered as the rightful property of some one or other of their daughters." In contending with these grammatically complex sentences, some students were drawn to the abstract nouns ("truth," "minds," "property") while others circled the weighty adjectives attached to them. They noted that "universal truth," "fixed minds," and even notions of "rightful property" all become the moving targets of the narrator's unsparing but still ambiguous irony. The "Blow Up" format allowed my students to confront directly the nuances of Austen's style—which they variously and precisely described as "powerful," "enigmatic," and "potentially hostile"—while also providing them with the literal, material space to draw out, write around, or even deface Austen's own destabilizing prose.

Part of the enchantment of this exercise derives from rendering a written text into an oral experience. Through the two oral readings, you can extend to your (especially quiet) students a low-stakes, seemingly straightforward opportunity to participate and have their voices heard in class. What surprises me is how the shyest students, who shudder to offer a "literary critical" comment, can read aloud with the most uninhibited flair. "Blow Up" enables lively impromptu performances, in which students must unwittingly make important interpretive decisions about pacing, pauses, cadence, and volume, sparking a discussion about elements such as character and scene. (The direction to read loudly and slowly creates a baseline of elocution, making performers' decisions even more pronounced.) Students are listening to and learning from each other, inevitably provoking such observations as "I hadn't realized how funny that part was!"

"The Blow Up" emphasizes the closeness of close reading, but it also grounds and enlivens more general discussions in the text—removing parts from the whole and putting the whole back into conversation with its parts. After having extracted, magnified, transformed, performed, and resituated individual sentences, students will feel more authoritative when the conversation widens to larger themes and ideas. They will also not be afraid to take apart the text, to zoom in and out of any page, drawing in or blocking out what they already know for the sake of testing new claims or ideas. Students will not only feel comfortable referring to specific passages, but they will find it easier to refer to one another's readings as evidence and counterevidence. Most importantly, they will enjoy the opportunity to converse freely with each other (instead of answering the instructor's questions), tracking their own interpretative moves and choices in a collective and creative encounter.

· ·

The Cut Up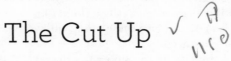

Diana Fuss

A warm-up close-reading exercise that invites students to repair rather than dissect texts.

Genre: *poetry or prose*
Course Level: *introductory or intermediate*
Student Difficulty: *moderate*
Teacher Preparation: *medium*
Class Size: *any*
Semester Time: *early*
Writing Component: *none*
Close Reading: *high*
Estimated Time: *30 to 50 minutes*

EXERCISE

Choose a short poem or a short prose passage—nearly any poem or passage will suffice. For this simple exercise, which invites students to take up pieces of a text and put it back together again, the text you select will depend largely on the level of challenge you want to present. In fiction classes, students will have a much easier time with contemporary examples written in a familiar language or style than with the elongated sentences and complicated syntax of eighteenth- and nineteenth-century stories. In poetry courses the exact opposite holds: early poems (ballads, sonnets, odes) that have a fixed meter and rhyme prove easier test cases for students than do free verse poems that have fewer auditory or visual signposts. In either case, no more than eight to ten sentences or verse lines work best.

Reproduce your poem or prose passage on a handout and keep this in reserve. Then digitally cut the text into parts: for poems, make the cuts after every line break; for prose, make the cuts after every sentence. Place each individual line or sentence on a separate page and be sure to increase the font size (to 20, 30, or whatever size font your single page will bear). Before printing out each isolated enlarged line or sentence, format the page on its horizontal (landscape) side for more room. (You can use smaller slips of paper instead, though students working and standing in groups find the larger sheets easier to see.) Shuffle all the sheets so the lines are in random order.

In class, separate students into groups of three or four and give each group a full set of the cut-up passages. You might disclose in advance the author's name, but if you are using a poem, do not identify which of the lines is the poem's title. You can give every group the same text or different texts, depending on your needs.

Now ask each group to reconstruct the text. Tell them that, without the aid of electronic devices, their mission is to place the cut-up lines in their proper order. Invite groups to move around the room and use any surface: table, wall, floor, blackboard. Tables work best, providing a flat surface and ample room for students to stand and shuffle the sheets as they debate different sequencings. Taping the sheets to the wall (you will need to provide painter's tape) or writing on blackboards and whiteboards works almost as well. Allow fifteen to twenty minutes for students to experiment with different line placements and arrive at a possible order.

Let groups strategize on their own, discussing among themselves the best way to put the mystery text back together. Part of the point of the exercise is to alert students to some of the more subtle formal features that convey style and carry meaning, so resist the impulse to give them clues. As they grapple with what might go where, you will see them suddenly start to look carefully at punctuation marks, listen for aural resonances, or check for verb tenses. Sit back and watch, taking notes for your own purposes on the things that seem to puzzle them most.

When the students are reasonably confident of their final order, mark off for them exactly which of their lines are in the right places. Give them a couple more minutes to try to reorder the text one more time with this new information in hand. For groups that have put all or nearly all of the lines in the wrong place, offer them the first and the last line of the poem or passage.

For groups that have succeeded in reconstructing all or nearly all of the text, move directly to the final phase.

Hand out the original text and let each group discover exactly how close or how far they came to getting everything where it belongs. Reconvene the whole class and begin a conversation. If a particular group did well, ask them how they did it—what did they look for and what clues did they follow? If they were off base, ask them what obstacles they encountered or misdirections they followed, and why. Reassure students that "getting it wrong" can be as instructive for this exercise as "getting it right." They will know, either way, what formal features to look for next time.

As students reflect afterward on their experience suturing (Frankenstein-style) small pieces into functional wholes, keep a record on the board of every formal feature they mention: language, tone, punctuation, and so on. This listing activity is especially crucial. It allows you to bring the exercise to a satisfying close by doing a group close reading that uses the terms on the board as a checklist of sorts, thus guiding the class to a more sophisticated understanding of how literature works.

REFLECTIONS

Most close reading exercises deploy a method that students often label "dissection": taking a whole poem or passage and breaking it into parts. "The Cut Up" inverts this method by deploying a strategy not of dissection but of repair: beginning with the parts and putting the whole back together. This shift in emphasis productively subverts expectations while offering an alternative approach to understanding literary formalism. It works especially well early in the semester as a warm-up exercise.

For example, in a poetry survey, I like to begin the course by using cut-ups of Emily Dickinson poems, which provide a particular challenge because of her twisty syntax and unconventional punctuation (the Dickinson dash). Recently I handed out cut-ups of two poems, "Pain—has an Element of Blank" and "I've seen a Dying Eye," each lyric containing eight lines (two quatrains) and little or no end rhyme. Student groups had no trouble sequencing the first two lines of these poems correctly, but they had a much more difficult time with the last lines—interestingly, not unlike Dickinson herself, whose manuscripts include more textual variants at the ends of poems than at their beginnings.

Deprived of rhyme as an obvious guide, students tried other strategies to identify underlying patterns. They focused on internal sounds (listening for both alliteration and assonance). They measured line lengths (fixing on a long/short pattern I later explained was ballad form). They talked about tone (asking if certain sequencings produced a more solemn effect). They counted beats (wondering if particular rhythms might regulate the flow).

And they looked for narrative elements (searching for a buried story that organized the whole). Later, when I asked them which tactic they tried first to make sense of the jumbled lines, all the groups agreed that, without even thinking about it consciously, they turned to basic grammar as their point of entry, initially attempting to sequence lines by subject-verb-object or another syntactical pattern.

The exercise proved to be an exceedingly quick way to introduce students to several key features that distinguish Dickinson's poetry: the problem of reference (those confusing "it"s), the challenge of mechanics (those seemingly random capitalizations), and the puzzle of parataxis (those repeated line openings "and then... and then"). It also proved to be an even more useful exercise for introducing students to the general properties of almost any poem. By the end students had generated a rather full checklist of formal features, which they listed in this order: grammar, referent, rhyme, syntax, sound, content, rhythm, meter, punctuation, tense, parallelism, story, imagery, form, tone, closure, diction, speaker, personification, and theme.

To drive the lesson home, I have also immediately repeated the exercise, this time cutting up the poem by stanzas rather than by individual lines, and putting a strict ten-minute time limit on the activity. Dickinson's "Grief is a Mouse" is a great candidate for a stanza cut-up because each of the poem's four stanzas begins with a different definition of grief: grief is a "Mouse," a "Thief," a "Juggler," and "Tongueless" (and a "Gourmand" too, one learns later in stanza three). With much less time, students zeroed in on figuration and personification to try to determine an internal logic that would make sense of these implied similes. No group got the stanza sequence exactly right, so after the big reveal I invited them to look harder at what the different personifications of Grief had in common and what precisely Dickinson might be saying about the lived experience of grief. The students concluded that mouse, thief, juggler, and gourmand are all active but silent figures; as one student phrased the poem's point, "Grief may render us speechless or tongueless but it is always industrious." Another student noticed a completely different set of figures organizing the four stanzas: Breast, Ear, Eye, and Tongue. She wondered if the cut-up stanzas, with their cut-up body parts, offered another perspective on grief's deep physical and emotional toll: "Grief mutilates and transforms bodies and language."

Inductive in method, "The Cut Up" offers a nice departure from the more common deductive approach to analyzing texts. It challenges students to get inside a writer's mind-set and reminds them of the infinite choices—in word and design—that any writer must negotiate. For me this approach to teaching close reading has felt liberating, perhaps because it carries a more creative and consequential feel overall: it combines the sportive play of solving a puzzle with the serious task of creating something meaningful.

The One-Liner

Kimberly J. Stern

A slowing-down exercise that encourages students to reflect on the importance of style.

Genre: *drama or prose*
Course Level: *any*
Student Difficulty: *easy or moderate*
Teacher Preparation: *low*
Class Size: *any*
Semester Time: *any*
Writing Component: *in class*
Close Reading: *high*
Estimated Time: *25 to 35 minutes*

EXERCISE

This exercise is all about style. In class, invite the students to spend some time flipping through the pages of their short story, novel, or play. As they peruse their reading assignment, ask them to take note of three or four sentences (they need not be consecutive) that catch their attention, writing each of these down on a separate sheet of paper. They should be sentences that are especially powerful, complicated, funny, or in some way idiosyncratic.

Now instruct your students to examine the style and grammar of each sentence, focusing especially on questions of syntax, tense, diction, and voice. Encourage them to label parts of speech, underline punctuation marks, circle suggestive words—in short, annotate each sentence. At this point, they should try to generate as many observations about the grammatical and stylistic details of the sentence as possible. As a final step, consider inviting students to select one of their chosen lines and paraphrase it, retaining its meaning but changing its style. Allow ten or fifteen minutes for students to select their lines and annotate them.

Next, invite the students to share their findings with the class. (For large classes, students can divide into pairs or groups of three; for smaller classes, proceed straight to the full-class discussion.) The class discussion portion of this exercise unfailingly generates striking insights into the relationship between literary style and content. It can be useful to copy or project a few of the students' sentences up on the board, so the class can examine and annotate the text collectively. This serves the secondary purpose of showing the students visually how many different details might contribute to their analysis of a single sentence. As arrows, circles, notes, and question marks fill the board, the students begin to realize that a lot happens at the level of the sentence.

REFLECTIONS

Students frequently tell me that prose is easier to interpret than poetry because it more closely approximates the language they use every day. Of course, familiarity sometimes breeds complacency. A student who eagerly devours the plot of a Charles Dickens novel may inadvertently miss some of the book's stylistic nuances. The first benefit of this exercise, then, is that it makes students slow down. In so doing, it reminds them that prose can be every bit as strange, performative, and meaningful as a ballad or a sonnet. Advanced students will find here a tool for engaging more rigorously with the text; less advanced students will find a way to enter the conversation and develop their analytical skills.

A single sentence can yield a variety of interpretations, often sparked by the word "why?" When reading Jane Austen's *Pride and Prejudice*, for example, my students spent several minutes examining that famous first line: "It is a truth universally acknowledged, that a single man in possession of a good fortune, must be in want of a wife." Why, students asked, does Austen begin her sentence with the impersonal subject "it"? Aren't all truths by definition "universally acknowledged"? Why not say a "wealthy bachelor" instead of a "single man in possession of a good fortune"? Why, in other words, does Austen use twenty-three words to say something she might just as easily have expressed in four?

For students less practiced in close reading strategies, the paraphrase step of this exercise can reap great results. Consider the example of Algernon Moncrieff, who remarks in Oscar Wilde's *The Importance of Being Earnest*, "In matters of grave importance, style, not sincerity, is the vital thing." Stripping the sentence of its most noticeable stylistic elements, one of my students revised the sentence in this way: "Style is more important than sincerity." From here, we began to ask questions about how this version of the sentence differs from the original. What does Wilde's introduction of words like "vital" and "grave" (words that seem to frame this as a matter of "life or death") add to the sentence? Is it significant that Wilde uses the phrase "not sincerity," thus not only prioritizing style but actually dismissing the value of sincerity?

The great reward of this exercise is that it allows students to pursue a focused and formal reading of the text while also inviting multiple interpretations of it. A single word or sentence does not simply move a plot forward or help to build a larger narrative structure. It can harbor many potential meanings, some working together and others openly contradicting one another to complicate and enrich the interpretive process. "The One-Liner" raises questions, performs meaning, and multiplies our perspectives on the text. To this extent at least, style is indeed the "vital thing."

. . . .

The New Title

Johanna Winant

A simple exercise that teaches students to identify important themes and images by asking them to retitle a text.

Genre: *any*
Course Level: *any*
Student Difficulty: *moderate*
Teacher Preparation: *low*
Class Size: *any*
Semester Time: *any*
Writing Component: *before class or in class*
Close Reading: *low to medium*
Estimated Time: *10 to 20 minutes*

EXERCISE

Once a class is familiar with a text—after students have read a poem or are at least partway through a novel or play—ask them to choose and write down a new title for the text. This can be done as homework or in the first few minutes of class time.

It's fine to leave the assignment open-ended, but depending on the level of the class, the themes of the course, and the genres under discussion, you could offer a number of different guidelines for choosing a new title. If you're discussing a novel, you could ask students to choose a single word that could work as an alternative title. Or ask them to choose a quote that a character says. Or ask them to choose a noun, an adjective, or a verb. If you're discussing a poem, suggest finding a line in the poem that could work as a title. To make it more difficult or to review different poetic terms, require the quotation be a metaphor or an iamb.

After everyone in the class has written down a new title for the text, ask students what their titles are and why they chose them. List them on the board for all to see. For example, if you are teaching Ian McEwan's *Atonement*, students might suggest "Liars! Liars! Liars!," appropriating Mrs. Turner's quote from the end of Part I, or such thematic titles as "The Library." If you are teaching John Keats's "Ode on a Grecian Urn," students might suggest titles based on quotations, such as "Cold Pastoral," or formal or thematic titles, such as "Questions and Answers" or "Ars Poetica." If you've asked students to use quotations as titles, it is easy to segue into a close reading of the passage that includes the quotations they have chosen. If you have asked students to choose titles that are not quotations, this can lead to a broader discussion about the text's themes and images.

REFLECTIONS

The first goal of this exercise is to teach students that texts are not natural objects but rather are deliberately made artifacts. Students often forget or ignore that literary texts are the results of purposeful decisions. While I do not encourage students to interpret the author's intention as the meaning of the text, I find that reminding them that the text was intentionally created improves their ability to interpret it. Asking students to choose a new title for a text reminds them that a title was carefully chosen in the first place. Students are fascinated to learn whether a text had an earlier or provisional title—such as *Mrs. Dalloway*'s initial title, "The Hours," or *A Raisin in the Sun*'s working title, "The Crystal Stair," or *The Waste Land*'s pre–Ezra Pound title, "He Do the Police in Different Voices"—and to think about how Virginia Woolf's novel or Lorraine Hansberry's play or T. S. Eliot's poem would have been different with a different title. The first benefit of this exercise, then, is that it shows students how every piece of a text, even a supposedly straightforward title, is open to interpretation because it is the result of deliberation.

The second goal of "The New Title" is to teach students that identifying the themes and images they consider important in the text can be the starting point for their own independent literary analysis. By choosing a quotation or a word they think could be titular, students are making a judgment about what is significant in that text and, as a result, how to understand it. One of my students who thought he had nothing to say about *Much Ado About Nothing* contributed the title "Beatrice and Benedick." Even that fairly uncreative title led to a discussion about why *Much Ado* is not named after its lovers the way that *Romeo and Juliet* is and why, more generally, the comedies are not named for characters the way the tragedies are. This student eventually came to the conclusion that *Much Ado* is a transitional play, a comedy that veers toward tragedy because of the lovers' excessive self-satisfaction.

This exercise works with nearly any text, although I would not try it with poems shorter than sonnets. I also would not use it with texts that students find very difficult: it does not make a frustrating text easier but rather shows how apparently easy aspects of stories, poems, or plays are actually rich with significance.

I have used "The New Title" with great success teaching everything from Renaissance plays to postmodern novels. Every time I do it, I find that students talk and listen and learn from one another. They are surprised that the titles chosen by their classmates differ so much from their own. They laugh at the funny titles and compliment the insightful ones. And they learn that they each approach the text with their own invisible subtitles.

· ·

The Descriptive Word

Erwin Rosinberg

An exercise that both solicits and questions students' preexisting ideas about a literary genre or period.

Genre: *any*
Course Level: *any*
Student Difficulty: *easy or moderate*
Teacher Preparation: *low*
Class Size: *any*
Semester Time: *first day and last day*
Writing Component: *none*
Close Reading: *none*
Estimated Time: *10 to 20 minutes*

EXERCISE

Disrupt some of the usual opening-day classroom protocols by instead engaging directly with what students may already know about the course's topic. Choose a key term that the course will revisit and refine throughout the semester, and ask students to share any descriptive words that immediately come to mind. In a period-based course, you might ask students what adjectives they would associate with the medieval period, the Renaissance, the Victorian era, and so forth; in a genre course or a topic-based course, you could ask them to think about how they would describe the ideas and images suggested by, for example, "Gothic" or "Romance."

You can further encourage and direct your students' feedback by asking them to think beyond literature to other forms of expression that they associate with the period or genre under examination, such as art, architecture, or music. It's helpful to reassure students that you're simply soliciting their preexisting impressions, which may come from anywhere: a Hollywood film about medieval knights, a television serial set in Victorian London, an abstract painting they once saw in a museum.

Keep track of your students' responses on the board. As they continue to contribute descriptive words, begin grouping their thoughts into categories of affinity, linking similar responses to one another. Ultimately, you can use the variety of responses generated to show that periods and genres are not monolithic entities and that students will be engaged in confronting the complexities and contradictions inherent in their assumptions throughout the semester.

This exercise is also worth returning to on the last day of class as a way of demonstrating to students what they have learned, both individually and collectively, about the topic at hand. Remind students of their initial impressions of the key term you selected at the beginning of the semester, and ask them to reconsider their earlier responses: Do the descriptive words that first came to mind still apply? How have their impressions of the period or genre evolved in response to the course material? What unexpected new impressions have the texts generated?

REFLECTIONS

I find this exercise valuable for two reasons: first, it gets students in the habit of talking on the first day of class, and second, it encourages students to let go of the idea that studying literature is about "locking in" particular definitions or creating airtight aesthetic and historical categories. By asking them to contribute the knowledge they already bring to a course from a variety of cultural sources, and to see how their own assumptions may differ from those of their classmates, you can begin to give your students a sense of the course material as a living body of work, however much it may be rooted in the past.

I use this exercise most frequently in my courses on modernist literature. I ask students for adjectives that communicate what "modern" or "modernism" mean to them. Most often, the descriptive terms they contribute tend to fall into two main categories, almost perfectly in contradiction with one another: some students associate modernism with a pared-down aesthetic, using adjectives like "simplified," "direct," or "minimalist," while others convey a sense (or a fear) of challenge and intricacy, using adjectives like "fragmented," "dense," and "difficult." After the board is covered with an array of terms, I ask students to reflect upon the definitional categories they have created. How is it that both groups of terms can be equally relevant to the study of modernism? Does modernism still cohere as a movement or a period if it is grounded in such contradictory aesthetics? Such complex questions, generated from the students' own insights, provide a rich entry into the semester's reading.

Student feedback may also prompt questions that move beyond aesthetic complication, addressing the social and cultural circumstances of literary production as well. For example, in one course students offered the terms "avant-garde" and "democratic" in response to my query about modernism. Again, both ideas are relevant, since modernist writing frequently finds itself answering to charges of exclusivity or elitism while, at times, advocating a radically egalitarian social renewal. We continued to address this apparent contradiction throughout the semester. Indeed, the efficacy of this exercise lies, I believe, in foregrounding contradiction rather than ignoring it. Our definitions of literary periods and genres only remain "true" if they also remain open to complexity and revision, and so soliciting and discussing students' preexisting definitions helps set an agenda for literary study as a continued act of discovery.

· ·

The Common Thread

Simon Grote

A versatile exercise in comparative thinking that enables students to analyze multiple texts when time is short.

Genre: *any*
Course Level: *any*
Student Difficulty: *moderate*
Teacher Preparation: *medium*
Class Size: *any*
Semester Time: *early, midterm, last day*
Writing Component: *in class*
Close Reading: *low to medium*
Estimated Time: *20 to 60 minutes*

EXERCISE

Choose some theme, subject, formal quality, generic category, or other characteristic that you want students to analyze across several texts (the "common thread"): the elegiac qualities in a set of poems, for example, or demagoguery exhibited in a variety of speeches, or the relative impartiality of several historical narratives. Concepts such as *elegy*, *demagoguery*, and *impartiality*, which admit of degrees, tend to work best, since the exercise eventually involves asking students to assess the degree to which the common thread is present in each text.

In class, after listing the relevant assigned texts on the blackboard, announce the common thread and ask students to describe its essential qualities in the abstract, so that they can approach the texts with a shared set of criteria. As you write their responses on the blackboard, you may wish to prime them to notice particular features of individual texts by asking them about relevant essential qualities they may have overlooked.

When the students seem to have a reasonably robust understanding of the common thread, ask each student to list the texts on a piece of paper in rank order, according to the degree to which the common thread is present in each. This may take them longer than a few minutes. As they make their lists, encourage them to keep the shared criteria in mind and to write a few notes justifying each text's placement in the list. (Naturally, the ranking process goes more smoothly when students have read carefully in advance. I sometimes find it helpful to announce the common thread before class or even ask students to read with it in mind.)

Once everyone has finished writing, tally the results on the blackboard. Now the stage is set for discussion of the texts. Begin by proposing that the class try to agree about the correct ranking. Whether or not the students ultimately reach a consensus, the difficulties they encounter along the way should produce vigorous and inclusive discussion. As students defend their choices and get drawn into a comparative analysis of the texts, their movement from text to text may become too fast for comfort, in which case I usually insist that they anchor their judgments in particular passages from each text and test those passages against the criteria they established together at the outset.

REFLECTIONS

In many courses, especially survey courses, multiple texts often need to be discussed in a single class meeting. In such situations, when time is short and the agenda is long, this exercise ensures that no text—and no student—gets left out.

The exercise is also designed to help students practice several skills: comparative analysis, attention to nuance, definition of key terms, and the application of general concepts to concrete cases. Ranking all the texts in a specific order requires students to pay attention to small differences in degree rather than comparing in broad strokes. Discussing the meaning of the common thread, and then returning to the results of that discussion when the students' rankings are up for debate, can illustrate the value of defining analytic categories precisely and in a way that others, after perhaps a little persuasion, are willing to accept.

This exercise works particularly well after students have built up a repertoire of readings suitable for comparison, and it can help them identify important course themes, such as in preparation for a test or final exam. A more time-consuming variation of the exercise, in which you solicit a common thread from the students instead of determining it yourself, can also serve this purpose.

That said, the exercise can also be useful early in the semester, especially when the concepts or key terms that students are asked to define at the outset provide them with a common thread not only through the texts up for discussion during that particular session but also through the rest of the course. As the semester continues and students move on to other texts, they can be encouraged to add those texts to their initial ranking and progressively refine their understanding of the common thread.

For this reason, if you use this exercise early in the semester, the common thread is worth choosing carefully, with a view to its usefulness later in the course. I discovered this after asking students in the second week of a Western civilization class to rank a group of four texts (Aeschylus's *Prometheus Bound*, Hesiod's *Theogony* and *Works and Days*, and the first four chapters of the Book of Genesis) by the degree to which each text portrays God or the gods as just. We spent a good fifteen minutes constructing a pair of definitions and descriptions for the two terms I thought most relevant: *justice* and (in order to clarify *justice* by contrast with its opposite) *tyranny*. As students volunteered elements for our description of each term, prompted sometimes by my questions about issues I knew might come up in our future readings and discussions (Is nepotism necessarily characteristic of a tyrant? Is mercy necessarily at odds with justice?), I wrote their contributions on the blackboard and observed most students copying my blackboard scrawls into their own notebooks. Justice and tyranny proved to be frequently recurrent themes in our course, and throughout the semester I noticed students flipping back to these original notes to defend their use of the terms in class discussion. Sometimes they even made new annotations in the margins of those old pages on occasions when, I imagine, discussing new texts had expanded or otherwise changed their understanding of the old terms.

STORIES

Prose fiction is at once the most familiar literary genre and also the least well understood. Stories, after all, can feel almost transparent in their effects, especially when compared to the linguistic challenges of poetry or the performative dimensions of drama. It's all the more important, then, to be able to help students recognize the distinctive elements through which novels and short stories create those effects, from the macro level of narrative, plot, setting, and structure, to the micro level of characterization and point of view, to the heightened dynamics of beginnings, endings, and—when the stakes are at their highest—ethics.

The fifteen exercises in this section instruct students in the art of storytelling. The first four activities on narrative and plot ("The Six-Word Story," "Narrative Rounds," "Splicing," and "Is It in Your Body?") ask students to think broadly about the nature of narrative itself: what makes a story a story, what it means to fictionalize experience, how narratives revisit (and rewrite) other narratives, and how stories end up inside readers. The exercises on setting and structure ("Mapmaker," "Diagram This," and "Bridges") maintain a wide perspective, helping students visualize and theorize the often hidden ways in which authors put stories together. The next four activities tighten the focus, to consider some of the most consequential choices storytellers make, including the representation of individual characters ("Intersectional Reading" and "Proust Questionnaire") and the perspective provided by the narrative's point of view ("Understanding Point of View" and "Flip the Script").

The three exercises in the next-to-last set ("First Paragraphs," "Script Doctor," and "Alternate Endings") zero in on two of the most distinctive components of any narrative—how it begins and how it ends—to highlight the ways stories create expectations and achieve closure. The final exercise ("The Great Debate") zooms in and then pulls back out, bringing to light powerful moments of conflict that offer no easy answers, in order to help students probe the ethical wagers of, and the diversity of values within, literary narratives. Taken as a whole, these exercises will ensure that even the most experienced readers will no longer take the workings of fiction for granted.

The Six-Word Story

Jacquelyn Ardam

A collaborative exercise that explores narrative condensation.

Genre: *fiction, especially short stories*
Course Level: *introductory*
Student Difficulty: *easy*
Teacher Preparation: *low*
Class Size: *small to medium*
Semester Time: *any*
Writing Component: *in class*
Close Reading: *high*
Estimated Time: *45 to 50 minutes*

EXERCISE

Legend has it that Hemingway's favorite piece of his own writing was a six-word short story that he wrote to win a bet:

For sale: baby shoes, never worn.

This six-word story is a great jumping-off point for a classroom exercise on narrative fiction, particularly the short story. Instead of beginning class by talking about that day's reading assignment, write Hemingway's six-word story on the board and ask the students for their thoughts on it. Let the class brainstorm for several minutes, encouraging them to say anything that comes to mind about the story, and write their ideas on the board as well. Ask some questions to get them thinking: Do you think that Hemingway's piece *is* a short story? How short can a story be and still be a story? Can you express a narrative in just six words? Characters? Who is narrating this story? How important are punctuation and syntax to its telling? What differentiates it from a poem?

After this discussion, divide your students into pairs and ask each pair to transform that day's reading assignment into a six-word story. Give them about ten minutes to compose, and then ask them to write their stories on the board. Once everyone has regrouped, ask each pair to present its six-word story to the class. To get the conversation going, consider posing one or two of the following questions to the pairs: Which elements of the original story did you absolutely need to include and why? What does your six-word story leave out? How important is punctuation to your six-word story? Diction? Tone? Do you see your six-word story as a summary of the reading assignment? As a tagline? Is there a narrative arc to your story? Is there an epiphany? What is the relationship between the two texts? Are your six-word story and the original story even in the same genre?

Here the conversation might naturally lead into a more general discussion of the genre of the short story. How short can a short story be? Conversely, how long can a short story be? How do long and short versions of narrative fiction work differently? If you wish, take notes on the board as your students come up with definitions in order to organize their thoughts. Ideally, your class will, as a group, come up with a framework and vocabulary for discussing fiction that you can employ throughout the rest of the class. You might encourage your students to define such key terms as point of view, plot, tone, or epiphany. If your course covers multiple narrative genres—flash fiction, the short story, prose poetry, the novella, the novel—you might also work with your students to define and distinguish one genre from another. Allow at least thirty to thirty-five minutes for the pair presentations and the conversations to follow.

REFLECTIONS

"The Six-Word Story" (an activity sometimes also assigned in creative writing classrooms) is designed to help students think about how and why we define narratives by genre, and also about the possible pitfalls of doing so. I have done this exercise several times in an introductory course, usually in the middle of a unit on short stories, but it can be done successfully at any point in a class on fiction or the short story in particular.

When doing this exercise, I often pair Hemingway's six-word story with Flannery O'Connor's "Good Country People," which has made for some deliciously humorous narratives. A sampling from my students:

- Leg lost: Christian country person wanted.
- Dude, where's my leg? That's country!
- Simple good country boy: leg thief.
- A woman loses her leg twice.

"The Six-Word Story" can also lead class conversations in many different and productive directions. I've talked with my students about Hemingway's "iceberg theory," the role of the gothic in American literature, the relationship between the comedic and the ironic, and the effects of terseness and brevity in literature. In addition to O'Connor's "Good Country People," I have also paired Hemingway's story with James Joyce's "Araby" and would recommend pairing the six-word story with any short story that exhibits a significant shift in tone or an epiphany. Other short stories that I'd recommend are Nathaniel Hawthorne's "The Birthmark," Michael Cunningham's "Pearls," Junot Díaz's "The Cheater's Guide to Love," and Jhumpa Lahiri's

"Sexy." If you're interested in a Hemingway-specific lesson, you could discuss his six-word story alongside "The End of Something" or another short story from *In Our Time*.

What I have found most valuable in this exercise is the group discussion of the students' writing process: how they narrow the original story down to just six words, how they decide what matters (and *how* it matters) in the story, how many of their six-word stories make use of the author's distinctive vocabulary, tone, or point of view. When you put students in an active authorial position, they are able to think about style from a completely different perspective and see a text's diction, syntax, and punctuation as deliberate.

Additionally, this exercise builds strong close-reading skills. It encourages students to read fiction as closely and carefully as they read poetry. While my students are often more than willing to debate the role of a semicolon in a poem, they are much more resistant to doing so in a short story. This exercise opens students up to reading fiction—even very, very short fiction—from a new perspective.

Narrative Rounds *in actual build*

Joyce Coleman

An icebreaker exercise that teaches the most basic elements of oral storytelling.

Genre: *fiction*
Course Level: *introductory*
Student Difficulty: *easy*
Teacher Preparation: *low*
Class Size: *small to medium*
Semester Time: *first day, early*
Writing Component: *optional after class*
Close Reading: *none*
Estimated Time: *35 to 40 minutes*

EXERCISE

Begin by putting students into pairs (for small classes) or groups of three (for medium classes). Ask each student to tell the other member or members of the group a story. The story should last no more than five minutes, and it must be about the storyteller him- or herself (what folklorists call a "personal experience narrative" or "memorat"). The tellers should choose a story that they are comfortable sharing and that is likely to interest the audience, and they should tell it with conviction. The listeners should pay close attention and respond supportively.

Once all the students have told their stories, ask the entire class to get up and form two concentric circles. (Move furniture to the sides of the room as needed; if you are in a classroom with bolted-down chairs, bring everyone to the front of the room.) Ask each circle to walk slowly, in opposite directions, until you tell the circles to stop and face each other. Then ask each student to choose one of the stories she or he just heard and tell it to the person standing opposite. That person will then tell the first speaker a story he or she had just heard. Because the retellings of the stories tend to be notably shorter than the originals, this portion of the exercise typically takes just five to seven minutes.

Now ask the circles to walk forward again until you stop them. Have the new facing pairs tell each other the story they have *just* heard from their previous partner. This next round will take even less time than the previous one, usually only four to five minutes.

Have the students return to their seats, then call on one person at random to tell the last story she or he heard to the entire class. Ask the other members of the class to help trace this version of the story back to the intermediate and original tellers, noting which aspects of the story have changed along the way. After the class has traced a few stories back this way, invite the students to consider the changes that seem to occur in transition. Although some parts of stories may become garbled, as in the game of telephone, students typically find that the changes are meaningful: action has been tightened, less important details have been dropped, and the story has moved more firmly into one or another narrative mode (usually comic). They may also find that common themes emerge. List these observations on the board and encourage students to reflect on what their discoveries might say about storytelling more generally.

REFLECTIONS

"Narrative Rounds" invites students to discover some of the most basic components of effective narrative through their own lived experience. The learning is augmented by many nonintellectual factors: the intimacy of the storytelling group at the beginning, the physical activity of walking, and the excitement or anxiety of encountering random listeners in the circle and plunging into engagement with them. The exercise takes narrative back to its source in face-to-face interaction, connecting it to the high-context, multisensory experience of oral literature. This can be used as a teaching point later on if you are reading texts derived from oral traditions; you can also use these observations to ask students how written narratives differ from oral ones. Finally, as an icebreaker, the exercise gives students a way to meet each other and begin to feel comfortable interacting.

For example, in one of my classes a student told a story about a trip from North Dakota to Manhattan with her father and two of her high-school friends. The father sent the three young women into the city with lots of good advice, which they promptly disregarded. They got pulled into a game of three-card monte, lost money, got the money back when a cop intervened, and were chased by the card dealer. They finally got back safely to their hotel, where they lied to the father about what had happened.

In tracing the story back to its original version, the class discovered that various details had dropped away in the retelling: for example, information about the women involved and the exact sequence of their bets in the card game. Other elements were augmented to create more excitement, such as how far the women had to run to escape the angry dealer. The class recognized that the retellers had edited the story to make it more dramatic and engaging. At the same time, the real fear that the women had felt gave way, in retelling, to a comic tone.

Discussion of the story's theme pulled in another story, about a male student engaging in underage drinking, then driving, landing in jail, and having to be bailed out by his parents. Combining these stories, the class arrived at a general, age-appropriate theme of adolescents testing their limits but needing their parents to fall back on. As a result of the discussion, the students became more aware of basic elements of narrative construction and also more aware of their own preferences as audience or readers.

As a follow-up to this exercise, you can also design a take-home work sheet that guides students to a more detailed analysis of the experience. The work sheet could ask the students to consider why they chose the personal story they told, how and why they edited and possibly fictionalized it in the telling, what they thought the underlying message of the story was, and how their listeners' reactions affected them as they spoke. They could also be asked to comment on what they learned about narrative from their experience as listeners and retellers. The next class can be devoted to sharing these analyses and drawing further conclusions.

The results of this take-home exercise usually reinforce the principles that emerge in class discussion. Even the original tellers of the stories, it turns out, often fictionalize them to make them sound happier or funnier ("I altered the 'reality' of my story by making it humorous. Of course, at the time this really happened, none of this was funny") or to heighten the interest by exaggerating key details or dropping boring ones ("like where I stayed and what I ate"). But it also provides new insight into the role of audience in shaping narrative: "The more we nodded the more he told," one student wrote. In another case the listeners transformed the story as the teller was telling it: he changed his serious account of falling down a flight of stairs into a funny story because his audience kept laughing. Tales tend to form a chain: one person's story about New Year's Eve evokes from the next person yet another story about New Year's Eve. All these reactions show how storytelling becomes a reciprocal exchange between tellers and listeners.

. . . .

Splicing

Michael Wood

An introductory exercise on literary influence and adaptation.

Genre: *fiction, especially novels*
Course Level: *introductory*
Student Difficulty: *easy*
Teacher Preparation: *medium*
Class Size: *small to medium*
Semester Time: *any*
Writing Component: *none*
Close Reading: *medium*
Estimated Time: *20 to 25 minutes*

EXERCISE

Play the following game with your students: The night before class, choose two novels that share some connection. The novels might be from the same genre, for example, or they might include a similar character type, or make use of a particular kind of plot point or theme, or use language in a similar way: two novels, in other words, that make you say, even if only briefly, "Oh, this reminds me of that other novel." (They don't need to be novels on your current syllabus, but they can be.)

From each novel, select a few short excerpts that you might normally show to students side by side as evidence of the similarity between the texts. *Now splice the excerpts from each novel together.* You can simply alternate bits if you like, or you can splice them more creatively (half a line here, half a line there). Try to maintain narrative sense; try not to let the seams show. You don't have to use every word or even every sentence. (What you don't include will ultimately be as instructive as what you do include.)

In class, give the students a copy of this new passage. Tell them it is a hybrid—a text made up of actual phrases or sentences from two different novels. You can tell them the titles of the novels if you wish; for a higher degree of difficulty, keep that a secret. Now play the game: ask them to try to take the passage apart by identifying, as best they can, which pieces come from which text. You can have them do this individually or in small groups. (The arguments in small groups can be lively.) When everyone is ready—ten minutes is generally enough time for a short passage—ask each person or group to describe how and why they split up the passage the way they did. Once everyone has had a chance to weigh in, produce the original excerpts and let them see exactly which pieces came from which texts. Let them also see—and reflect on—which pieces you didn't splice together. Could those pieces have been spliced in just as easily? Why or why not?

REFLECTIONS

It has been said that there are only six or seven stories in the world—all other stories are variants upon them. This game gets students thinking about often quite subtle narrative questions—in particular, how literary texts adapt, repeat, and rewrite each other.

I first used this exercise in an introductory survey course on the reading of fiction, from Homer's *The Odyssey* to the present day. Texts included *The Arabian Nights,* Charles Dickens's *Hard Times,* Bram Stoker's *Dracula,* and a number of others, and one particular section was devoted to literary influence and intertextuality: Michael Cunningham's *The Hours* as a revision of Virginia Woolf's *Mrs. Dalloway*, Jean Rhys's *Wide Sargasso Sea* as a supplement to Charlotte Brontë's *Jane Eyre.* I spliced certain sentences from J. K. Rowling's *Harry Potter and the Sorcerer's Stone* into the text of *Jane Eyre*, as follows:

His mother had taken him home for a month or two, on account of his delicate health. In her opinion there was no finer boy anywhere. He hated exercise—unless of course it involved punching somebody. He was large and stout for his age, with a dingy and unwholesome skin. He gorged himself habitually at table, which made him bilious and gave him a dim and bleared eye and flabby cheeks. He had thick blond hair that lay smoothly on his thick, fat head. He bullied and punished me; not two or three times in the week, not once or twice in the day, but continually. He spent some minutes thrusting out his tongue as far as he could without damaging the roots.

Here are the source passages:

The Dursleys had a small son called Dudley and in their opinion there was no finer boy anywhere. . . . [They] didn't want their son mixing with a child like that.

Nearly ten years had passed. . . Dudley was very fat and hated exercise—unless of course it involved punching somebody. Dudley's favorite punching bag was Harry. . . Dudley was about four times bigger than he was. Harry. . . wore round glasses held together with a lot of Scotch tape because of all the times Dudley had punched him on the nose. . . Dudley. . . had a large pink face, not much neck, small, watery blue eyes, and thick blond hair that lay smoothly on his thick, fat head. Aunt Petunia often said that Dudley looked like an angel—Harry often said that Dudley looked like a pig in a wig.

—Rowling, *Harry Potter and the Sorcerer's Stone*

His mother had taken him home for a month or two, 'on account of his delicate health.'
[He was] large and stout for his age, with a dingy and unwholesome skin. . . . He gorged himself habitually at table, which made him bilious and gave him a dim and bleared eye and flabby cheeks. . . . The master. . . affirmed that he would do very well if he had fewer cakes. . . sent from home.
He bullied and punished me; not two or three times in the week, not once or twice in the day, but continually. . . . [He] spent some minutes thrusting out his tongue. . . as far as he could without damaging the roots.

—Brontë, *Jane Eyre*

Student groups were quick to spy the recurring figure of the spoiled bully—in both cases the son of the family our orphan hero/heroine has come to live with. Some groups even guessed, correctly, the identities of the two novels I had commingled together, more at first from the composite character portrait of the bully than anything else, such as narrative point of view, tone of voice, irony, diction, recognizable metaphors or tricks of syntax, and so on. And that's when things got more interesting: How is it exactly that these two novels, from two different centuries, speak so well to one another? And what kind of "story" can be said to emerge from this act of irreverent coupling?

When we reconvened, conversation turned immediately to the subject of literary influence. Students concluded that the important thing was not just that Rowling had read *Jane Eyre*, which she certainly had, but that both Brontë and Rowling are working interestingly with a stereotype, involving readers in what they already know and what they want from such a story. They liked the "new" story the spliced version presented, noting how the sentences slip seamlessly from one book into another, and also the way sentences I did not include matched other sentences so well: "delicate health" / "no finer boy"; "large and stout" / "very fat"; "dim and bleared eye" / "small, watery blue eyes"; "flabby cheeks" / "pink face." The interest in intertextuality, we finally concluded, is not, as it may at first seem, in what looks like copying, but in shared use of material.

And it is with this thought in mind that the exercise could be developed or adapted to help students think about genre (revenge tragedy, the epic, the western, the sentimental romance); about the way individual texts can talk to each other across genres; about many of the basic building blocks of character and narrative. You can use the exercise to teach plot or theme or character or language, depending on your needs and interests. You can even use it to teach style (most style exercises focus on stylistic differences between writers; this one plays on their unexpected harmonies). But in each case the point is to put together one or more texts and invite students to take them apart and wonder why the job is so easy or so difficult. And then, with practice, you can ask them to make their own collations from texts they have read for the course.

. . . .

Is It in Your Body?

Kathryn Bond Stockton

An exercise in recall that helps students think about how—and why—texts get "inside" us.

Genre: *fiction*
Course Level: *intermediate or advanced*
Student Difficulty: *moderate or hard*
Teacher Preparation: *low*
Class Size: *any*
Semester Time: *any*
Writing Component: *in class*
Close Reading: *medium*
Estimated Time: *50 to 60 minutes*

EXERCISE

Assign a ten- to twenty-page scene from a novel for students to read outside of class. Choose something juicy, even upsetting. Make sure it is rich in detail and word choice. Ideally, it should be interpretively dense—for example, the scene from Jean Genet's *Querelle* in which the sailor Querelle murders Vic, or the scene in Vladimir Nabokov's *Lolita* where Humbert has a wiggling Lolita in his lap. Passages less salacious but lush include the protagonist's drug-dream scene in Charlotte Brontë's *Villette* or the emotional "shipwreck" scene between Dorothea and Rosamond in George Eliot's monumental *Middlemarch*. Instruct the students, when you assign the passage, to expect an in-class written exercise that will require them to have read carefully.

When class convenes, divide students into groups of three or four. Ask each group, with their books closed, to record on paper as many details as the students can remember about the scene they've read. (Have one student serve as group recorder.) Tell them first to list only the words or phrases they recall verbatim. Then have them sequence the general happenings and features (dialogue, descriptions, and so on) of the scene, using the left-hand part of the paper for verbatim details and the right-hand part for sequencing and summarizing. Allow about twenty minutes for the students to work in their groups. State the time limit. You want to convey a bit of excitement, even urgency, but also allow for the students' thoughtfulness.

In the next twenty minutes, assign two scribes to each side of the board at the front of the room (chalkboard or whiteboard). Call on each group in turn to offer a single detail or a happening, the student-scribes writing these on the board: verbatim details on the left, paraphrase/summation on the right. The point is to get a snapshot of *how much text* and *what of the text* students have internalized. Ideally, the groups keep adding details one at a time, until all their details appear on the board. (This part of the exercise can also be shortened or even skipped; it's fun to compare different groups' recall but not required for the lesson's overall force and effect.)

Once the students have established how much of the text is "in" their bodies, invite the class to reflect on these results: To what extent did groups (and individuals in groups) recall the same details or features from the scene? For details recalled in common (which ones?), what is the reason: Shock value? Salaciousness? Beauty? Repugnance? Unusual word choice? (Un)familiar concept? Do we as readers all have the same novel *in* us while discussing it? Is the novel functionally reducible, then, to the bundle of words and summations we extract from it and carry in our bodies? Why or why not? Wind up the conversation by encompassing the work students and their teachers perform in the classroom. Is our differential recall a problem for proffering interpretations or readings—in short, for doing literary criticism? How or how not?

REFLECTIONS

Students have serious fun with this text-in-the-body experiment. With the right passage, they're intrigued to think deeply about why certain details got inside them and then remained verbatim or became altered or just petered out. As you can imagine, most undergraduates have never thought of words having penetrative force—and never thought of readers having different novels "in" them after they've read the exact same text.

For example, in my class Theories of Gender and Sexuality, I taught *Lolita* and had a riotous but truly illuminating time with this exercise. I assigned the famous lap scene, along with short chapters that precede and follow it (chapters 12–14, nine pages total). Images commonly recalled verbatim: "Eden-red apple" (with a few students adding from memory the critical adjective "banal" that Humbert attaches to this phrase), "hidden tumor" and "gagged, bursting beast" (phrases describing Humbert's erection), "tactile correspondence" (euphemism for his penis being rubbed by her monkeyish movements in his lap), "innocent cotton frock" (indicating innocence attributed to Lolita's dress, not to her), "safely solipsized" (for Humbert's confidence that he's preserved her innocence), "Turk" and "slave" (Humbert's tumescent sense of their positions), "bruise. . . on thigh," "huge hairy hand," "thumb. . . reaching. . . groin," "giggling child," "shrill voice," "squirmed," "crushed against buttock. . . throb," "man or monster," "[her] cheeks aflame, hair awry," "Blessed be the Lord, she had noticed nothing!" (all from the crucial sequence leading to Humbert's climax).

Who does what to whom and to what effect (Is Lolita aroused by Humbert's "beast"? Does she, too, ecstatically arrive?) caused intense debate—and laughter—demonstrating how much hangs on *what of the text* gets "in" us. Many students sheepishly admitted that they *wanted* to commit to memory this "beautiful" passage, despite their being repulsed by its content. Given what students did and didn't memorize, even in the face of enormous effort, we as a class decided that the passage positions the *reader* as both attracted pedophile and distracted child. That is to say, like Humbert, we ourselves experience a strange attraction that time will erode—our attraction to the very words on the page (dense, lyrical, rhythmic, funny, euphemistically fresh, and clearly antinormative)—and these words distract us (much as Humbert tries to distract Lolita with his Carmen ditty) from the bewildering goal being sought. We were left wondering which and how many of these words would still be in us at semester's end.

For a greater challenge in a more advanced class, especially in a literary theory class, launch this exercise after you have taught Ferdinand de Saussure's concept of the sign from his treatise *Course in General Linguistics*, Jacques Derrida's notions of difference and deferral, or even Roland Barthes's "The Death of the Author" (which views the reader as the text's "destination"). The exercise helps to show and explore the materiality of the signifier. In my class, our discussions kept turning back, for example, to the sound of the words, to their rhythmic flow. In some instances, the signifier's satisfying sound ("plop," "safely solipsized," "gagged, bursting beast") aided students' recall. But we also noticed that certain sentences were so precise and dense that we were defeated in committing them to memory, despite our intense desire to do so ("Lola, the bobby-soxer, devouring her immemorial fruit, singing through its juice, losing her slipper, rubbing the heel of her slipperless foot in its sloppy anklet"), making us like Humbert, who can't keep hold of what he has only momentarily possessed. In addition, you can illustrate how the text inside us (only ever partially there, due to its tendency to drain from us) contributes to meanings being plural and partial but not subjective in the way many students think the text can mean anything they think or say it does. Of course, you don't need Saussure or Derrida to make such points. You can simply use the exercise itself to stage these questions in ordinary discourse any undergraduate is bound to understand.

. . . .

Mapmaker

Kenyon Gradert

A cartographic adventure that helps students visualize plot, themes, and literary place.

> Genre: *fiction*
> Course Level: *any*
> Student Difficulty: *easy*
> Teacher Preparation: *low*
> Class Size: *small to medium*
> Semester Time: *any*
> Writing Component: *none*
> Close Reading: *medium to high*
> Estimated Time: *50 minutes*

EXERCISE

Choose any extended work of fiction that has a strong element of place. After your students have read the entire work, spend a final discussion day in class by collectively drawing and annotating a map. Begin by drawing a giant rectangle on the board to serve as your map's borders—you'll need lots of space. In a bottom corner, draw a compass with the cardinal directions. Then ask students to recount the four or five most important locations of the plot, starting with the geographically largest and moving to the smallest: In what country does this story take place? What cities? What houses, cafés, or parks? (The size and scope of the locations will of course vary by text.) As students answer, ask them to come up and draw the location, depicted either by its geographic outline or by some clever symbol: a log cabin for Uncle Tom's cabin, for example. It often helps if you, as the instructor, draw the largest-scale location first and set a relaxed mood by poking fun at your own lack of cartographic precision.

After you have this handful of primary places on your map (this part of the exercise usually takes ten to fifteen minutes), divide the students into small groups and assign each group to a particular place on the map. Give groups ten minutes to convene and discuss their place, focusing on such questions as these: What kind of language does the author use to depict this place? What sort of things tend to happen in this neck of the woods? Which characters are most connected to the place, and how do they feel about it? Does the place change as the plot progresses? What key themes in the work are best expressed here? Could this place be considered, in its own way, a character in the text, and if so, how? What other places on the map is this place connected to? Reconvene the class and allow another ten minutes for groups to present (briefly) key thoughts on their place. Annotate the map with these observations as the groups present their findings.

Finally, devote fifteen to twenty minutes to a conversation about the "big picture" of the map. Ask students, for example, to trace the story's journey on the map; have them literally draw lines on it for a visual reminder of plot. Ideally, these lines will form a good transition into the concluding discussion of big questions: How do these places work together, or in tension, to form a narrative experience? How are place and plot, in this text, related? In addition, consider how these places inform the author's vision of the world: how does the Chicago of Dreiser's *Sister Carrie*, the Middle East of Melville's *Clarel*, or the Rome of Hawthorne's *The Marble Faun*, for example, reveal the authors' beliefs about God, human beings, and society? Bring the journey full circle by tying these authors' visions to your students' visions of their own place: Where do they come from, and how does this inform their vision of the world? Does a student's suburban upbringing chafe against Faulkner's Yoknapatawpha County? (See Cowley's *Portable Faulkner* for a great model.) Does your university campus stand with or in contrast to the works you're reading? Ideally, students will reveal their diverse backgrounds and illustrate how it forms the basis for their own unique interaction with the map's big picture.

If the text under discussion focuses on an actual or metaphorical journey, you might also broaden this closing conversation to discuss the nature of travel more generally. What kind of journey are the characters on? Are they pilgrims? Aimless wanderers? Gaudy tourists? Imperial conquerors? Are some characters more stationary than others?

As class draws to a close, ask the students if they would change anything on the map—either by addition, subtraction, or reconfiguration—in light of the discussion they've just had. Some students may wish to hear more about a certain character; others may think a certain side journey is irrelevant to the main plot; yet others may express frustration with go-nowhere characters. Reactions vary (and opinions may change as discussion progresses), but students tend to enjoy discovering their own agency within the story through expressing opinions about how the work's world might change.

REFLECTIONS

This mapping exercise is a memorable way to reexamine major characters, plots, and themes one final time before you move on to another work. Students enjoy the visual aspect of the mapmaking and find that tracing connections between places is a helpful way to make vivid the key components of the text. The exercise also can be a springboard for the discussion of critical approaches to literature and space, including postcolonial, ecocritical, feminist, Marxist, new historicist, borderlands, and queer theory interpretations. It can even function as an introduction to GIS and spatial projects in the digital humanities.

"Mapmaker" helps students draw connections not only within the work at hand but also to previously read works, as students perform their own sort of journey within the literature. In my classroom the exercise has worked well to enable this very journey. At the conclusion of Benjamin Franklin's hectic *Autobiography*, for example, a map helped our class synthesize the rambling course of the author's life. By listing all of Franklin's varied activities in Philadelphia, London, and the frontier, students were able to visualize the marvelous breadth and depth of his life. Noting this spatial rambling, we transitioned smoothly into a discussion of Max Weber's analysis of Franklin's restlessness in *The Protestant Ethic and the Spirit of Capitalism* and discussed how Franklin's geography may have informed his famous discussion of morality in Part Two of the autobiography.

In addition, students noted that Franklin, supposedly a quintessentially American figure, was thoroughly transatlantic in his scientific studies and diplomatic missions. (Here I pulled up a digital map comparing Franklin's transatlantic and Voltaire's Eurocentric letter correspondences, from the "Visualizing Benjamin Franklin's Correspondence Network" case study within Stanford University's wonderful *Mapping the Republic of Letters* project.) Finally, we discussed how Franklin's extended descriptions of public spaces (libraries, streets, fire stations) inform his vision of democracy and republicanism. Discussion could have continued long after, reaching into contemporary politics of space and debates about whether Franklin still has something to say to the Occupy generation or to postcolonial peoples. At its best, "Mapmaker" poignantly brings the author's world into contact with students' own sense of space and place.

This exercise also gives students a new appreciation for narrative structure—the ways stories take (and make) their journeys. One student may note that the journey in *The Sound and the Fury* is nauseatingly cyclical; another that many works of the American Renaissance feature a movement out from society and back; yet another that Spenser's *The Faerie Queene* seems more interested in labyrinthine wandering than in getting anywhere in particular. In discussing and arguing with each other about the nature of the literary journey at hand, students make a collective trip, not unlike Chaucer's travelers: "In felaweshipe, and pilgrimes were they alle."

. . . .

Diagram This

Erin G. Carlston

An exercise that asks student to think visually about narrative structures and patterns.

Genre: *fiction*
Course Level: *introductory*
Student Difficulty: *easy or moderate*
Teacher Preparation: *low*
Class Size: *small to medium*
Semester Time: *any*
Writing Component: *in class*
Close Reading: *medium*
Estimated Time: *50 minutes*

EXERCISE

This exercise asks students to create a diagram of a work of fiction. The range of structures and patterns you can ask your class to visualize is quite broad. I have used this exercise, for example, to ask students to diagram the relationship between the provinces, the metropole, and the British Empire in Arnold Bennett's *Old Wives' Tale*; the interaction of race and class in Dorothy West's novel *The Living Is Easy*; the connections among Dorian Gray, Dorian's picture, Basil Hallward, Lord Henry, Life, and Art in Oscar Wilde's *The Picture of Dorian Gray*; and the chronology suggested by the first hundred lines of Homer's *Iliad* compared to the first hundred lines of the *Odyssey*.

At the beginning of class, divide the students into groups of three or four and provide them with pencils, erasers, and 8.5 × 11–inch sheets of paper. Then choose one of the following aspects of that day's text for the groups to diagram: either the structure of the work as a whole, or the relationship among a set of characters, places, events and/or themes (which you will specify) in that work. Give the students your chosen prompt, along with two simple rules: (1) don't draw representational pictures—no stick figures or symbols like smiley faces, and (2) use absolutely no written text. Instead, ask the students to think in terms of pattern, shape, and relationship.

To help them get started, offer examples of diagram types or invite them to brainstorm a list as a class before beginning. Possibilities include flow charts, Venn diagrams, timelines, food pyramids, geometric forms, graphs, and abstract transit maps, among other forms. Stress that this isn't a test of drawing ability and that students won't be judged on their artistic talents. Ask each group to designate one member who will do the actual drawing.

After they have finished drawing their diagrams (this should take about fifteen minutes), ask each group to pass its diagram to the group on the right. Each group should now spend five minutes trying to figure out what the group to their left is getting at—*without asking that group any questions*. When everyone is ready, have each group present the diagram they were given and propose their interpretation of it to the rest of the class. Project each diagram in the front of the room for everyone to see, if possible. Let students from the other groups offer comments or questions, and before moving on to the next group, invite the students who drew the diagram to say whether the interpretation accurately captured their intention. (If you are pressed for time, you can also simply have each group present its diagram to the rest of the class directly without passing it to the right first, though passing introduces an extra layer of interactivity and interpretation that students particularly enjoy.) In the last ten minutes of class, ask the class as a whole how the diagrams have shaped their understanding of the text and whether, after seeing other diagrams, they would alter their own in any way.

REFLECTIONS

The primary goal of "Diagram This" is to get students, especially first-year students or nonmajors, to think about narrative fiction in terms of structure and pattern rather than the more accessible character and plot. It teaches them that the way a work is constructed affects what it says. While many students are perplexed by the exercise for the first few minutes and often ask for examples—which I refuse to give them because then they'll just copy the model—almost all of them rise to the challenge. The visual act of diagramming encourages students who are less comfortable with written and spoken language to get their ideas about a story into a form in which they can literally see what they think. And for students who *are* adept at written or verbal analysis, the assignment requires that they temporarily set aside the tools with which they're comfortable and conceptualize more abstractly how texts function.

When I use this exercise with Virginia Woolf's short story "Slater's Pins Have No Points," I ask students to diagram its structure and then, if they need more prompting, encourage them to think specifically about how time works in the story: it begins and ends in almost the same second, and the entire body of the story consists of flashbacks and mental associations. Some students end up drawing two fixed points connected by squiggly lines or large tangled loops. Others have drawn parallel lines representing "real time" and "internal time" and have added elements suggesting how they're connected. Some have shown external reality as a very small element contained within a much larger figure representing the psychological interpretation of reality. Within the short space of a fifty-minute class period, students can go from being baffled by Woolf's elliptical methods to working out quite successfully how she weaves in and out through time and memory.

For a variation useful for small classes (under fifteen students), you can have each student draw an individual diagram and, again, if you prefer, eliminate the step in which they pass around the drawings. Instead, go straight to asking a few students to share with the whole class. Done in this fashion near the beginning of the class, the exercise is a more concise way of starting off discussion and close reading of the text, rather than a task occupying the entire hour.

. . . .

Bridges

Joseph Fruscione

A flexible exercise that teaches narrative structure.

> Genre: *fiction*
> Course Level: *any*
> Student Difficulty: *moderate*
> Teacher Preparation: *low to medium*
> Class Size: *small to medium*
> Semester Time: *any*

Writing Component: *in class, optional after class*
Close Reading: *high*
Estimated Time: *45 to 50 minutes*

EXERCISE

Assign any fictional work with an interesting or innovative structure. Novels are best, but short stories with sufficiently complex narrative designs also work nicely. Consider, for example, Joyce's "The Dead" (layers of consciousness and flashback), Woolf's *Mrs. Dalloway* (parallel perspectives in a novel spanning only one day), Melville's "Benito Cereno" (flawed narrative consciousness, flashbacks, and a plot twist), Chopin's *The Awakening* (internal harmony and repetition, layers of memory, and subtle flashbacks), Nabokov's *Pale Fire* (postmodern metafiction with a hybrid structure), or any other work that plays with time and structure but can challenge first-time readers.

In class, you might begin by mapping out on the board with students what appear to be the different sections or larger movements of the work at hand. This part of the exercise can be a quick, general overview of the text's main chapters or sections, or it can be a slow, more careful diagramming of its many structural parts. (A useful starter exercise for "Bridges" could be the abbreviated version of the previous exercise, "Diagram This.") This opening step is not essential, but for introductory classes in which students may not know much about narrative structure, it can be helpful.

Invite students to choose any two consecutive sections, review them quickly, and write in response to this three-part prompt: What is each section doing individually? How are the two narrative pieces linked stylistically or thematically? What is new or clearer through rereading them in sequence? Give students fifteen to twenty minutes for this in-class writing component, which will strengthen and specify the group discussion to follow (the writing component can also function as prewriting for an eventual essay). If you like, you can pair students off and ask them to perform the exercise together, keeping a more casual record of their findings.

After the students have done their rereading and writing, have them share the *what* and *why* of their choices. Encourage them to read out loud the key lines or passages that capture the links they've identified, and help keep them focused on what they most want the class to see about their structural pairing. Highlight those fortuitous moments when students pick the same pairing but draw very different conclusions, or when they choose overlapping sections (one's second piece is another's first)—a happy coincidence that can add considerable momentum to the discussion.

Conclude by posing a set of more general questions about narrative structure and about the exercise itself: How exactly do authors create textual bridges, and what is their relation to other literary devices like plot, characterization, point of view, or theme? How are a text's internal motifs and connections easier to identify by locating and examining these narrative bridges? What can we learn from this method that we might have missed otherwise?

REFLECTIONS

"Bridges" focuses on the always important, often invisible, and sometimes complex structures of literary narratives. It pointedly directs students' attention to how an author connects and perhaps counterpoints a story's individual pieces to advance a larger unified purpose. Studying a narrative's consecutive clusters helps students identify internal tensions or ironies, explore complementary themes or images, understand narrative pacing or movement, and analyze narration or shifting points of view.

The exercise can work well for eighteenth- or nineteenth-century novels and stories, though I find it tailor-made for modernist texts, in which a narrative's internal transitions or overall cohesiveness may at first strike students as disjointed, even confusing. I have tried it on a number of story collections and novels from the early twentieth century, including Jean Toomer's *Cane* (1923), Ernest Hemingway's *In Our Time* (1925), and William Faulkner's *As I Lay Dying* (1930). In Toomer's *Cane*, one student group examined the juxtaposition of "Harvest Song" (a narrative poem) and "Bona and Paul" (a story) to ask why Toomer sequenced, side by side in the collection's urban section, characters of such different cultural and racial experiences. In linking this poem and story of this rich but challenging text, they concluded that Toomer deploys repetition, revision, and region to capture the richness of interracial voices and identities. For Hemingway's *In Our Time*, the juxtaposition of the seemingly different narratives "Indian Camp" and "Chapter 2" ("Minarets stuck up. . .") struck one group as, in truth, variations on a set of common themes: interpersonal struggle, parent-child relations, gender fluidity, and strained childbirth.

Faulkner's *As I Lay Dying*—with its fifteen narrators—posed to students a difficult challenge but also offered one of the strongest examples of how authors construct meaning by creating narrative bridges. For example, Vardaman's "My mother is a fish" chapter, placed back-to-back with Cash's methodical, thirteen-step description of making his mother's coffin ("I made it on the bevel," he begins), highlights how Faulkner presents the Bundrens as foils for each other throughout the novel. Here the students argued, quite insightfully, that Faulkner showcases Cash's meticulousness in counterpoint to Vardaman's confusion to illustrate different kinds of grief. I like to end my course section on narrative structure by noting how Toomer, Hemingway, and Faulkner all shared a common mentor, Sherwood Anderson, whose short-story cycle *Winesburg, Ohio* (1919) may have influenced their stylistic innovation, flexible handling of time, and broader identity as artists of the avant-garde.

As this example intimates, the exercise can also work progressively. For courses that arrange the readings chronologically, like mine, instructors can revise the exercise and heighten its level of difficulty when they get to later texts: by asking students to connect *three* consecutive sections in one work or by requiring them to make thematic pairings across texts (for example, a race-gender-place juxtaposition in Faulkner might echo yet complicate one from Toomer). I like this cumulative, more advanced version of "Bridges" because it goes beyond a single day and can yield for students deeper critical insights about both period (the avant-garde form of modernist texts) and genre (the forms of fictional works). In my experience, these kinds of fictional texts have worked particularly well because we often approach modernist works in nontraditional ways, while uncovering how fiction can be distinctive in its embrace of nonlinear structure and reading practices.

· ·

Intersectional Reading

Maureen Meharg Kentoff

A comparative exercise that examines character through the theory of intersectionality.

Genre: *fiction*
Course Level: *any*
Student Difficulty: *moderate*
Teacher Preparation: *low*
Class Size: *small to medium*
Semester Time: *any*
Writing Component: *none*
Close Reading: *high*
Estimated Time: *45 to 50 minutes*

EXERCISE

Intersectionality is an approach to literary analysis that invites students to consider how a range of identity factors, such as gender, race, nationality, class, sexuality, age, physical ability, corporeality, role, or setting, interact to shape character. Novels with richly rendered social worlds—texts like Kate Chopin's *The Awakening*, Edith Wharton's *The House of Mirth*, Nella

Larsen's *Passing*, or Toni Morrison's *Sula*, for example—are particularly good candidates for this comparative exercise in intersectional reading.

Before class, choose two characters from the assigned text that make a good pair for comparison across a range of factors like the ones listed above. Decide on the scope of material you want your students to analyze: the entire text, a particular chapter or section, or a specific selection of passages that provide rich character detail. Then prepare two handouts, each with three columns and four rows. Orient these two handouts in landscape mode and maximize the size of the chart so that there is ample space in each box.

On the first handout, label the first column header "Subjectivity Factor" and the remaining two column headers with the names of the characters. Then, under the first column header, label each of the three remaining rows with a particular subjectivity factor pertinent to the characters you've selected, such as "gender," "class," and "race." Title this handout "Close Character Reading."

On the second handout, keep the character names the same but change the first column header to "Intersecting Factors." Under this header, list the factors from the first handout as intersecting pairs: for example, "gender and class"; "gender and race"; "class and race." Title this handout "Intersectional Reading," and copy it on a different color paper, so the forms are easy to differentiate. If you were asking students to compare main characters Clare Kendry and Irene Redfield in Larsen's *Passing*, for example, your handouts might look something like this:

Handout #1: Close Character Reading

Subjectivity Factor	Clare Kendry	Irene Redfield
Gender		
Class		
Race		

Handout #2: Intersectional Reading

Intersecting Factors	Clare Kendry	Irene Redfield
Gender and Class		
Gender and Race		
Class and Race		

In class, spend the first few minutes briefly reviewing the concept of intersectionality and its potential for a more complete analysis of a character's lived experience. Then divide the class into groups of three or four and distribute copies of handout #1. Ask each group to spend fifteen to twenty minutes completing the boxes on the chart as they consider how each sub-jectivity factor is addressed in the text for each character. (If you like, you can offer an example for each factor to get them started.) Tell the groups to be specific in recalling character descriptions and events, including direct references to words, phrases, scenes, interactions, dialogue, and plot trajec-tory; remind them to cite page numbers when possible. (Be sure to specify what portion of the text they are responsible for.) At this point the groups should *not* compare characters but simply consider each individual character in terms of the factors listed. If they discover overlap between categories, tell them to place each detail in the box that seems most appropriate.

After the students have completed the first handout, pass out copies of handout #2. Ask each group to spend the next fifteen to twenty minutes completing the boxes on the new chart by considering how the two subjec-tivity factors that are listed *intersect* with each other. Encourage the groups to refer to the first handout for specific details and to note how these factors differ when compared across characters. Remind the groups again to list di-rect references, with page numbers. As with the first handout, you can offer examples to help them get started. During the group work, it can also be helpful to move around the room, listening in on the deliberations and pos-ing questions or offering suggestions for fine-tuning ideas.

Once the groups have completed the second handout, bring the class as a whole back together and spend the remaining class time discussing each intersection. Invite groups to share their findings on how a particular set of intersecting factors shapes, enriches, or constrains each character's lived experience. In what ways do these intersections reveal similarities and differ-ences across characters? Ask the groups to cite specific language used by the author and to acknowledge both literal and figurative descriptions within the text. If possible, list the group responses on a shared chart in the front of the room, either on the board or a projection screen. Given the "messiness" of intersectionality, your discussion will likely not be an orderly process. En-courage students to embrace this quality, and underscore how it is evidence of the complexity of characters (and humans!). Also note that intersectional reading will help students recognize and tease out this messiness as they con-duct literary analyses in formal and informal written assignments.

REFLECTIONS

The goal of this exercise is to help students develop a more tangible and pro-found understanding of the complex theory of intersectionality. (For a fur-ther overview of intersectionality, I have found Michele Tracy Berger and Kathleen Guidroz's edited volume *The Intersectional Approach: Transform-ing the Academy through Race, Class, and Gender* particularly helpful.) The process achieves a number of objectives: students practice close reading of the text in general and close reading of characters in particular; they generate concrete ways in which to explicate a character's intersectionality; and they are given additional opportunities to "unpack" the author's language and various literary devices (imagery, symbolism, dialect, and so on) that elicit multiple interpretations across characters.

My favorite text for teaching intersectionality is Stephen Crane's *Maggie: A Girl of the Streets*. I typically ask students to compare siblings Jimmie and Maggie Johnson, or Maggie and her lover Pete across such factors as "gender," "class," and "setting." Sometimes I offer a few examples to help the class get started, but students usually need only a little prompting before tackling the handout. In completing the first chart for the character of Maggie, for example, my students have cited allusions to "gender" in her family position (she is a daughter, an older and younger sister, a caretaker, and a family domestic), in her appearance (she is described as a pretty girl "who blossomed in a mud puddle"), and in her changing roles throughout the story (initially a romantic who desires marriage and feminine finery, she ends up a scorned lover and finally a prostitute). When we move to the second chart, the conversation quickly focuses on the impact of gender difference, as the life trajectories and even physical spaces available to Maggie contrast sharply with those available to the male characters Jimmie or Pete, despite their shared class status. This intersectional comparison helps students develop a multilayered analysis of Crane's commentary on "how the other half lives" (to borrow a phrase from Jacob Riis) rather than simply focus on a single characteristic such as class.

"Intersectional Reading" can be adapted to any course level and tailored in multiple ways. For an introductory class, you might focus on only two subjectivity factors or only one character (but note that the act of comparing characters can elicit a more complete understanding of intersectionality). For an advanced class, you can delve into subjectivity factors that are more tacitly implied by the author. In *Maggie*, for example, I have used such factors as capitalism, urban geography, and domestic abuse. In Larsen's *Passing*, I have asked students to explore the themes of sexuality or miscegenation by comparing Irene and Clare across various intersections of race, gender, family, and marriage. Another option is to choose topics specific to a particular course: for example, consumer culture, vernacular speech, or religion. You can also assign less fully drawn characters (in *Passing*, try Brian Redfield or Jack Bellew). I have also invited students to compare characters from two different texts, such as an intersectional analysis of class, gender, and setting focused on Edna Pontellier from Chopin's *The Awakening* and Lily Bart from Wharton's *The House of Mirth*.

Regardless of the course level, it can be helpful to offer examples of concepts that might fall under a given factor. For example, for "class," tell the students that they might consider depictions of work, income, liquid assets, possessions, attire, education, language, home life, or financial future. For "setting," they might focus on location, landscape, weather, home, material surroundings, public venues, corporeal space, architecture, workplace, street life, transportation, or mobility. You can also list these concepts on the board or even print them on the first handout.

My students react with great enthusiasm to "Intersectional Reading." They enjoy the challenge of tackling what is often perceived as a very abstract and difficult theoretical model. After the exercise, they report feeling more confident in their ability to generate specific and complex analyses not just of the characters but also of various themes and literary devices throughout the text. Some requested that we schedule the activity a few times throughout the semester. Given the growing prominence of intersectional interpretations across the humanities, this exercise also offers insight into how intersectional reading can be applied to a variety of literary genres. In sum, students are grateful for the practice and the open forum in which they are challenged to explore more fully and concretely how a key concept of lived experience affects literary representation.

. . . .

Proust Questionnaire

John Bugg

An exercise that encourages critical distance in the study of characterization.

Genre: *fiction, especially novels*
Course Level: *any*
Student Difficulty: *easy or moderate*
Teacher Preparation: *low*
Class Size: *any*
Semester Time: *any*
Writing Component: *in class*
Close Reading: *medium*
Estimated Time: *50 minutes*

EXERCISE

This exercise uses a version of the famous Proust Questionnaire as a springboard for a discussion of characterization. When French author Marcel Proust was a teenager, a friend asked him to answer a series of questions.

He answered the same questions again when he was twenty (both questionnaires survive today). The Proust Questionnaire later became popular for interviews in magazines and on television shows, and today *Vanity Fair* regularly asks celebrities to respond to a modified version.

The "Proust Questionnaire" exercise works well with almost any type of novel: realism or romance, historical fiction or metafiction, even crime thrillers and graphic novels. Any work with a roster of multidimensional characters will do. Some good candidates include Jane Austen's *Pride and Prejudice* (with hidden connections among characters who at first appear very different); Charlotte Brontë's *Jane Eyre* (with Jane's first-person narration contouring the depiction of every other character in the novel); and Alan Hollinghurst's *The Line of Beauty* (with characters' inner lives coordinated according to a handful of repeating ideas about Thatcher-era Britain). The "Proust Questionnaire" also works brilliantly with any volume of Proust's own *In Search of Lost Time*, with its density of personalities and a narrator who is himself a constellation of selves.

To begin the exercise, distribute copies of the Proust Questionnaire (see the end of this chapter for an example with selected answers from the young Proust) to each member of the class and explain its origin. Next, hand out a template of the questionnaire with Proust's answers removed. Ask your students to fill out the questionnaire from the point of view of one of the characters in the text you are reading. But here's the crucial step: ask students to craft their answers in such a way that they could plausibly have come from *more than one character*. Challenge your students to perplex both you as the instructor and their classmates. Offer an example. Let's say you are doing the exercise with Austen's *Pride and Prejudice*, and the character in question is Mrs. Bennet. For the question "What do you regard as the lowest depth of misery?" ask students not to write "Failing to marry off my daughters to rich men" but to craft a less obvious answer, one that could apply to other characters, perhaps something like "To have no control over whom people marry." You can see how, in these more abstract terms, the answer could plausibly have come from other characters in *Pride and Prejudice* (Lady Catherine de Burgh, for instance). Give students about fifteen minutes to complete the quiz on behalf of their character.

When they are done, break up the class into groups of about five students each. Have each group switch questionnaires with one other group. (If you have an odd number, just ask each group to hand off its quizzes to the group next to them.) Instruct groups to determine together which literary character filled out each questionnaire and to prepare justifications for their answers. This portion of the exercise takes roughly twenty minutes. Afterward, reconvene for a full-class discussion. Invite each group to share their best guesses and the reasons for those guesses, before the author of each questionnaire confirms if they got it right. (As a variant for this exercise, you can also split it across two class periods. In the first class, ask students to fill out the questionnaires before they leave. Make copies of the five questionnaires that are most difficult to figure out, and then distribute these in the following class, a complete set to each group.)

Once all the guesses have been made, use some of the following questions to lead discussion toward the real purpose of the exercise: discovering the structural logic of characterization. It can be useful to move from queries specific to their individual answers to those that address broader issues:

- What made the characters seem different from each other before we did this exercise? (Social status? Age?)
- What makes them seem similar after doing this exercise? (Internal motivations? Emotional states? Attachments to particular people or things?)
- Were there any characters who simply couldn't be mistaken for anyone else in the text, no matter how craftily you disguised their answers? What are their unique qualities? What is their role in the novel? Did this tend to happen with major or minor characters?
- Was any one question especially useful for illuminating underlying similarities or differences among the characters?
- Was any question particularly difficult to answer for your character? Was this because you didn't know the answer or because you didn't know how to disguise that it belonged to your character?
- What did this difficulty reveal about your character or about how the novelist characterizes this figure?
- Which characters were most frequently mistaken for each other? Why do you think these confusions happened? Did they tend to happen between characters you already associated with each other or between those that seemed to have little in common at first glance? What does this confusion reveal?

Bring things to a close by asking students to expand from what they learned about specific characters and the relationships among them to what they learned about the technique of literary characterization.

REFLECTIONS

The quiz format of this exercise is inviting, and students enjoy the challenge of "fooling" everyone with their answers. But as students craft their responses, something counterintuitive happens: rather than becoming immersed in intense psychological profiles of their favorite characters, students begin to think about characterization in structural terms. Because the aim in filling out the questionnaire is precisely not to pretend to be one character but to hold two or more characters in mind at the same time (through the process of disguising their answers), students come to recognize the craftedness of character delineation, so often a transparent part of the reading experience. In other words, the larger aim of the exercise is to help students pull back from an uncritical absorption in the novel or too close an identification with any one character.

I often use this exercise when teaching Jane Austen's *Emma*. It gets students talking about how Austen delineates character and about the importance of differentiation in this process. Are characters in novels knowable only by their difference from one another, or are they knowable in other ways? What might it mean if we can't tell whether the questionnaire has been filled out by Emma Woodhouse or Robert Martin? We ran into this very question when one student filled out the questionnaire so cleverly that the class was evenly split on "whose" answers we were reading. In response to the question about "the lowest depth of misery," for instance, the student wrote that it would be "to lose the respect of Mr. Knightley." Everyone assumed that this answer must have come from Emma, and there was great surprise when it turned out to be Robert Martin.

Before doing the exercise, students had never considered the possibility that these two characters have qualities in common or that they might serve a similar structural role in the novel: to establish Mr. Knightley's status as community mentor. This led us to an interesting recognition of some of the other things these characters might have in common. Students mentioned their mutual interest in creating and maintaining a stable household, caring for the spectrum of social life that makes up Highbury, an attachment to Harriet Smith, and, more complexly, a relationship to social striving that can be difficult to define. Ultimately the questionnaire led us to think about how, for Emma, antipathy might be masking similarity, which brought us in turn to a broader discussion of a recurring dynamic in Austen: her characters tend to dislike those who share certain qualities that they also possess.

I have also used this exercise successfully with Mary Shelley's *Frankenstein*. Here, discussion often leads to the recognition that Walton, Frankenstein, and the Creature are startlingly similar. Several questions on the questionnaire bring these similarities to light. For instance, for the questions "What is your idea of earthly happiness?" and "What is your favorite occupation?," the answers given from the point of view of Walton, Frankenstein, or the Creature tend to emphasize a desire for learning. Before doing this exercise, students had not noticed how strongly all three characters were driven by the common motivation to acquire knowledge. But when we used the disguised "Proust Questionnaire" answers to explore what each character valued most, students often simply could not distinguish the novel's central male characters from one other. This conversation led to a larger discussion about how the genre of science fiction (for which *Frankenstein* is an important source text) tends to function through a nonrealist, mythological, or archetypal logic of doubling and mirroring.

PROUST QUESTIONNAIRE

What do you regard as the lowest depth of misery?
— *To be separated from Mama.*

Where would you like to live?
— *In the country of the Ideal, or, rather, of my ideal.*

What is your idea of earthly happiness?
— *To live in contact with those I love, with the beauties of nature, with a quantity of books and music, and to have, within easy distance, a French theater.*

To what faults do you feel most indulgent?
— *To a life deprived of the works of genius.*

Who are your favorite heroes of fiction?
— *Those of romance and poetry, those who are the expression of an ideal rather than an imitation of the real.*

Who are your favorite characters in history?
— *A mixture of Socrates, Pericles, Mahomet, Pliny the Younger and Augustin Thierry.*

Who are your favorite heroines in real life?
— *A woman of genius leading an ordinary life.*

Who are your favorite heroines of fiction?
— *Those who are more than women without ceasing to be womanly; everything that is tender, poetic, pure and in every way beautiful.*

Your favorite painter?
— *Meissonier.*

Your favorite musician?
— *Mozart.*

The quality you most admire in a man?
— *Intelligence, moral sense.*

The quality you most admire in a woman?
— *Gentleness, naturalness, intelligence.*

Your favorite virtue?
— *All virtues that are not limited to a sect: the universal virtues.*

Your favorite occupation?
— *Reading, dreaming, and writing verse.*

Who would you have liked to be?
— *Since the question does not arise, I prefer not to answer it. All the same, I should very much have liked to be Pliny the Younger.*

Understanding
Point of View ✓ ✓

Pamela Regis

An exercise that teaches the mechanics of narrative point of view.

Genre: *fiction*
Course Level: *any*
Student Difficulty: *moderate*
Teacher Preparation: *low*
Class Size: *small to medium*
Semester Time: *any*
Writing Component: *in class*
Close Reading: *medium*
Estimated Time: *50 minutes*

EXERCISE

Choose one or more passages from a work of fiction—five sentences from any novel or short story will do, but a longer passage will also work—and ask the class to determine the point of view that the author has employed. Project the passage on a screen or distribute it in a handout. Have students point out the pronouns that help identify the point of view. Beginnings are particularly useful passages for this exercise, because authors must establish a work's point of view immediately. Also useful are passages that report the thoughts of characters.

Next, solicit from the students a list of all the *other* point of view possibilities the author could have employed, and list these on the board. For example, a paragraph written in third-person omniscient could have been written in third-person objective or third-person limited. Include the various focal character possibilities as well. For example, the focal character in a third-person limited point of view could have been a major character or minor one. Or the passage could have been written in the second person, which, although rarely used, is helpful in this exercise, the goal of which is to uncover all of the other possibilities that the author could have employed. Finally, the passage could have been written in the first person with, again, any focal character recounting the events.

Now ask the students, either singly, in pairs, or in small groups, to rewrite the passage in one of the points of view that the author did not employ.

Assign each student (or group) a specific point of view. (If you have more students or groups than point of view possibilities, you can assign the same point of view more than once.) Students will have to figure out how to cut, supplement, or otherwise rework the details of the passage to follow the rules of the point of view they have been assigned. They should add or delete details in order to get as close to the original as possible while still observing the limitations imposed by the new point of view. Give students about fifteen minutes for this section of the exercise.

When the revisions are done, taking each revision in turn, invite the reviser(s) to present the new passage to the rest of the class. If possible, have revisers write the passage on a flip chart, display it on an overhead projector or via a document camera, or put it on a PowerPoint slide so that the whole class can see the rewrite.

Ask the class if the rewritten passage follows the rules of the new point of view. You can prompt them with questions: Have the pronouns been shifted appropriately? Have the rules of who is allowed to "think" in the new point of view been adhered to? Have limited or first-person points of view truly kept within the knowledge that the focal character could have had? Does third-person objective stay out of characters' heads? In first person and third-person limited, has knowledge that the narrator knows but that a given character cannot know been deleted or attributed to a character in a plausible way?

Then ask the revisers to explain a few of the changes they had to make in order to rewrite the passage. What was lost? What was gained? How has the overall impact of the passage been changed by the rewriting?

Finally, ask the class several questions: What has the *reader* gained or lost by the shift? What information does he or she now have that the original did not include? What information has been lost that the original did include? Ask students whether or not the original author chose the best possible point of view, given the work's focus and themes. If not, which point of view would have been more effective? Why? Repeat this sequence with the next rewritten passage. Allow roughly four to five minutes per student or group; in a fifty-minute class, for example, you can comfortably cover seven to eight rewritten passages.

For a variation on this exercise, have students prepare their rewrites for homework and bring them to the following class. This will eliminate the small-group discussion (unless you assign this as an out-of-class group activity) but will also give you more time to discuss the rewrites themselves during the class period.

REFLECTIONS

The goal of this hands-on exercise is to help students understand the nature of point of view and the control that it exercises over every aspect of a work of fiction. The exercise makes apparent the decisions that an author makes in deploying a given point of view, as well as the extent to which a reader's information about the events and characters in a work of fiction is a direct consequence of the point of view that the author has chosen. This exercise also provides a good introduction to modernist and postmodernist departures from traditional point of view, such as stream of consciousness.

Any work of fiction will provide a passage for rewriting. Take, for example, Terry L. Tilton's extremely brief short story, "That Settles That." Here it is in its entirety:

> Tom was a handsome, fun-loving young man, albeit a bit drunk when he got into an argument with Sam, his room mate of just two months.
> "You can't. You can not write a short story in just 55 words, you idiot!"
> Sam shot him dead on the spot.
> "Oh yes you can," Sam said, smiling.

For this particular story, before I assign complete rewrites, I ask the entire class to identify the two instances of description that we need to delete to change the omniscient narrator, who can see into characters' minds and souls, into an objective one, who limits the narration to what can be known through the senses, particularly sight and sound. Omit "fun-loving" and "a bit drunk," which require knowledge of Tom's inner states, and the third-person omniscient narration becomes objective.

Then I ask groups of students to rewrite the story, extending it beyond the fifty-five-word limit if they wish, and inventing details, as long as they observe the rules of the point of view they have been assigned. Different individuals or groups rewrite the story

- in the first person, using Tom as the focal character;
- in the first person, using Sam as the focal character;
- in third-person limited, using Tom as the character whose observations, thoughts, and impressions the reader is privy to;
- in third-person limited, using Sam as the character whose observations, thoughts, and impressions the reader is privy to;
- in third-person objective, which prohibits the narrator from reporting the inner state of any character; or
- in second person, a rarely used point of view, but useful for this exercise.

Students quickly realize that rewriting the story using first-person narration from the point of view of the shooter, Sam, permits them fairly wide latitude in drawing Sam's character, and that Sam is very much a filter for the reader's perception of Tom's character, assuming that Sam characterizes his victim at all. When Tom narrates, the opposite is true, and students realize that conveying "Sam shot him dead on the spot" from Tom's point of view presents them with a challenge, which they typically overcome using an ellipsis. The third-person limited rewrites permit students to provide the thoughts of the focal characters, and rewrites typically include the motives of Sam and Tom.

Third-person objective rewrites force students to confine the narration to the action only. (Raymond Carver deploys third-person objective point of view to chilling effect in "Popular Mechanics.") The biggest challenge is to rewrite the story in the second person, which provides an opportunity to discuss the difficulties posed by this point of view. (See "Videotape" by Don DeLillo for a fine example of a second-person narrator: "You know about families and their video cameras," DeLillo's narrator explains.)

For English majors, I follow this exercise with a paper assignment that asks them to assess the contribution of point of view to the theme of a given work of fiction. If you'd like to offer your class an extended opportunity to explore the ways in which writers deploy point of view, consider pairing Joyce Carol Oates's 1972 rewrite of Anton Chekhov's 1899 short story "The Lady with the Pet Dog" with Chekhov's original. Both authors employ third-person limited point of view. Chekhov uses the male protagonist as the focal character; Oates uses the female protagonist.

. . . .

√

Flip the Script

Stephen M. Park

An exercise that teaches point of view through creative rewriting.

Genre: *fiction*
Course Level: *any*
Student Difficulty: *easy or moderate*
Teacher Preparation: *low*
Class Size: *small to medium*
Semester Time: *any*
Writing Component: *in class, optional after class*
Close Reading: *medium*
Estimated Time: *50 to 60 minutes*

EXERCISE

Choose a passage from the novel or short story your students are reading and ask them to review it before coming to class. The passage should be a page or two in length, though slightly longer passages can work for take-home versions of the exercise. Stories told in the third person work well: Charles

Dickens's *Hard Times*, Susan Glaspell's "A Jury of Her Peers," Salman Rushdie's *The Satanic Verses*. Novels with first-person narrators work even better: Jonathan Swift's *Gulliver's Travels*, F. Scott Fitzgerald's *The Great Gatsby*, Albert Camus's *The Stranger*, Alice Walker's *The Color Purple*.

At the start of class, project the passage on the board and ask students to discuss the point of view from which the passage or story is told. Who gets to tell the story, and why?

Now, it's the students' job to "flip" things around and look at the same story from another angle. Organize the class into small groups and tell them to rewrite the passage from the point of view of another character in the story. Give them at least fifteen minutes both to choose a character and to start writing, though this part of the exercise could easily run longer. When they've had enough time, have each group (1) identify the character whose point of view they chose (and why they chose him or her), (2) explain how the shift in point of view changes the understanding of the passage, and (3) read a little bit of what they wrote. (As a variation, you can also assign each group a specific character into whose point of view you would like them to rewrite the passage, or even assign the same character to all the groups.)

During the presentations (allow five to seven minutes per group), you may find that some groups struggle with the second task: although they have rewritten the passage in a provocative way, they are not able to articulate fully the significance of the changes they have made. If that happens, encourage the other groups to offer suggestions, or step in to point out how important the change is ("Rewriting the passage from *Benito Cereno* from Babo's perspective really makes clear how naive Melville's original narrator is"). Be sure to ask the students to reflect on why the author has made the narrative choices that appear in the original text in the first place ("Why has Melville constructed a narrator who misinterprets his surroundings while still allowing the reader enough information to come to other conclusions?"). The larger question to keep students thinking about during this exercise is this: if the reader of the original text were deprived of the narrative perspective that they have just rewritten, what is lost and what is gained?

This exercise can also work well if you invite students to insert characters from other novels or stories you've read in the course. For instance, if Stephen Crane's Maggie suddenly landed in the middle of Henry James's *Daisy Miller: A Study*, how might she describe the experiences of this other young American woman? In more-advanced courses, you might ask students to insert a literary theorist or historical figure as a character in the story and narrate from that point of view. How would Karl Marx narrate the visit to the flax mill in Gustave Flaubert's *Madame Bovary*? How would Simone de Beauvoir narrate the opening pages of Jane Austen's *Pride and Prejudice*? There really are no limits to how you might have your students reimagine a piece of fiction.

REFLECTIONS

"Flip the Script" allows students to approach a text in new ways, think about reading as an imaginative act, and study the formal element of point of view. By rewriting a story from the perspective of a minor character, or by shifting the perspective from third to first person, students become more aware of the author's original narrative choices and the reasons behind them. This exercise is similar in approach to "Understanding Point of View" (see the preceding exercise) but allows for more creative latitude, works best with comparatively longer passages, and provides the option of working across literary texts.

In my Introduction to Literature class, students experimented with Charlotte Perkins Gilman's first-person short story "The Yellow Wall-Paper" by rewriting the beginning using a third-person narrator. Whereas Gilman's original narrator observes of her husband, "John laughs at me, of course, but one expects that in marriage," without providing further details, I asked my students to imagine the scene more fully. What is John's laugh like? Is it a hearty laugh, a nervous laugh, or perhaps a condescending one? What was actually said between the characters? In their rewrites, students drew on different clichés of patriarchal husbands, and by discussing such attitudes and behaviors, they were able to understand more fully the meaning behind Gilman's phrase "one expects that in marriage." We then spent more time thinking about the narrative choices in Gilman's original text and the ultimate effect of leaving such scenes out. My students noticed how the narrator's presumption that such scenes go without saying tells us something about her worldview, thus adding to the richness of Gilman's first-person narrative.

Inviting in the students' creativity can also serve as an opportunity to challenge the text you are reading. Looking at a story from the point of view of a minor character or an invented one enables students to explore the gaps in the text and consider how presumptions about gender, race, or class have shaped the way the story has been told. When reading Sherman Alexie's *Flight*, for example, my students often notice how the novel's adolescent male narrator voices a number of patriarchal attitudes, especially in his descriptions of women. So when asking students to flip the script on this novel, I encourage them to rewrite a passage from the point of view of one of the stronger female characters we've seen in other texts, such as Paula Gunn Allen's "Deer Woman" or Leslie Marmon Silko's "Yellow Woman." The result is a variety of new stories that leads to a great discussion of Alexie's novel. For instance, Allen's "Deer Woman" (itself a rewrite of a folktale) tells the story of two women who lure two sexist male characters away, not to their deaths but rather toward a chance for a renewed appreciation of strong Native American women. So, in writing a scene in which Allen's characters present Alexie's narrator with the same option to change, the question emerges: would he?

This scenario has generated all sorts of student rewrites, ranging from an unrepentant narrator who fixates on the women's bodies to a more enlightened narrator who ends up chastising a fictionalized Sherman Alexie for the descriptions of women in his novel. These speculations about what the narrator would do always divide the class, and our conversation naturally moves from their creative rewrites to an analytical debate regarding Alexie's novel and the complexity of his characters, during which I make sure that the students support their claims about the narrator with evidence from *Flight*. To wrap up the class, I stress that just as Allen as a writer inserts resistant characters into her story, students as imaginative readers can challenge texts in similar ways.

This is an exercise that brings everyone into the conversation. Since it gets away from traditional modes of literary analysis, students can speak up in class without having to worry whether their insights into the story are "correct." Their rewrites themselves constitute creative critical acts, allowing students to make interpretive statements about the text by thinking about the author's narrative choices and by considering which perspectives are absent from the story. What's more, these rewrites can create some hilarious and memorable moments when they're read aloud, which may be why my students often refer to what they learned in this exercise months later.

In a follow-up to "Flip the Script," I have sometimes asked students to continue writing at home, further embellishing their rewrite of the story. Or I have had them write a short critical reflection that explains what their group's rewrite reveals about the original text or the technique of novel writing. In any case, this act of rethinking a text's narrative point of view helps students become more imaginative and resistant readers of fiction.

I would like to thank Gretel Vera-Rosas for developing this lesson with me in a class we taught together.

First Paragraphs

Abigail Burnham Bloom

A first-day exercise in which the texts introduce themselves to your students.

Genre: *fiction*
Course Level: *any*
Student Difficulty: *easy*
Teacher Preparation: *low*

Class Size: *any*
Semester Time: *first day*
Writing Component: *none*
Close Reading: *high*
Estimated Time: *variable, from 20 to 50 minutes*

EXERCISE

For the first day of class, type up (or cut and paste) the first paragraph of each work of fiction you will read in the course and arrange them on a handout in the order they appear on your syllabus. Limit the number of paragraphs to novels or major works of the course so that all can be discussed during the time allotted for the exercise. When class begins, distribute the handout or project it in the front of the room.

Ask a student volunteer to read the first paragraph. Then invite the class to offer their first impressions, posing questions such as these: Who is speaking in the paragraph? What seems striking or significant about it? How does the paragraph draw you in—or push you away? Next, ask students to make some predictions: What kind of story does this opening paragraph seem to be preparing you to read? What do you think will happen in this story? (When you pose these last questions, ask any students who may have already read the work to let their uninitiated classmates venture the predictions!)

Spend four to five minutes on each paragraph before moving on, as it's important to make sure students "meet" each one before the class is over. (Four examples might take just twenty minutes; ten examples a full fifty minutes.) Encourage students to comment on whatever elements seem striking, including voice, tone, diction, imagery, vocabulary, sentence structure, and theme. Remind them that there are no incorrect responses—they are simply giving initial impressions. When students venture answers, ask follow-up questions to encourage even closer reading: Where do you see that in the paragraph? Does this remind you of other works you have read? As you introduce more paragraphs, ask the students to note similarities and differences among them. After all the paragraphs have been introduced, ask the class to compare them. Do they show a progression or a change of emphasis?

Often the first paragraph will reveal concerns of the author in an oblique way that you can help your students realize. Bring up ideas that would suggest what an author might be trying to accomplish in the first paragraph and what an astute reader might be able to comprehend. You might ask: Based on what you've seen, how do authors use the first paragraph of a work to interest a reader in continuing to read the work? At the end of class, take a straw poll: based just on the opening paragraphs, which work would the students most like to read, and why?

REFLECTIONS

"First Paragraphs" encourages students to think about how narratives draw in their readers, an appropriate activity for the first day of a class on fiction. It also introduces, in a low-key and enjoyable way, some of the analytical terminology and methods to which you'll return throughout the semester. For students new to literary analysis, after all, starting to read a new work of fiction can be intimidating. The start of a novel like Mary Shelley's *Frankenstein* can provide the context for discussing the use of letters or diaries within fiction. Students need to be reminded that even if the start seems slow, if they stick with the novel, it will become comprehensible and even exciting. A text such as Joseph Conrad's *Heart of Darkness* may be less daunting to students later in the semester after a "First Paragraphs" introduction to the style and themes of the work. And all students look forward to finding out whether their initial predictions about a work are correct.

This exercise also introduces students to the rudiments of close reading, and shows them how to listen and respond to the opinions of their classmates from the start of the semester. As they discuss the works and their reactions to them, moreover, students will become more comfortable not only with the literature but also with your style of questioning. For this reason, it's important to model the methods that you'll use during the term in this first class. For example, if you want students to see that they will be encouraged to volunteer or that they will be called on and asked for their opinion, be sure to call on students during this first class.

Depending on the class and its structure, this exercise might yield different kinds of results. In a course devoted to a single author, for example, the first paragraphs might highlight the range of, or shifts in, an author's concerns or techniques. In a course devoted to Jane Austen, students can see a similarity of theme and tone but differences in emphasis. In a period survey class, in which the syllabus is organized chronologically, the progression of the paragraphs may show the developing concerns and literary styles of the era itself. Works in a history of the novel course may reveal a progression from an impersonal voice to a more psychologically penetrating approach. If the students don't notice these patterns, try drawing their attention to them. Regardless of the course, the exercise will also help you assess the reading abilities of your students and gain familiarity with the expectations and assumptions they will bring to the works on your syllabus.

In a summer class on Victorian novels, we read the first paragraphs of *Wuthering Heights*, *Great Expectations*, *Dr. Jekyll and Mr. Hyde*, and *Dracula*. Many students were confused by the openings of *Wuthering Heights* and *Dr. Jekyll and Mr. Hyde*. After reading the first paragraph of *Wuthering*

Heights, one student guessed that the narrator was a woman who was in love with Heathcliff. When he had finished the novel, he recounted his confusion over the start and reflected that the author had intended the reader to be as disoriented as the narrator. Another student commented that he wondered why such a long first paragraph as that of *Dr. Jekyll and Mr. Hyde* made no reference to the title characters and contained so many difficult references (Mr. Utterson is described as "austere with himself" and states, "I incline to Caine's heresy"). Many students worried that *Dr. Jekyll and Mr. Hyde* itself would be lengthy and off point, which it definitely didn't turn out to be. Students believed correctly from the opening of *Great Expectations* that the novel would be about Pip's discovery of his own identity and enjoyed seeing how the fact that his name is a palindrome accentuates that theme. With the first paragraph of *Dracula*, students caught on immediately to the differences between the East and West that are established, and they enjoyed that the novel began as a diary entry, just like *Wuthering Heights*.

During the comparative discussion, students were impressed by the diversity of opening structures. They came to see that what they think they know about a work because of cultural references or previous readings in high school may not be true when they read the novel in college. The opening paragraphs also brought out what may be difficult for students in reading Victorian novels—a different vocabulary from ours today, a tendency to verbosity, and a multitude of characters and plots. In the straw poll students voted for *Great Expectations* as the novel they most wanted to read, because the first paragraph was direct and clear. However, at the end of the semester, when they voted again, they chose *Dracula* as their favorite novel, mainly because of its subject matter and plot, which they found "so modern."

As you study each new text in the semester, ask students if the work matches their expectations from having read the first paragraph on the first day of class. (If not, what changed?) At the end of the semester, you can do a parallel exercise with "last paragraphs." Are the tones, images, and themes that are most important in the work reflected in the final paragraphs of the book? What's particularly striking about the ways these narratives bring their stories to a close? Conclude the semester by letting students vote for their favorite closing paragraph—or even their favorite read of the semester.

Script Doctor

Diana Fuss

A high-energy exercise for thinking about narrative closure.

Genre: *any, especially fiction*
Course Level: *any*
Student Difficulty: *moderate*
Teacher Preparation: *low*
Class Size: *small to medium*
Semester Time: *any*
Writing Component: *in class*
Close Reading: *medium*
Estimated Time: *40 to 50 minutes*

EXERCISE

Choose a novel, short story, or play with a curious ending—an ending that is complex, unsatisfying, disturbing, controversial, unnerving, or simply surprising. Script doctoring for narrative closure can be performed on almost any fictional or dramatic text and even on poems like Robert Browning's dramatic monologues ("My Last Duchess" or "Porphyria's Lover"), with their strong narrative thrust and complicated, demented speakers. I find it works best, though, for novels with sad or tragic endings: George Eliot's *The Mill on the Floss*, Henry James's *The Turn of the Screw*, Thomas Hardy's *Tess of the d'Urbervilles*, Nella Larsen's *Passing*, Edith Wharton's *The House of Mirth*, Ralph Ellison's *Invisible Man*, Salvador Plascencia's *The People of Paper*.

If the passage you have selected is short, begin by asking a student to read it out loud; if the passage is long, invite students to refresh their memories by skimming it quickly. Then identify some general problems with the ending—interpretive questions that have preoccupied scholars for years, or simply things that have long puzzled, worried, or intrigued you. If there is time, pause and ask students why these problems and debates might be important, or whether they have questions and concerns of their own about how the text comes to rest. This preliminary discussion might take ten minutes or so.

Next, invite students to think like script doctors: if they were charged with rewriting the ending, how might they conclude it differently? Remind them that script doctors are those unsung, uncredited writers whose primary job is to retool specific elements of scripts that need fixing—be it plot, dialogue, characterization, tempo, or theme. Give students roughly five to six minutes to jot down one or more proposals for an alternate ending. Students may have several ideas: ask them to pick one. Then ask them to share their ideas with the class as a whole. Make a first pass around the room, so everyone has a chance to talk about at least one of their doctored endings. Consider using a one-minute time limit so that everyone has a chance to speak and no one gets too carried away. And leave a few minutes at the end of the round for comments and conversation. For a small class this portion of the exercise should take roughly twenty minutes.

If your class is medium sized, it is better at the outset to divide students into small groups of three to four. Ask them to generate together one or more new endings within a ten- to fifteen-minute time frame. I find that even when done collaboratively, "Script Doctor" works most efficiently if students still have a moment to generate some of their own thoughts first, so recommend that each group take a contemplative moment before they begin discussing ideas. When the groups are done, ask each group to share what they agree is their best or favorite idea first. If there is time, you can go around the room a second or even a third time to solicit more endings. Leave time for other students to respond, or even vote as a class on the ending they like best. For this group work and class discussion, you'll need at least thirty minutes.

To bring things to a satisfying close, take at least ten minutes at the end to circle back and reconsider the logic, purpose, or value of the story's original ending in light of its many possible alternatives. What have the new endings made more legible about the original text? What crucial elements of the original might be lost in the alternative endings considered as a whole? Is there anything about the original ending that no one dared to change? Why or why not?

REFLECTIONS

Script doctoring provides a high-energy (and often hilarious) way to talk about larger questions of narrative form and literary endings. Teaching closure is more challenging than it looks, posing any number of literary conventions to unknot: plot, character, structure, framing, sequencing, foreshadowing, denouement, resolution, suspense, irony. Working with students' doctored revisions as points of contrast immediately helps to sharpen both local questions of authorial choice (why does the author choose this incident, this image, this word, this tone?) and larger questions of narrative closure (What constitutes a successful ending? What changes when an ending changes? Why does a story conclude the way it does?).

The results can be fascinating, as I discovered teaching Kate Chopin's *The Awakening*, a novel that famously concludes with the heroine swimming languidly out to sea. While students usually wish to debate the meaning of Edna Pontellier's ambiguous act (choice or fate? action or passivity? triumph or tragedy?), an exercise like this can yield much fresher results. The alternate endings students imagined were notably diverse: Edna returning to the beach, Edna swimming across the channel, Edna washing up on shore, Edna dreaming of swimming, Edna painting the scene. But the one thing every doctored script had in common was the return of Edna's body (dead or alive) to land.

This strong desire to put the body back on terra firma, and back into the text, returned us to what we had not yet understood about the body of the novel itself—namely, its gradual dematerialization of language, its wavelike and oceanic structure, and its subtle narrative drift. An ending that at first seemed so disappointingly vague suddenly made perfect sense. And the novel's narrative problems actually appeared more like literary strategies—a fitting finale to an exercise all about endings.

There are several variations for a script-doctoring exercise like this one. For longer classes or seminars with an emphasis on in-class writing exercises, you can really kick things up a notch. Consider asking students to rewrite the text's final paragraph. Or invite them to craft a short epilogue to the tale. Or, if you have already spent some time on narrative exposition, invite them to draft the first paragraph of a proposed sequel. Once again, be sure to allow enough time for students to read their efforts aloud and to comment on one another's literary imaginations. The point of this exercise is to augment and amplify the method of close reading with the practice of creative revision.

· ·

Alternate Endings

Melina Moe

A comparative exercise for thinking about endings.

Genre: *fiction*
Course Level: *any*
Student Difficulty: *moderate*
Teacher Preparation: *low*
Class Size: *small to medium*
Semester Time: *midterm or late*

Writing Component: *optional in class*
Close Reading: *medium to high*
Estimated Time: *25 to 30 minutes*

EXERCISE

Choose the closing passage of a short story or novel whose ending exists in multiple forms, either in print or manuscript. The selection could be a couple of paragraphs or up to a chapter in length, depending on how much time you allot for the exercise. Good candidates for this exercise include any fictional work for which the author drafted more than one ending: Charles Dickens's *Great Expectations* (focusing on the "shadow of parting," compare the original ending to the 1863 edition), Julio Cortázar's *Hopscotch* (with multiple scripted endings, this novel facilitates a good discussion about what Cortázar meant when he called it a "counter-novel"), Herman Melville's *Moby-Dick* (compare the first British edition to the first American edition), Ernest Hemingway's *A Farewell to Arms* (he wrote *forty-seven* different endings!).

After a first day of discussion about the published version of your fictional work, surprise students by circulating the alternate ending. Ask them, as they read it for the next class meeting, to attend to how the two endings affect their interpretation of the narrative as a whole. Let them know that when class reconvenes, you will be inviting them to choose which ending they prefer. If the alternate ending is not very long, and if there is sufficient time, you can also perform this exercise in the same class period, without sending them home first.

Frame the ensuing discussion according to your needs. If your primary focus is narrative plotting or structure, divide the class into two (or more) groups, assign each a different ending, and give the groups ten minutes to work together to generate arguments in defense of their endings. Then reconvene and let each side argue why their ending may (or may not) be suggestive, successful, or otherwise suitable. For texts with multiple endings, like *A Farewell to Arms*, use multiple groups to collaboratively argue for (or, if they like, against) their particular assigned ending. Allow ten minutes for the actual group debates.

If your primary focus is the precise stylistic techniques of narrative closure, consider using pairs instead. Have students study more closely the language and tone of the two different endings, being sure to list the precise ways the wording or mood of the ending changes from version to version. Then have each pair choose their most interesting finding to report back to the class as a whole. The pair version of this exercise also takes roughly twenty minutes of class time.

To wind up this exercise, take a bit more time to pose some larger questions: What kinds of problems does each of the endings resolve? What uncertainties do they raise? Why do you think the author finally settled on the ending he or she did? Did he or she make the best decision?

REFLECTIONS

"Alternate Endings" presents narrative as a site of interpretive complexity, for both readers and authors. While it emphasizes close reading, it also shows students how a single passage (or the omission of a single passage) can change the meaning of the entire narrative. For example, my students have been genuinely surprised by the ending to the first British printing of *Moby-Dick*, in which it remains a mystery how Ishmael, and thus the story of the *Pequod* itself, escapes the whirlpool. This exercise introduces students to various techniques of narrative closure and facilitates discussion about how endings can focus and guide our interpretation of works that can in other ways be quite imposing.

For works that have been the subject of editorial controversy, this exercise works particularly well for thinking about the circulation of a text from author to printer to reader. For example, I frequently teach the two different published endings of Nella Larsen's *Passing*. Larsen's modernist novella describes the social and psychological upheaval following an unexpected meeting between two friends whose paths had diverged many years before when one of them left the black community to "pass" as a white woman. One version ends with the ambiguous breakdown of one of the story's main protagonists, Irene Redfield, after her friend Clare falls to her death from a Harlem apartment building; the other concludes with an anonymous police officer offering the closing words about the accident. Both endings were printed in the same year (the text changed between the second and third editions), and the surviving paratextual archives provide few clues as to who, or what, is responsible for the change. It is unclear if Larsen oversaw the alteration, if the editorial staff pushed for a different ending, or if the change was the product of contingency in the typesetting or publishing process. I always provide students with details of the manuscript's preparation and tell them that Larsen's original ending was on a single plate of stereotype that might have been accidentally dropped in the third edition.

The American Women Writers paperback edition of *Passing*, from Rutgers University Press (packaged with Larsen's *Quicksand*), includes an editorial footnote that claims the change of endings makes little difference, so I begin there, separating students into small groups and asking them if they agree or disagree. To give students a flavor of what it is like to edit a text, I ask each group to generate their own footnote: if they were editing an edition of the novel, what would they say about the two endings? In one of my classes, one group focused on narrative style, arguing that the original version of Larson's ending was an experiment in using first-person perspective to alert us to unreliable narrators. Another group defended the revised ending and described how the appearance of a police officer at the conclusion of the book framed what was otherwise an intensely psychological tale in a specific historical moment of urbanization and American racial conflict. Both groups said that whatever footnote they wrote about Larson's ending would color their interpretation of the novel as a whole. It is a short leap for them from writing editorial footnotes to talking about how these interpretive claims can guide a reading of major themes in the novel.

· ·

The Great Debate

Jay Dickson

An exercise that analyzes the wider ethical and cultural stakes of crucial conflicts in literary texts.

> Genre: *fiction or drama*
> Course Level: *introductory or intermediate*
> Student Difficulty: *moderate*
> Teacher Preparation: *low*
> Class Size: *any*
> Semester Time: *any*
> Writing Component: *none*
> Close Reading: *medium*
> Estimated Time: *50 minutes*

EXERCISE

Choose an extended, complex, structurally important debate from a fictional or dramatic literary text, a debate in which choosing sides or determining the eventual resolution is neither simple nor immediately clear. Examples might include the famous *agons* of the Greek tragedies (the disagreement over Polynices's burial in Sophocles's *Antigone*, or the Carpet Scene in Aeschylus's *Agamemnon*, wherein the title character argues with his wife Clytemnestra about whether he is as despotic as she would make out), the debate in Mary Shelley's *Frankenstein* between Victor and his creature over whether to create a bride for the monster, or the Wilcox family's argument over whether to fulfill the request of Ruth Wilcox's penciled will in E. M. Forster's *Howards End*. You might also choose a dilemma that takes place mostly within a character's mind (such as Hamlet's reluctance to kill his uncle) or even an important *implicit* textual conflict (such as whether Clarissa Dalloway made the right decision about whom to marry years before).

Identify the debate you wish students to examine. If you like, you can alert students beforehand by asking them to pay especially close attention, as they read the assigned work, to a particular chapter, scene, or section. On the day of the discussion, tell the class that the purpose of the exercise is not to hash out who is "right" in the debate but rather to identify the terms of the debate and, most importantly, to explore why these terms matter.

Prepare a handout with the following eight questions:

1. What are the main positions taken in the debate?
2. What is the main core argument of each position?
3. Is the core argument for your position refuted, and if so, how?
4. Who speaks for your position, and for what reasons?
5. What cultural, social, political, or economic interests does your "side" in the debate represent? Which values are really being debated?
6. Why does the author place the debate where it is within the text? What kinds of structural purposes does this placement serve?
7. If the decision is adjudicated, who acts as judge? What interests does the judge represent?
8. Are there other positions that the debate allows for but that are not pursued or staged?

After circulating the handout, begin with a full-group brainstorming discussion of no more than ten minutes, simply to get the lay of the land. Limit this portion of the exercise to the handout's first two questions only: what are the main positions in the debate, and what appears to be the main argument behind each position? Quickly sum up the students' answers on the board, choosing a large column for each of the major positions so everyone can see the general terms of the debate.

Once you have the positions on the board, break the class into small groups—anywhere from three to five students per group. Assign each group a "side" in the debate. (If there are more groups than sides, assign multiple groups the same position.) Give each group no more than twenty minutes to discuss the remaining six questions on the handout. Let them know that, while they might touch on all sides of the debate if they wish, they should attend most closely to the side they have been assigned.

For the next twenty minutes, have each group report back to the larger class. As groups delve more closely into each side of the debate, continue to fill out the information on the board, recording and defining each position with the detail and nuance students provide. If you like, you can ask groups to hold off on discussing the last two questions on the handout until each individual position has been more deeply explored. Then, at the end of the exercise, ask students to explain how the conflict is ultimately decided and how the stakes of the conflict might be at play elsewhere within the text. Talking through alternative outcomes also will help students understand why the author structured the text as she or he did, and will clarify the writer's core thematic or ethical commitments.

REFLECTIONS

This a great exercise for getting students to understand the ethical wagers of literature. The guided questions lead students to grasp more fully the specific underlying beliefs, codes, customs, or ideals that a text analyzes and contests. And the focus on opposing or multiple sides encourages students to explore and examine a real diversity of values, especially in cultures or eras of which they are less informed. Such an approach seeks to attune students historically to the tremendous ethical possibilities for literature as a whole. This exercise highlights why the humanities matter.

Usually, when confronted with an important and difficult conflict within a text, students immediately wish to judge who is "right," a decision based on their own experiences and emotions. For example, when I did this exercise with Jane Austen's *Mansfield Park* and focused on the debate over whether Edmund Bertram and then Fanny Price should participate in the amateur theatricals, my students initially found it unimaginable that the two should not participate, given how casually such activities are treated today. But asking students to spell out the terms of the debate by rehearsing Fanny's position against performing *Lovers' Vows* against Mr. Yates's position for it, they ultimately were able to see why amateur theatricals might be viewed as dangerously socially destabilizing in late eighteenth-century and Regency society. My students also noted that the challenge to static patriarchal authority represented by the theatricals is mounted later in *Mansfield Park* when Maria Rushworth leaves her husband for Henry Crawford. When I finally asked the class to brainstorm alternative resolutions for the conflict not proposed by the text, they came up with two especially clarifying questions: Could the young people gathered at Mansfield Park have chosen a safer play to perform, or were any theatricals socially dangerous without Sir Thomas Bertram's explicit permission? And, did the Bertram children and their friends actually *need* to choose as risqué a play as *Lovers' Vows* in order to release their pent-up rebellious energies?

Although this exercise works particularly well with novels and with plays, I have also successfully tried it with at least one poem marked by moral conflict, Homer's great epic *The Iliad*. The heated debate in Book I between

Achilles and Agamemnon before the assembled Achaeans as to who deserves the Trojan woman Briseis as a prize concubine brings out in students strong emotions and a bit of initial confusion. Many don't fully understand why the warlords are fighting or why this particular conflict should begin Homer's poem, while others wonder why Briseis should herself be denied a voice in the disagreement entirely. By assuming sides and talking through the actual terms of the debate, my students began to understand more clearly the complex role of women in ancient Greek culture. Students were also able to discover and delve more deeply into competing models of leadership at play in the positions taken by Agamemnon and Achilles. My students, for example, noted that the shame-based warrior ethos is staged most strikingly when Agamemnon publicly tells the mighty warrior Achilles—with nearly fatal consequences—that the latter's anger and arguments "mean nothing" to him.

Working through this debate, which transpires at the beginning of *The Iliad*, also prepared the students well for discussing other contesting values elsewhere in the poem, most particularly the two different models of heroism represented by the epic's major combatants: Achilles (the figure of the older war-based culture) and Hector (the representative of the emerging order that values domestic life). "The Great Debate" proved to be a great way to highlight how ancient Greek culture routinely worked through its cultural values in agonistic form, whether in the Socratic dialogues, in the political debates staged in the histories of Herodotus and Thucydides, or in the conflicts enacted in the tragic Greek dramas.

. . . .

For more exercises that can be used to teach stories, try these:

Specific relevance	*General relevance*
Read, Reread, Close Read (Discussions)	The Sixty Second Game (Discussions)
Reverse Entropy (Discussions)	Fishbowl (Discussions)
The Blow Up (Essentials)	Put the Question (Discussions)
The Cut Up (Essentials)	It's Time We Talked (Discussions)
The One-Liner (Essentials)	Debate (Discussions)
Let's Get Heretical (Poems)	Leader, Skeptic, Scribe (Discussions)
Dramatic Monologue (Poems)	The New Title (Essentials)
Talk Show Host (Plays)	The Descriptive Word (Essentials)
Introduction to Genre Fiction (Genres)	The Common Thread (Essentials)

Social Media Meets Classic Literature (Genres)

Is This Book Literature? (Canons)

Judge a Book by Its Cover (Canons)

Le Mot Juste (Words)

Word Clouds (Words)

First Things First (Styles)

One-Sentence Pastiche (Styles)

Imitate This (Styles)

Draw Me a Picture (Pictures)

Island Mapping (Pictures)

Reverse Ekphrasis (Pictures)

Novel Portraits (Pictures)

Close Reading Comics (Pictures)

Making It Graphic (Pictures)

Digital Literacy (Pictures)

Vote with Your Feet (Plays)

How to Read a Bookstore (Genres)

Mixtape Maker (Genres)

To Thine Own Tweet Be True (Genres)

What is "Literature"? (Canons)

Putting a Face to a Name (Canons)

Literature Class Band (Canons)

The Blank Syllabus (Canons)

Build-A-Canon (Canons)

Keywords (Words)

Vocabulary Bites (Words)

Aphorisms (Words)

Fill in the Blanks (Words)

Punctuation Matters (Styles)

Reading without Reading (Objects)

Making Manuscripts (Objects)

Online Commonplace Book (Objects)

Object Lesson (Objects)

The Things Inside Books (Objects)

POEMS

Of all forms of literary expression, poems can be especially challenging for students. As a medium that routinely takes liberties with the standard conventions of both written and spoken language, poetry delights in turning sentences, words, and even syllables inside out and upside down. But even so, poems rely on an inner logic of their own, achieving an organic unity in which meaning is conveyed through the precise synchronization of parts—content, form, language, sound, meter. The fifteen lessons in this section cover all five of these parts, each exercise instructing students in the complex inner workings of poetry.

The first three exercises on content ("Let's Get Heretical," "Great [and Not So Great] Expectations," and "Piece by Piece") help students get their bearings in a poem while simultaneously moving them beyond summary and into analysis. The exercises on form ("Form and Content," "Sonnet Sampler," and "Dramatic Monologue") go a step further, demonstrating how particular poetic forms and voices give shape and meaning to a poem's elusive subject matter. Language marries content and form, as the next set of exercises ("Parts of Speech," "Tenor and Vehicle," and "Be Pedantic") suggests in its focus on grammar, figuration, and imagery. Another set of exercises on sound ("Karaoke Poetry," "Explode the Poem," and "Close Listening") highlight poetry's early roots in music and song by focusing on assonance, alliteration, rhyme, repetition, refrain, and other sonic effects.

The "Poems" section concludes with several methods ("Don't Get Stressed by Meter," "Your Line," and "Versification") for introducing students to poetry's most technical feature: versification. These final lessons on the art of scansion demonstrate how rhythm and meter, the hardest poetic techniques for students to master, operate as the fundamental baseline of poetry. The trick in teaching students how to get the most out of a poem is letting them experience themselves how all the different parts of the poem work together to produce a distinct mood or message. As the following exercises demonstrate, there are a number of creative ways to teach the formal properties of poetry, among them literary paraphrase, voice imitation, linguistic experiment, oral reading, or line annotation. Poetry may indeed be difficult, but it is also eminently teachable.

Let's Get Heretical

Patrick Thomas Morgan

A systematic close-reading exercise that empowers students to commit the "heresy of paraphrase" with pride.

Genre: *poetry*
Course Level: *any*
Student Difficulty: *moderate*
Teacher Preparation: *medium*
Class Size: *any*
Semester Time: *early*
Writing Component: *before class, in class*
Close Reading: *high*
Estimated Time: *25 to 30 minutes*

EXERCISE

Choose a poem from the syllabus (lyric poems work best) and give students the following assignment: "Get ready to be excommunicated, because you're about to commit a heresy. In poetics, paraphrasing has a dirty reputation. Cleanth Brooks once said that it's impossible to paraphrase a poem, and those who try are committing 'the heresy of paraphrase.' Read the poem we're discussing in our next class and distill the lyric into its poetic essence. What lies at the heart of this poem? As succinctly as possible—while trying to capture the 'work' this poem 'does'—write a single sentence paraphrase. Be prepared to share your description with your fellow heretics."

After students have completed their paraphrase (this can take three to five minutes, depending on the poem's length and difficulty), ask a student to read the poem aloud. Then have each student share his or her paraphrase with the rest of the class, and intermingle their paraphrases with your own questions to help the students think about the similarities and differences between everyone's poetic distillations: Are there any trends? What are the possible lenses through which we can view a poem? What makes a good paraphrase? Is it even possible to paraphrase this poem? Once students begin to notice that their paraphrases are largely thematic (this won't take long), it's time to jump things up a level.

Introduce the class to what I call an "analytic paraphrase," a method of reading I learned years ago as a student of Helen Vendler's. Provide students with a handout explaining three general methods for moving their paraphrase beyond summary and toward analysis. Ask them, individually or in pairs, to do the following: (1) *Content*: Provide a one- or two-word summary of the poem's main mission or type: for example, landscape poem, travel poem, aubade, elegy, love poem, friendship poem, occasional poem, war poem, or spring/winter/summer/fall poem. You can list the major poetic types on the handout, while also encouraging students to be creative and use their own verbal tags. (2) *Address*: Classify each thought unit in the poem according to its rhetorical utterance: for example, command, exclamation, question, declaration, apology, narration, conversation, instruction, lament, or supposition. It's helpful to list on the handout the most common addresses and to explain that the easiest way to find the most appropriate address is to first discover what attitude the thought unit is trying to express: for example, if the language represents an expression of sorrow, the address is labeled a "lament," and if the language evokes a submissive attitude organized around the asking of permission—and isn't earnest enough to be called a "plea"—the address is labeled a "request." (3) *Form*: Identify the rhythm, rhyme, meter, stanza shape, and (if applicable) formal genre: for example, sonnet, sestina, terza rima, or prose poem. Cater the formal terms and definitions provided on your handout according to the needs of your students and the formal possibilities of the poems you consider.

Now ask students to return to their initial paraphrase and revise it once more, including this time all three levels of their analytic paraphrase (content, address, and form). Leave enough time for the class to discuss in a general way the difference between their first thematic paraphrase and their final analytic paraphrase. You might ask them these questions: What does an analytic paraphrase accomplish that a thematic paraphrase does not? Which descriptive method creates the more effective poetic distillation? Did the analytic paraphrase yield any surprises about the poem? Since everyone is paraphrasing the same poem, it can be highly instructive to end this activity by inviting students not just to read their new and improved paraphrases out loud but also to explore the most striking differences between them. Asking students where their paraphrases seem to diverge the most can provide a useful point of entry into a deeper discussion of the poem's ambiguities, nuances, and complexities.

REFLECTIONS

Students tend to react with enthusiasm to this exercise because they're eager to learn concrete methods for approaching poetry. By following a three-step system for "getting into" a poem, they can keep practicing this interpretive strategy until it becomes habitual. After sharing and discussing their final efforts, students are usually surprised at how much more sophisticated the analytical paraphrases are compared to the more thematic ones. By the end of the exercise, the students should feel they have encountered an entirely different lyric, in which form and content, address and audience, genre and theme all work in tandem to create a fuller, richer experience of the poem.

For example, looking at Emily Dickinson's poem "I Died for Beauty," one of my students offered this initial paraphrase: "The poem is about two deceased individuals who realize they died for the same thing: Beauty and Truth." Her analytical paraphrase read: "This is a death poem composed of three ballad stanzas, opening with the self-presentation of a persona who died for Beauty, followed by a narration in which the persona is joined by a character who died for Truth. Upon realizing via dialogue that they died for the same cause, the poem ends with a revised, relational self-presentation and narrative of union." Because poems are often composed of multiple types of addresses, it's common—and entirely permissible—for the analytic paraphrase to be longer than the thematic one. The analytical paraphrase inevitably facilitates closer reading. With the Dickinson poem, for instance, several students noted the way the first and last quatrains are composed of the same two speech acts (self-presentation and narration), opening up a fruitful discussion on how and why poetic voice transforms over the course of this short lyric.

Although "Let's Get Heretical" is intended for poetry, it is adaptable for both fiction and nonfiction. Try it with Henry David Thoreau's *Walden*, a text chock-full of identifiable speech acts (rhetorical questions, boasts, narrations, instructions, self-presentations, exclamations, apologies, generalizations, requests, surmises) and figures of speech (metonymy, synecdoche, metaphor, simile, epistrophe, syllepsis, litotes, anaphora, puns, parables). Sometimes students take so readily to analytic paraphrasing that you need to remind them at the end that this method is a bit like the Wikipedia of poetics: a good tool to begin describing and analyzing texts, but never the final word.

Great (and Not So Great) Expectations

Sophie Gee

An exercise that helps students distinguish literary analysis from simple description.

Genre: *poetry, especially early poems*
Course Level: *intermediate*
Student Difficulty: *easy or moderate*
Teacher Preparation: *low*
Class Size: *any*
Semester Time: *early, midterm*
Writing Component: *in class*
Close Reading: *high*
Estimated Time: *25 to 30 minutes*

EXERCISE

Choose ten to fifteen lines from a poem and copy the passage for the class. Explain to the students that they will be doing an exercise in which they distinguish between items they are expecting to see in the passage and items they are not. The really crucial instruction is that the term "expectation" can cover almost any aspect of a reader's response. Reassure the students that this isn't about already knowing what to expect from a sixteenth-century sonnet or an eighteenth-century pastoral. It's about using their reader's instincts to figure out how the author is being unconventional. Let them know that the everyday meaning of words, their connotations, their syntactical position, their frequency of use, and even their omission are all important and that most important of all are the associations that words and images trigger in the reader's mind.

To begin, offer students the following instruction: "As you read each word or phrase, what does it make you expect about what might come next, and why?" Then ask the students to make two columns in their notebooks: *Expected* and *Unexpected*. Read the poem aloud three times, inviting a different student to read the passage each time. (The class will appreciate the opportunity to really *hear* the passage, since sound no less than sense creates reader expectations.) Then invite students to work through the text and place as many words as they can in one of the two columns. Tell them to try keeping each list item to single words, not phrases.

Give an example to get people started. Here's a favorite of mine for this exercise, the opening couplet from Alexander Pope's *The Rape of the Lock*:

What dire offence from am'rous causes springs,
What mighty contests rise from trivial things . . .

A reader might not expect the word "amorous" to follow "dire," or "trivial" to follow "mighty." Alternatively, a reader might not expect to encounter serious words in a singsong rhyming couplet. So "springs" and "things" could go in the *Expected* column and "offence" and "contests" could go in the *Unexpected* column.

Allow students roughly ten minutes to draw up their lists. Then begin making one master list on the blackboard, encouraging conversation about whether particular items should be on the *Expected* or *Unexpected* side. (Remember to keep your chosen passage brief, or this part of the exercise takes too long.) Emphasize that it is perfectly acceptable for everyone's list and explanations to be different.

Finally, have students discuss their lists, and the experience of making them, with the class. Which column is longer? (It would be fine, for instance, for a list to be all *Unexpected*. Sometimes that's the reading experience.) What part of speech tends to dominate, if any? Does that change from the beginning of the list to the end? Do all the elements on the *Expected* side of the list go together, or could that list be further divided? You can conclude by asking how the exercise may have changed or shaped some of the students' own expectations, about how poems work or how they work on readers. What larger expectations do we routinely bring to the reading of poetry?

REFLECTIONS

The purpose of "Great (and Not So Great) Expectations" is to develop techniques for moving from description to analysis in critical reading. Distinguishing analysis from description is probably the hardest skill for undergraduates to achieve, and it is also difficult to explain well. The "list" constraint of this interpretive exercise is what compels students to move away from simply describing the story within the poem and toward analyzing the poem's formal elements, such as language, sound, rhythm, and tone.

This little exercise can't go wrong in showing students that they understand more than they think. It is especially useful for teaching early poetry; with poems like Chaucer's *The Canterbury Tales*, Spenser's *Faerie Queene*, or Milton's *Paradise Lost*, it is incredibly difficult for students to know what is unexpected in the poem and what is not. It is also the case with early poems that, understandably, students tend to focus on *what* the poem might be saying at the expense of *how* it is saying it. In making their lists, they will discover that they must necessarily read against the grain of the poem's narrative. At least half of what they write down (words, phrases, images: whatever jumps out at them) complicates or contradicts what the text appears to be overtly telling them. Poems, they will realize, provide as much that is unexpected as expected. Students will make other valuable discoveries, such as that we read by forming expectations about what will come next based on what we have just seen. And they will experience how expectations change from moment to moment when we read poetry because the most interesting or memorable poems change constantly too.

I first developed this exercise because I kept telling my students to say something "interesting" about the poem, and I defined interesting as "weird or unexpected." One day a canny student pointed out that the things I often called attention to were neither weird nor unexpected but incredibly ordinary, like how Adam and Eve get hungry all the time in *Paradise Lost*, or how their relationship with Satan is an adulterous love-triangle like one we might see in a nineteenth-century novel. In a breakthrough moment, the whole class realized that the paradoxical sign of something being truly unexpected about a poem is that it feels intensely recognizable in a text where otherwise much is alienating. In the end it can be the most familiar moments in a poem that are the most unexpected, which suggests that the function of poetry is not always or only defamiliarization. To paraphrase the German Romantic poet Novalis, a poem makes the familiar strange and the strange familiar.

. . . .

Piece by Piece

William A. Gleason

An exercise that uses section breaks to help students understand content.

Genre: *poetry*
Course Level: *any*
Student Difficulty: *easy*
Teacher Preparation: *low*
Class Size: *any*
Semester Time: *any, especially early*
Writing Component: *none*
Close Reading: *high*
Estimated Time: *40 to 45 minutes*

EXERCISE

Students new to the analysis of poetry often need help tackling poems of moderate length—anywhere from, say, thirty to sixty-five lines—that are not already separated into stanzas or that have few if any clearly marked sections. By dividing such poems into smaller units and then tracing the connections between them, this exercise helps students develop a clearer sense of the poem's content while also discovering its underlying structure. You can use poems from almost any period and written in almost any form, including blank verse, free verse, or couplets. Poems that use conventional punctuation tend to work best, because they create natural opportunities for division into smaller units. Poems that contain narrative or descriptive elements also work well, because they often provide their own internal markers to follow. Some good midlength poems for this exercise include Anne Bradstreet's "Verses upon the Burning of our House" (fifty-four lines), William Wordsworth's "Nutting" (fifty-six lines), and Robert Frost's "Directive" (sixty-two lines).

Photocopy the poem onto a sheet of paper and give it out at the beginning of class. If you can get the complete poem onto one side of the page, all the better. (Use two columns if necessary.) You'll also need a copy of the poem that you can project at the front of the room—and annotate—for later in the exercise. Have the students begin by reading the poem aloud, either by asking one student to read the entire poem or by having students take turns reading a few lines each. Then invite the students to help you divide the poem, at least provisionally, into sections, using content as their guide. Where does the poem seem to pause, or the action to turn? Where do the meaningful breaks occur? This should take no more than five to ten minutes. It's less crucial that the students divide the poem "correctly" than that they agree, for now, on where to mark the sections. (If you prefer, or are pressed for time, you can skip this step and mark these divisions on the handout yourself, but having the students do this preliminary work gets them thinking about the relationship between content and structure right from the start.) Poems of this length will typically divide into four to six sections.

Now divide the class into small groups and assign each group one section of the poem. (If you have a large class, with more groups than sections to assign, you can assign the same section of the poem to more than one group.) Tell each group to look closely at its section and to mark the most striking elements of that section on their handouts. What words or phrases stand out? What are the most notable images? Are there any repeated sounds? Any unusual pauses or pacing? Tell the groups to feel free to consider any elements that might seem worth noticing, including diction, rhythm, rhyme, tone, imagery, point of view, and so on. Tell them they will be reporting back to the class on what they discover in their section, so they should also think about how to prioritize their findings.

Let the groups work on their sections for roughly ten minutes, then call all the groups back to report. Project your copy of the poem at the front of the room. Next, starting at the beginning of the poem, solicit each group's findings, highlighting their most significant notations on your projected copy—using circles, squiggly lines, different colors, whatever seems best—for the entire class to see. After you do this for the first two sections of the poem, ask the class as a whole whether there are any elements that might link the second section to the first. A recurring phrase or image? A particular sound? A grammatical pattern? *What do you see?* Feel free to encourage them to point out more abstract connections as well: anything that seems to link the sections in a striking way—or, indeed, that separates them. (Perhaps one section introduces an image or idea that seems to oppose or negate one from the previous section.) Mark each of these, drawing lines to connect the elements students have identified. Encourage the students to mark up their own copies of the poem in this way, too, so that they have a record of the work you are doing together.

Continue this process until you reach the last group. (It might take twenty minutes or so to work through the entire poem.) As you move further into the poem, encourage students to point out connections (or disconnections) between *any* sections, not just adjacent ones, and continue to mark all of these on the projected copy. (Connections between the first and last sections are often striking.) After all the groups have reported, your projected poem will likely be covered with notations and webbed with connecting lines.

Conclude the exercise by asking the students whether the initial divisions they proposed still seem the most appropriate. Do other divisions now present themselves more clearly? Why or why not? How would the students describe this poem—both its content and its structure—to another class of students? How is this poem put together, and why?

REFLECTIONS

The basic premise of "Piece by Piece" is a simple one: in order to tackle a moderately long work, break it down into its component parts and let the students "teach" the work to each other, section by section. (This approach can also be used with prose.) As the students piece the work together, they are also identifying larger structural patterns and connections that they might not have seen as easily on their own. The discoveries seem to arise out of the poem itself ("Hey, look!") rather than from the instructor, which gives students, especially those new to the study of poetry, a model for close reading they can replicate with other works. For all these reasons, this can be an exercise that works particularly well near the beginning of a course, when you are trying to establish good close-reading habits.

In my course on late nineteenth- and early twentieth-century American literature, I have used a version of this exercise with "Joe," by the Canadian poet E. Pauline Johnson (Tekahionwake). On first read, Johnson's thirty-four-line poem might be taken as a largely genial depiction of a young boy resting from work in fields of "Indian corn." But as the students look closely at the poem's different sections, they gradually remark the more negative imagery that clusters at the scene, from the "drunken" fence that "staggers" along the edge of the fields in the opening section, to the pioneer's axe and settler's plough that, at the end of the poem, stand soberly ready to turn what was likely Indian land into farmers' stumps. What might have seemed comically harmless (a fence that can't "walk" straight) or charmingly innocent (a boy with "vagrant" freckles and "vagabond" hair) eventually comes to look sinister and threatening, as the students link the boy's "shambling" walk and "lazy" yawns in the poem's final section with the drunken assault of the "zig-zag" fence on the landscape in the first—the repeated *z* sounds perhaps even mimicking the violent sawing that the trees themselves await and that the "semi-savage" boy will undoubtedly learn to do.

For a variation on this exercise, you can also have students tackle poems that are already divided into stanzas or sections, giving each group its own piece to work with and then report back to the class as a whole. This works well with a poem like Paul Laurence Dunbar's "Ere Sleep Comes Down to Soothe the Weary Eyes," for example, a fifty-four-line poem divided into six stanzas of nine lines apiece, following an ABABACDCD rhyme scheme. Despite its regularity and clear divisions, Dunbar's poem makes a prominent turn in the final stanza (from a single night's sleep to "the last dear sleep," or death), a turn that becomes more anticipatable once students follow the progression of imagery from section to section. The main principle here is the same: when working with a text whose length might initially be daunting, let the students "divide and conquer" by teaching it to each other, piece by piece.

Form and Content

Andrew Benjamin Bricker

An exercise that shows how poetic form affects meaning, by tracing a story through its poetic retellings.

Genre: *poetry*
Course Level: *introductory*
Student Difficulty: *easy or moderate*

Teacher Preparation: *medium*
Class Size: *any*
Semester Time: *early*
Writing Component: *none*
Close Reading: *high*
Estimated Time: *30 to 45 minutes*

EXERCISE

Choose a story from a classical or biblical text, one of particular fascination to later poets, such as the myth of Prometheus, David's seduction of Bathsheba from the second book of Samuel, or the fall of Icarus in Ovid's *Metamorphoses*. On a handout, reproduce the story in its simplest or earliest form (this may be in prose or verse, an original or a transcription, depending on your needs). Then add two or more poetic retellings of the same story. For Prometheus, you might use passages from Hesiod's *Theogony* or Aeschylus's grim *Prometheus Unbound*, or later retellings, like Percy Bysshe Shelley's *Prometheus Unbound*, Byron's "Prometheus," or William Blake's painting, *Prometheus Bound*. For David's seduction, try two first-person pieces, written centuries apart: "Hot Sun, Cool Fire" (sometimes known as "Bethsabe's Song") from George Peele's *The Love of King David and Fair Bethsabe*, and Robert Calvin Whitford's "Bathsheba" (or, for contrast, the mildly bawdy ballad *The Story of David and Berseba*). For the fall of Icarus, consider using the sixteenth-century painting *Landscape with the Fall of Icarus* and two very different ekphrastic poems inspired by it: W. H. Auden's "Musée des Beaux Arts" and William Carlos Williams's "Landscape with the Fall of Icarus." Put everything on the same handout and circulate it among the students. If possible, also have these texts ready to project at the front of the room.

Begin class by explaining to students the difference between what a poem says (its content) and how it says it (its form). As a quick and easy example, I use the opening lines of Samuel Taylor Coleridge's "Kubla Khan": "In Xanadu did Kubla Khan / A stately pleasure-dome decree." With their inverted syntax, the lines offer an immediate analog for the surreal disorientation of Coleridge's dream vision—the form in effect mimics the content. From there, you can begin to give a more in-depth understanding of the difference between content and form. Focus first on the "what." Give the students some time to read the classical or biblical story (which they may well be familiar with) and to summarize, in a single sentence, its main plot or action. Invite volunteers to share their one-sentence summaries to see if there are any disagreements on what actually happens in the tale.

Once the content, or "what," is clear, move directly into a discussion of the "how." Have the students read two more retellings of the same story.

(Having several points of comparison helps students see how wildly the form can change even if the content remains largely the same.) At this point, you can separate the students into pairs for a few minutes or lead a full-group discussion. Ask students to discuss the differences between the pieces they have read or looked at. To guide the students, project or write on the board some key formal terms—tone, diction, syntax, imagery, audience. Ask students to describe the tone of each poem and to point to specific language or imagery that conveys that tone. Focus on adjectives: what mood do they create? (You might even have students recite the lines in their stagiest voices, asking them what disposition they intuitively strike: Are they serious? comic? melancholy? wry?) How does the syntax foreground certain words or shape the speaker's voice? What about the meter? Even if students don't know their iambs from their spondees, most will be able to sense whether the poem has a solemn or singsong quality, whether the lines use breathless enjambment or end in punchy couplets. Finally, ask them, Who is the projected audience, and how can we tell?

After the students have had time to discuss the poems (and perhaps paintings) among themselves, begin a group discussion, going over each keyword to gather the students' impressions. Focus specifically on how, in each instance, formal aspects of the work shape our sense of the story's meaning. For students new to poetic analysis, they might be surprised at just how similar their impressions are.

To close, remind students that form is the nuts and bolts of poetic analysis. Urge them, when reading poems for class, to attend first to the formal aspects of the poem by asking themselves each time, how does form shape content? Remember to insist that this is the kind of analysis you want—not summaries or impressions of content alone, but analyses based on the concrete technical and linguistic aspects of each work.

REFLECTIONS

Form produces meaning. This proposition is perhaps so obvious that we often neglect to mention it to our students. But it is also abstract and general, and difficult to illustrate without a concrete example. This is an exercise that teaches students to distinguish between form and content—to understand how the form in which something is written affects its meaning, tone, and projected audience.

One of the great virtues of a broadly formalist approach to the study of poetry is the way it encourages students to go beyond simply noting what a poem is "about." Instead, students learn to ground their readings concretely in a poem's formal properties: its language, tone, syntax, and sound, and its line breaks, meter, and rhyme scheme. By showing a poetic recycling of an accessible story, students have an easier time shifting their focus from the poem's subject matter to its form, learning as they move from one poetic retelling to another how different forms can shape and recast similar content.

For teachers inclined to use literature in context, as a medium for history and cultural analysis, poems deployed for allegorical or analogical purposes also offer a way to understand not only the poet's selection of a recycled story but also how the poet's formal and linguistic choices shape the projected reader's understanding of that tale. I use some version of this exercise in almost every poetry class I teach; it is a first step for students to learn how to read closely.

My favorite primary text for this exercise is Genesis. Most students already know the story and can summarize it easily. Here is one student's synopsis: "Nothing, then something, six days of work, then Adam, Eve, the snake, and an unfortunate trip to the farmer's market." This is the "what"—the content of Genesis. The "how" is trickier. I immediately turn to a facsimile page from the original 1611 King James Version (KJV) of the Bible (available free online at http://kingjamesbibleonline.org/Genesis-Chapter-1_Original-1611-KJV) with its gothic lettering, bizarre early modern spellings, long *s*'s and Latinate *v*'s for *u*'s and *i*'s for *j*'s. I project the page onto the screen and have someone in the class read a few verses aloud. We start a conversation: What do you notice right away? (Usual answer: unusual spellings, long *s*'s.) But slowly we get into the poetry of the KJV: its calming, confident authority and its incantatory repetitions. I ask a few pointed questions: How do we know the audience? How does the KJV create its solemn tone? How is the perceived authority of a vernacular Bible created through its lineation, presentation, and poetic and rhetorical devices? The story's the same, but something has changed.

Students slowly realize that the authority and meaning we attach to the KJV is not simply a product of its content (the story of Genesis), but a necessary effect of its presentation. Even by 1611, gothic lettering and ye-olde spellings were purposefully archaic, but they connected a modern, vernacular Bible to a distant, authoritative past. Similarly, the translators' lineation and rhetorical devices intimate, at a verbal level, both the originary power of God and the perfection of his creation. Students see it in the anaphoric "And God" that begins each verse (always active, the first mover), in the epistrophic "and it was so" that concludes many verses, and in the declarative "and God saw that it was good" that repeats throughout.

But I don't leave the "how" there. I replay the story twice more. The second time, we turn to Brendan Powell Smith's *The Brick Testament* and his magnificently detailed Lego-block retelling of Genesis (http://thebricktestament .com/genesis/index.html). Broken up into discrete scenes, each retelling is done in bold, eye-catching colors, and every line of dialogue appears in word bubbles written in that most cartoonish of fonts, Comic Sans. The contrast between the KJV and this version is instant. Students immediately notice something has changed about the tone and the projected audience, even if the story has remained the same. Maybe this is for children, some students suggest. Or maybe it is parody or burlesque.

The same happens with the third retelling, when we hit closest to home with God's Facebook Page (http://collegehumor.com/article/3739519 /the-facebook-of-genesis), an admittedly juvenile version produced by the website CollegeHumor, complete with Facebook status updates, photos, and news feeds. My students know immediately how to read this version. They are, after all, its main audience, and they have no difficulty understanding the ways in which the filter of Facebook is the latest formal reshaping of the biblical story: a Genesis for the Internet age.

Sonnet Sampler

Amber Foster

A group activity for teaching sonnet patterns and the importance of rhyme.

Genre: *poetry*
Course Level: *introductory or intermediate*
Student Difficulty: *moderate*
Teacher Preparation: *medium*
Class Size: *any*
Semester Time: *early, midterm*
Writing Component: *none*
Close Reading: *high*
Estimated Time: *50 to 60 minutes*

EXERCISE

Choose a selection of sonnets distinguished by their different rhyme schemes: the Petrarchan sonnet, the Shakespearean sonnet, the Spenserian sonnet, and the terza rima sonnet. Be sure to select your sonnets from a broad spectrum of literary periods. Some good candidates include Edmund Spenser's "What guile is this, that those her golden tresses," William Shakespeare's "From fairest creatures we desire increase," John Milton's "When I consider how my light is spent," Percy Bysshe Shelley's "O Wild West Wind, thou breath of Autumn's being," and Edna St. Vincent Millay's "Only until this cigarette is ended."

Begin by providing a "quick and easy" guide to the more common sonnet patterns and their defining rhyme schemes. You can project the guide on a screen or write the patterns on a board, but providing a simple handout like this one—which should also include the sonnets you have chosen—works best:

A Quick Guide to Identifying (Some) Sonnet Patterns

Petrarchan Sonnet:
abba-abba-cde-cde
  Alternate sestet rhymes:
cdc-cdc, or cde-dce.

Terza Rima Sonnet:
aba-bcb-cdc-ded-ee
  Often has a rhyming couplet at the end.

Shakespearean Sonnet:
abab-cdcd-efef-gg
  Usually 14 lines, iambic pentameter.

Spenserian Sonnet:
abab-bcbc-cdcd-ee

Take some time briefly to explain how rhyme controls form. In the Petrarchan sonnet, the octave's two quatrains present and develop the sonnet's general themes, while the sestet's two tercets reflect upon these themes. The Shakespearean sonnet will permit a break between octave and sestet but is composed of three quatrains and a closing couplet. The Spenserian sonnet deploys rhyme to link its quatrains more tightly, while the terza rima sonnet abandons quatrains altogether and uses tercets with interlocking rhymes to create even greater continuity. Explain to the students how rhyme schemes help to establish and distinguish different types of sonnets.

Then create groups of three to four students and, according to your needs, assign each group either the same sonnet or different ones from the handout. Explain that students have twenty minutes to discuss the poem and decide which type of sonnet it might be. Their work does not end there, however. Tell them in advance that each group will report back to the class on not just the sonnet's form and rhyme scheme but on the poem's other formal properties, such as diction, figurative language, and tone. Let them know they will have roughly five minutes for their presentation, in which they will read their poem aloud to the class, identify the sonnet pattern, show where and why the sonnet may break that pattern or "bend the rules," and note anything else about the poem's language, tone, structure, or meaning that captures their attention. To help them work efficiently and stay on task, provide them with some concise sample questions (these may also be included on the handout).

Sample Questions for Sonnet Presentations

1. What sonnet pattern and rhyme scheme did the poet use?
2. What is the sonnet about?
3. Who is the speaker?
4. What is the tone (melancholy, cheerful)?
5. What figurative language or other techniques did your group find interesting?
6. What themes appear in the sonnet?
7. What is the "meaning" or "significance" of the poem?

You might recommend that members of the group divvy up these questions, but leave plenty of time to put all the pieces of their explication together for a more compelling group presentation. Give students a five-minute warning before you conclude this portion of the exercise, so every group has time to address the final question on the handout, about the poem's meaning or significance. For a more advanced variation on this group exercise, consider asking groups to prepare two or three discussable questions about their sonnet, either in lieu of a formal presentation or to facilitate class discussion afterward. A supplemental or extra-credit activity might also include having students write their own sonnets. I like to end this exercise with a five-minute in-class writing reflection, in which students report on what they learned about the sonnet as a form and how their understanding of the sonnet had changed after participating in this activity.

REFLECTIONS

"Sonnet Sampler" is ideal for survey or poetry courses that must cover a great deal of literary ground in a short time. It works well at the beginning of the semester, though students should already have a basic understanding of poetic meter (especially iambic pentameter). Designed to both introduce students to a versatile poetic form and further develop their powers of explication, this exercise may also be modified to accommodate varying class sizes and durations.

At the beginning of this activity, I allow students to use dictionaries on their mobile devices, an invitation that encourages them to puzzle out difficult words for themselves. While groups work, I circulate around the room, offering hints for particularly difficult elements. For example, on the day I assigned all the groups Shakespeare's "From fairest creatures we desire increase," I found myself assisting with some of the more challenging diction. When one group struggled to see past the archaic language, I indicated that "increase" is an Old English term for reproduction. Almost immediately, the group members began to grasp a main theme of the poem, pointing out that the speaker had to be an old man giving advice to someone young. When another group seemed to be missing all the figuration, I simply asked, "Why does Shakespeare describe the spring as 'gaudy' here?" Very specific questions or targeted information work best for facilitating individual group discussion and deeper textual analysis. Monitoring groups in this way also keeps them from going off track.

This exercise gives students a greater appreciation for the importance of rhyme in poetry. One of my groups pointed out the presence of slant rhymes (a student exclaimed, "Even Shakespeare wasn't perfect!"). Another noticed the way a rhyming couplet at the end of a sonnet could add emphasis ("like a punch line"). In the informal written survey I did at the end of the exercise, still another student acknowledged, "rhyme can really make a difference in the reading, interpretation, feel, and impact of a poem."

Other students reported, more generally, that they enjoyed the collaborative nature of this activity. "I enjoyed working in a group because it made it easier to understand the poem, and it was interesting to hear different interpretations," a student wrote. Indeed, the written responses to the exercise revealed that groups had spent the most amount of time debating the poem's "meaning," something I had hoped to foster as I walked around the room, nudging students to provide textual evidence to support a single interpretation of the poem.

This activity has proven effective in both my literature and creative writing courses. It provides a good foundation from which to build a deeper understanding of poetic form and content. "Sonnet Sampler" also tends to leave the students keen to learn more.

Dramatic Monologue

Renée Fox

An imitation exercise that deepens students' understanding of character and form in the dramatic monologue.

Genre: *poetry*
Course Level: *intermediate*
Student Difficulty: *moderate or hard*
Teacher Preparation: *low*
Class Size: *any*
Semester Time: *midterm*

Writing Component: *before class, optional in class*
Close Reading: *medium*
Estimated Time: *40 to 50 minutes (longer with optional in-class writing)*

EXERCISE

Select a group of dramatic monologues—poems voiced entirely from the perspective of a single speaker (who is clearly not the poet) and usually addressed to an implied listener. Some good picks: any of the poems from Richard Howard's *Untitled Subjects*; T. S. Eliot's "The Love Song of J. Alfred Prufrock"; Ezra Pound's "Portrait d'une Femme"; Robert Browning's "The Laboratory," "Fra Lippo Lippi," "Andrea Del Sarto," and "My Last Duchess"; and Alfred Lord Tennyson's "Ulysses."

Assign at least four students to each monologue. For homework, tell them that this is their chance to talk back to the poems, but with one catch: they need to talk back using the same formal constraints the original monologues use. Ask each student to write an imitation of the monologue they've been assigned (paying close attention to meter, stanza form, and tone) from the point of view of *either* the monologue's presumed listener *or* the speaker's "victim." Different dramatic monologues will lend themselves to one or the other, some monologues will allow for either one, and in some monologues the listener and victim might be the same character. But leave the decision about which point of view to adopt up to the students.

Remind them that their sense of the character they are voicing must come from the original monologue—they can be creative, but their speakers have to emerge from the original poem. Ask them to think about the strategies the original monologue uses to develop the character of *its* speaker and how that speaker's character shapes students' sense of the other possible characters in the poem (including its presumed, desired, or even "worst nightmare" listener). Ask students to ponder how the character that they choose to voice does or doesn't conform to the original monologue's depiction of that character: Is the students' Duchess from Browning's "My Last Duchess" really as free with her affections as the Duke says she is? Might students' Telemachus from Tennyson's "Ulysses" be less content to rule Ithaca than his father says he is? Ask students to consider what the original speaker needs or wants from the monologue's implied "you": sympathy? companionship? assistance? a scratching post? nothing but an excuse to talk? Tell students that they can be inventive in their responses and can certainly resist the original speaker's demands but that their imitation needs to use its own speaker's particular perspective to interpret and to judge the original speaker's character.

In class on the day the imitation is due, put students into their respective monologue groups. Have them read each other's versions and discuss the different choices that they made in their responses. Prepare a list of questions: From whose points of view have they chosen to write, and why? How have they differently developed the poem's victims or interlocutors? How does the original speaker's character change, depending on how they've chosen to write the voice that talks back? Does the form of the original poem lend itself better to certain new speakers than to others? How do these differences translate into different interpretations of the original poems?

This exercise takes between thirty and forty minutes, with an additional ten minutes for a general class discussion. For longer classes like seminars, you can also incorporate, as a follow-up, an in-class critical writing exercise. Ask students to write a paragraph in which they analyze their own imitation and how it interprets the original monologue. Or have students swap poems with someone in their group and do the same thing with another student's imitation. Whatever you do, be sure to leave five or ten minutes at the end of class for a full group debriefing. You might close by asking them questions about the self-reflexive nature of the dramatic monologue: In what ways do dramatic monologues seem to be thinking about the creative process and about the ethics of making art/poetry? What relationship do they articulate between art and gender? What about between art and history, or art and memory?

REFLECTIONS

When students read dramatic monologues, they understand instinctively that there's a huge difference between how the story of the poem looks from the speaker's point of view and how it would look if the poem were written from anyone else's point of view. The purpose of this exercise is to draw students' attention to the relationship between voice and character in the dramatic monologue: to the subjective nature of the speaker's "reality," to the strategies by which the speaker engages his or her listener's/reader's sympathies, and to the complex multiplicity of voices and alternative stories that the univocal dramatic monologue so cleverly implies. Writing imitations of the poems from alternative perspectives gives students a fun way to think more deeply about the tactics the poet uses to allow the poem's "story" to emerge from its speaker's subjectivity.

I often assign this exercise when I teach Robert Browning's dramatic monologues. For instance, in a group of four students writing back to the speaker of "Porphyria's Lover," I have had one student write in the voice of an angry Porphyria, one in the voice of an abused and broken Porphyria, one in the voice of an overeager psychiatrist, and one in the voice of a weary police detective. In each case, the position the student chose to occupy allowed him or her to move past simple judgment of the original monologue's speaker—"That guy's a delusional psycho"—and to think instead about the ambiguities, possibilities, and uncertainties that a detailed response to this speaker's story exposes.

One variation of this exercise that I use in a mixed genre course is to have students return to a novel we've already read and write dramatic monologues that narrate, in poetic form, a morally suspect event from the "offending" character's point of view (for example, Bertha Mason's setting Thornfield on fire in Charlotte Brontë's *Jane Eyre,* or Miss Havisham's deciding to adopt Estella and turn her into a man trap in Charles Dickens's *Great Expectations*). Like the "talk back" exercise, this version draws students' attention to the idiosyncrasies of the speakers in dramatic monologues and to the way the drama of the monologues emerges from the tension between the speaker's engagement of our sympathies and our own desire to judge the speaker's morality. But this version also asks them to reevaluate a text the class has already read and discussed and to imagine its story from an alternative point of view: to draw an analogy between the insistent subjectivity of the dramatic monologue and the way narrative bias in fiction can create its own creepy silences.

. . . .

Parts of Speech

Katherine Bergren

A dissection of lexical categories that teaches students to analyze poems quantitatively, then qualitatively.

Genre: *poetry*
Course Level: *any*
Student Difficulty: *easy*
Teacher Preparation: *low*
Class Size: *any*
Semester Time: *early*
Writing Component: *none*
Close Reading: *high*
Estimated Time: *35 to 40 minutes*

EXERCISE

Choose a relatively short poem—sonnet length or a little longer is perfect—that you anticipate will challenge your students' interpretive abilities. Two types of poem spring to mind: enigmatic poems that befuddle students, and simpler-sounding poems that lend themselves to generalities about symbolism or emotion. Some possibilities include Emily Dickinson's "She staked her Feathers" or selections from Gertrude Stein's *Tender Buttons* (all befuddlers); or William Blake's "The Sick Rose," Claude McKay's "The Tropics in New York," or William Wordsworth's "I wandered lonely as a cloud" (all generalizers).

Distribute a copy of the poem and begin by reading it slowly aloud. Then give students several minutes to jot down a text-message-length summary of the poem (no more than twenty words). Emphasize that this summary should not include any analysis—just the basic plot or content of the poem. Ask for volunteers to share their summaries. (Sometimes it takes a few minutes to find a true summary, as opposed to a burgeoning interpretation.)

Next, divide the class into four groups. Assign each group to a part of speech: group 1 gets the nouns, group 2 the verbs, group 3 the adjectives and adverbs, and group 4 the "small words"—the prepositions, conjunctions, articles, and interjections. Depending on the poem and the size of the class, I vary the parts of speech. (If there are lots of adjectives and adverbs, I split those up and cut the "small words." If one stanza features lots of prepositional phrases, I'll make prepositions its own group.) Give students five minutes to underline every instance of their part(s) of speech in the poem. The underlining is done solo. If your class is an introductory one, this is a good moment to review parts of speech: how to identify them and what work they do.

Next, ask students to pair off within their groups (matching each student with someone assigned to the same part of speech). Invite them to discuss their findings and to brainstorm trends they see among their underlined words. Is their part of speech prevalent in the poem or not? Is this prevalence constant throughout the poem, or is it specific to certain stanzas? Most important, is there a thematic continuity among the words they underlined? This should take another five minutes or so.

Finally, create four columns on the blackboard for the different parts of speech. Solicit pairs to share their findings with the class, and write their observations on the board. When everyone has contributed, go a little deeper into what work these parts of speech are performing in the poem as a whole. What does it mean for a poem to have lots of adjectives, or virtually no prepositions? Why might a poem shift from being verb heavy to noun heavy? Then bring in the summaries the students wrote at the beginning of class. What is the relationship between the trends on the board and these text-message summaries? How do the poem's various parts of speech support or subvert, clarify, or complicate the content of the poem?

REFLECTIONS

While "Parts of Speech" is suitable for students at all levels, I find it particularly effective in classes with a high number of nonmajors—students often more comfortable in science or social science classes than in literature ones. I add a tally to the columns on the board, allowing students to analyze numerically the grammatical makeup of the poem. The process of quantifying parts of speech teaches many resistant readers that humanistic inquiry is not based simply on feelings and opinions but also on how the facts or details of a text conspire to produce such feelings and opinions. Because the exercise offers a step-by-step procedure for connecting poetic form and content, it works best at the start of the semester as a technique students can repeat later as needed.

I have had success with this exercise using poems that are from very different literary periods and that pose different interpretive challenges. For example, with William Blake's "Introduction" to the *Songs of Innocence*, a seemingly straightforward Romantic poem, my students found they could easily write their short summary of the poem's action but had a hard time saying more. With selections from Gertrude Stein's abstract *Tender Buttons* (like "Milk" and "Single Fish"), the students discovered that summarizing the poem's plot or content was almost impossible, far more difficult than identifying its parts of speech. Both types of poems (the seemingly simple and the frustratingly opaque) can prove stumbling blocks for students: How can we dig deeper? How do we even scratch the surface? In both instances, immersion in the specific details of a poem's parts of speech can jump-start a serious literary analysis.

The results for the Blake and Stein poems, which I assigned in the same week, were illuminating. In Blake's "Introduction," students who underlined small words noticed the repetition of "and" toward the end of the poem and suggested it gave the poem a "continuous" sound. When I asked them to connect this continuity with the action of the poem, one student mentioned the poem's shift in focus from the spoken to the written word and thought that the repetition of "and," and the continuity it engenders, makes the transition smoother. When faced with Stein's *Tender Buttons*, students typically have difficulty saying anything about the poems other than "they're difficult." But by focusing on parts of speech, my students were able to seize on a few key trends in Stein's experimental poetry. One student pair who focused on Stein's nouns noticed, for instance, that the "Food" section of the book features not just food products but also other domestic objects and chores. And a pair studying Stein's small words were able to comment on the speaker's tone, which can sound imperious or bossy: "Please shade it a play. It is necessary and beside the large sort is puff." Soon, a student connected these two trends, domesticity and the speaker's imperious tone, in a nuanced feminist reading that had seemed impossible fifteen minutes earlier.

Tenor and Vehicle

Miriam Chirico

A charting exercise that teaches the duality of metaphor.

Genre: *poetry*
Course Level: *introductory or intermediate*
Student Difficulty: *moderate*
Teacher Preparation: *low*
Class Size: *small or medium*
Semester Time: *early*
Writing Component: *in class*
Close Reading: *high*
Estimated Time: *30 to 35 minutes*

EXERCISE

Before beginning the exercise, take some time with students to define metaphor in its clearest terms: figurative language that asserts a comparison between two things of unlike nature. The word "metaphor" comes from the Greek meaning "to carry over" (*meta* meaning "over, across" and *pherein* meaning "to carry, to bear"). It may help students to think of a metaphor as a vessel or a bucket (or an *amphora*) that carries the properties associated with one thing over to the second. If you start with this description of a container traveling back and forth, then I. A. Richards's model of metaphor as possessing the two components of vehicle and tenor will make more sense.

According to Richards, the "tenor" is the object in the poem, the thing that is being described, while the "vehicle" is the object external to the poem that provides traits for the description. When we say "David was a lion in battle," the vehicle (lion) is the language that carries the comparison (ferocity, bravery), and the tenor (David) is the subject to which this language is applied. Write some more examples on the board: in Homer's description of the "rosy-fingered dawn," the tenor is the dawn, and the vehicle is a hand; in Walt Whitman's "the beautiful uncut hair of graves," the *implied* tenor is grass, and the vehicle is uncut hair; in Emily Dickinson's "Hope is the thing with feathers," the tenor is Hope, and the vehicle is a bird. Emphasize that metaphor is really a transaction, a relationship between two things, and that the purpose of this exercise is to show how vehicle and tenor in tandem will point students toward the poem's more elusive theme.

To make the nature of such metaphoric figuration clear to the students, use T-charts to diagram the tenors and vehicles throughout the poem. Begin by creating handouts of a T-chart: one line across the top of the page and another line down the middle. (T-charts can be generated for free at the website "worksheetworks.com.") T-charts, typically used to list pros and cons, or the two sides of a balance sheet, provide an effective visual tool for helping students understand the essential duality of metaphor.

After choosing poems or sections of poems that are short, about fifteen to sixteen lines (sonnets work well for this exercise), divide the students into small groups and provide them with the T-chart work sheet. Have them title the left column "Tenor" and the right column "Vehicle" (or, if you prefer, "Object Described" and "Object Lending Its Traits"). You may choose to have all groups work on the same poem the first time you do this exercise, and later to have each group analyze a different poem and present their T-chart to the class (reproducing their work on the board or an overhead projector).

Have a student read the poem aloud. Then explain the rules for filling out the T-charts. Instruct them that the Tenor column must contain actual words from the poems (usually these will be nouns, occasionally verbs), but the Vehicle column should note whatever traits or associations these particular words and phrases suggest. Encourage students to include as much of the poem's main subject on the left side of the chart, while listing as many possible corresponding ideas, images, or sensations on the right side. The only rule groups must follow is to list the Tenor words vertically in the T-chart in the sequential order in which they appear in the poem.

Allow fifteen to twenty minutes for this portion of the exercise; less advanced students usually need some encouragement to think more deeply about associations. Reconvene the class for a concluding discussion about the T-charts students created and the poem's themes. Students should be able to deduce the "meaning" or the "imaginative statement" the poet is making by connecting the various ideas listed in the right-hand Vehicle column of their T-charts. You can give groups a few minutes to write collectively a statement of theme, or you can perform this exercise with the class as a whole. (If you have time, you could invite each group to draw their T-chart on the board, explain their choices and the patterns that emerged, and then share their statements of theme.) Conclude the exercise by discussing and honing these final statements, weighing which themes seem especially central to the poem and also which metaphors appear crucial for conveying the poem's message.

REFLECTIONS

Drawing the connections between a poem's concrete language and its larger imaginative statement can be a real challenge for students. Without a full understanding of how metaphoric language conveys meaning, students often find it difficult to access a poem's deeper significance or—if they have intuitively identified the meaning—to trace the textual support for their interpretation. Though hardly new, the tenor and vehicle approach to metaphor, paired with the compulsory linearity, spatial representation, and one-to-one correspondence demanded by the T-chart, offers a particularly effective way to teach students how to perceive the subtle metaphoric twists and turns so fundamental to poetry.

I have tried this exercise with a range of poems of varying degrees of difficulty. Nearly any passage from Shakespeare makes a good candidate for teaching the one-to-one correspondence of metaphor. Here's one I have tried from *As You Like It*:

> All the world's a stage,
> And all the men and women merely players:
> They have their exits and their entrances;
> And one man in his time plays many parts,
> His acts being seven ages. (Jacques, *As You Like It*)

Tenor	*Vehicle*
World	**stage** Theater, a play; implies a director (God?) and an audience
Men and women	**players** Actors who perform their prescripted roles in a play
Deaths and births or the arrivals and departures of people; perhaps projects/relationships beginning and ending	**exits and entrances** Departures and arrivals on the stage
Identities Any individual possesses different identities in his/her lifetime, such as occupations or relational identities (father, neighbor, friend).	**one man. . . plays many parts** An actor takes on various character roles in different plays.
Developmental stages Every seven years a person passes through a different developmental stage (infancy, childhood, adolescence, etc.).	**his acts being seven ages** An actor plays his part through various acts.

This student T-chart yielded a number of metaphorical associations in the Vehicle column, which students linked together to arrive at Shakespeare's theme: human lives are theatrical. But looking more closely at their own chart, they also recognized the fatalism behind this premise. The character Jacques suggests that a particular script has been planned for us with a fixed beginning and ending. But (as the class ultimately agreed) in introducing the idea of role-playing, Shakespeare complicates this idea of human destiny by reminding us that we are free to play various parts and that these parts change over time.

We tend to distinguish similes from metaphors based on the degree to which the comparison is made, but in actuality a simile is a type of metaphor. Metaphors assert an identity—"It was evening all afternoon" (Wallace Stevens)—while similes rely upon some degree of heterogeneity or difference between the two things being compared: "His hanging face, like a devil's sick of sin" (Wilfred Owen). In the first case the metaphor works through compression, while in the second the simile encourages discursiveness. However, in both instances one thing is being understood based on the properties of another.

Thus the T-chart exercise can be applied to poems using similes as well as metaphors. Here is a T-chart my students produced for a more contemporary poem, N. Scott Momaday's aptly titled "Simile":

What did we say to each other
that now we are as the deer
who walk in single file
with heads high
with ears forward
with eyes watchful
with hooves always placed on firm ground
in whose limbs there is latent flight.

Tenor (describing "we")	Vehicle
We (the noncommunicative couple): skittish, frail and prone to flight	**deer**
Not seeing eye-to-eye, one subservient to the other, not acting in unison or in harmony	**walk in single file**
Arrogant, proud, overly confident, on the lookout for danger	**heads high**
Overly sensitive to comments; sensing offence in a casual remark; self-protective	**ears forward / eyes watchful**

Not wishing to take risks or expose one's vulnerability	**hooves on firm ground**
Tendency to leave the relationship at slightest provocation; dormant desire to abandon the other	**limbs there is latent flight**

While the similitude between the couple and two deer was obvious to students upon first reading, we needed to tease out the precise analogy between the deer's behavior and the couple's wariness in order to understand the theme of estrangement at the center of the poem. From the descriptive traits listed in the Tenor column—skittishness, arrogance, pride, oversensitivity, defensiveness, and an unwillingness to be vulnerable—students found they could not just identify the lovers' estrangement but also diagnose some of its causes. Thematically, the poem poses a question: what is necessary for stability in a relationship? Metaphorically, it gives the answer: honest communication. By calling attention to its own figurative language, "Simile" suggests that it can be difficult to discuss affairs of the heart in objective or realistic terms.

For more advanced classes, you can use this exercise to go much deeper into types of metaphor: for example, *mixed* metaphors (in which the comparison is untenable), *dead* metaphors (in which words and phrases have historically lost their tenors), or *extended* metaphors (in which the vehicle is often quite elaborate). You can also use this metaphor exercise to lay the groundwork for later lessons on related rhetorical devices, like *allegory* (an extended metaphor in which a character or event personifies a more abstract idea) or *symbol* (a metaphor with an especially rich tenor that often carries deep emotional power).

. . . .

Be Pedantic

Andrew Cole

An advanced exercise in textual annotation that offers students a new approach to writing about poetic language.

Genre: *poetry, especially medieval*
Course Level: *advanced*
Student Difficulty: *hard*
Teacher Preparation: *medium to high*

Class Size: *small to medium*
Semester Time: *any*
Writing Component: *before class*
Close Reading: *high*
Estimated Time: *50 to 60 minutes (per session)*

EXERCISE

To prepare students for this intensive exercise in annotating medieval poetry (Chaucer works best here), begin by spending an entire class (fifty to sixty minutes) reviewing rudimentary editorial principles. Place on screen an image of an original manuscript page, a fragment of which might look like this, though you should use a larger image with more text. (I offer here an excerpt from William Caxton's print of Geoffrey Chaucer's *Anelida and Arcite*, circa 1477. Notice that the typeface resembles manuscript. This is the first example I use to introduce students to basic features of late medieval vernacular letterforms, abbreviations, and diacritical marks.)

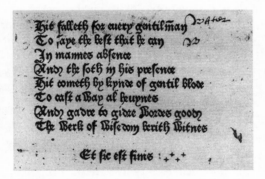

Ask students to discuss what they see. Invite them first to identify and list everything that puzzles them: mysterious marks, confusing letters, puzzling words, strange abbreviations. Then juxtapose on the screen the original page with its latest scholarly edition—in this case, *The Riverside Chaucer* (Boston: Houghton Mifflin, 1987).

Talk about the variation of the scribe's penmanship, or "hand," and offer strategies for deciphering difficult letterforms. Train students' eyes to distinguish a long *s* from an *f*, and how to use context clues to read blotchy letters. Sleuth around in the minutiae. After you've covered some ground, supply students with a different manuscript page and give them ten minutes or so to test, individually or in pairs, their chops. Instruct them to transcribe the manuscript, drawing on what they've just learned in class. Then check in with the class as a whole, addressing any remaining questions. This entire portion of the first day exercise usually takes twenty to thirty minutes.

Once students have a feel for medieval penmanship and letterforms, spend another twenty to thirty minutes discussing two different models of editorial practice: a variorum, or "best text," edition and a "diplomatic" edition. A "best text" edition collates readings from a number of manuscripts to construct a single and presumably error-free archetype, a text thought to resemble what the author originally wrote or even intended to write but didn't quite do so without making mistakes. A diplomatic edition transcribes or records the text exactly as it appears on the manuscript page, leaving abbreviations intact and errors (if any) preserved. Select another text—say, Chaucer's Envoy in the *Clerk's Tale* as presented in the *Riverside Chaucer* and in the Chaucer Society's diplomatic editions produced by Walter W. Skeat in the late nineteenth century. Pass around hard copies of these two examples for students to share, or continue to use a screen or handouts if the real thing is not readily at hand.

Talk about the degrees of editorial involvement. Are there differences in punctuation, capitalization, phrasing, and how do these differences affect the meaning of the poetry? In particular, ask your students to consider how much editorial intervention is too meddlesome. Ask them to weigh the advantages and disadvantages of a "best text" that may, in fact, never have existed. Ask them to contemplate the role of the editor in reproducing medieval literary texts for the general reader. Conclude by having a conversation about whether, or how, we should respect medieval artifacts as "witnesses" speaking to us from the distant past.

Then give students this assignment, to be completed before the following class:

> You're an editor now! Transcribe, punctuate, correct, and annotate one of the many short fifteenth-century Chaucerian poems contained in the variorum facsimiles on reserve in the library. Choose a poem of at least ten lines but no more than twenty-five. All the thinking you ordinarily put into an academic essay you must now put into the footnotes to your edition. Pause over any letterform, any stray mark, any word, any phrase, any allusion, any editorial decision you've made about punctuation or emendation that affects our interpretation, and explain it in a footnote. Educate your reader: if the poem asks you to supply philological, imagistic, historical, or literary information, no matter how particular, then gladly accept the invitation to be pedantic. And last but not least: write a two-page introduction that explains your editorial principles, your approach to emendation, punctuation, word division, and capitalization. This introduction will serve as your in-class presentation on what you've discovered in completing this exercise. Finally, make sure to include a copy of the manuscript page you are transcribing.

When the next class convenes, ask the students to form into pairs or groups of three and exchange minieditions, double-checking each other's transcriptions and reading carefully their scholarly introductions. Focus should be on what students have learned in reading someone else's edition and on what (in turn) they may have done differently when producing their own. This activity can take at least twenty to thirty minutes, after which point the class can come together again for a general discussion for the remainder of the time slot.

This discussion, as I like to conduct it, involves each group sharing what they've learned. Remember each student will be working on a different poem or a different part of the same poem, so when the class regroups, everyone is truly assembling a larger picture of what it means to edit medieval texts in all of their variety. To be sure, some texts pose more special challenges than others, as when there is a hole or tear in the manuscript and the text is obliterated (a situation that requires the student editor to consider using a strong form of the "best text" approach to reconstruct the text with the help of rhyme scheme and meter). What's fun about this final part of the assignment is that everyone gets to hear something about another medieval poem they might not encounter otherwise, and what they'll hear will be something that is wonderfully technical and idiosyncratic, generated out of the dialogue between student and artifact.

REFLECTIONS

It's no secret: when students encounter medieval English literature (poetry and prose) in its original language—Middle English—they feel accomplished by simply making it to the end of the text and remembering its basic plot. In other words, there's often little time for complex interpretative work, which is why this particular exercise is so crucial, in that it offers a limited textual sample with many interpretive possibilities. Despite the difficulty of medieval poetry, students enjoy the practice of annotating because it allows them to take it slow in their reading and do detailed, even patient work on small passages. In this respect, the invitation to "be pedantic" appeals to English majors because it encourages them to indulge what they often have to defend or hide: the love of obsessive, even nerdy, literary criticism. Students can engage in close reading and historical interpretation at once—without the teacher having to pronounce, ex cathedra, on the virtues of one critical mode in relation to another. Here, the close reading *is* the historicism, and vice versa!

What's more, the exercise channels the effort of traditional essay writing into the scholarly apparatus; what drives students to keep on annotating is the edifying process itself, the building up of a structure of interpretation, the making of a thing of meaning. By shifting the work of paper writing from center to margin, it offers a change of perspective: students look at the poem from above and write about it from below, while the literary object remains, visually, in the center. Even the traditional essay introduction, which students often view as a hurdle on the way to the essay proper, is repurposed as a necessary guide to the reader, a place for the editor to reflect on his or her meticulous practices, rather than a paragraph with the predictable nonce formulas.

For their selections of passages to annotate, my students gravitated toward Chaucer, even though many of the aforementioned facsimiles contain the work of other major poets like Thomas Hoccleve and John Lydgate. You will often find that the students' work on their passages coalesces into a theme—that is, a little something on top of the requirement to edit and annotate. For example, one of my students looked at the short poem known as the "Complaynt D'Amours," which is readily available in two well-known facsimiles of manuscripts housed in the Bodleian Library at the University of Oxford: Bodley 638 and Fairfax 16. (Most college and university libraries will own facsimiles of these two manuscripts; select images of the latter, however, can be found via the University of Oxford's online portal, LUNA.) Learning that the "Complaynt D'Amours" is not attributed to Chaucer but nonetheless included in the authoritative *Riverside Chaucer*, this student went about trying to prove that the poet had written this work.

This quest to demonstrate authorship made for an especially productive conversation in class when the student presented her findings, because the students debated what makes Chaucer's poetry (or any other poetry for that matter) distinctively "Chaucerian." They forensically contested each other with information marshaled from sources such as the *Middle English Dictionary*, the online Chaucer Concordance, and the online *Linguistic Atlas of Late Medieval England*—all of which can be used to dig deep into the language, meaning, and even location of the poem's copying. (I have these sources already listed on my course syllabus, but you can just as well include them on the assignment sheet itself as online resources necessary for the completion of the assignment.) When one student perceptively exclaimed that Chaucer never uses such-and-such a word in any of his other works, another countered by saying that indeed the poet coins many terms, and at any rate, the dialect is that of London, where Chaucer worked and wrote for most of his life, so take that! Of course, nothing is proven conclusively, but it's quite a joy to kick back, as a teacher, and watch this conversation unfold.

Students loved this approach to reading medieval literature. By transcribing and editing poems in this fashion, they experience medieval literature in intimate, material terms and discover that the initial strangeness of the literary artifact becomes oddly comforting as they familiarize themselves with the poem, word by word. They also have to read *slowly*, which is an advantage today when so much social media has conditioned us to respond quickly to texts or even read them "distantly," as one modern scholar suggests we do, without close and careful attention to their local meanings, word by word, letter by letter. The whole point of this exercise is to offer students a new approach to writing about poetry that is, in some ways, an old approach.

. . . .

Karaoke Poetry

Patricia M. García

A karaoke-like performance that emphasizes the power of the spoken word.

Genre: *poetry or drama*
Course Level: *any*
Student Difficulty: *easy*
Teacher Preparation: *medium*
Class Size: *any, especially medium to large*
Semester Time: *any*
Writing Component: *none*
Close Reading: *medium*
Estimated Time: *15 to 30 minutes*

EXERCISE

Choose a poem that uses repetition to create rhythm and tone. As you select your text, look for a poem rich in such formal elements as alliteration, anaphora, parallelism, and rhyme. For a choral performance, somewhat longer poems work best, poems with an abundance of repetitions or refrains, like Edgar Allan Poe's "The Bells" or Alfred, Lord Tennyson's "The Lady of Shalott." But some shorter poems make good candidates as well, particularly highly musical poems like Elizabeth Barrett Browning's "How Do I Love Thee?" or William Blake's "The Lamb" and "The Tyger" (paired together). This exercise can also be used to teach a Shakespeare play. Simply choose a speech relying upon parallelism and repetition, such as Shylock's "Hath not a Jew . . . ?" or Portia's "The quality of mercy" from *The Merchant of Venice*, or Juliet's soliloquy "What's in a name?" from *Romeo and Juliet*.

Next, write a script for a choral reading of the poem to be performed in class. You will be asking the class to read aloud those lines with the repeating elements while a single reader, most likely yourself, will read the remaining parts of the poem. Designate these assigned lines by color choice or by font.

On the day of the lesson, announce that today is poetry karaoke day. Distribute the script and, if possible, project it at the front of the class. Explain that the group will be doing a choral reading of the poem and that they will be assigned to read lines aloud. Stress that this works best if the class reads energetically and at the same pace. Before you begin, explain the rationale behind the exercise: to highlight the sound effects of a poem and identify its structure, rhyme, and rhythm. Alternating their choral reading with your single voice will illustrate the contrast between those parts of the poem that repeat and those that do not. If you like, you can even divide the class into smaller groups and have each group read different sections of the poem. (Hearing parts of the poem voiced chorally from around the classroom can help demonstrate a poem's movement.) Designate the concluding line or lines for the entire class to read for a final, powerful emphasis.

Have the class perform the poem at least once; if you have time, a second performance once students are familiar with the exercise is worthwhile. Typically, this choral reading helps students recognize the importance of line breaks and caesuras, but if this doesn't happen in the first reading, a second reading is an opportunity to teach these important elements.

When the performance concludes, ask students to discuss the effect of the choral reading. What sounds did they hear, and how might this have been easier to hear aloud rather than in a silent reading? If they are familiar with poetic terminology such as alliteration, anaphora, parallelism, rhyme, or rhythm, what examples did they notice? Or if not, this would be a good opportunity to introduce poetic terminology. Ask them, What rhythms and rhymes do you hear in the poem? Did you notice tension building in the poem as phrases were constantly repeated? What is the poet emphasizing through his or her use of repetition, and how does this help develop the poem's meaning?

REFLECTIONS

The purpose of this exercise is to introduce students to the value of reading poetry aloud, to help them identify important formal elements in poetry, and to show them how to use their observations about poetic form to begin building an argument about a poem's effect as well as its meaning. A choral reading is a helpful introduction to a poetry unit because it relies upon the first lesson in understanding poetry: reading it aloud. Students act as both performers and audience in this exercise, allowing them to appreciate the sound of the poem before considering its meaning. They respond well to the choral reading because it creates a team atmosphere that eases their anxiety about reading aloud in class and, more importantly, about "not getting" poetry. Once they have completed the performance, students are better able to see how and why particular phrases and rhythms were repeated, which then develops organically into an analysis of theme.

Edgar Allan Poe's "The Bells" is my favorite poem for a choral reading. The poem is divided into four sections, and in each section the word "bells" repeats along with other onomatopoeic words like "tinkle," "ring," and "throb." Not surprisingly, since this is Poe, the poem's tone begins light-heartedly with the sound of silver bells and moves toward the darker, frightening death bells. I always divide the class into three groups situated from left to right in the classroom: group 1 reads the highlighted words in the first section of the poem, group 2 does the same for the second section, and group 3 the same for the third section. For the fourth and final section of the poem, we all read the highlighted words together. Because of the placement of groups, students hear the rhythm of the poem as the vocal chorus moves across the room. And when the entire class joins in for the final section, the increased volume matches the intensity of the poem as it hastens to its dark conclusion: the tolling of the death bell.

There is some nervous laughter when we begin, but it quickly stops as students become more used to reading in unison. When the reading of "The Bells" is over, my students are generally pleased with their group performance and ready to talk about Poe's precise aural techniques (onomatopoeia, anaphora, rhyme, rhythm) and how they support the poem's themes. The poem's first two sections celebrate life, with references to winter sledge bells and wedding bells that ring sweetly. Students in the first two groups have fun saying "twinkle" and "sprinkle" aloud and are quick to note the lighthearted effect of Poe's word choices. Students who perform the third section, which describes loud alarm bells, scream out, or at least speak loudly, the words "shriek," "clang," and "crash." Afterward, as we discuss the tone of these lines, group 3 is often more attuned to the growing dread of the poem, which a student once described as "becoming much darker, like life itself." The poem's final section announces the tolling of the death bell. Asking the entire class to read aloud the highlighted words of this section emphasizes the universality of death. Because the death bell is one we all hear one day, my students often describe this last section as something frightening, even "something out of a horror movie"—an observation that speaks eloquently to the power of language to excite and terrify us.

This exercise on rhyme and repetition, which teaches students to *hear* poetry through an actual experience rather than a lecture, works well at any point in the semester and is itself worth repeating. Inviting the class periodically to perform choral readings of a poem focuses attention on the writer's language, a helpful strategy when students face a complex poem or when classroom discussion needs refocusing. "Karaoke Poetry" is also a fun lesson, even and especially when the poem itself is a bit maudlin, like "The Bells." Despite the long aural history of lyric poetry (lyrics were composed to be sung), reading poems aloud is not a skill we practice or teach often. But this lesson creates the opportunity to return to poetry's origins in recitation, chant, or song and to appreciate a poem more fully for its musical notes.

. . . .

Explode the Poem

Jennifer Minnen

A collaborative close-reading exercise that opens discussion to multiple voices.

Genre: *poetry*
Course Level: *introductory*
Student Difficulty: *easy*
Teacher Preparation: *low*
Class Size: *small to medium*
Semester Time: *any*
Writing Component: *none*
Close Reading: *medium to high*
Estimated Time: *25 to 30 minutes*

EXERCISE

Select a poem or a section of a poem that can be read out loud in about two minutes. (Students will be inserting their voices into the poem to break open meaning, so the reading's length will extend quickly.) Prepare handouts with roomy margins for students to write on and around the poem.

To get started, explain to students that you will read the poem three times and that each time their task will change. For the first reading, they will simply listen to the poem. For the second reading, they will choose and annotate a line (only one!) with a short question or comment; these annotations can easily range from formal concerns to historical perspectives to affective or associative responses. For the third reading, the class will "explode" the poem by sharing what they wrote directly after the line is read.

With each performance of the poem, read slowly and pause meaningfully in order to give students time to collect their thoughts. When you reach the crucial third stage of the exercise, the point when students share their single-line annotation, read even more slowly to give everyone time to speak.

Certain lines will elicit multiple responses. While students may initially find this awkward, assure them (*before* you start round three) that repetition and contrast will add welcome texture to both the aural experience and the discussion that follows. Remember that the goal is for students to hear the poem and their own annotations in conversation with each other, so avoid commenting or attempting to direct traffic with more than eye contact and an encouraging smile. Students will also listen more closely to each other if you leave the timing up to them.

Afterward, ask students to consider what they heard in their "explosion," and record their thoughts on the board as a catalyst for discussion. Helpful questions include the following: What did you hear? What surprised you and why? What patterns did you notice? Which lines drew more attention and why? Where did contrasting ideas or opinions appear, and what do you make of this? Once you have collected a healthy number of comments, ask students to categorize and evaluate the group's annotations. What types of annotations do they see? What analytic moves do these different types make? This final, reflective step encourages students to step back and articulate the close-reading process, modeling its application for future use.

REFLECTIONS

Exploding the poem sparks discussion grounded in textual evidence, helps students identify formal patterns, and improves group dynamics by explicitly sequencing listening before speaking. The three-step process creates time for practiced comments while also encouraging each student to speak at least once before anyone (including the instructor) can take over. The chief purpose of the exercise is to show students how to leave summary behind and step confidently into analysis.

Almost any short verse explodes well, though I have found that those with clear speakers usually provoke the most extended and lively student analysis. Poems like Li Young Lee's "Mnemonic," Mahmoud Darwish's "Identity Card," Elizabeth Bishop's "The Map," and a stanza from Tennyson's "Ulysses" all work quite nicely. Enjambment warrants a caveat, since it can affect your reading of the poem. I usually pause at the end of every line break, whether enjambed or not, to avoid accidentally cutting off any annotations.

When I recently used the strategy to teach Keats's "On First Looking into Chapman's Homer," I wanted to offer a way inside its deceptive compactness without giving a prechewed analysis or a bland list of references. I learned that while no single student could be expected to pick up on the poem's central allusions or to grasp wholly the poem's tone of wonderment, together the class could amass an impressive array of responses to the poem's many nuances. Several key student annotations came at the poem's volta, as this sonnet turns from Keats's past Homeric encounters to the revelations of Chapman's translation. The most helpful of these annotations parsed literal and vicarious voyage by exclaiming, "Wait a minute! Is this guy going somewhere or only thinking about it?"

Another particularly vibrant set of student annotations centered on the poem's closure and what Keats might be saying about epiphany's risks, through reference to New World exploration. At the poem's end, Hernando Cortés takes a firm first glance at the Pacific while his crew looks wildly at each other. Interested in the crew's reaction, several students debated whether this "wild looking" was evidence of excitement or fear and whether the crew wanted to follow Cortez across the ocean or mutiny and go home. After exploding the whole poem, the students decided that journeys of discovery (literal or figurative) come with risks: it is impossible to reach new territory without embracing the unknown.

Later, while discussing the exercise itself and categorizing their annotations, students singled out, as their initial points of textual entry, three things: direct questions, vocabulary guesses, and what they called "stating the obvious." We ended by noting how these starting moves, which taken alone can end in summary, had together produced more analytic moves—larger, indeed braver, interpretive claims that can push a reading forward into uncharted terrain.

. . . .

Close Listening

Veronica Alfano

An introductory exercise that attunes students to the distinctive sound of poetry.

Genre: *poetry*
Course Level: *introductory*
Student Difficulty: *moderate*
Teacher Preparation: *low*
Class Size: *any*
Semester Time: *early*
Writing Component: *before class and in class, or in class only*
Close Reading: *high*
Estimated Time: *45 to 50 minutes*

EXERCISE

Either as homework or during the first few minutes of class, have each student select a line or so of recently assigned poetry that sticks in his or her mind due to a particularly conspicuous or suggestive sonic feature: perhaps a multisyllabic rhyme, a prominent rhythmic violation, an instance of exaggerated assonance or insistent alliteration, a caesura that forces the reader to slow down as she reads the line aloud, or an enjambment that rushes him across the line break. If you like, you can instead bring to class a handout of poems with especially noteworthy acoustic properties. Works by William Shakespeare, Christina Rossetti, John Donne, Gerard Manley Hopkins, Thomas Hardy, William Blake, Emily Dickinson, Robert Frost, John Keats, or Sylvia Plath—to give just a handful of examples—are a good place to start.

Ask students to copy onto a sheet of paper the lines that (quite literally) sound most interesting to them. Then give the students five to ten minutes to rewrite these chosen lines. Their mission: to preserve the paraphrasable meaning of the lines as much as possible but *eliminate* the sonic feature in question.

For example, the sibilant echoes of Edgar Allan Poe's "And the silken, sad, uncertain rustling of each purple curtain" might become "And the soft, unhappy, doubtful moving of each purple curtain"; the multiple stressed syllables of Robert Browning's "Whence, then, this quite new quick cold thrill—cloud-like" might become "Why do I feel this cold and cloudy thrill"; the truncated nonrhyme of George Herbert's "My heart was in my knee, / But no hearing" might become "My heart was in my knee, / But God did not hear me."

When they are done, invite students to exchange their revisions with a partner. Ask each pair to read their lines aloud—both the original lines and their revisions—and discuss together the similarities and differences between them. You might provide a few guiding questions for the students as they engage in conversation: Exactly what changes when the sound of a line changes? Why might the author have chosen (for instance) to use an internal rhyme at this point in the poem? Could the author have achieved the same emotional effect in any other way? Give the pairs roughly ten to fifteen minutes to peruse one another's work, and to coauthor a brief paragraph explaining why their experience of the rewritten lines is so different from their experience of the originals.

Finally, devote a generous portion of the remaining time to a full-group discussion of this exercise, talking through several examples in detail. Questions to consider: Were there any lines that two or more people singled out? Why might these lines have been especially striking? More generally, to what extent does the class agree that the meaning of a poem is synonymous with its formal or aural presentation? Can we establish a stable distinction between manner and matter, sound and sense? If several different schools of thought on this subject emerge, you might expand the exercise by having students come to the next class ready to defend their point of view in a formal debate.

REFLECTIONS

Many students have trouble understanding precisely why the sound of a poem matters so much. They often find it difficult to make interpretive claims based on the acoustic features of a poem rather than relying solely on its summarizable narrative content, or to realize that a complex of sonic and rhetorical structures necessarily shapes the "plot" of a poem. Although this exercise could certainly be useful near the beginning of the semester in an upper-level poetry course, it works extremely well in introductory poetry classes, since once the class is at ease with this way of thinking, you can smoothly incorporate topics such as rhyme and rhythm into discussion questions ("Let's talk about what might have happened if Adrienne Rich had written her poem in couplets"). Such fruitful destabilization of the text can also provide a convenient segue into a conversation about the ways in which authors revise their work, for which you may find it useful to bring into class manuscript versions of the poems on the syllabus.

The last time I did this exercise with one of my classes, the students showed a strong—and, given the nature of the assignment, understandable—preference for lines from traditionally rhymed and metered poems over lines from poems written in free verse. Prone to regard a poetic text as sacrosanct, they rather enjoyed running roughshod over Thomas Hardy's dactylic tetrameter ("Woman much missed, how you call to me, call to me" became "I missed you, lady, and I hear your calls") and speeding up the exhausted plaints of Alfred Lord Tennyson's forlorn Mariana ("She said, 'I am aweary, aweary, / I would that I were dead!'" became "'I am just beat,' she said; / She wanted to be dead").

But while these revisions certainly got laughs, they also generated a productive discussion. Working in pairs, the students discovered that Hardy uses dactyls as his lost wife Emma's sonic signature in "The Voice"; the dactylic pattern disappears as her imagined presence fades, and so meter here not only underscores but also helps to create and constitute meaning. They realized that the radical deceleration of that repeated "aweary, aweary" is not just an interesting aural effect but is absolutely crucial to depicting Mariana's crushing despair. And to return to an example mentioned above, the student who added an extra rhyme to Herbert's "Denial" proposed that this poet's withholding of rhyme creates an effect of chaotic disconnection, which is entirely appropriate for a poem about alienation from and eventual reconciliation with God.

In our full-group discussion, we were able to see firsthand that the stories poets tell are dependent on—are, indeed, inextricable from—their formal and sonic choices. I concluded this conversation with a caveat that poets who compose in free verse also make these choices. They may not offer end rhymes, but they still repeat important words and iterate vowel and consonant sounds. They may not write in a single identifiable meter, but their patterns of syllabic emphasis and line length are still significant. I encouraged the class to engage in close reading and close listening when encountering all sorts of poetry—and, for that matter, when encountering prose!

For this exercise on the mechanics of sound in poetry, some students may also be eager to grapple with theoretical questions, asking whether paraphrase is always heresy (see Patrick Thomas Morgan's "Let's Get Heretical" in this section) and perhaps debating why scholars may be more comfortable summarizing plays and novels than poems. Moreover, this exercise cues many students to take a more creative approach in their own critical writing. In my classes, it has inspired a paper that asked how Christina Rossetti's *Goblin Market* would work differently in iambic pentameter, a paper that experimented with adjusting the line breaks in E. E. Cummings's lyrics, and a paper that explored the ways in which adding rhyme would affect William Wordsworth's blank verse.

Many thanks to James Richardson of Princeton University, whose paper assignment for an undergraduate course called Reading Poetry inspired this exercise.

· ·

Don't Get Stressed by Meter

Johanna Winant

A basic introduction to meter and scansion that teaches students what it means to call a syllable "stressed" or "unstressed."

Genre: *poetry*
Course Level: *any*
Student Difficulty: *easy*
Teacher Preparation: *low*
Class Size: *any*
Semester Time: *any*
Writing Component: *none*
Close Reading: *high*
Estimated Time: *20 to 30 minutes*

EXERCISE

First, disarm the students by telling them that if learning scansion in high school was traumatic or confusing, you are here to help. After all, if they speak English, they already know whether the syllables in a given word are stressed or unstressed. (Indeed, all languages except tonal languages operate this way.) Teach them the poetic symbols for stressed (/) and unstressed (u) syllables, and then give them examples of words to scan: ask them to scan their names, ask them to distinguish between the noun and verb versions of "permit," and ask them to mispronounce words by putting the stress in the wrong place.

Second, teach poetic vocabulary. Teach students that a "foot" is usually two syllables, but almost always only one stressed syllable (you can reserve the spondee for later). Teach them that scansion is the activity of identifying stresses and that meter is the pattern of stresses. Teach them what iambs and trochees are (and that the rhythm of the human heartbeat is iambic). Teach them to count the number of feet in a line and work from monometer to hexameter. Remind students that iambic pentameter is the most common meter because it imitates the rhythm of natural English speech; some examples are "Are Brad and Angelina getting hitched?" and the poet Elizabeth Bishop's favorite example, taken from a blues song, "I hate to see that evenin' sun go down."

This is the important part: teach them that stress is comparative; calling a syllable "stressed" or "unstressed" is like calling a person "tall" or "short"— *it just depends on what they are standing next to*. Nearly any person is short standing in between NBA players, and nearly any person is tall standing between toddlers. Similarly, calling a syllable "stressed" or "unstressed" is not a black-or-white decision; when you label a syllable with a / or a **u**, you are making a *comparative judgment*.

End on a fun note: Ask for ten volunteers and have them stand in a line in the front of the classroom. Tell the class that each of the students represents a syllable and ask them to arrange the volunteers in "iambic pentameter," with taller students being more "stressed" than shorter students. What the students will quickly find is that Sarah counts as "stressed" because she is in between two shorter students, while Ali is the same height as Sarah but is "unstressed" because he is in between two taller ones. Students will find that Max and Sam are essentially the same height but, in order for them to fit the pattern, Sam will count as "stressed." Ask each "foot" to raise their hands. Then ask the line to become trochaic. I have done this "stand and be counted" portion of the exercise in classes where everyone is average in height. If you expect that this activity may make anyone uncomfortable, you can use any characteristic where students are arrayed on a spectrum: say, the brightness of their shirts or the length of their hair.

REFLECTIONS

This exercise is designed to teach students not to be afraid of meter. It is tremendously enabling for students to realize that they already know if a syllable is stressed or unstressed, and that "stressed" and "unstressed" are comparative rather than absolute labels. By learning a handful of poetic terms, students can identify any iambic or trochaic meter. I like to teach meter on the first day of a poetry class or relatively early in a literature survey course, because it demystifies for students (majors and nonmajors alike) the thing they are often most worried about, poetic scansion. A general familiarity with scansion ensures that, as the course progresses, even if a student does not understand a poem's content, he or she can still comment on its form.

One poem I especially like to use is Shakespeare's Sonnet 18, "Shall I compare thee to a summer's day?" We first discuss how the speaker feints toward the adoration of the beloved but then shifts to self-adoration. Then I ask students about the first foot, "Shall I," and we discuss how in those first two words, the speaker is weighing what to praise: if the "Shall" is stressed, the first line reads as a simple, if rhetorical, question; if the "I" is stressed, the speaker is already subtly touting his powers. I have used many other poems to teach students the inextricability of meter and message. Emily Dickinson's "I taste a liquor never brewed" and Theodore Roethke's "My Papa's Waltz" both provide students with memorable examples of drunkenly stumbling meter, while Robert Louis Stevenson's "From a Railway Carriage" can show them mechanically regular meter.

Students often assume that every line must fit a metrical pattern exactly. But in fact no line scans entirely perfectly unless it is imitating a machine. The true payoff of scansion is showing how a poem might vary the dominant metrical pattern, introducing ambiguity or difficulty because it betrays a speaker's unregulated—and so metrically irregular—emotion, thought, or behavior. The message students take away from this exercise is that identifying moments of metrical variation, along with moments of ambiguity or difficulty—noticing when syllables are the same "height" or spying a particularly stressed or unstressed syllable—is where literary analysis can begin.

Your Line

Kristen Case

A creative exercise for understanding poetic meter.

Genre: *poetry*
Course Level: *any*
Student Difficulty: *easy*
Teacher Preparation: *medium*
Class Size: *any*
Semester Time: *any*
Writing Component: *in class*
Close Reading: *high*
Estimated Time: *50 to 60 minutes*

EXERCISE

Choose a short poem that has a decisive, easily identifiable metrical pattern—for beginning students, iambic pentameter works best. Your options are many: poems by Shakespeare, Keats, Donne, Millay, and Bishop all make especially good candidates. Print copies of the poem for the class, with one metrically significant line omitted.

Before class convenes, write the entire poem on the board with a space left for the omitted line and with space between lines for adding stress marks. (You can inform students you have omitted a line or surprise them later.) Begin by having a student read the poem aloud. Then ask the class what is literally being described in the poem. Spend some time (ten to fifteen minutes or so) clarifying ambiguous or difficult lines, and have students look up (in a class dictionary or online) words they don't know.

Now move on to meter. Beginning with the first line, give students an exaggerated sense of what iambic pentameter sounds like and help them grasp the basic pattern. You might pause here to ask a couple of volunteers to invent nonsense iambic pentameter lines or to make up a few yourself. Then look at the other lines of the poem and see which lines correspond neatly with the metrical pattern and which are variations, perhaps sounding more like everyday speech. Going line by line, students will be able to see that certain lines have a much stricter rhythmic pattern than others. Encourage students to debate borderline cases: this will help them understand that metrical scansion is an art rather than a science. On the board mark the strictly iambic lines "SAME" and the more varied lines "DIFFERENT." Then ask students why they think the poem alternates between lines that have a stable, recognizable meter and lines that are more varied: how does this alternation between sameness and difference reflect the meaning of the poem? This portion of the exercise takes roughly twenty minutes.

Next, ask students to write a line to replace the missing one. Encourage them to think about whether they want the line to be strictly or loosely metrical, and what the rhyme scheme suggests the last word of the line should rhyme with. Encourage students to depart from this pattern, too, if they want, but be ready to say why they chose to do so. After giving students a few minutes to think and write, ask them to share their lines and explain why they made the choices they did. Finally, add the actual missing line to the poem on the board. This is a dramatic moment, and it rounds out the exercise nicely by provoking discussion on how a single line can often change the entire meaning of a poem.

REFLECTIONS

The purpose of this exercise is twofold: to enable students to begin hearing the rhythms of metered poetry and to help them explore the relation between meter and meaning. The exercise helps students lose their fear of metrical analysis by enabling them to get a handle on a basic rhythm. Once they get a feel for an underlying metrical pattern, they'll also begin to notice when that pattern is being disrupted and how both meter and variation are part of a poem's meaning. Writing their own lines (even if they struggle with the task) enables students to make the big leap of the lesson, which is from understanding the mechanics of scansion to discovering how metrics contributes to a poem's theme. Though sophisticated metrical analysis can take a good deal more practice, this exercise will allow even inexperienced students to see how sound can contribute to the sense of a poem.

My favorite text for teaching scansion is Robert Frost's "Hyla Brook," a fifteen-line iambic pentameter poem dealing with the constancy of love in the face of change in the loved thing, in this case a brook that has dried up in the summer heat, thus ceasing to be what it was. I usually omit the last line, with its final, paradoxical statement about love and identity, in order to allow the students free rein in imagining how the metrical and semantic elements of the poem resolve—or don't. To get conversation rolling, I stick first to what is being described in the poem (How big is Hyla Brook? Do you think you'd be able to see it on a map? If not, why does it have a name?) before challenging students with a few more interpretive questions (How does the speaker feel about the brook? How many and what kinds of temporal markers do you notice in the poem, and what are their effect? What do you make of the repetition of the word "song"?).

Then I move the conversation to meter, scanning with students a couple of regular lines first, such as "By June our brook's run out of song and speed," before spending more time on trickier lines that seem to break or push against the dominant meter, such as "Weak foliage that is blown upon and bent." For each line of the poem I ask a different student to call out the meter, which I initially mark on the board without comment, letting other students jump in first and suggest alternate scansions. Highlighting those lines that are truly borderline often leads to a productive discussion of how much voice, emphasis, or even accent come into play. At this point I ask the students to spend a few minutes composing their own final lines, and I have several volunteers read their lines aloud. I focus particularly on the question of how closely the line follows the iambic pattern and ask the students to explain their reasons for departing from or adhering strictly to that rhythm.

Finally, I write Frost's final line, "We love the things we love for what they are," on the board. Student response is usually a positive one: attuned to the role rhythmic consistency plays in this poem about love and change, they immediately feel the quality of closure and certainty that this line creates with its monosyllabic and evenly iambic rhythm. Further discussion of the meaning of this line in the context of the poem as a whole, however, opens up more questions. This line *sounds* quite resolved about the constancy of love in the face of time and change, but what does it mean to love things "for what they are" if things, like the brook, have no stable identity? The discussion usually ends with an examination of the way the poem's stable and unstable elements, meter chief among them, contribute to the complexity of its meaning, and a debate about whether the poem is finally a consoling one or not, a point on which the students are often evenly divided. In this way, the exercise demonstrates the richness of meter as an element of meaning that can reinforce or pull against the semantic meaning of a given line, stanza, or poem.

· ·

Versification

Meredith Martin

An introduction to versification that melds the classic and the contemporary.

Genre: *poetry*
Course Level: *introductory*
Student Difficulty: *moderate*

Teacher Preparation: *medium*
Class Size: *small*
Semester Time: *any*
Writing Component: *in class*
Close Reading: *high*
Estimated Time: *30 to 40 minutes*

EXERCISE

This exercise teaches the fundamentals of versification to students by first invoking the poems and songs they already know. Its purpose is to teach students classical meter (foot-based scansion) as well as poetry's sonic properties: rhyme, assonance, alliteration, consonance, and repetition. You need not select poems for discussion in advance; indeed, the success of this introductory exercise depends largely upon letting students provide their own examples.

Begin class with a general conversation: ask students what lines they happen to have memorized—anything from hip-hop songs to advertising jingles. Put four or five of these lines up on the board (or ask the students to do so) and start an open discussion about why they think they have memorized these particular snippets.

As students present their theories, list on the board each sonic concept that, directly or indirectly, enters the conversation. Ask them what they hear first in the song: Are they vowels? Are they consonants? Define appropriate poetic terms as you go and underline any vowels or consonants students comment upon. As they begin to notice things like assonance, alliteration, repetition, internal rhyme, slant rhyme, or other sounds and patterns in the song lyric or jingle, keep expanding your list of basic poetic vocabulary on the board.

When you have generated a handful of sonic terms, slowly start shifting into a discussion of meter. Begin talking students through emphasis and performance, using the easy example of "How are you?" Ask what it means when you say those three words as "HOW are YOU?" versus "How ARE you?" or "How are YOU?" Talk about the difference between stress and emphasis, thinking about the subtle ways that performance influences meaning. (For a companion exercise on poetic scansion, see Johanna Winant's "Don't Get Stressed by Meter" in this section.)

In rap songs, the temporal structure of the verse is often hurried or slowed. For the rap lyrics on the board, ask the students if they can agree on the song's beat, and put the beat of the song below the lyric. Ask how they would like to mark beat (With a *B*? An *X*? It's up to them). Then, together, come to a consensus on the stressed syllables above. Again, ask how they would like to mark the stress (an *S*?).

Note the way that the stress (and in some cases, even the emphasis) inter-acts with the beat of the song. Is there another level of rhythm in the line? If there is, see if you can mark the second level of rhythm and, again, make sure that students agree on *how* this should be marked. (This is a good introduc-tion to the arbitrary nature of most scansion.) Have fun thinking together and talking about what certain rappers might be good at—a certain kind of flow that moves incredibly quickly through syllables that have a lot of allit-eration, for instance, or a way of using extreme slant rhyme to make words that don't seem to rhyme work in a song. The most important thing is to listen to what students already know about meter and rhythm and to steer them toward seeing influence and intertext in contemporary music culture.

Next comes the tricky part. Ask if anyone has studied Greek or Latin. If a student has, invite him or her to describe how Greek or Latin poetry is measured. If no one has, briefly tell them that Greek poetry was measured by quantity, and Latin poetry by quantity and stress. To explain what "quantity" means, go over long and short vowels. Ask "What do you notice? It feels like it takes longer to say 'eeeee' than 'eh,' right?" In classical meter, the rule was generally that a "long" syllable took twice as long as a short syllable, and that was one of the ways that meter was measured. Remind them that "meter" sim-ply means "measure," and that in classical prosody the measure was mostly quantity. Teach students what a macron (¯) looks like, and a breve (˘), and that macron means "long" and breve (brief!) means "short." Ask them why it might be harder to measure by quantity in English, coaxing them to under-stand how pronunciation is intertwined with emphasis. Ask "What would happen if all English words had measurable quantity?" You can usually dem-onstrate the pitfalls of this by giving an example or two of different English dialects—how British English speakers typically pronounce "advertisement" (adVERTisement) differently from American English speakers (adverTISE-ment), for example, or how some regional American English dialects might change the length of certain syllables (as when my Virginia uncle pronounces "hair" as "hay-er"). Smoothing out quantity, in these cases, would homogenize speech dialects. Also tell them how "long" becomes "heavy" and "short" be-comes "light" and how these, in turn, become "stressed" and "unstressed" in discussions of English meter so that students understand why English poems are generally only measured by stress and not by quantity. Then show them the traditional sign for stress, the ictus (´), and explain how the names for patterns of stress ("feet") are left over from the Greek.

Next, write the classical names for feet on the board and show how lines are divided into them, making certain students know that the classical meters have a far larger variety of complicated names for feet and that these are, in English, entirely arbitrary. Return to the lines on the board and invite the class to scan them using the ictus for accented syllables and slash marks for dividing the feet. Or consider ending with an actual short poem or couplet that you happen to have memorized ("But, soft! what light through yonder window breaks? / It is the east, and Juliet is the sun"). Write the lines on the board and invite students to apply everything they have learned so far to this single poetic example.

REFLECTIONS

This exercise is designed to teach students how much they already know about poetic rhythm and sonic effects. It demonstrates that meter is an unstable measure and that understanding a poem's context (When was it written? How did it circulate? Was it memorized or read silently? What was its intended audience?) can help us understand how the rhythm and meter of a poem are working on multiple levels that are at once formal and cultural. Students learn the terms of traditional accentual-syllabic scansion, but they also learn that this is not the only way to hear the rhythm of a poem and to talk about it. This exercise allows students to hear and recognize poetic effects of meter on their own terms first, before learning how poets manipulate meter for particular technical ends. I have found that beginning with what the students already know not only engages them but also helps them see how poetic communities are formed and how poetry has often been addressed to certain audiences but not to others.

Students have a lot of fun working through their own and one another's lines, whether the line they offer up for group analysis is a complicated rap lyric or a simple advertising jingle. The shorter the line, I have noticed, the more quickly students rise to the challenge. One of my students offered the advertising jingle for a jewelry store, "Every kiss begins with Kay." Everyone caught immediately the repetition of the hard "k" sound in "kiss" and "Kay" (I wrote consonance on the board), but the internal rhyme in "kiss begins with" took longer to notice.

For this same phrase I asked students where they thought the emphasis should go, and why. We marked the possibilities on the board and talked a bit about stress: should the stress fall on "kiss" and "Kay" or on "kiss" and "beGINS" and "Kay"? "Every" generated the greatest debate among the students: Is it three syllables? Two? Can it be both? When would we say it as three syllables? How do we *know*, looking at this and hearing it, that it should be two? I ended our discussion of this particular student example by rewriting the phrase on the board in segments (Every kiss / begins / with Kay), inviting students to think about the way the line works temporally, hurrying a bit through "every" and dwelling a little on "kiss," in effect slant rhyming "kiss" with "begins" before elongating on the "Kay."

This exercise is ideal for teaching students about "rhythmic communities." Folks who listen to a lot of opera, or a lot of pop music, or a lot of rap music will have ears that are better tuned to hear certain rhythmic patterns in the songs. And it can show to them as well the importance of "metrical communities": why poets who would have had a classical education might have used more classical meters, and why professional readers have to practice in order to hear and see certain effects in poems of the past that most contemporary audiences miss.

Meter, which has many varieties, is one way that poets communicate with one another and with an audience. It is also a way we can learn about the past. In courses that deal with mostly metered poetry, I believe it is important not just to practice scansion with students but to show them what historical role meter might play in a poem's meaning. It is perfectly understandable that students today cannot easily identify the metrical structure of a poem written hundreds of years ago. Indeed, we should not take for granted that the classical system is the only system at work. Shakespeare may not have known what to do with a contemporary rapper, but, like my students, Shakespeare would have been both incredibly impressed by the rapper's skills as well as challenged by how to talk about these skills.

For more exercises that can be used to teach poems, try these:

Specific relevance

Read, Reread, Close Read
(Discussions)
The Cut Up (Essentials)
Dramatic Scansion in Everyday Life
(Plays)
Translating Sonnets (Genres)
The Fascination of What's Difficult
(Words)
The Forgers' Circle (Styles)
Imitate This (Styles)
Convolution (Styles)
Draw Me a Picture (Pictures)
Reverse Ekphrasis (Pictures)
Poetry Broadside Gallery (Objects)

General relevance

The Sixty Second Game
(Discussions)
Fishbowl (Discussions)
Put the Question (Discussions)
It's Time We Talked (Discussions)
Reverse Entropy (Discussions)
Debate (Discussions)
Leader, Skeptic, Scribe (Discussions)
The Blow Up (Essentials)
The New Title (Essentials)
The Descriptive Word (Essentials)
The Common Thread (Essentials)
Vote with Your Feet (Plays)
How to Read a Bookstore (Genres)
Mixtape Maker (Genres)
To Thine Own Tweet Be True
(Genres)
What is "Literature"? (Canons)
Putting a Face to a Name (Canons)
Literature Class Band (Canons)
The Blank Syllabus (Canons)
Build-A-Canon (Canons)
Keywords (Words)
Vocabulary Bites (Words)
Le Mot Juste (Words)
Aphorisms (Words)
Fill in the Blanks (Words)
Punctuation Matters (Styles)
Digital Literacy (Pictures)
Reading without Reading (Objects)
Making Manuscripts (Objects)
Online Commonplace Book
(Objects)
Object Lesson (Objects)
The Things Inside Books (Objects)

PLAYS

Plays are literature's most embodied genre. Stories written on the page to be enacted on the stage, plays must be taught with careful attention paid not just to literary elements like plot, language, or style but also to performance elements like action, speech, and setting. Teaching drama frequently entails helping students negotiate the tensions and transitions between page and stage. Building a critical vocabulary for drama (dramatis personae and chorus, exposition and dénouement, rising and falling action, climax and catastrophe, monologue and soliloquy) instructs students in the distinct performance element of plays, be they classical tragedies, romantic tragedies, or domestic tragedies; sentimental comedies, bourgeois comedies, or satirical comedies; pastoral plays, political plays, or problem plays; verse dramas, musical dramas, or melodramas. From the Greek word for *action*, drama lends itself particularly well to active learning exercises. Drama texts are ideally suited for any number of engaged classroom activities, and in any number of combinations: translating, role-playing, acting, directing, rehearsing, adapting, diagramming, improvising, choreographing, reviewing, and historicizing.

The fifteen exercises in this section cover all these approaches in six major groupings: interpretation, genre, character, staging, performance, and context. The first two exercises on interpretation ("Vote with Your Feet" and "Statues") bring out the performance aspect of dramatic interpretation itself by asking students to use their bodies to respond to the play. The next three exercises on genre ("Dramatic Scansion in Everyday Life," "Playing with Genre," and "Whose Line Is It, Anyway?") highlight the multiplicity and complexity of dramatic form by illustrating drama's reliance on other genres, in particular poetry, prose, and music. The two exercises on character ("We've Got the Beat" and "Talk Show Host") next offer strategies for getting inside the minds, motivations, and mannerisms of characters and for understanding the interactions and relationships between characters.

The remaining exercises in this section place a more direct emphasis on learning about performing or learning through performing. The two exercises on staging ("Set Design" and "Staging the Scene") invite students to analyze a play first by making their own creative choices about its set design and then by controlling the movement and actions of characters on the stage.

The three exercises on performance ("Adaptation," "Soliloquy," and "Director's Cut") take the next step and ask students to adapt, enact, or direct a scene, often in more than one version. The final three exercises, on context ("Moving Scenes," "Reading the Reviews," and "Spin the Globe, Shakespeare"), place the play's dramatic performance back into its social, cultural, or historical framework, broadening student understanding of the time and place in which the play was first produced or later restaged. As students learn to move from play text to performance, they will discover that the best way to understand an embodied literary form like drama—a genre that is at heart a story come to life—is simply to jump feet first into its imaginative world.

· ·

Vote with Your Feet

Jill Dolan

A classic early-semester exercise that loosens students up by asking them literally to "take a stand."

Genre: *any, especially drama*
Course Level: *any*
Student Difficulty: *easy*
Teacher Preparation: *medium*
Class Size: *any*
Semester Time: *early*
Writing Component: *none*
Close Reading: *none*
Estimated Time: *variable, from 5 to 30 minutes*

EXERCISE

This popular teaching technique works well with all genres, but particularly drama. Draw an imaginary line across the space of the classroom, pushing back tables, desks, or chairs as necessary to leave the space as empty as possible. Suggest that one end of this line represents an emphatic "yes," while the opposite end symbolizes an equally firm "no." Tell the students that the middle signifies various shades of gray, reaching across a spectrum of potential responses to your pending prompts. Once the line is drawn and students are up and moving around the classroom, propose a few general questions or statements to begin a conversation about the play or text under discussion. Select statements to which no "right" responses can be assayed but which instead require students to hazard their own opinions.

For instance, for a discussion of *Death of a Salesman*, you might prompt students with "Willy Loman is a failure." With that bald statement in mind, give them no time to mull their responses, but instead, ask them to position themselves somewhere along the "yes" or "no" continuum. Those students who think Loman is certainly a failure should stand at the "yes" end of this presumptive continuum, and those who think he's most definitely not should stand at the opposite. Those students contemplating a more ambivalent response should put themselves on the line at whatever point they think represents their reading of the character's success or failure.

Once all students in the room have placed themselves somewhere, ask students standing in different locations to justify their choice. A simple

149

"Why are you standing here?" should be enough to encourage them to share their reading of Loman's relative success or failure, and subsequent probing might allow them to amplify or specify their views. Asking students near to or far from one another demonstrates the range of potential responses to this deceptively simple question. Because students can see one another's positions, responses that feel abstract when discussed behind a desk become clear, concrete, and active.

As they share their views, encourage students to move to other places in the room as their own opinions are changed by their fellow students. Ask several sets of yes or no questions (however reductive they might at first seem) to allow students to literally vote with their feet. Metaquestions that probe their thoughts on the status of the text are also useful. For instance, "Should *Death of a Salesman* remain in the canon of 'good American drama'?" often gets students riled up and eager to plant themselves at one end of the line or the other. Students frequently have to jockey for space at particular points on the continuum when statements find unanimity of response, in which case outliers' opinions are visible and encourage much discussion and debate.

REFLECTIONS

In any seminar in which discussion is based on questions for which no empirically correct answer is possible, students often hesitate to offer their own analytical opinions. One way to loosen them up is to ask them to embody their responses to the text by literally placing themselves in the room according to their views. The exercise allows students to take a stand physically and unmasks the typical anonymity of response by requiring them to put their bodies behind their analysis. Encouraging them to move positions when their opinions are changed by fellow students' arguments also illustrates that analysis is a form of persuasion. Whether you use the exercise as a quick five-minute pace changer (use a single question) or as a more elaborate thirty-minute debate prompt (use interlocking questions), the goal is to teach students how changing one's mind on the basis of reasonable evidence is part of good critical practice.

I recently taught *Death of a Salesman*—with my colleague Stacy Wolf—in a course on Jewish American theater and performance. Directly after *Salesman*, we taught Donald Margulies's *The Loman Family Picnic* (1989), which riffs on Miller's play. Although the characters' names are different and the play takes place in the present rather than the 1940s, Margulies's themes and concerns purposefully mirror those of Miller's tragedy. Margulies updates the Lomans into a highly dysfunctional, explicitly Jewish family, whose oldest, rather arrogant and moneygrubbing son is just about to celebrate his bar mitzvah; whose youngest son clamors for his father's attention and writes a musical called *Willy!*; whose mother is anxious and lonely but socially ambitious; and whose father is a weary salesman with a track record even more miserable than Willy Loman's.

As we discussed the play, we used "Vote with Your Feet" to ask students whether they thought it was necessary for readers or spectators to be familiar with *Death of a Salesman* to understand *The Loman Family Picnic*. Their strongly held opinions at first positioned them at opposite ends of the line we drew across the classroom. But as some argued that *Loman Family Picnic*'s characters and themes are familiar enough to stand on their own, certain students moved from the "yes" end toward the "no." Then again, as other students argued just as strongly that knowledge of the original would only enhance audiences' understanding of Margulies's satire, some students edged away from "no" closer to the "yes" position. As we continued to discuss the play, students stayed almost constantly in motion, adjusting their position to their peers' arguments.

This exercise is often useful early in a semester, when students don't know one another well. It encourages them to break from the individualized, chair-centered format of seminar discussions, to see themselves as a malleable group, and to encourage clear, well-supported responses to the text. "Vote with Your Feet" is also useful when a group seems listless and inattentive. Standing on their feet and moving about the room in proximity to and in relationship with their classmates helps students focus on the text and the issues raised and allows the instructor to point out similarities and differences, congruencies and surprises among a variety of student responses. Returning to a more structured discussion after this exercise lets the instructor use the insights "Vote with Your Feet" yields, integrating students' responses to the text into subsequent analysis.

. . . .

Statues

Stacy Wolf

A lively small-group exercise that asks students to express ideas with their bodies.

Genre: *drama*
Course Level: *any*
Student Difficulty: *moderate*

Teacher Preparation: *low*
Class Size: *small to medium*
Semester Time: *any, especially early*
Writing Component: *none*
Close Reading: *none*
Estimated Time: *50 to 60 minutes*

EXERCISE

Depending on the size of the class, divide the students into small groups of three to eight (three to four groups is ideal). Tell them to make a sculpture with their bodies that captures the essence of the play or other dramatic reading assigned for class that day. Give them about ten minutes to create the statue, sculpture, or tableau.

Each group then shares its statue in turn, holding the position as the rest of the class comments. Have everyone walk around the statue to observe it from all sides. Ask the observing students first to describe merely what they see (for example, the positions of the bodies in relation to one another). Then ask them to talk about how this statue expresses the play and what it seems to be saying about it. Continually press the students to be specific about what they see and how it relates to the play.

Next, ask the group to break the pose and explain their intentions and what they wanted the statue to mean. After all the groups have shared their statues, invite the class to compare the choices of the different groups: Did everyone understand the text in the same way? Were some of the statues representational and others more abstract? What were the similarities and differences across the statues, and what do these different choices say about the play and its range of meanings?

Finally, ask the students to reflect on the exercise itself: Why this kind of exercise? Why not, for example, write a sentence that articulates the main themes of the drama? Why bodies? Why a statue? What does this exercise do, and why does it matter? Be sure to allow a full class period (roughly fifty to sixty minutes) for this exercise, so students have time to be creative in their statues and thoughtful in their responses.

REFLECTIONS

This exercise forces the students to (1) get to know each other as they work together and negotiate different understandings of the text, (2) articulate to one another and then to the rest of the class what they see as the essence of the work, (3) translate that spoken idea into a physical representation, (4) analyze the images that their classmates produce, and (5) see the variations of not only what the text means but how its meaning (or theme) might be presented differently.

With plays, you'll find that some groups will typically assign each student to a particular character, while other groups will present more abstract models of what they think the play means. For example, when I tried this exercise with Amiri Baraka's *Dutchman*, one group placed chairs in a configuration that looked like the inside of a subway car. A student played Clay and another played Lula, and they sat in the seats closest to and directly facing the audience. The rest of the students in the group sat on the other chairs and played bystanders on the subway, and one student stood far upstage and portrayed the conductor.

The student actors carefully chose their physical poses and facial expressions. The conductor, for example, looked up and out with a distant, absent expression, and the passengers pretended to look down at "newspapers" or out the window. Only Lula and Clay connected with each other, their eyes locked. Lula's body leaned toward Clay's and she held in her hand an "apple" (again, a mimed gesture). Clay looked scared and trapped. Lula looked at Clay with evil intention and a casual threat, unsmiling and with her eyebrows raised. When the other students described the "sculpture" in front of them, they quickly identified it as a literal representation of Lula and Clay's relationship, staging the power of the white woman over the African American man.

Another group took a completely different tack. One student stood in the center, his legs spread and his arms raised in a V shape. His face was contorted into an expression of pain, his mouth open in a silent scream. The other students formed a circle around him, and each found a different pose of powerlessness: one sat cross-legged on the floor with her head buried in her hands; another kneeled with shoulders hunched and palms raised as if protecting his face; a third lay face up on the floor like a corpse; and a fourth stood with arms extended and wrists crossed as if they were handcuffed together. The observing students surmised that the central figure represented Clay, who explodes in rage in his final monologue, and that the other figures showed different states of entrapment or fear or death. The play, this group argued, is about the terribly limited options for black men in the 1960s.

A third group focused again on the struggle between Lula and Clay but more abstractly than the first group. Two students faced each other, crossed their wrists, joined hands, and then leaned back, clearly depending on the other's weight to keep them from falling on the ground. Behind the first leaning student, three others kneeled with arms extended, ready to catch her if she fell. And behind the other leaning student, three more stood but all were busy: the first posed as if playing the saxophone, a second looked like she was writing, and the third seemed to be painting. The student audience identified one "leaner" as Lula and thought that the others behind her portrayed the white society that protected her. They saw Clay on the other side, with black society represented as artists whose work might not protect Clay should he fall. This group, as we then discussed, homed in on Baraka's notion of art making as a sublimation of black America's rage. The sculpture led us to a larger debate about Baraka's views on art's power and purpose for political change.

For each sculpture, we followed a strict format. The observing students began simply by describing what they saw: "Jessica's body is leaning into David's"; "Ben's arms are raised and his mouth is open"; "Keith looks like he's playing the saxophone." Then students offered thoughts on what the sculpture represented: "This looks like a scene in the play where Lula is threatening Clay"; "This looks like Clay in the center, and he's screaming"; "This looks like Lula and Clay in a battle, and they're dependent on each other to hold them up." And finally, we moved to interpretation. Importantly, we never decided which sculpture was best or which offered the most persuasive reading of the play. We simply used this exercise and the multiple examples of *Dutchman* in the form of a statue as a jumping-off point for discussion.

Explaining their choices allows groups to reflect on how their decisions were made and which ideas were mentioned that got rejected or adapted. Inevitably, students perform their analytical collaboration as they explain their choices. In addition, by being asked to put down their books and pens, move around the room, and use their bodies to express a point of view, students are usually surprised by a classroom exercise that generates so much energy, laughter, and fun. This activity, which encourages students to concentrate and work together in an especially dynamic fashion, almost always succeeds in creating a congenial intellectual community in the class. "Statues" values a different learning style and conveys to the students that a range of modes to describe and analyze texts will be welcome in your course.

This is a surefire winner for the first day's discussion of virtually any dramatic text. (While it works beautifully with plays, it can be easily adapted to all genres of writing, including critical theory.) And although "Statues" is an ideal icebreaker for early in the semester, it is also fascinating to try after your class has discussed multiple texts. For two plays, for example, ask students to make two different sculptures and to choreograph the transition between them. This variation works well with dramas that comment on or are based on another—for example, Jean Racine's *Phèdre* and Marina Carr's *Phaedra Backwards*; or Shakespeare's *Othello* and Paula Vogel's *Desdemona: A Play about a Handkerchief*; or Arthur Miller's *Death of a Salesman* and Donald Margulies's *The Loman Family Picnic*.

This activity becomes increasingly easy if it is repeated over the course of the semester, as students become more practiced at translating their ideas into sculpture. I typically use this exercise once very early in the semester and maybe once or twice later on. And I have used it in virtually every course that I have taught in theater and performance studies (including Modern Drama, Contemporary Drama, Musical Theater History, Feminist Theory, 1960s Performance, and Jewish Theater). Ironically, nothing works as well as frozen statues to animate students.

. . . .

Dramatic Scansion in Everyday Life

Daniel Jump

A quick and easy introduction to scanning dramatic verse.

Genre: *drama or poetry*
Course Level: *introductory*
Student Difficulty: *moderate*
Teacher Preparation: *low*
Class Size: *any*
Semester Time: *any*
Writing Component: *none*
Close Reading: *high*
Estimated Time: *15 to 20 minutes*

EXERCISE

On a chalkboard or whiteboard, write the words *how do you know*. Ask your students to imagine that they are standing on the seashore: a wave crashes in, recedes, and these words are left in the sand. Then ask them what other information they would need in order to understand the meaning of the words. Someone will tell you that you need a question mark; add this to the end of the phrase. Is this sufficient to communicate to us what the words—now an interrogative sentence—mean?

It will be clear to your students rather quickly that it is not, and they will hunt around for a proper language to express what is lacking. It won't take long for someone to suggest that the meaning "depends on how it is read" or "depends on the speaker's tone"; some precocious students will tell you that it "depends on how the words are stressed." Ask them where the stress should fall. Experiment with their suggestions, placing stress marks over one or another of the single-syllable words. Ask the students to read the question with that stress, and then ask them what they learn about the significance of the words when so stressed. What does the stress pattern imply about the attitude of the question asker to his or her interlocutor? Is there more than one possibility? Can they come up with an example of the type of sentence the interlocutor might have spoken just before that drew this voicing of the question as a response? In what kind of situation might one find a question voiced in just this way? Go through each of the possibilities in turn, erasing the stress just discussed and placing it elsewhere, inviting students to discuss the various meanings that emerge as you do so.

Then replace your humble question with a few lines of dramatic verse. Choose a passage (Shakespeare is a good candidate here) for which at least two distinct interpretations emerge from variously stressed readings. Consider, say, the first few lines of Prospero's great "Our revels now are ended" speech from *The Tempest* (act 4, scene 1, 148–50), or the first three lines of Lear's bloodcurdling speech on the heath in *King Lear* (act 3, scene 2, 1–3). Ask students to experiment with different ways of stressing each passage. Invite them to think about the dramatic and interpretive implications of different ways of stressing these lines. (This part of the exercise can be done as a whole class or in smaller groups.)

At an appropriate point in the discussion, you may want to introduce students to the rudiments of English prosody: the concept of meter and how it is measured, the definition of metrical feet and their types, and the distinction between "meter" and "rhythm." See, for example, the last three exercises on versification in the "Poems" section of this volume.

REFLECTIONS

While scansion is a staple lesson of poetry courses, we often gloss over its importance in drama classes, privileging direction and performance over rhythm and metrics. But plays no less than poems need to be scanned if students are to achieve a fuller and more visceral understanding of dramatic verse. This exercise also demonstrates to students how formal prosody—a practice that can seem at first like an intimidating and pointless exercise—is in truth not so far from everyday practices of meaning making and employs many of the same basic cognitive processes. Unlike other exercises in the literature classroom that promote "defamiliarization," this one practices "familiarization"—a pedagogical approach especially helpful for those students who find the process of literary interpretation in general, and prosody in particular, mystifying.

"Dramatic Scansion in Everyday Life" is best suited for teaching early verse plays from the Renaissance through the eighteenth century and on to Romanticism. Practically any passage from *King Lear, Volpone,* or *Doctor Faustus* will show unsuspected nuances when treated in this way. Apply it to the verse prologues or epilogues of Restoration comedies (like Wycherley's *The Country Wife* or Etherege's *The Man of Mode*) and see how the play's characters use metrical effects to cajole, flatter, criticize, abuse, or otherwise appeal to their audiences. Or use it for Romantic-period dramas like Byron's *Manfred*, Keats's *Hyperion*, or Shelley's *Prometheus Unbound* to kick-start a discussion about what happens when drama detaches from theatrical practice and becomes something to be read rather than to be staged or seen. In all of these cases, the act of scansion not only draws students' attention to the language of the play text but also often highlights what is missing and left to readers' imaginations: implied stage directions, bodily gestures, voicing of lines, stagecraft, and blocking. In this way, the exercise provides a useful bridge between textual close reading and what scholars of theatrical performance call "dramaturgical reading."

For example, I have found this scansion exercise useful in grappling with the meaning of the end of Shakespeare's great play about endings, *All's Well that Ends Well*. After some discussion of *how do you know*, I replaced that phrase with the play's final couplet, spoken by the King: "All yet seems well; and if it end so meet, / The bitter past, more welcome is the sweet." How should this scan? One student, confident in his prosody, marked it as a perfectly regular iambic line. Such metrical regularity, he said, was appropriate for the stately summation of the play's action that the king is offering here; it's a moment of consolation, with the voice of royal authority behind it, encouraging us to forget the conflicts that have gotten the characters where they are, and to relax, with him, into a peaceful resolution. Another student chimed in to agree but suggested that this reading of the King's tone would be strengthened if we read a rather heavy stress on the first syllable "all." (This seemed a good place for me to add that this effect has a name: trochaic inversion). A third student wondered if the king himself might have doubted the truth of the resolution he voices. What if, the student suggested, we hear the heaviest stress in that crucial first clause falling not on "all" or "well" but rather on "seems"? Is the king voicing, perhaps anxiously, perhaps knowingly, a skeptical doubt about whether what seems well is in fact so?

At this point we were off to the races. Another student tried out a reading that stressed "yet," and wondered whether that word should be read as a contrastive or as a marker of time. Pretty soon the students were looking back to other parts of the final scene to help adjudicate between all these different takes on the King's last lines. Might the King have seen something in the final interaction between Bertram and Helena that would give him cause for concern? And if so, is he motivated to cover it up? Expose it? Both at once, perhaps? Finally, a quiet student piped up: "When I read the play by myself, I was pretty satisfied with the ending. But now I see that it's much darker than I thought." This student went on to note the "frustration, resentment, and uncertainty" simmering beneath the play's surface. It really is a revelation how much can turn on a seemingly minute matter of stress. Give your students the tools for producing such insights and you will find that, far from being drudgery, scansion may become something they do without your having to guide them.

· ·

Playing with Genre

Joel B. Lande

A preparatory exercise that teaches students what's distinctive about drama.

Genre: *drama*
Course Level: *any*
Student Difficulty: *moderate*
Teacher Preparation: *low*
Class Size: *small to medium*
Semester Time: *any*
Writing Component: *before class*
Close Reading: *medium*
Estimated Time: *60 to 80 minutes*

EXERCISE

Choose a crucial and preferably compact scene from a dramatic text, and ask students to rewrite this scene in narrative form in preparation for class. If you like, for greater coverage, you might select several passages from the same play (or from a single act) and then divvy the scenes up among smaller groups. It is helpful to keep in mind while selecting your passage(s) that dense or ambiguous sections of dramatic dialogue, especially from decisive moments in a drama, will provide students the opportunity to be more insightful and imaginative in their rewritings.

Consider giving students a word-count limit for their translations of dramatic verse into narrative prose, since students can get carried away and since you want enough class time for as many students as possible to read their creative revisions. (I recommend no more than four hundred words or a length not to exceed one page.) Encourage students to include in their rewritings narrative details not explicitly named in the dramatic scene but details for which they find implicit support. Such implicit features might include gestural details, facial expressions, tone of voice, scene descriptions, or character motivations. And be sure to instruct students to avoid direct citation of dialogue.

When class convenes, ask for volunteers and begin with a dramatic reading of the scene in question. Then have students read their narrative renderings aloud in class. (If your class is large, this can be done in groups.) Ask students not to read one immediately after the other but instead to allow time for discussion after each student presents his or her translation. As students present (and others respond to) their narrative translations, keep guiding them back to the original dramatic passage, encouraging them to explain the choices they made while translating from one genre to another.

To keep the conversation focused, ask some pointed questions about the passage: What stage directions, if any, are provided in the original? Why these and not others? To what extent does the play's dialogue provide explicit or implicit information about tone and gesture? Then wrap up the exercise by opening a wider conversation about literary genre. How much paralinguistic information is present in a narrative text as opposed to a dramatic one? Where and why do students feel there is a gap in the dramatic text that needs to be filled in when translating into prose? What does the inclusion of a narrator add or subtract? What sorts of details do you require to make a scene convincing in a prose text that plays leave undetermined?

REFLECTIONS

Translating a dramatic scene into a narrative one allows students to discover dimensions of dramatic texts they have never noticed before. Because undergraduates are almost always more familiar and comfortable with prose narrative, this exercise is a helpful way for them to develop attentiveness to specific features of dramatic form. I find it especially productive to have students discuss moments within the selected passage that introduce ambiguity or uncertainty, prompting them to consider why information is being omitted or only implicitly provided. You may also wish to encourage students to talk about places in the text where they felt uncertain how best to proceed. Such moments are often particularly good for discussion because they point to concrete differences between genres.

If you are teaching Aeschylus's *Oresteia*, for example, the scene in which Clytemnestra welcomes Agamemnon home works very well. A less commonly taught ancient tragedy that really appeals to undergraduate students (perhaps due to its gruesome detail) is Seneca's *Thyestes*, from which you might discuss the concluding dialogue between Thyestes and Atreus. Among the canonical modern plays, you can choose something as obvious as Hamlet's monologue or the opening dialogue between Phèdre and her nurse Oenone in Racine's great classical tragedy. If you are looking for something more comic, you can also use the second study scene from Goethe's *Faust*, when Mephistopheles pulls one over on an unsuspecting student. If you are feeling experimental and particularly want to challenge your students' imagination, try Hamm's final monologue of Beckett's *Endgame*, with its staccato rhythm and abundance of seemingly disconnected stage directions. These are all scenes rife with details and ambiguities that will allow your students to be creative and critical at the same time.

My own breakthrough experience with this exercise came while teaching the first part of Goethe's *Faust*. This play works so well for a number of reasons: it moves at an alarmingly fast pace and can be productively slowed down; it alternates between comic and tragic registers that require different sorts of narrative translation; the monologues are astonishingly rich with images to be decoded; and there are scant but intensely meaningful stage directions that allow students lots of room to think creatively. I asked my class to create a prose translation of the scene "Forest and Cavern," which begins with a monologue by Faust and then feeds into a dialogue with Mephistopheles. Because I really wanted to get into the nitty-gritty, I devoted an entire class meeting (eighty minutes) to this scene. Beforehand, I provided a few questions to guide students: Why does this dialogue take place in a cavern located within a forest? What does this scene tell us about Faust's state of mind? What differences are noticeable between the two protagonists? I also suggested that students should make certain their prose rewritings capture what they regard as the crucial feature or features of the scene. I encouraged them to imagine what the play would be like without the scene and then to ask themselves what essential pieces of the complete puzzle would be missing if this scene were excised. (If students can successfully identify these pieces, they are well on their way to figuring out what is really important in the scene.)

The classroom discussion of the Goethe scene impressed me for a number of reasons. The first major takeaway for the students was the realization that there are different forms of mise-en-scène in prose texts and in plays. Some students were very imaginative when introducing the setting, while others jumped immediately into a narrative recasting of Faust's opening monologue. This discovery allowed us to talk briefly about the variety of decisions that have to be made in order for a dramatic text to become a theatrical performance. My second goal was to facilitate discussion about the structural role of stage instructions, monologue, and dialogue.

As each student presented his or her narrative translation, I invited the rest of the class to identify not just salient details from the play that were highlighted but also other details from the original that were missing. That way, each student could explain his or her choices, while classmates could present alternative takes on the same material. A third major discovery for the students was the variations in voice, tone, and intention between Faust and Mephistopheles. Only a few students initially realized that the play's eponymous hero is reflective and melancholy, while his diabolic companion is playful and droll. Most of the students at first elided the differences between these two characters and were thus surprised to discover from their peers' prose translations just how slippery Mephistopheles really is.

The most rewarding feature of this exercise is how effectively it can help students grasp that a play, while (usually) written by a single person, includes a multiplicity of different voices and personas. By the end of "Playing with Genre," students will be speculating about methods for translating the internal heterogeneity of any dramatic text into a narrative text. They may even be comfortable and informed enough to start doing the reverse, having gained a deeper knowledge of drama's own formal and distinct mode of presentation.

. . . .

Whose Line Is It, Anyway?

Roy Scranton

A musical theater exercise that teaches students the fundamentals of dramatic form and the interplay of song and speech.

Genre: *drama, especially musical theater*
Course Level: *any*
Student Difficulty: *easy*
Teacher Preparation: *low*
Class Size: *any*
Semester Time: *early, midterm*
Writing Component: *in class*
Close Reading: *medium*
Estimated Time: *20 minutes*

EXERCISE

This exercise is primarily for musical theater (or opera), though it could be adapted to conventional theater. Choose a scene with music, in which both soloists and chorus sing. Any scene in which the music and singing dramatize some conflicted relation between singers and their community is especially suitable: "Tonight (Quintet and Chorus)" from *West Side Story* (excluding the introductory verses), "The Farmer and the Cowman" from *Oklahoma!*, "The Rain in Spain" from *My Fair Lady*.

Ideally, the scene you select should have three or four different identifiable singing parts, preferably with very distinctive characters. It is even better if the scene includes a shift from speech to song, or vice versa. Make sure the piece is long enough so that most of the voices sing at least twice. While it is easier to pick a scene from a work the students have already studied, you can also pick a scene they haven't yet considered if the characters and their relations are briefly explained.

Reproduce the lyrics of the scene you have chosen in one continuous paragraph, with both attributions and line breaks edited out. Take the quartet reprise of "Johanna," for example, from Act II of Sondheim and Wheeler's *Sweeney Todd: The Demon Barber of Fleet Street*. That reprise is sung by Anthony, the Beggar Woman, Johanna, and Sweeney Todd, and in performance their voices interweave and overlap. A section of the song containing all four voices can be excerpted and reformatted so that the material flows from one character to another, one line to another, without explicit marking. Reproduced on your handout, the lyrics would appear as a single paragraph of prose.

In class, distribute the new, unattributed text and separate students into small groups (pairs or triads work best). Have the groups then work out which lyrics belong to whom, and where they think the line breaks fall. Students should also identify any shifts from speech to song or vice versa.

Once the groups have finished working out who is singing where, lead them in a discussion of the specific decisions they made and why. Why did they attribute certain lines to one character rather than another? How could they tell if the lines were sung by a soloist or by the chorus? How were they able to figure out where the line breaks occurred?

As the students discuss their decisions, issues of lyric structure will begin to emerge. Ask them about the relations between formal structure and semantic content. Draw their attention to how the different voices interact: are they dialogic, additive, or monadic? Where and how do they blend and resonate, or do they resist each other? These questions can direct attention to technical and thematic aspects of the work, and the interrelation between the two, as rhyme, rhythm, melody, and music work to shape dramatic tension. Then, as class discussion winds down, play the relevant music for the students, having them listen specifically for the ways the instrumentation identifies and works with each singer.

REFLECTIONS

Through this exercise, the most fundamental aspect of musical theater—the differentiation of single actor and chorus—comes to the forefront in a strange and illuminating way. By working through the decisions of who should sing, when, and why, students are provoked to consider the technical issues that arise in musicals, and the theoretical and thematic issues that take shape through those choices. Whether viewed in terms of figure and ground, individual and collective, or dialectics and integration, the mechanics of individuation in musical theater opens up rich and provocative possibilities for understanding the complex interplay of song and speech. In this exercise there are certainly correct answers (swiftly revealed by the actual script), yet the very possibility of divergence raises the critical question of why the lyricist made the decisions he or she did. Having students "rewrite" lyrics can also reveal that, as modes of linguistic activity, creative writing and critical practice might be less distinct than we assume.

Reframing and examining the question of lyrical individuation line by line can be immensely productive. When I used this exercise with Gilbert and Sullivan's *The Mikado*, focusing on the scene at the end of the first act when Katisha arrives at Titipu and threatens to unmask Nanki-Poo as the son of the Mikado, I found it shook students out of their usual interpretive stance by requiring them to merge the practices of close reading, dramaturgy, and creative writing. As they considered resemblance and difference in the play's individual lines, one group spied new connections between seemingly antipathetic characters. Another group noted aptly how important shared rhymes are to the scene's dramatic tension. Most importantly, all the groups focused eventually on the curious role of the chorus in *The Mikado*, and how it works to both produce and repress individual agency. In our larger group discussion, students came to the conclusion that the chorus's repetitions work first to resist Katisha, then to support her, suggesting that the chorus's allegiances might differ from those of the audience, and forcing us to ask what role the chorus is supposed to be playing.

This exercise offers a way to open up fundamental questions about musical theater. As such, it works best toward the beginning of a course and always in pairs or small groups, which helps students feel more comfortable engaging in a highly creative task that still has a "right answer" (though with low stakes). By opening up the mechanics of writing to student control and discussion, "Whose Line Is It, Anyway?" helps demystify the dramatic work, empower students, and shift the act of interpretation from a posttextual performance of appreciation to an intertextual engagement of understanding and evaluation.

We've Got the Beat

Nick Salvato

A conversation-driven exercise that helps students grasp "invisible" dramatic form and nuances of characterization.

Genre: *drama*
Course Level: *any*
Student Difficulty: *moderate*
Teacher Preparation: *low*
Class Size: *small to medium*
Semester Time: *any*
Writing Component: *none*
Close Reading: *medium*
Estimated Time: *50 to 60 minutes*

EXERCISE

Begin by explaining to students the meaning of a *beat*. Some literature students may be familiar with the use of the word *beat* in poetics to describe a rhythmic emphasis. And theater students may even have observed the regularity with which modern and contemporary dramatists use the word *beat* as a stage direction to indicate a slight pause in conversation or action. But in the interpretation of drama and the making of theater, the word *beat* has yet a third meaning: it designates a textually unmarked moment in a dialogic encounter among characters—most vividly between two characters—when some shift alters the dynamic between or among those characters. The shift constituted by this beat may be seismic or subtle, but it is worth reiterating to students that the strongest beats alter not just the general dynamic but also the power dynamic between or among characters.

Pick a scene or part of a scene in which the shifting dynamics between characters are numerous and pointed enough to warrant the counting of each beat. Some good candidates for this exercise include the passage in act 1 of Anton Chekhov's *The Cherry Orchard*, in which Lopakhin remembers his childhood and first tries (unsuccessfully) to convince Ranevskaya to sell the cherry orchard; the latter part of scene 3 in Tennessee Williams's *A Streetcar Named Desire*, in which Stanley beats Stella, then cries and begs for forgiveness; the pivotal argument between Hally and Sam in Athol Fugard's one-act *"Master Harold". . . and the Boys*, which culminates in Hally's order to be addressed as Master Harold; and the portion of act 2, scene 9 in Tony

Kushner's *Angels in America: Millennium Approaches* that focuses on Prior's indictment of Louis for leaving him.

Ask a couple of students to read aloud the chosen scene. (You can identify these student readers in advance and give them time to prepare the scene before class, but this step is not strictly necessary, and the exercise can work very well on the fly during the course of a class meeting.) While the scene is read aloud, ask the rest of the students to follow along in their copies of the text and mark each beat that they discern with a notational slash.

Then divide the students into groups of three to five and give each group twenty minutes to synthesize their efforts. Instruct them to focus on the differences among their beat analyses, explaining why they made the choices they did. Every (or almost every) member of the class will have identified some major, obvious beats. A smaller set of students will likely be attuned to more nuanced, "quieter" beats. Let them debate which of their beats seem clear or compelling and which may have been misidentified and might, by collective judgment, be struck from the final tally of the scene's beats. Make it clear that the end goal of their group discussion is to produce a new beat analysis, one different from what they heard in the initial oral reading. Encourage students to focus on character dynamics as they consider other imaginative and interpretive possibilities for the speaking of these same lines. Have them test some lines aloud and mark down the new beats as they go.

Once each group has come to interpretive agreement, ask groups to select (as time allows) a section of their newly "beated" scene to read aloud to the class. Prompt the members of the groups to choose bits of their differently beated scene that they will inflect in such a way that the class can hear and then discuss the revised interpretations of character and action. Allow for some further debate and discussion of these revised interpretations as the class as a whole considers them. Then wind up the exercise by transitioning back to a broader conversation about character, tone, or any other formal properties of the play that you wish to highlight.

REFLECTIONS

"We've Got the Beat" gives students a good set of tools for interpreting dramatic structure, theme, dialogue, tone, and style—though, first and foremost, it is an exercise for reading character in a more sophisticated way. It can work well at any point in the semester in which dramatic beat analysis is a suitable response to an assigned play, though I like to use it early in the term to teach the fundamentals of dramatic characterization (including motivation and objective) as they play out in relational scenarios.

This exercise gives students a concrete way to understand what doesn't appear explicitly on the page but nonetheless defines a good deal of skillful playwriting: the shaping of a scene and the movements within the scene as those movements are guided by characters' relationships. Part of the fun, but also the great purchase, of the exercise comes from the genuine surprise with which students tend to recognize just how many beats, especially subtle rather than seismic ones, can accrete over the course of even a short scene. Ticking off a scene's beats—and, in the process, developing a vocabulary to account for how and why the beats emerge when and where they do—enables students to appreciate that such scenes have been carefully crafted to have specific trajectories for their characters, expressive of desires, negotiations, and transformations.

My favorite play for this exercise is Derek Walcott's *Pantomime* (1978). Many scenes between English hotel-owner Harry Trewe and his Trinidadian "factotum" Jackson Phillips work well for the exercise, given Walcott's leveraging of these characters' one-upmanship of each other to reflect on colonialism's legacies. Most memorably, I have asked students to focus on the passage in act 1 in which Harry and Jackson discuss Jackson's theatrical reinterpretation of the Robinson Crusoe story in a pointed take on the English panto tradition. In the first oral reading of the scene, the student enactors encouraged a "beating" of the conversation with an emphasis on obvious moments in which the dynamic between Harry and Jackson shifted: Jackson's response to Harry's goad, "I challenge you," for instance, or Harry's initiation of a new action with the line "Two can play this game, Jackson."

But then some groups produced a much more nuanced and detailed beat analysis of the scene in question. They noticed how much irony pervades certain lines of Jackson's ("I surrender," "All you win") and how much power Jackson exerts by using this irony to mock his boss. This particular analysis and the discussion it prompted enabled a deeper penetration into Jackson's character; more specifically, it made the students understand better a key monologue that immediately precedes the passage in question and in which Jackson waxes poetically and elliptically about the (post) colonial subject's use of mimicry as mockery. If the tricky monologue entails a complex sort of "thesis" about this mimicry as mockery, then the ensuing, combative conversation—many of whose combative elements are sly and understated—enact the thesis. Beat analysis enabled students to connect the two passages to each other, to see how their interplay unfolds a powerful idea about colonialism's aftereffects, and to appreciate this idea's manifestation in the characterization of Jackson as he interacts with Harry.

Not every play will be a suitable candidate for a beat exercise. The beat-driven scene is more a feature of modernist drama in its turn toward realism than of either earlier plays like Restoration comedies or more experimental plays (say, futurist *sintesi* or symbolist dream plays) that work more radically with form. I like to end the exercise by comparing the play at hand to previous plays we have read, discussing with students larger genre questions posed by the importance of dramatic beats. Can we plausibly say that there are beats of this sort in an experimental play like Gertrude Stein's *The Mother of Us All* or in a historical one like William Shakespeare's *Measure for Measure*, or are there other energies and movements driving the dialogic encounters between these plays' characters? Does the notion of characterization *as such* historically change from the early modern to the modern period? Students often note that the kind of beat-driven writing we see in many nineteenth- and twentieth-century realist plays seems to have its corollary in cinema and television, two other modern mediums that also feature power plays and shifting dynamics among characters, especially in realist dramas, sitcoms, and dramedies.

. . . .

Talk Show Host

Ralph Crane

A lively exercise that uses role-play to teach dramatic characterization.

Genre: *drama or fiction*
Course Level: *any*
Student Difficulty: *moderate or hard*
Teacher Preparation: *high*
Class Size: *small to medium*
Semester Time: *any*
Writing Component: *before class*
Close Reading: *low to medium*
Estimated Time: *1 hour*

EXERCISE

"Talk Show Host" uses role-play to help students analyze the roles of selected characters in a play. (The exercise can work with a novel as well, though its performative elements make it especially suitable for drama courses.) It works best with plays that have a cast with a number of spirited or richly de-veloped characters, like William Shakespeare's *Twelfth Night*, Arthur Miller's *Death of a Salesman*, or Caryl Churchill's *Top Girls*.

In advance, assign each student a character so that they can prepare for their role. Ask them to read the play carefully, focusing on the role of their character, and gathering as many details of their character's backstory as possible. Remind students that they will need to be prepared to answer questions about what happens to their character in the play in a general sense and, more specifically, about his or her interactions with other characters.

If the group is a larger one, students who have not been assigned a character will act as a studio audience. Their task is to prepare questions they can ask of the "characters" (focusing on such issues as social relationships, plot, or theme). For these students, provide some sample questions, which for *Twelfth Night* might include the following:

- (to Olivia) What lay behind your refusal to marry Orsino?
- (to Sir Toby Belch) Do you think the practical joke you and Maria played on Malvolio went too far?
- (to Viola) How did it feel talking to people while disguised as a male? Did you ever think you were going to be caught out?

Emphasize that their questions should not be overly complex but instead more typical of the talk show variety: general questions that address character or motivation.

As instructor, you will play the role of talk show host, so you too will need to prepare a suite of questions for each character in advance, and perhaps for the audience as well. Your questions for the characters will be similar to those you have asked the student audience to prepare, but you may also want to prepare a few questions for the audience:

- How did you respond to the practical joke you witnessed being played on Malvolio?
- Do you think Sir Toby and Maria will have a happy marriage?

Arrange the classroom to simulate a talk show environment. If the class is small and all the students have been assigned roles to play, then arrange the characters in a semicircle. If the class is large and there is a studio audience, it is better to have the characters arranged on either side of the host and facing the studio audience. In this situation a small, tiered lecture theater (or black-box space) works well, as it helps create the feel of a studio setting, but most ordinary classrooms can be rearranged to suit. Props, such as lights, small tables, and water jugs and glasses, can add atmosphere and help the characters get into the spirit of their role-play. Before you begin, remind the role-playing students that they need to answer every question in character.

Begin the talk show with the host welcoming both the characters and the studio audience. The host should then pose at least one question to each character before inviting questions from the studio audience. This gives each character the opportunity to speak and get into their role before the discussion becomes livelier with audience questions. The host will need to be an active moderator, ensuring that questions are directed to each character and interjecting with his or her own questions if necessary to make sure this happens. You can hold a "talk show" for as long as time permits (less than an hour is never enough time but more than an hour can be exhausting). The talk show should be brought to a close by indicating that time is running out and by thanking each of the characters and the studio audience for their participation.

REFLECTIONS

"Talk Show Host" challenges students to work actively with a text in order to think more complexly about dramatic character: What makes a character tick? Why do particular characters act and think the way they do? How do characters relate to other characters? Why are secondary characters necessary to the plot or theme? The main goal of the exercise is to allow students to inhabit a play fully, interpreting it from the inside out by becoming, for a moment, part of the world they are analyzing. It offers a different way of getting inside the play—something between close reading and performance.

This exercise works best when the instructor takes on the role of talk show host, since the person in that role needs to know the text very well, and since the success of the exercise often depends on the opening questions and the way they are asked. For advanced classes, however, you might consider deputizing an enthusiastic student to play the role of host. If there is no studio audience but only characters, and you are posing all the questions as host, try a variation on this exercise by encouraging the "characters" to respond to each other rather than to wait for you to direct questions to them. This gradually shifts the emphasis from a question-and-answer format to a livelier discussion format, which promotes a more animated conversation with students working hard, often with amusing results, to stay in character.

This exercise has worked particularly well when students have taken on controversial characters like Petruchio in Shakespeare's *The Taming of the Shrew*. The "studio audience" love to interrogate Petruchio about his attitudes toward women and marriage. My students wanted to know, for example, whether he married for money or for love and whether he really has "tamed" Kate by the end of the play. I have found that the questions the audience asks can lead to some especially productive discussions about issues that are not resolved in the play, such as whether or not Petruchio and Kate planned her display of obedience in act 5 in order to trick the other characters.

For drama students, exploring such questions provides practical experience of the kinds of choices actors have to make when preparing for a performance and gives insight into the varied options for character interpretation contained within the dialogue of a dramatic text. The exercise can also illustrate how much of a character's backstory is absent from the play script and highlight the need for close attention to the nuances of speech and interaction when studying plays.

. . . .

Set Design

Robert Yeates

An exercise for interpreting the significance of stage directions in plays.

Genre: *drama*
Course Level: *introductory or intermediate*
Student Difficulty: *easy or moderate*
Teacher Preparation: *low*
Class Size: *any*
Semester Time: *early*
Writing Component: *none*
Close Reading: *low*
Estimated Time: *45 to 60 minutes*

EXERCISE

Before class, prepare a handout of a theater stage: this is best kept to showing just essential elements such as upstage and downstage, stage left and right, the shape and elevation of the stage, and the proscenium line (see diagram). When class convenes, begin by briefly explaining the shape of a theater and its stage by diagramming it on the board; then distribute the handout. Split the students into groups of two or three and direct them to a specific set of stage directions from the play they are currently reading for your course. (This exercise works best once students have read through the play and have some understanding of the plot.) Give each group their own blank sheet of paper, the larger the better. Their task is to fill in this blank paper with a set diagram.

Ask students to assume the mind-set of director or stage designer and to imagine how they might fill the space of the stage based on the playwright's instructions alone. Where would they place walls or the rooms of a house, doors and windows, tables and chairs? Would they use backgrounds, or would they project words or images onto a backdrop? Are there other,

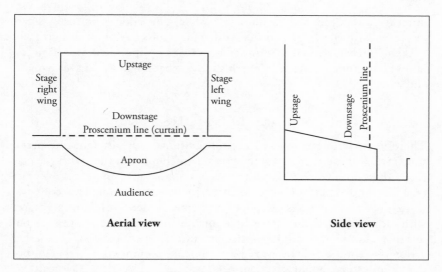

Aerial view   **Side view**

smaller props that are integral to the narrative? Where would these smaller props be placed? Modern dramas—Samuel Beckett's *Endgame* and *Krapp's Last Tape*, or Tennessee Williams's *A Streetcar Named Desire*—that feature extensive and particular stage directions are particularly useful for this exercise.

Remind students to draw it all on paper, while simultaneously reassuring them that they need not worry about their drawing skills. The point of the exercise is to examine the importance of stage directions to the action of a play and to question to what extent these stage directions can realistically be followed in practice. Emphasize that stagehands and funds might be limited and that students should maximize the functionality of the space so that it need change only a little over the course of the performance. Students will typically need ten to fifteen minutes for this portion of the exercise.

Now ask each group to briefly explain their stage design to the class, starting with the basic layout and moving on to more specific details. Have each group tape their sheet to the wall where everyone can see it and informally present their staging ideas. This will typically take three to five minutes per group. Feel free occasionally to weigh in and ask how the action of the play might work in these physical environments or how actors might use the set design in their performances. As each group explains its reasoning, encourage other students to respond. Invite them to identify what they like best about each set design, but also encourage them to offer suggestions for how each one might be tweaked or improved.

Time permitting, you can conclude the exercise by showing a brief clip from a film adaptation of the play, asking students to pay close attention to the setting rather than the camerawork. How does the layout of the film set differ from the students' own designs? Were some choices especially smart or particularly puzzling? Did the set designers miss any potentially fruitful tricks? (You can freeze the frame to help focus on specific details, if necessary.) If the students were filming this scene, what might they have changed, and why?

REFLECTIONS

There are no wrong answers to staging questions, only different interpretations. Still, some creative staging ideas are much more in tune with the play than others, so encouraging students to agree or disagree on something practical like set design can lead to constructive debate about a play's core dramatic elements: character, action, tone, theme. Students sometimes disagree with the playwright's own stage directions. Such disagreements are a real bonus since they tend to inspire particularly interesting discussions of whether action or setting should be viewed with more importance or whether authorial intent can or should affect our readings.

When I tried this exercise with Williams's *The Glass Menagerie*, a play that opens with extensive descriptions of the set, students were surprised to discover that despite the level of detail stage directions may give, no two interpretations are identical. Much of Williams's detail, they learned, provides the poetic setting of the play's mood, which a set designer can choose to represent visually on stage in a number of ways. For example, one group saw the "cellular living units" of the tenement block as evocative of a jail cell, so they created an austere interior with barred windows and doors. Another group gave this same set description a biological spin, drawing the apartments as identical, living clones placed in close proximity to one another. Both groups constructed a nonrealistic but expressive set, in part to emphasize how the setting in *The Glass Menagerie* is in fact part of the memory of the character Tom.

With the jail-cell apartment, characters could look through barred windows when expressing dreams or hopes, the closing of a door could express their participation in their own imprisonment, and the domineering Amanda's pacing could be reminiscent of a jailor. With the biological-cell apartment, Tom could have difficulty traversing the narrow alleys and mistake his own front door for another identical door, and the living, breathing space could expand or contract between scenes to reflect the feelings expressed within the walls. The differences explored in the interpretation of a single word of stage directions ("cellular") showed students that even Williams's precise directions could be liberating rather than rigid and that interpretations of a written play can manifest in a number of ways.

The personal engagement with drama that students often gain from an exercise like "Set Design" makes it particularly suited to early in the semester. It primes students to get in the habit of imagining visually the precise spaces in which a play's action takes place, and it demonstrates as well the subtle (and sometimes considerable) impact set design can have on a play's action, mood, and meaning. After completing this exercise, some students will report that they "see" the play far more clearly—a testament perhaps to drama's dual ambition to be not just a text we read but a performance we watch.

. . . .

Staging the Scene

Benjamin Jude Wright

A multifaceted investigation of the production of one dramatic scene.

Genre: *drama*
Course Level: *any*
Student Difficulty: *moderate*
Teacher Preparation: *medium*
Class Size: *any*
Semester Time: *any*
Writing Component: *before class, in class*
Close Reading: *medium*
Estimated Time: *45 to 60 minutes*

EXERCISE

Choose a scene from a play that poses interesting staging questions. Dramas that work well are those with set descriptions (even sometimes detailed ones) that nonetheless leave considerable room for creative staging. Good candidates include the first part of act 2 of Henrik Ibsen's *Hedda Gabler* (for staging realism); act 1, scene 1 of Tennessee Williams's *The Glass Menagerie* (for staging memory); and act 1 of Arthur Miller's *Death of a Salesman* (for staging fantasy). Both *Hedda Gabler* and *Death of a Salesman* lack specific scene divisions, providing greater flexibility for selecting appropriate starting and stopping points.

Begin by giving students the following preclass assignment:
Read the scene, paying particularly close attention to the scene description and stage directions provided by your text. Now pretend that you are designing a production of the play. How would you present the physical space of this scene on stage? Study the play's language for any

clues it may provide on the space in which the scene is set. Then describe in words what you think the stage should look like. You are welcome to consult outside sources, but you should use those sources only in order to inform your own vision of how the scene should be staged. Ask yourself questions about what the room should look like: What are the essential physical elements the scene needs in order to work? Should there be furniture? What kind, and why? Should there be a backdrop? What should it look like? Should there be doors and windows, staircases and balconies, lighting and shadows? If so, where? Write a description of the space, being sure to explain why you have made certain choices. What in the text are you drawing from? Are there outside sources you are inspired by? How do they relate to the play? If you want to attach a sketch to your discussion, you may, but this is not required. If you do draw a design, make sure that you explain its various elements and why you believe they suit the scene.

In lieu of this preclass assignment, you might also consider devoting an entire class lesson to diagramming stage sets (see "Set Design," which precedes this exercise).

When class assembles, hand out a copy of the scene without footnotes and with wide margins, something like what an actor's text might look like. Number the students off into small groups and assign each student a role. Instruct them to each take ten to fifteen minutes to reread the text, this time annotating it based on how they believe their own role should be staged. Encourage students to take notes in the margins of the script in front of them. What kind of physical actions should their character perform? Which gestures would be appropriate? What should their voice sound like? Is the character angry, sad, somber, something else? How would they act the character out? Then ask the students to take a moment to imagine their characters performing on the stage set that they have described or drawn. How much space do the characters need to perform their roles to greatest effect? How, exactly, will they occupy the space? When they are done, ask students to share with one another their thoughts about the set design. Give them fifteen to twenty minutes within their groups to discuss their staging ideas and their roles, directing them to explain why they chose to portray the physical space and their character in that particular way, based upon the text.

For a variation, have each group share their set designs first. Tell them to select one design they all agree is particularly successful or workable, and then annotate their character roles with a single, shared set design in mind. Another fun variation for more advanced drama classes: consider designating student groups in advance of the preclass set-design assignment, assigning each group a different scene from the play. Providing students with different scenes opens up the possibility for group presentations (even group performances) and can allow you to cover in class more material from the play.

Once the group discussions are finished (again, give students about ten to fifteen minutes to annotate, fifteen to twenty minutes to discuss as a group), ask groups to report back to the class as a whole about the decisions they came to. Start with the physical spaces: How did their views of the stage differ? Which of their stage designs seemed most striking or interesting? Then add in character portrayal: How difficult was it to place the character imaginatively into the space? Did the stage set the students designed give them ideas for how to portray the character? Or did the stage set limit in any way what the character could do? Conclude by drawing their attention to the interdependence of design and performance: how much is the design dependent on characters and their actions, and how much are characters and their actions beholden to design? If students work efficiently, this portion can easily take another twenty minutes.

When groups have reported back, you might consider using any remaining time showing one or two different interpretations of the scene from films or filmed stage adaptations. Ask students to think about what choices the directors, set designers, and actors made when confronted with the same questions the class was confronted with. What kind of rationale did these professionals use to create the scenes? Did the participants in the different stagings or adaptations make similar or different choices? Do those choices have an effect on how we think of the scene and the characters in it?

REFLECTIONS

"Staging the Scene" is designed to get students thinking about how the production of a play relies on multiple levels of interpretation. All plays require careful, considered interpretive choices to move from page to stage. Stage producers must think not only about plot or action but also character, mood, and theme. This exercise offers students a more active way into the world of drama by inviting them to make their own interpretive choices about design, lighting, and staging, as well as to look closely at the literary components that suggested these choices.

My favorite scene to use for this exercise is the closet scene in Shakespeare's *Hamlet* (act 3, scene 4). The stage directions and description are minimal (the Norton edition refers to the space as "The Queen's Private Chamber," and Polonius refers to it in the play as "The Queen's Closet"), yet there is a highly developed tradition of staging that significantly impacts how the scene is interpreted. I try a slight variation, first numbering the students off into groups of just two, with one student focused on Hamlet's role and the other on Gertrude's. I ask students to focus on Hamlet and

Gertrude and their interactions (as opposed to Polonius and the ghost). I assign the two roles randomly, without concern for gender; if a male student objects to finding himself assigned Gertrude rather than Hamlet, I take the opportunity to slip in a few words about gender roles and acting conventions on the Elizabethan stage.

After students have annotated their scripts, I then combine the pairs into groups of four so that each group ideally has two Hamlets and two Gertrudes. This doubling up of character pairs allows groups to debate how much character interpretations shape a scene (Were there differences? Were there similarities? Where are the possible conflicts between interpretations?). When the whole group reassembles, I always leave time to show one or more screen takes on the closet scene, by Franco Zeffirelli (1990), Kenneth Branagh (1996), or Michael Almereyda (2000). I have found that the BBC production of *Hamlet* (1980), from its *Complete Works of William Shakespeare* series, tends to interest students the most, since it has no cuts and has minimal scenery—a film staging that comes closest to an actual theatrical production. The Zeffirelli version is also very useful, as the sequence is so obviously designed and directed around a specific interpretation (the Oedipal reading of the play), allowing the class to see very clearly the relationship these elements have to the construction of a play's meaning.

In the end, each of my student groups produced a very different staging of the closet scene. One group, which opted to include a bed in their set design, had a vigorous debate about its significance; they noted that inclusion of this single piece of furniture turns Hamlet into an aggressor violently entering his mother's private space, and also highlights the dubiousness of Polonius's presence in those same chambers. Another group focused more on the context surrounding the scene, Gertrude's summoning of Hamlet, as a touchstone for their design. They pondered the pros and cons of including formal elements, like a dais, to represent visually Gertrude's attempt under pressure to maintain her authority as both a queen and a mother.

"Staging the Scene" works because it couples adaptation with interpretation. In our full-class discussion that followed, the students acknowledged that their adapted set designs were based entirely on their quite different interpretations—interpretations that depended in this case more on the language, tone, dialogue, and characters in the scene than on the playwright's minimal stage directions. They also experienced, many of them for the first time, how creative staging itself functions as an act of literary interpretation, refining and shaping how we understand a play.

Adaptation

Jennifer Waldron

An exercise that uses performance to provoke debate about a scene's language, characters, and themes.

Genre: *drama*
Course Level: *intermediate or advanced*
Student Difficulty: *moderate*
Teacher Preparation: *low*
Class Size: *small to medium*
Semester Time: *midterm, late*
Writing Component: *optional, either before class or in class*
Close Reading: *medium*
Estimated Time: *variable, from 50 to 80 minutes*

EXERCISE

This exercise has two parts. For the first part, which takes place before class, assign students a short scene and ask them to read it carefully, marking important words and phrases. For the second part, which takes place in class, ask students to work together in small groups to develop two starkly different dramatic readings of the scene. The first part invites students to exercise close-reading skills: What cues does the script give us about the emotions, gestures, or motivations of the characters? What larger ideas and problems does the language suggest? The second part asks students to develop and debate their interpretations of a scene in relation to the kinds of decisions that are required for live performance: What are the larger effects of small changes in tone, pacing, movement? What kind of social world do these characters inhabit? Because students are asked to perform the scene two very different ways, they are encouraged to make interpretive decisions and to evaluate the effects of their choices, engaging actively in producing the meaning of the scene.

Choose the scene you want to work on carefully. In addition to selecting a scene that presents interpretive challenges of some kind, the section you choose should be approximately one hundred to two hundred lines long, depending on the density and complexity of the lines. Good options are Antigone's debate with her sister at the opening of Sophocles's *Antigone*, the comic resolution of Shakespeare's *As You Like It*, the closing dialogue between Nora and her husband in Ibsen's *A Doll's House*, or John Proctor's resistance when authorities arrest his wife at the end of act 2 of Miller's *The Crucible*. Take into consideration the number of parts required for the scene, since this will affect your division of the students into small groups. For instance, if you have a class of thirty students, you might have six groups of five students working on a scene with five characters. You can also assign one student to be the director, which gives you flexibility in case one group is larger than the others.

For the first phase of the exercise, make sure students have a copy of the scene that can be marked up and used for the class performances. Consider giving them a handout that is either a photocopy of the scene or (even better) a Word document with large text and wide margins. Ask them to read it carefully and to mark any important or confusing words or phrases: Where are the key points where the tone shifts? What cues do we have for the emotions and relationships among the characters? Where might characters move, gesture, or be still? Whom would students cast in the lead roles if they could use contemporary actors? Students might focus on their particular characters, if you have assigned parts in advance, or on the scene as a whole. Ask them to begin thinking about how they want to adapt this scene, reminding them that the best performances often take creative risks that depend on particular interpretations of the play's themes and characters.

If you have time, show students DVD or YouTube clips that illustrate two very different adaptations of a scene. Rather than showing the scene they will be working on, which can overly influence their own interpretations, you might choose a different scene from the same play or from another play by that author. I often show students Hamlet's first encounter with the ghost of his father, contrasting Laurence Olivier's film with Kenneth Branagh's. You might show these clips at the end of the previous class, when you give out the copies of the scene they will adapt. Or you could do it at the beginning of the class in which they will do their own performances.

For the in-class exercise, divide students into groups of two to five, depending on the number of characters in the scene. Explain that during the last part of class, they will perform the scene two different ways and receive feedback from the rest of the class about the interpretive choices they have made. Encourage students to be creative, and give examples of adaptations that stretch boundaries: perhaps silent characters steal the show with gestures and antics; perhaps the group will use cross gender or cross race casting; perhaps some of the lines will be cut or delivered as asides. As the students break into groups, ask them to begin by comparing notes about important words, phrases, and turning points: What might each character want in this scene? What larger ideas and themes are active?

After five to ten minutes have passed, ask the groups to begin developing the scenes. Encourage them to brainstorm surprising approaches to these characters and to the world of the play: What contemporary situations or problems does it recall? For instance, do the justifications for going to war with France in Shakespeare's *Henry V* resonate with contemporary debates about intervention in foreign conflicts? Challenge students to generate strong interpretations of the scene by drawing on their own emotions about relevant topics, from the personal to the political. Remind them that these larger decisions and interpretations can and should influence very small decisions: How loudly or softly should a character speak? How close do two characters stand? How quickly does each one move about the stage? This portion of the exercise should take approximately twenty-five to thirty minutes.

When the groups are ready, gather the class for performances, asking for volunteers to go first. The performances can take a fairly long time, depending on the size of your group. If you have only a sixty-minute class, be prepared to cut short the feedback sessions, set aside time during the next class meeting for the last groups to perform, or allow the groups who are reluctant to perform to bow out. After each group performs their two versions of the scene, ask the rest of the class to offer feedback: what was the overall impact of the different performance choices? Make clear that the audience should comment before anyone inside the group reveals the guiding ideas. This way, the performers can see whether their choices came through. After the audience has commented, ask the performers if they'd like to respond.

Wrap things up by asking students to comment on what they learned from the exercise. How do creative adaptation and critical analysis feed one another? To what extent does the text dictate how the performance should be carried out? What are the advantages of adaptations that depart from tradition or abandon certain elements of the original script? Of course, depending on the playwright and the scene, there is a lot of variation: a play like *The Crucible*, for example, provides extensive stage directions and even descriptive commentary, while a play like *King Lear* has few directions and does not exist in a single authoritative edition.

REFLECTIONS

Students often assume that the meaning of the play (especially a canonical one) is fixed in the words themselves or in a past history of stage performance that is now inert. This exercise instead encourages students to engage actively in producing the scene's meaning rather than assuming that the text speaks for itself. In the discussions that follow the performances, students are often able to articulate the ways in which their decisions about language, tone, dialogue, and characterization coalesce around particular interpretations of the play that go far beyond the playwright's sparse stage directions. With this exercise, students also gain concrete experience that helps them engage in sophisticated discussions of artistic and cultural problems that might otherwise seem abstract: How do older cultural forms survive in the present? What is the relationship between text and performance, author and actor, actor and audience? Student discussions are often as deeply insightful as the performances are hilarious.

When I did this exercise using the mock marriage scene between Orlando and Rosalind (disguised as Ganymede) in Shakespeare's *As You Like It* (act 4, scene 1), students began to take positions on small and large questions about gender and role-playing in ways that they had not in discussions of the text alone. While some groups emphasized the homoerotic potential of Orlando's affectionate words and actions toward a person he thinks is a boy, others rendered the scene as one of discovery, in which Orlando slowly realizes that his beloved Rosalind is before him, disguised as a boy. Another group staged the scene as a farce about the fickleness of love and Orlando's detachment from reality. But in the process of the discussions, and in the space that opened up between these very different possibilities, students became curious about a range of complex problems. They wanted to know more about gender relations in Elizabethan England, noting that the very same gestures and words could have had a different cultural resonance in Shakespeare's time. They wondered which version fit better with the trajectory of the play as a whole: did the role-playing diminish the authenticity of love, or was it somehow bound up in that experience? And beyond their interpretations of this particular play, the students also asked questions that implicitly broached complex problems in the history of gender, the evolution of literary and cultural traditions, and the close relationship between critical and creative work.

There are several fun variations on this exercise. One alternative is to invite students to write their own words and use a different setting for one of their performances of the scene—a variation that works best as part of the take-home assignment. This approach has particular benefits for teaching early plays (Shakespeare, Christopher Marlowe, Ben Jonson), since students must actively interpret particular words and phrases in the process of modernizing them, but in truth it works well for any play, since it asks students to think about the cultural resonance of particular words and verbal styles. If students are working on early drama, this is also a great moment to introduce them to the *Oxford English Dictionary*, available online, as a way of thinking about how the meanings of particular words shift as they enter new cultural contexts: what are the modern equivalents for Shakespearean words like "fortune" or "fashion"?

You might also offer students examples of specific cultural moments and idioms they can draw on. My students have staged memorable scenes from Shakespeare in the style of film noir, Seinfeld episodes, and dystopian science fiction. Perhaps my favorite, however, was a melodramatic sock puppet performance of the death of Julius Caesar. Shakespeare's plays contain many self-conscious references to the vulgarizing effects of bringing classical personages and stories to the Elizabethan stage, where a boy actor with a "squeaking" voice might impersonate a royal personage such as Cleopatra. While students may assume that irreverent adaptation is an entirely modern approach to something as "classic" as a Shakespeare play, this exercise positions them to see that self-conscious adaptations are frequently built into plays themselves.

Soliloquy

Sean Keilen

An exercise that asks students to combine close reading and etymological research with structured improvisation.

Genre: *drama, especially early modern*
Course Level: *intermediate or advanced*
Student Difficulty: *moderate*
Teacher Preparation: *low*
Class Size: *any*
Semester Time: *midterm, late*
Writing Component: *before class*
Close Reading: *high*
Estimated Time: *2 hours*

EXERCISE

This exercise has two phases. In the first phase, which takes place outside class time, groups of two to three students read a soliloquy through the lens of the *Oxford English Dictionary* (*OED*). In the second phase, they work together during class—first to perform the soliloquy, then to transform it into a different kind of dramatic speech, which they also perform. The first phase of the exercise invites them to approach the soliloquy as a text for reading. The second phase invites them to approach it as a text for improvisation and performance.

Choose a soliloquy in which one or more key words or concepts of the play that you're studying is under examination, or in which the soliloquist disputes the way that other characters have used key words and concepts. If, like me, you teach Shakespeare, you'll have no shortage of good options: Bottom's attempt to verbalize his dream (*A Midsummer Night's Dream*, act 4, scene 1); Richard II's comparison between his mind, his prison cell, and the world (*Richard II*, act 5, scene 5); Hal's private declaration of independence from Falstaff (*1 Henry IV*, act 1, scene 2); Antony's vow to avenge Caesar, spoken over the dead man's corpse (*Julius Caesar*, act 3, scene 1); Hamlet's meditation on an actor's tears for Hecuba (*Hamlet*, act 2, scene 2); or Prospero's renunciation of his magic (*The Tempest*, act 5, scene 1). For most dramatists, soliloquy is a crucible in which words and ideas with ostensibly immutable meaning fluctuate and change, along with the soliloquist's sense of self.

In the first phase of the exercise, in which each group meets together outside class, ask groups to select a word from the soliloquy that you've chosen and, using the *OED*, to scrutinize the range of meanings that this word had during the dramatist's lifetime. Have each group decide which meanings are active in the soliloquy, then ask every student to write a brief response paper, explaining the decision that was reached and how it influences one's perception of the scene and of the play as a whole. Ask them to bring their response papers to class and use them as the basis for a preliminary discussion about the soliloquy.

When class convenes, begin the second phase of the exercise. Give students approximately twenty minutes to devise a plan for performing the soliloquy in class. Have them decide when and how the soliloquist should raise and lower his or her voice, speak rapidly or slowly, pause before speaking, use gestures, and move about or remain still. Tell them that their goal is to fit the decisions that they make about performance to the decisions that they made about meaning during the first phase of the exercise. Keep their attention focused on the challenge of relating text and performance in this way.

Next, ask for volunteers from different groups to perform the soliloquy. Depending on the length of the passage that you have chosen, and the number of groups in your class, these performances could take twenty to twenty-five minutes. It is important that there be at least two performances, so that comparison is possible, but time will also be needed for discussion and the next part of the exercise. After the performance, discuss whether the decisions about delivery did justice to the text. For example, did the performance capture or convey the ambiguity and plasticity of the soliloquy's key words and concepts?

Now give the groups approximately fifteen minutes to devise a second plan for performance, different from the first. This time, give them the choice of converting the soliloquy into one of three options: a monologue with a silent, onstage audience of which the soliloquist is aware; a monologue with an onstage audience that makes side comments without the soliloquist noticing; or a dialogue between the soliloquist and another character from the play. (Shakespeare's works in particular offer numerous examples for each of these kinds of dramatic speech.) Remind the students to make their decisions about performance underscore the conclusions that they reached about the meaning of the (now transformed) soliloquy's words.

Leave lots of time (up to an hour) for all the groups to perform their new versions of the soliloquy (for a sixty- or ninety-minute class, this means devoting another session to the performances; for a seminar, you should have sufficient time). Wrap up by discussing with the students the results of the exercise as a whole. What specific moments in the different performances did they find most compelling, and why? And what in particular did they learn about the dramatic potential of soliloquies?

REFLECTIONS

Many undergraduates have a working understanding of soliloquies: in contrast to monologues, dialogues, and asides, soliloquies are speeches that are uttered when an actor is alone on stage. But no one is ever really alone in the theater. Drama is a genre of, and for, voyeurs and eavesdroppers. Every soliloquist has an audience (sometimes onstage and always offstage); it would be more accurate to say that a soliloquy is a speech that is uttered when a character wrongly *believes* that he or she is alone. This exercise clarifies for students that, from the theater's perspective, all privacy is a fiction.

When I performed this exercise with Hamlet's "O, what a rogue and peasant slave am I!" students were quick to realize that soliloquies actually have quite a lot in common with dialogues. The experience of performing the speech for the first time, with just one actor per group speaking the lines, helped them to understand that Hamlet is not only an orator alone; he is also a critical interlocutor—for himself. Hamlet poses questions and answers them from different points of view, much as one would expect from a conversation between two or more characters. By the same token, the students noted that as Hamlet's soliloquy moves through a range of topics and moods (self-criticism, anguish, readiness and procrastination, hatred, the difference between the ways we feel about theatrical illusion and our real circumstances, the utility of drama), it also gathers momentum, like passionate arguments between different persons that occur elsewhere in the play and in other plays.

The experience of revising the first performances to include the presence of other characters seemed to broaden and deepen the students' understanding of the soliloquy as something more than an uncomplicated expression of solipsism. The second performances were imaginative and diverse. One group rewrote the soliloquy as a disagreement between Hamlet and Horatio about the efficacy of the theater as a means of rousing the emotions and discovering the truth about the old king's death. Another group brought the Ghost back to the stage to criticize Hamlet for his lack of sympathy for Gertrude, his preoccupation with abstract questions, and his delay in getting revenge. A third group, whose response papers had focused on the similarities between Hamlet's pedantic statements about the theater and Polonius's style, incorporated the old man as an eavesdropper and speaker of increasingly agitated asides.

Students especially enjoy this activity's combination of scholarly assignment (the response papers) with creative work (the performances). I tell them that in the kind of grammar school that Shakespeare attended, this twofold approach to teaching was called *analysis* and *genesis*, and it was standard fare. In our colleges and universities, it is more of a novelty to combine scholarly and creative forms of engagement, but as Nietzsche said, "the only time when we can actually *recognize* something is when we endeavor to *make* it." For me, the appeal of this soliloquy exercise is that it puts scholarly research in the service of creative discovery.

· ·

Director's Cut

Michael Komorowski

A performance-based activity to get students talking about what history means for Shakespeare.

Genre: *drama*
Course Level: *advanced*
Student Difficulty: *hard*
Teacher Preparation: *medium*
Class Size: *small to medium*
Semester Time: *any*
Writing Component: *none*
Close Reading: *low*
Estimated Time: *45 to 60 minutes*

EXERCISE

This performance exercise works with any of Shakespeare's history plays, but especially with *1 Henry IV*. At the beginning of class, distribute and/or project on a screen copies of several ornate frontispieces from early modern

English histories. Good choices include William Camden's *Britannia* with its map of Britain, Raphael Holinshed's *Chronicles* with its border of stern-faced kings, Walter Raleigh's *History of the World* with its God's eye looking down the page, and John Speed's *Theatre of the Empire of Great Britain* with its succession of ethnic representatives of British peoples. Tell students that these authors were Shakespeare's contemporaries (and in the case of Holinshed, an important source) and that these frontispieces are elaborate advertisements for a particular approach to history. Ask students to speculate about the content of these books, based on their initial impressions of the frontispieces.

With these visualizations in mind, divide the class into groups of four to five students and ask each group to put on a brief performance of a significant scene in the play, imagining that Camden, Holinshed, Raleigh, or Speed were their director. For *1 Henry IV*, certain pairings work particularly well. The play's opening scene with King Henry and Westmoreland that describes a clash of ethnic customs on the battlefield (act 1, scene 1) lends itself well to Speed. To the group performing the scene in which Falstaff parodies King Henry chiding his wastrel son (act 2, scene 5), assign Holinshed. To the group putting on the map scene with Mortimer, Hotspur, and Glendower (act 3, scene 1), assign Camden. And to the group performing the final battlefield scene during which Hal slays Hotspur and Falstaff comically seems to rise from the dead (act 5, scene 4), assign Raleigh. For a variation on this exercise, assign the groups each a different frontispiece, but ask them to act out the same scene.

Students will need direction in selecting relatively brief passages from these scenes to perform. Other than this guidance (mostly in the interest of managing time), I prefer not to give detailed instructions about acting these scenes: I want my students to think about how they can communicate a message from one of the frontispieces through tone, emphasis, and gesture. Depending on the amount of class time available, allot about fifteen minutes for the planning and informal rehearsal of these scenes and, again depending on the length of the class, three or four minutes for each performance.

Save time at the end (at least ten minutes) for a summary class discussion of the performances and the questions they raise. Ask students whether these scenes seemed like dramatized history or whether they were closer to comedy or tragedy. It may be helpful to point out that *1 Henry IV* contains more invented material than any other of Shakespeare's history plays. Ask students why that may be. This may be a good time to mention that Shakespeare had originally intended to name Falstaff's character "Oldcastle," the name of the knight who was executed as a Lollard in 1417 and who was memorialized in Shakespeare's day as a Protestant martyr. Does Falstaff seem to be a less "historical" character because he appears under a different name than, say, Hotspur or Hal? It's also helpful to ask students to share some of the challenges they faced in translating a picture into a performance. How did the frontispieces help or hinder their emphases of the comic, tragic, or romance elements of these scenes? With these impressions on the seminar table, students are ready to approach some of the thematic questions that the play raises, including the nature of heroism, the justification for dissent, or the vexed relationship between language and intention.

REFLECTIONS

Shakespeare's history plays can be difficult. It's not immediately clear to most students what Shakespeare is up to with these texts. This activity helps students to think about the history plays as more than dramatized chronicles. The frontispieces also remind students that Shakespeare's works have a material history as books and that his plays participated in a culture in which competing representations of the past jostled for attention.

It's exciting to see that competitive process come alive in these brief performances. The students' productions almost always exaggerate the comic features of Shakespeare's play (and indeed this exercise is designed to elicit exaggerated acting and declamation), helping to show in isolation one of his techniques for bringing history to the stage. Shakespeare is not retelling a bare chronology of long-dead monarchs, students are quick to grasp, but is selecting stories about the past for their ethical or political resonance. Shakespeare's history plays may, in fact, question the reasons why a contemporary audience chooses to manipulate the past as much as they question the motives of the historical actors represented on stage. Usually, students are eager to share their sense of an agenda behind their scene when they've interpreted it in light of one of the frontispieces. Push students to think more about how Shakespeare may be asking his audience to reflect on who makes history and how stories are remembered long after the events they describe.

After their performances, students especially like to talk about the genre mixing that is a typical feature of Shakespeare's history plays. In the case of *1 Henry IV*, some students feel that the range of characters and their peculiar idioms make this play especially hard to categorize as a history play. They readily note that the Welsh rebel Glendower uses strange locutions while his daughter speaks only Welsh; King Henry remains cloistered at court and has his myopic way of reading events; Falstaff and his friends at the Boar's Head tavern speak a coarser dialect. Shakespeare's histories can be as funny as his comedies and can probe the depths of human emotions as well as any tragedy. By detaching some key scenes from the rest of the play, students see more clearly that Wales can be a land of romance, Hotspur can be a potentially tragic hero, and a tavern can be a scene of comedy. Understanding this variegated texture, I tell my students, is a big part of the pleasure of reading or seeing a Shakespeare history play.

Moving Scenes

Douglas A. Jones Jr.

A dynamic small-group exercise that strengthens students' knowledge of dramatic movements.

Genre: *drama*
Course Level: *intermediate or advanced*
Student Difficulty: *hard*
Teacher Preparation: *low*
Class Size: *small to medium*
Semester Time: *midterm, late*
Writing Component: *before class*
Close Reading: *low*
Estimated Time: *15 minutes per performance*

EXERCISE

Sometime before the midpoint of the course, divide the class into small groups of three to five students. Have each group choose a scene from one of the plays the class has read that semester, preferably something well known: Oedipus's epiphany in Sophocles's *Oedipus Rex* or Nora's final exit in Ibsen's *A Doll's House*, for example. The students' mission will be to "displace" or "move" that scene elsewhere; that is, to reimagine it through one or more different dramatic movements. (By "dramatic movements" I mean both discrete movements, such as Sturm und Drang or naturalism, and historical periods, such as ancient Greece or the Restoration.) For example, students might restage the balcony scene in Shakespeare's *Romeo and Juliet* as Theater of the Absurd, or Walter Lee's confrontation with Lindner in Lorraine Hansberry's *A Raisin in the Sun* as early Roman comedy.

Instruct the student groups first to write a script and second to prepare to perform it for the class. Encourage them to perform their script with as much production as possible (costumes, set pieces, lights, props). This takes some work and coordination, so save this exercise for a final presentation at the end of the semester, although it also works well as a post-midterm project. If instructors have had students read scenes out loud throughout the semester—a habit I strongly encourage for every drama course—then by the end of the semester most students will be comfortable performing their "moving scenes" in front of their classmates. The number of groups and length of class period will ultimately determine how much time you can allow for each presentation, but this assignment is most productive when each group has roughly fifteen minutes to perform, leaving additional time for other students to respond.

For a wrap-up discussion, be sure to ask students what they think of the exercise itself. How does it differ from the close reading they might be used to? What specific insights into drama did they learn that they might not have discovered otherwise? This is a good time to stress to students that "Moving Scenes" is an exercise in dramatic theory and that the point of such an approach is to recognize how specific plots, characters, dictions, resolutions, and sequencings do not lend themselves to certain literary movements and modes of dramaturgical praxis. Students are quick to understand from the start that this performance lesson is not about creating a smooth adaptation in the vein of, say, Aimé Césaire's *A Tempest* for Shakespeare's *The Tempest*. By the end, the class will be comfortable embracing the formal discord and narrative incongruities that emerge from the students' staged displacements.

REFLECTIONS

Displacing scenes from one dramatic movement to another offers an effective and highly entertaining way to bolster (and gauge) your students' understanding of the particularities of dramatic and performance theory as well as the intimate relationship between form and content. Having to write and stage the displacements themselves, students discover firsthand the possibilities and limitations of particular dramaturgical, theatrical, and performance practices.

Further, this fun but challenging activity deepens students' knowledge of how literary movements and theories of drama reflect broader political concerns and social preoccupations. For example, in a survey course on the history of theater before modernism, one of my student groups elected to displace the final scene of Euripides's *Medea* onto the mid-seventeenth-century French stage. The students quickly discovered the difficulty of negotiating the neoclassical insistence on decorum: Should the dead bodies of Jason and Medea's sons appear onstage? If not, how should Medea reveal her filicide? They asked, Doesn't the very act of filicide contravene decorum? Doesn't her marriage to Jason?

Like most, this group of students found that the dynamics of such scenes cannot help but violate the dictates of French neoclassicism. And yet, their presentation was most creative and instructive when it embraced that violation: specifically, the group used it as an opportunity to explore the broader moral and sociopolitical function that Richelieu and his *Académie français* demanded the stage should serve. In this "moving scene," students came away with a better grasp of not only the poetics of French neoclassical drama but also the often fraught relationship between the theater and the state in the early modern period.

"Moving Scenes" fosters a robust dynamic of collaboration; it requires a good deal of out-of-class preparation and group bonding, so it is best to let students know that up front. Indeed, every displacement calls on groups to get down to the fine details of how each theatrical job (playwright, director, actor, designer) should be performed. Remarkably, students often note that the time they spend outside the classroom working on the project does not feel like research—but it certainly is. For the *Medea*-as-French-neoclassicism example, students learned how to write the characters' verse, establish their social and gender relationships through stage positions, act out decorous affects and corporeal gestures, and construct appropriate set and costume properties for the mise-en-scène. If you are facing time limits or other types of constraints, consider having students (individually or in groups) write the script only, which is in itself an extremely valuable exercise, leaving time for students to comment on one another's work. However, I suggest assigning the full version of "Moving Scenes" whenever possible, because its greatest pedagogical impact emerges from its forms of embodied praxis.

Reading the Reviews

Sunny Stalter-Pace

A historical-context exercise based on theater reviews.

Genre: *drama*
Course Level: *introductory or intermediate*
Student Difficulty: *easy or moderate*
Teacher Preparation: *medium*
Class Size: *any*
Semester Time: *any*
Writing Component: *none*
Close Reading: *high*
Estimated Time: *30 to 50 minutes*

EXERCISE

This exercise invites students to reconstruct the contemporary historical context and reception of a single stage play. For the most interesting results, try this exercise with a controversial play like Frank Wedekind's *Spring*

Awakening or Sarah Kane's *Blasted* or an era-defining play like Tony Kushner's *Angels in America*. These qualities increase the chances that your reviews will contain within them multiple historical or cultural references and that the reviews will express especially strong opinions. You might also use this exercise with a play that's so canonical that your students don't think of it in historical terms, perhaps Arthur Miller's *Death of a Salesman* or Lorraine Hansberry's *A Raisin in the Sun*.

Choose a single review from the period when the play was first performed. Useful databases will differ according to the author's nationality and time period. For British plays you might consult British Newspapers 1600–1950 or the Times Digital Archive. For American plays, try Chronicling America (the Library of Congress database of American newspapers until 1922) and the Historical *New York Times*. If you'd like students to use a particular historical database for later research papers, then that might be a good one to incorporate into this exercise.

If the review is long, choose an extract from it that the class can tackle in an appropriate amount of time. (With older plays, a single paragraph with difficult language and historical references can take about twenty minutes; a two-page review can take twice that long.) If the extract is sufficiently brief, you may want to project it onto a screen. Otherwise, make photocopies and plan on giving students time in class to read the review on their own.

Begin the classroom exercise by informing students of its ultimate purpose: to place the play into its original historical and cultural context by using a primary source from the period. Ask them what they expect when they read a theater review; typical answers will include things like opinionated language, plot description, or assessments of the acting. Then let them know what else they can expect in this particular review, such as unfamiliar references or old-fashioned slang.

Once you've given them plenty of time to read the review, invite students to let you know which words, phrases, and references are unfamiliar. Write them on the board and ask volunteers to look up the definitions on their phones or laptops. Once the common vocabulary is established, invite the class to summarize the reviewer's thoughts on the play by working through the text sentence by sentence, even clause by clause. As you go, ask some guiding questions: What does the reviewer express or imply about the play? What do we find out about the performance that we wouldn't know from reading the published script? How does the reviewer connect the play to current events and issues of the day?

This process endorses the value of close reading—paying attention to how small details support larger interpretations—while simultaneously turning up interesting contextual tidbits about the play's direction, set design, performance, or audience. When you're done, take some time to talk with students about what one can learn by placing a literary work back into its original time period.

REFLECTIONS

Theater reviews are a useful jumping-off point for approaching plays, especially ones that can seem quite obscure at first. Reviews help students go beyond the words on the page and envision a play as a live performance in a particular place and time; in this way, reviews are useful complements to other resources for teaching drama, such as photographs, sketches, and videos. Approaching the play first from the perspective of a reviewer can offer students the context that they need to understand why the play *mattered*—the events, language, or issues that struck a chord at the time of its production. Finally, reading theater reviews in class models the process of research for students, showing them that even the most opaque references can usually be understood with a little sleuthing.

One of the pleasures of this exercise is seeing students broaden their understanding of what can be gained from reading a review. I like to remind students that primary materials like these are good sources of information about particular theater productions; students are often surprised that the only record of a play's sets, acting, or costumes might be in the reviews. Since it is a familiar genre, I've found it easy to move our discussion from elements that the class expects in a review—like the thumbs up / thumbs down judgment of the critic—into complicated analysis of authorial persona, audience, and taste. Reviews offer particularly opinionated takes on the plays, and my students have often felt emboldened to respond to and even disagree with them in a way that they don't feel they have the authority to do with a critical essay.

After a particularly productive discussion of a *Spring Awakening* review, for example, my students understood just how much anger the play's antiauthoritarian stance stirred up when the English translation of this German play was first produced in New York City on March 30, 1917. I invited them to read a particularly opinionated *New York Times* piece that appeared the next day—an anonymous review titled "Wedekind Play Abused." The reviewer calls Wedekind's play "unpresentable in the theater," even in Germany. From this part of the review, students discovered something about literary genres: controversial topics that can be addressed in novels are often considered obscene when set onstage.

As we moved paragraph by paragraph through the review, students noted how the author ignores the play's plot, themes, and performances until the third of the review's four paragraphs. Instead, he spends most of the time mocking the audience as pretentious and strange. One old man in particular was said to have "whiled away" the intermission reading the *Birth Control*

Review. Students found this detail to be funny but telling: the reviewer obviously found the man's attitude and reading matter to be incongruous. One of the major issues raised in *Spring Awakening* is the need for more frank discussions about sexuality, but the reviewer, students concluded, saw these discussions as the domain of creepy bohemians and not his readers.

Reading *Spring Awakening* today, it's easy for students to identify with the perils of teenage sexual curiosity but far more difficult to put themselves in the mind-set of the middle-class adults that Melchior and Wendla rebel against. But with its dry condemnatory tone, the review helped my students do just that. They enjoyed thinking about which parts of the play would have been "tasteless" and "unpresentable" in 1917 (Hansy's masturbation scene) and which parts still seemed to shock today (Melchior's rape of Wendla). And in a course that considers the transnational circulation of expressionist drama, the review introduced issues of translation and cultural relativism that recurred throughout our semester.

"Reading the Reviews" lends itself to a number of variations, either later in the same semester or with upper-level classes. Once students have practice reading reviews, you can ask them to find another review in the same database and respond in writing to the argument made by the critic. (After we had already dissected one review together, my students were far more comfortable looking up reviews for other plays on their laptops and analyzing them.) In a more advanced course, you can invite students to unearth a range of reviews across different time periods. Ask them to make some historical argument based on the reviews—for instance, how *Death of a Salesman* plays in times of economic prosperity versus times of economic crisis. At its most successful, this exercise can teach close reading, research, and cultural analysis skills all at once.

. . . .

Spin the Globe, Shakespeare

Benjamin Hilb

An explorative exercise that helps students to appreciate transnational, intercultural theater.

Genre: *drama*
Course Level: *intermediate or advanced*
Student Difficulty: *moderate*

Teacher Preparation: *high*
Class Size: *any*
Semester Time: *any*
Writing Component: *optional*
Close Reading: *none*
Estimated Time: *2 hours*

EXERCISE

This exercise (especially suited to seminars) is an intellectual variation of the classic "spin the globe and stop it to see where you'll go" game. Students spin a globe, stop it at random with an index finger, and then read about a Shakespeare production produced or set in the country on which their finger lands.

If your classroom is not Internet-friendly, print out brief (two-to-four-page) reviews or essay segments on well-known Shakespeare plays produced or set in countries besides England. Look in particular for reviews or discussions of productions that adapted Shakespeare into a non-English culture, preferably with one or more images included. You won't be able to cover every country on the planet, of course, but the more diverse your collection, the better. Begin with three to five countries per continent (excluding Antarctica), and add as you can. Maintain a folder for each continent, and file the reviews in alphabetical order by country (Asia folder: Afghanistan, Armenia, Azerbaijan, etc.). The greater the number of culturally distinctive elements highlighted and explained in the reviews and essay pieces, the better.

Along with your folders, bring to class one or several globes that spin on their axes. Again, the more the merrier, and the bigger the better. Students can do the spinning individually, or you can divide them into small groups, depending on class size. Have each student, or one from each group, give the globe a spin and use his or her finger to stop it. Give the student a review or discussion of a Shakespeare play produced or set in the country thus spotted. When a nation pops up that doesn't seem to offer any Shakespeareana, pick one near it. Maldives? Try nearby Sri Lanka, where the well-publicized Inter School Shakespeare Drama Competition takes place annually. Did a student land in the big blue? Offer her the short *Times Higher Education* review of Steve Mentz's fascinating volume *At the Bottom of Shakespeare's Ocean.* If students have access to their own computers in class (in a laptop-friendly setting), you can turn this into an interactive online activity they can start in class. In lieu of handing out preselected pieces, let them find a review, article, blog post or wiki, even a video clip of or about a Shakespeare play produced or set in the country they've spotted.

If you don't have a spinning globe, simply direct students to one of several free online versions of the spin-the-globe game, such as SpinFirst.com. It is best to begin by detailing and demonstrating what constitutes a good piece for the assignment. Encourage them to look for documents of suitable length (two to four pages, two to five minutes for video) on productions clearly adapted into a non-Anglocentric culture. You can assist by listing helpful online resources such as *Shakespeare Quarterly*'s World Shakespeare Bibliography Online, MIT's Global Shakespeares, or the Year of Shakespeare website. It is helpful, too, to bring your own collection of reviews, articles, and videos, to have good backup pieces on hand in case of difficulty.

Once each student or group has a piece on a play produced or set in a different culture or country, have them read (or watch) their respective pieces and then present them to the class. Make visible (for example, with chalk, whiteboard, or projection screen) a few guiding questions for their presentations: Which play, which country? What was culturally distinctive about the adaptation? What surprised you? In hour-long classes, the search will take one class period, and students can present their findings in the next class. In seminars, the first hour or so can be spent on the students' online search, with the remaining time devoted to informal presentations and classroom discussion.

REFLECTIONS

Many students come to college well aware of Shakespeare's worldwide influence but have never actually read about, seen, or learned from the Bard's global reach. This exercise helps them not only to imagine Shakespeare's plays in different cultural contexts but also to engage diverse national cultures through widely familiar plays. It encourages students to think about global theater and intercultural exchange and can provoke lively discussions about art and globalization. If students perform their own online searches, it will increase their awareness of and encourage them to use invaluable Internet resources on Shakespeare to explore the vast and growing worlds of Shakespearean theater. Hopefully this, in turn, will inspire students to explore the increasingly intercultural worlds of other theater, literature, and art.

In one memorable instance of the exercise, one of my students, who spotted Japan, presented a beautiful clip of Miyagi Satoshi's *Othello* titled "Desdemona's Spirit in Final Dance," made available by MIT's Shakespeare's Performance in Asia website. Without much knowledge of Japanese culture, he analyzed the performance as a representation of the unity of lovers, citing the New Testament's "and the two shall become one flesh" (Mark 10:8). I highlighted this student's use of the New Testament as an interesting moment of cross-cultural interpretation and asked if anyone could interpret the clip from a Japanese perspective. Another student raised her hand and suggested the performance resembles Butoh, a twentieth-century Japanese performance style conceived in opposition to governmental and artistic authority. We then discussed Desdemona's haunting dance as a conflicted act of resistance to the man she loves.

In another class, a student landed on New Zealand and presented on Catherine Silverstone's blog review for Shakespeare's Globe of Ngākau Toa's *A Toroihi rāua ko Kāhira, a Maori translation and adaptation of Troilus and Cressida*. Incited by a few guiding questions, he cleverly noted that while the Shakespeare play was used to promote Maori language and culture amidst their ongoing endangerment, that endangerment is largely a consequence of the nineteenth-century British colonization of New Zealand. The observation that British (colonizer) culture was paradoxically being used to sustain Maori (colonized) culture led to a keen discussion of postcolonialism and justice.

The exercise works best when students already have some Shakespeare under their belt. It is a great way, for example, to conclude a general survey course on Shakespeare by placing the bard in a more international context. And for majors it can be used to anchor an early modern comparative literature or drama class, or even to kick-start an entire seminar on "global Shakespeare." Students are particularly drawn to images and videos of Shakespeare productions adapted into different cultures and languages. When sources have a visual component, students become curious about what in the world they're seeing—Why these flamboyant costumes? Why the masks? What is the meaning of the ritual dance?—and together begin to rethink the stories and scenes many of them thought they knew. In my writing-intensive Shakespeare course, I also invite students to expand their discovery into a formal essay, using their initial curiosity and excitement to motivate an in-depth (and original) research paper.

For more exercises that can be used to teach plays, try these:

Specific relevance	*General relevance*
Read, Reread, Close Read (Discussions)	The Sixty Second Game (Discussions)
The One-Liner (Essentials)	Fishbowl (Discussions)
The Great Debate (Stories)	Put the Question (Discussions)
Karaoke Poetry (Poems)	It's Time We Talked (Discussions)

Updating a Classic (Genres)

Social Media Meets Classic Literature (Genres)

Dramatic Echoes (Styles)

Island Mapping (Pictures)

Chekhov's Gun (Objects)

Reverse Entropy (Discussions)

Debate (Discussions)

Leader, Skeptic, Scribe (Discussions)

The Blow Up (Essentials)

The New Title (Essentials)

The Descriptive Word (Essentials)

The Common Thread (Essentials)

How to Read a Bookstore (Genres)

Mixtape Maker (Genres)

To Thine Own Tweet Be True (Genres)

What is "Literature"? (Canons)

Putting a Face to a Name (Canons)

Literature Class Band (Canons)

The Blank Syllabus (Canons)

Build-A-Canon (Canons)

Keywords (Words)

Vocabulary Bites (Words)

Le Mot Juste (Words)

Aphorisms (Words)

Fill in the Blanks (Words)

Punctuation Matters (Styles)

Digital Literacy (Pictures)

Reading without Reading (Objects)

Making Manuscripts (Objects)

Online Commonplace Book (Objects)

Object Lesson (Objects)

The Things Inside Books (Objects)

GENRES

Each of the three preceding sections attends to a major literary genre. The exercises here focus on the idea of genre itself. What makes a genre a genre? How do genres function in the wider world? And what can we learn about one literary form by transforming it into another genre entirely? In the process of identifying, rethinking, and switching genres, students will develop a clearer sense of the conventions and expectations that make genre possible, uncover the cultural codings embedded in seemingly neutral categories, and probe the powerful relationship between form and content.

How do genres present themselves to readers? The first two exercises ("Introduction to Genre Fiction" and "How to Read a Bookstore") concentrate on the defining and marketing of genre, putting students in contact with popular forms and physical bookstores. Next up are three classic exercises in genre switching ("Translating Sonnets," "Updating a Classic," and "Mixtape Maker"), in which students discover what's gained—and lost—when they turn poetry into prose, drama into film, or literature into music. The final pair ("Social Media Meets Classic Literature" and "To Thine Own Tweet Be True") update the classic switch for our social media–saturated moment, asking students to reflect on what happens when they translate literary texts into the tweets, posts, and hashtags through which they already communicate in their daily lives. Whether you go old school or new school, these activities will help students rethink the boundaries that give literary texts their particular form.

Introduction to Genre Fiction

Christy Tidwell

An exercise that introduces students to concepts and definitions of genre fiction.

Genre: *fiction*
Course Level: *introductory or intermediate*
Student Difficulty: *easy*
Teacher Preparation: *medium*
Class Size: *any*
Semester Time: *early, or at the beginning of relevant unit*
Writing Component: *none*
Close Reading: *none*
Estimated Time: *30 to 40 minutes*

EXERCISE

This structured discussion of the conventions and expectations of genre fiction works well in courses devoted to a single genre (science fiction, fantasy, mystery, romance) or courses that explore multiple genres. In the former, introduce the exercise at the beginning of the course; in the latter, introduce it each time you begin a new genre.

Begin by having the class generate two lists. For the first list, ask students to describe the characteristics they associate with the genre at hand; put their responses in one column on the board. Encourage them to suggest both atmospheric and narrative elements, as well as typical attitudes toward the genre—any associations at all. It is helpful to ask a series of questions to draw out these associations, such as the following: What elements does a story need to have to be in this genre? What kinds of characters, relationships, or events would you expect to encounter? What kinds of beginnings or endings? What kind of setting or time period? Why? Is there a typical consumer of this genre? If so, who? Why do people who enjoy this genre enjoy it? A wide range of associations is important because it allows the class to talk freely about conventions as well as misperceptions of the genre. To encourage this variety, refrain from commenting on the responses until after completing both this list and the following one.

Building on their initial associations, now ask students to brainstorm the second list: examples of the genre from literature, film, television, video games, or other media. Put these examples in a new column on the board. Again, refrain from commenting on the examples until both lists are complete.

After generating these lists, which should take fifteen to twenty minutes, move on to the discussion portion of the exercise, which should take an equal amount of time. Ask the students whether there is anything in either list they might question or disagree with—ideas or examples that do *not* seem characteristic of the genre. What disqualifies them? Do they belong more properly to another genre? This will help students think about the genre's boundaries and also the boundaries between related genres. (If the students do not offer any questions or disagreements, you should feel free to raise them yourself.) Before moving on, ask the students to propose a working definition of the genre. Based on the lists they have generated (and the elements they have excluded), what are this genre's essential features? Put this working definition on the board.

Once the students have proposed a working definition, introduce them to some of the relevant critical terms and debates that scholars have generated to analyze this genre. Write these terms on the board as well. Show the students where their definitions and the critical terminology overlap (or, if appropriate, where the critical terminology captures an aspect of the genre they may not have considered). After a full-group discussion of these relevant terms, encourage the students to revise their working definition, and write the final working definition on the board.

REFLECTIONS

This exercise requires a lot of knowledge on the instructor's part but very little explicit knowledge from the students. Its purpose is to draw out what the students already know and help them organize that knowledge. Most students, even if they are not fans of a given genre, have seen enough in the wider culture that they have some information on which to draw. Doing so helps give those students confidence going forward in the course or unit. Students who already know a great deal about the genre as fans may nonetheless not have specific language to discuss the genre analytically or may not be aware of the larger debates about it. This exercise thus allows them to take on the role of "expert" while also introducing them to established critical approaches to the genre. Whether students are fans or not, this group exercise helps develop a set of common references for the class as you move forward, which builds a sense of community. It also establishes a way of thinking about genre as a set of conventions and reading practices that are both identifiable and flexible.

For example, when I use this exercise to teach science fiction, students (fans and nonfans alike) are able to generate lists of associations and expectations, including concrete terms like "aliens," "space," "the future," and "science" alongside more abstract evaluative terms like "fantastic" or "unrealistic." Students usually develop a working definition for the genre based either on its reliance on science (it is in the name, after all) or on its speculative nature. At that point, I am able to introduce them to some of the terminology and debates surrounding the genre, including the following:

1. *Science fiction versus fantasy.* Drawing on definitions that highlight the differences between the two genres (although I note that this is not agreed upon by all scholars and fans), I define science fiction as writing that creates worlds we could get to from our present, and fantasy as writing that creates worlds we could not reach.
2. *Extrapolation.* This term helps clarify the previous point, highlighting the logical connection between present and imagined worlds.
3. *Cognitive estrangement.* This term is crucial to a discussion of science fiction and can be defined as the way in which science fiction allows readers to see the familiar patterns of our own world anew as they are presented in the unfamiliar context of the imagined world.

In our discussions of these terms, we are able to further refine the students' working definition and address any misconceptions about the genre the class may have.

Other genre fiction offers different terms and debates. With mystery, for example, you might discuss whether the genre requires a murder or a hard-boiled style; with westerns, you might discuss the importance of landscape and setting or the genre's sharp lines between good and evil; with romance, you might discuss distinctions between sex and pornography or the definition of romance provided by the Romance Writers of America, which requires a central love story and a happy ending.

The ultimate goal of this exercise is to lay the groundwork for continuing discussion rather than to define the genre in some final way. Some students may not be convinced by the working definition, but they will need to refer to it to make their own arguments later. Encourage students to write these definitions down so that they can easily refer to them in future discussions (or on papers or exams).

How to Read a Bookstore

Seth Studer

An exercise that helps students analyze how physical spaces such as bookstores and libraries influence their reading practices.

Genre: *any*
Course Level: *introductory or intermediate*
Student Difficulty: *easy*
Teacher Preparation: *medium*
Class Size: *small*
Semester Time: *early, midterm*
Writing Component: *in class*
Close Reading: *none*
Estimated Time: *45 to 50 minutes*

EXERCISE

Identify the most prominent bookstore on or near campus—perhaps the campus bookstore, an independent bookstore, or a large chain retailer—and schedule one class there. It is good to scope out the store in advance: you will want to find a space in or near the store where you can sit or stand comfortably with your students.

Before class, prepare a list of six or seven questions related to your students' experience of the bookstore (you will use these questions partway through class). Ask your students to bring pen and paper, and meet them at the bookstore. Depending on your class length, give the students between fifteen and thirty minutes to browse and explore the store on their own. Give them a handout with general instructions: Ask them to log observations about the bookstore's layout, design, selection, and ambiance. Ask them to locate the literature sections and note their placement within the store (you might even encourage students to draw a simple map). If your class deals with a specific genre, ask them to locate that genre within the store.

When your students are finished exploring, reconvene at the designated meeting place and begin a group discussion, using the questions you have prepared as a guide. Begin with observational questions: What was the first thing you saw when you entered the store? What types of books are most prominently displayed, and how are they displayed? Did you feel comfortable browsing? Were the aisles wide or narrow? Then introduce more evaluative or critical questions: Why are the literature sections located where they are? Why are certain works of literature prominently displayed and others not? Why are different types of literature (for example, drama, poetry, best sellers) separated from each other? What types of literature *aren't* represented in the bookstore? In short, ask questions that prompt your students to analyze the bookstore as a space of literary marketing and circulation. Ask them to consider how a bookstore shapes the practice of reading.

If you want to expand this exercise, pass out the list of questions you prepared and ask students to visit another bookstore before the next class. They should jot down brief answers to these questions while visiting the second bookstore. Their answers can serve as a basis for in-class discussion. Alternately, you might ask students to visit an online bookseller such as Amazon or Powell's. How does the experience of a brick-and-mortar bookstore compare to that of a digital bookseller? Does one have a more pronounced impact on the reader?

REFLECTIONS

This exercise helps students analyze the impact of public spaces on their experience of literature. It could be easily modified to work in a library, museum, or theater. Introductory-level cultural studies courses frequently conduct similar public space analyses (How is this gym gendered?). These exercises help students uncover cultural coding embedded in seemingly neutral spaces. Literature majors sometimes assume that the work of literary studies is restricted to the classroom and to a continual honing of proper reading practices. They may not reflect on how spaces and markets outside the classroom shape the reading practices they bring to class. This exercise encourages such reflection.

Depending on the focus of the course, you might develop genre-specific questions for your bookstore excursion. Instructors teaching a drama or poetry course might ask, Why is the drama section so small? or Why is the poetry section located beside the philosophy section? An instructor of contemporary literature in translation might ask students which writers from the syllabus are not represented in the bookstore. An instructor of science fiction might ask students to compare the sci-fi section to other fiction sections. Instructors of *any* literature course can ask, Who do you think names these different sections? Do these names imply certain ideas or attitudes about literature?

I first conducted this exercise in a big-box bookstore. My students dispersed in multiple directions, but when it came time for discussion, their first observations were uniform: the bookstore was pushing e-readers in enormous, unavoidable displays. One student was appalled: "Every customer had to walk around the e-reader display to get to the actual books!"

Another student defended e-readers. She had chatted with the salesperson, and this prompted a third student to ask if anyone else had been approached by a salesperson while browsing the aisles (only one or two had). A thoughtful conversation ensued about how the market priorities of booksellers can shape literary experience.

In a science fiction class, my students observed that Kurt Vonnegut is not shelved in the sci-fi section but is instead lumped into the more general "fiction and literature" section. One student speculated that Vonnegut's cheekiness, a mark of postmodern literary ambition, muted his sci-fi roots. The bookstore's categorization, he argued, both reflected and reinforced the perception of Vonnegut as "literary," separate from other sci-fi authors. Meanwhile, several students observed that the featured sci-fi authors were overwhelmingly men, while our syllabus featured numerous women writers. In science fiction, concluded one student, the academic canon and the marketplace were badly out of sync.

This exercise changes dramatically from bookstore to bookstore. A darkly lit, densely shelved used bookstore will yield different observations than a big-box store will. But the questions that students confront remain the same: How and where do we access, encounter, and form ideas about literature? And how do these spaces and modes of access, often without our noticing, instruct us to read literature?

. . . .

Translating Sonnets

Arthur Bahr

A genre-switching exercise that highlights the relationship between literary form and content.

Genre: *poetry*
Course Level: *introductory*
Student Difficulty: *moderate*
Teacher Preparation: *medium*
Class Size: *small to medium*
Semester Time: *early*
Writing Component: *before class*
Close Reading: *medium*
Estimated Time: *35 to 40 minutes*

EXERCISE

Pick a Shakespeare sonnet (or any other fixed-form poem that you're reading; villanelles and sestinas also work well), and, as homework, have students translate it into no more than 125 words of modern English prose. This word count is just slightly longer than the typical sonnet; adjust the word limit if you are using a substantially longer or shorter form. Give your students some version of the following instructions:

> First, read the poem several times, both silently and out loud. Decide what you think it is trying to say, and then write that down in no more than 125 words. (That limit is firm, so use your computer's word-count function!) Now go back to the sonnet and compare it to your translation. What aspects of the sonnet does your translation highlight, and what elements does it minimize or omit altogether? Reconsidering the sonnet in light of your answers to those questions, would you revise any elements of your prose translation? Finally, pick one aspect of the sonnet that you found significant but untranslatable. What makes it so?

Have students write answers to these questions (bullet-point form is fine) and e-mail them to you the day before class, along with their translations. When class convenes, divide students into groups of three or four and have them analyze the translations of another group's students, asking them to think about each prose translation as an interpretation of the poem.

To guide the group discussions, which typically take fifteen minutes or so, give students discussion questions like the following: What commonalities and contrasts between the translations seem most significant? What questions would you ask the translators? Does having multiple prose translations of the same poem shed new or additional light on the poem itself?

When you reconvene as a full class, allow at least twenty minutes for groups to share their answers. If they saw patterns among the translations, invite them to share these revelations. If they have questions for a translator, encourage them to pose them. And if they have deeper understandings of the original poem, take the time to do a final valedictory reading of the poem with these insights in mind. Be sure to reserve the last few minutes of class for a full-group discussion of what students think they've learned from the exercise. Focus on the main question at hand: what exactly changes when the genre changes?

REFLECTIONS

The goal of this genre-switching exercise is to help students see that understanding a poem's propositional content—what this exercise calls "translating"—is an act of interpretation. The lesson is useful in countering the belief, especially common among nonmajors, that summarizing the text is a critic's principal task. This exercise enables you to empathize with that belief ("Yes, understanding a poem is not easy") but also sets you up to push students further. I tell them that deciding what the poem says by translating it into a different genre is an interpretive move that is also a useful first step for close reading–based argumentation.

Another goal of this exercise is to ground students' appreciation of the relationship between form and content, since many students, especially nonmajors, see only the constraints inherent to poetic form, and not the interpretive and aesthetic potentialities that it creates. What is a sonnet (or villanelle or sestina) able to do *because* and not in spite of its form? What poetic flash points seem particularly resistant to paraphrase, and what makes them so? How do such flash points enable both literary appreciation and analytic argumentation?

For this exercise I often use *Astrophil and Stella,* Sonnet 1 ("Loving in truth, and fain in verse my love to show"), since it depicts an author struggling to find an authentic voice in the midst of old literary authorities—a position with which many students can identify as they try to write college-level essays for the first time. Elizabeth Bishop's "Sestina" also works well because its "plot" can be interpreted so variously. Debating these poems' inevitably wide range of translations forces students to attend closely to diction, tone, and syntax, all crucial skills for writing successful essays. Finally, doing this exercise with an overfamiliar Shakespeare poem, like Sonnet 18 ("Shall I compare thee to a summer's day?") or Sonnet 116 ("Let me not to the marriage of true minds"), can help students distinguish between such now-hackneyed sentiments and their artful construction—and so see how the poems became clichés in the first place.

A few more things I've found helpful about this exercise: The word limit forces students to make difficult decisions about what to include and emphasize in their translations, so I use that aspect of the exercise to illustrate the value of making tough choices about one's own prose. This exercise is also valuable as an early measure of students' ability to comprehend figurative language and difficult vocabulary; a translation that completely misunderstands the sonnet might indicate a student who could benefit from extra time in office hours or from an early visit to the academic support services on your campus. Finally, as someone who teaches a lot of scientists and engineers, I've found this exercise responds to many students' desire to understand how things *work*, concretely—how they are put together. I pitch the exercise to them as an opportunity to take apart a sonnet (which is, to most of them, an object just as forbiddingly complex as the interior of a laptop is to me). The tactic of translating one genre into another offers an opportunity to poke around at a text's springs and guts and wiring and to learn from what students find there.

Updating a Classic

Rosemary Gaby

A stage-to-screen adaptation exercise that asks students to modernize an early drama.

Genre: *drama, especially early modern*
Course Level: *any*
Student Difficulty: *moderate*
Teacher Preparation: *medium*
Class Size: *small to medium*
Semester Time: *any*
Writing Component: *in class*
Close Reading: *low*
Estimated Time: *90 minutes, or two 45-minute sessions*

EXERCISE

This genre-switching exercise asks students to imagine themselves as film-makers adapting a much older drama (ideally an early modern play) to the silver screen for contemporary viewers. It can be conducted during one long class period (seminars are perfect) or spread out over two shorter classes.

Begin class by inviting students to think about film adaptations of early modern drama they have already seen (these will be mostly adaptations of Shakespeare's plays, such as *Romeo and Juliet, Much Ado About Nothing*, or *Hamlet*). Ask them to name the adaptations they feel have worked best, and why. Then ask the class for a list of pros and cons for updating the setting of an early modern play in the first place. Record their responses in two columns on the board as you ask them to think in particular about what might be gained, and what might be lost, in the adaptation of these older plays for a contemporary movie audience. Allow ten to fifteen minutes for this opening discussion.

Next, divide the class into small groups and assign each a significant dramatic element from the early modern play they will be adapting to the screen. (The play you choose does not need to have been adapted to film before.) It is important to choose elements that are closely associated with the play's time period and require some imaginative effort to update. For Shakespeare's *Macbeth*, for example, assign such elements as the opening battle, the castles, the witches, Banquo's ghost, Lady Macbeth's sleepwalking scene, and so on. These elements could all be represented in visually striking ways on film. Tell each group to come up with an innovative way of presenting their element in a film with a contemporary setting. Once they've had time to develop their ideas (ten to fifteen minutes is usually sufficient), ask each group to share their concept with the class as a whole, which altogether might take another ten to fifteen minutes.

Now it's time for each group to plan an entire film. Instead of a single element, ask groups to adapt the play under discussion by emphasizing a particular theme prominent in the original. (Students planning a film of *King Lear*, for example, might be asked to focus on parent-child relationships, sibling rivalry, the struggle for power, madness, or social injustice.) Each group's film should have an updated setting and use film genre conventions that seem appropriate for their theme.

Invite the groups to complete two short written tasks to encapsulate their ideas:

1. Prepare a short press release describing the film (this might mention such aspects as casting, locations, soundtrack, target audience).
2. Choose a line from the play that will be used to promote the film on posters and DVD covers.

This part of the exercise requires at least thirty minutes. If the exercise is spread over two shorter classes, students can make some basic decisions about the setting for their film at the end of one class, take those ideas away, and then develop them more fully in the next class.

Once this part of the exercise has been completed, reassemble all the groups and ask each to describe their film concept and read their completed press release and promotional line. Be sure to invite other students to respond. This whole process, which might take twenty to thirty minutes, can unearth some remarkably varied and inventive ideas. After students have discussed each other's ideas for adapting the text, the exercise can conclude with a return to the opening discussion of the pros and cons of updating the text for film, now informed by the students' own experiences.

REFLECTIONS

The primary aim of this exercise is to encourage students to think critically about the process of adaptation and the multiple interpretative possibilities early modern play scripts offer. It provides a timely reminder that the adaptations we watch are necessarily interpretations of the original text, with their own specific aims and agendas. It also asks students to think carefully about the specific textual elements that resonate easily within a modern context and those elements that are more stubbornly tied to the past. The activity of choosing a line from the play to promote their film adaptation sends students back to the text and the demands of its distinctive language. While the press releases may at times be humorously exaggerated, the promo line task encourages a more thoughtful focus on the business of bridging the gap between the period text and the contemporary medium of film.

My students have particularly enjoyed undertaking this exercise while working on *Hamlet*. They have reimagined Elsinore in varied guises, from a luxury hotel to an Australian outback cattle station. They have considered having Polonius stabbed through a shower curtain. And they have envisioned the players' performance as an after-dinner cabaret. For their full-scale adaptations, I ask them to focus on themes such as revenge, madness, romantic love, dysfunctional families, political intrigue, and growing up. Revenge has proven the easiest for students to imagine within film genre conventions, usually in the context of a western or gangster movie. Their promo lines range from the predictable ("Something is rotten in the state of Denmark") to the chilling ("Now could I drink hot blood"). Students usually find the political context of *Hamlet* the most difficult aspect to modernize, but this can produce interesting discussion about the specific political situation that generates the plot and foster a broader conversation around questions of universality and the historicity of the text.

A secondary aim of this exercise is to dispel anxieties about studying early modern drama by giving students a sense of ownership of the text. By the end of the class, students have developed a sense of how their contemporary adaptation might look on screen and can carry those ideas with them when they analyze the play in greater depth. Although this exercise works well with early modern drama, it could also be adapted to work with other canonical texts, especially ones that have been frequently adapted for film or television.

Mixtape Maker

Clark Barwick

A creative final exercise that invites students to synthesize literature, music, and visual art.

Genre: *any*
Course Level: *any*
Student Difficulty: *moderate*
Teacher Preparation: *medium*

Class Size: *small to medium*
Semester Time: *late, last day*
Writing Component: *before class*
Close Reading: *none to low*
Estimated Time: *variable, 1 to 2 hours*

EXERCISE

In lieu of a final paper or final exam, ask students instead to prepare a "mix-tape" compilation. Explain that "Mixtape Maker" is a creative assignment that invites them to thematically connect a selection of literary texts from the period the class is studying with music from the same era.

Tell the students that this project can take a number of different shapes. For example, they might pair poems having musical qualities or references with songs that were actually popular during that period. Or they might begin with a central concept from the course and match songs with liter-ary texts that express that concept thematically. If students are interested in poetry, they might join songs with poems according to certain rhythms or moods. They might even take on the challenge of soundtracking an entire literary text from start to finish. Reassure them that ultimately the governing logic of their mixtape is up to them. The point is for every textual and musi-cal selection to have a reason behind its inclusion and order on the album. Limit their final compilation to no more than ten to twelve songs.

To guide this process, ask students to compose two to four pages (a few sentences per song) of "liner notes" that provide context and explanation for the pairing of each song and text. If you like, you can circulate liner notes from one of your own favorite albums by way of example. To complete their albums, have students select artwork or photography from the period to grace the covers of their mixtapes. Throughout this entire assignment, en-courage students to be as creative as possible with their literary and musical connections. Final compilations can be submitted via compact disc, USB drive, a class website, or even a file-hosting service like Dropbox or Google Docs.

In order for students to have enough time to make these kinds of con-nections, announce the project as early as the second or third week of the course, and consider asking for a working outline from each student around the middle of the term. Then, at the end of the semester, ideally during your last class of the semester or during your scheduled final exam period, ask stu-dents to present their mixtapes to each other. Allow each class member up to five minutes to do the following: first, explain his or her compilation's title, theme, and visual design; second, briefly walk the class through the track list-ing; and third, conclude by setting up one song from the album (with help from a liner note) and then playing this selection. Typically, the sharing of mixtapes can take anywhere from one hour (for a small class) to two hours (for a medium class).

REFLECTIONS

One of the challenges of teaching literature in its historical context is trying to communicate to students exactly how multimodal and cross-pollinating periods of intense artistic production often are. Musicians often influence poets, poets often inspire painters, songs appear in literary works, and artists work across genres. "Mixtape Maker" is an activity designed to push students to reconceptualize a literary work (or set of literary works) in relationship to its broader cultural landscape. This exercise can be adapted for almost any period of literature, and it is also easily adjustable (lending itself to a group exercise as well). Certain literary moments—the Jazz Age, the Beat Movement, the Black Arts Movement—are particularly well suited for this activity.

As a capstone to a semester, this exercise is ideal because it requires students to do everything that a final paper or exam should do—review class material, think seriously and critically about course content, articulate thoughtful written and oral responses to subject matter—all while encouraging students to be as creative as possible. Undergraduates tend to become excited about this project in a way that they rarely would for a traditional paper or exam. For students, the assignment easily accommodates various learning styles, and for instructors, the results never cease to surprise.

I first developed "Mixtape Maker" to enhance my courses on the Harlem Renaissance. Although I have traditionally taught (and continue to teach) this exciting period from a literary angle, I found that my focus on writing de-emphasized the widespread and often exhilarating cross influence among artists of different mediums and perspectives. In my classroom, "Mixtape Maker" now prompts greater discussion of landmark developments by African Americans in music (especially jazz) and in painting, and the exercise also encourages students to draw connections that defy easy cultural and generic categories.

One particularly inventive mixtape, for example, deployed the concept of "Misbehavin'" (a reference to Fats Waller's popular "Ain't Misbehavin'") to match Harlem Renaissance poems with songs that shared themes of perceived nonnormative activity. The album was then illustrated with Hayden Palmer's provocative *Nous Quatre à Paris (We Four in Paris)*, a watercolor that shows four dapper, card-playing men each looking over his shoulder. During her presentation, this student compared how each artist coded (or chose not to code) various transgressions for a mass audience. Another creative student identified climactic cabaret scenes in Nella Larsen's *Quicksand*, Claude McKay's *Home to Harlem*, and Rudolph Fisher's *The Walls of Jericho,* where music was suggested but particular songs were not speci-fied. The student then selected three possible real-life 1920s songs that could have actually played in each setting. During his class presentation, this stu-dent explained how each musical composition would radically change the tone (and potentially our reading) of the particular passage. Ultimately, the possibilities for truly imaginative projects are endless, and the best mixtapes invite us to imagine each chosen cultural product anew.

Although most of my students draw from the literary works, musical com-positions, and visual art that we discuss in class, I urge students not to feel confined by traditional racial, gender, linguistic, and geographic boundaries that usually delineate the period. (This is often a good place to discuss the constructedness of canons and anthologies.) Some of the most provocative mixtapes I have received have paired the work of African American writers with Stravinsky, Gershwin, Picasso, and Lewis Hine. Although I generally require students to focus on the 1920s and 1930s, instructors could conceiv-ably allow students to pair course texts with music from any period. While this would likely change the emphasis of the projects, such an adjustment might also produce much more personal and eclectic compilations.

For those instructors who do not normally teach music in the classroom, I recommend directing students to online resources (such as the Smithso-nian's website) that will allow class members to listen for free to period-specific music. You may also want to set up your own password-protected course website for this purpose. At many colleges and universities, research librarians are happy to help locate music and set up ways for students to ac-cess songs legally.

· ·

Social Media Meets Classic Literature

Megan Lynne Hamilton

A role-play exercise in which students translate a classic literary character's voice into the vernacular of social media.

Genre: *any*
Course Level: *any*
Student Difficulty: *moderate*

Teacher Preparation: *low*
Class Size: *any*
Semester Time: *any*
Writing Component: *in class*
Close Reading: *none to low*
Estimated Time: *45 to 50 minutes*

EXERCISE

Choose a passage or scene from a text you're teaching and ask students, in pairs or small groups, to adapt it into a series of Facebook statuses or a Twitter feed. Depending on the scene you've chosen and your goals for the lesson, you might let each group select its own character, assign the same character to each group, or divide up the key characters throughout the class. This exercise is especially apt for passages that students may have found difficult, since it encourages them both to articulate what has occurred and to inhabit the perspective of a character involved in the action.

For instance, imagine status updates from the gravediggers in act 5 of *Hamlet*; a series of #havingaball *#Pride&Prejudice* tweets from Mr. Darcy, Mr. Bingley, Mr. Collins, Charlotte Lucas, and the Bennet sisters; or the way that a twenty-first-century Robinson Crusoe might have recorded his story 140 characters at a time. Give students about ten to fifteen minutes for this portion of the activity, although the length of time will depend on the difficulty and length of the scene you have chosen.

Once the pairs or groups have completed their adaptations, allow at least thirty minutes for students to share their efforts with the rest of the class. Ask the students to discuss the various ways they chose to adapt the source material: For example, what moments did they choose to emphasize? How did they depict their character's emotions and thoughts? How did they represent a character's voice in the language and style of social media?

Depending on how you've divided up the scene, it may be worth comparing how different groups interpret the same character or how different characters respond to the same moment. Prod the students to imagine further translations of a character's voice into other corners of social media: How would Hamlet's profile have reflected his mood? How would Robinson Crusoe have classified his relationship with Friday on Facebook? What persona would Lydia Bennet have put forward on Twitter? Encourage students to use evidence from the text to support their assertions. (Some might, for instance, cite Lydia's flirtatious exchanges to support the idea that her Twitter feed would have featured a revealing profile photo and lots of winking emoticons.) What happens at the level of language when you translate "literary" diction into the twenty-first-century vernacular of social media?

If you like, conclude the activity by comparing the world of the text with the world of the present on other levels as well. How would these characters and stories have been different if they had occurred in a moment already saturated in social media? Were there equivalent modes of communication available to these characters? Would social media have rendered that world or this story impossible? Why? As my students point out, while it is easy to imagine a flirtatious Lydia Bennet in the world of social media, it is difficult to picture the more reticent Fitzwilliam Darcy operating comfortably there.

REFLECTIONS

This genre-switching activity—inspired by Sarah Schmelling's *Ophelia Joined the Group Maidens Who Don't Float: Classic Lit Signs On to Facebook*—can be an energizing way to open up a conversation about a significant or complex passage. It not only helps students think about character and voice, it also helps them sort out both *what* is happening in a text and also *how* it happens, by focusing on "translating" a text from one expressive form to another. If your course is concerned with a canonical text that has given rise to multiple adaptations, this activity could also dovetail nicely with conversations about what makes works suitable for adaptation and how different moments in time interpret a work differently.

That said, some students—especially those less drawn to creative writing and social media—may feel uncertain at first about what this exercise wants them to do. If you think that may be true of your students, it might be worth bringing in an example from Schmelling's book or creating a short example of your own to help them get on board before they begin to write their adaptations. I have used Schmelling's *Hamlet* newsfeed, which was originally published online by *McSweeney's* and is still available at http://mcsweeneys.net/articles/hamlet-facebook-news-feed-edition.

To use this exercise with John Cheever's short story "The Enormous Radio," I divided my class into groups of three or four and asked each group to write a series of tweets recording Irene's responses as she listened to the radio's broadcasts of the lives of her neighbors. The exercise helped us chart Irene's transition from curiosity to obsession, and writing from Irene's perspective forced students to decide what, exactly, Irene finds so irresistible about eavesdropping. For instance, one group tweeted "Starting the day with a lullaby is better than coffee" #nevertooold, while another tweeted "overheard: no invitations for the introverted" #hellohighschool #adultmeangirls. As we more deeply considered the reasons for Irene's responses, we were forced to ask ourselves whether Irene's desire to listen to the radio comes from a feeling of superiority to her fellow apartment dwellers (as in the second example) or the comfort she gains from a heightened sense of connection to others (as in the first).

Interestingly, students felt it was both but found that they struggled to imagine Irene being able to articulate her desire to feel more deeply connected to others on Twitter or anywhere else. Why was that, I asked? As our conversation continued, students drew parallels between Irene's desire to keep up appearances and the posturing required of social media; that is, we realized neither Irene's fictional context—an upper-middle-class New Yorker at mid-twentieth century—nor the twenty-first-century social media context we had put her in encouraged authentic emotions or expressions of personal vulnerability. Recognizing the limitations of Irene's ability to express herself on social media helped us see the limitations in her world, which in turn became strangely familiar to us in ours.

· ·

To Thine Own Tweet Be True

Heather Alumbaugh

A creative exercise that uses social media to hone students' analytical skills.

Genre: *any*
Course Level: *introductory*
Student Difficulty: *moderate*
Teacher Preparation: *low*
Class Size: *small to medium*
Semester Time: *midterm*
Writing Component: *in class*
Close Reading: *medium*
Estimated Time: *80 to 90 minutes*

EXERCISE

For this genre-switching social media exercise, your classroom will need to have laptop projection capability. The exercise works best at midsemester, since it requires that students already have a good grasp of written and verbal literary analysis, and its length makes it especially suitable for seminars. I have used it to examine the theme of "dissembling" in Shakespeare's *Hamlet*, but it would work equally well with other Shakespeare plays (gender performance in *Twelfth Night*), with character-driven poetry (power in Robert Browning's "My Last Duchess"), or with fiction (self-discovery in Kate Chopin's *The Awakening*).

Divide the class into small groups of three to five students. Give each group a different principal section of the text you are studying. (For a play, give each group an act; for a novel, give each group a chapter; for a narrative poem or dramatic monologue, give each group a roughly equal portion of the text.) You do not have to divide up the entire text for this exercise to work; each group simply needs a representative sample.

Next, identify a specific idea or theme in the text you want all the groups to investigate, and ask each group, laptops at the ready, to perform five tasks. Let the student groups know in advance that they will be responsible for sharing their "translation" with the class and explaining each of the following steps:

1. Isolate a moment in your section of the text that you think is crucial to the development of the specific idea or theme. That moment should be dense in literal and figurative meaning but not too long—keep it to about twenty lines or less.
2. Paraphrase that moment.
3. Briefly and concretely explain why you chose this moment. Why is it so important? What makes it exemplary of the author's conceptual methods? *How* does it communicate what it does? (In other words, what literary techniques does the author use here?)
4. Now, create a Twitter, Instagram, Facebook, Tumblr, or other social media site entry for your selected passage. For this, you need to be able to capture, translate, and communicate the passage's essential meanings in another medium.
5. Explain why you created the "translation" that you did. [I leave this instruction purposefully vague.]

Groups might wish to appoint from among their ranks a "tech" person to do the actual mock-up of their entry, or they might all enjoy giving it a try. If you do not have a media-equipped classroom, you can invite students to use the board for their mock-ups, though it is more effective to have the real thing.

Let the groups spend roughly forty to forty-five minutes preparing their translations and allow another forty to forty-five minutes for groups to present their results. If you want to save time or spread the exercise across two class periods, simply have student groups work collaboratively outside of class to produce their translations (step 4 above). Then have them bring the translations to class on a USB drive or post them on a class website for viewing before the actual class meeting (this latter method opens up the entire class meeting for discussing their interpretations).

Whether you spend one class or two, as each group presents its work, encourage discussion by inviting the other groups to comment and ask questions. As discussion unfolds, coax students to link their statements back to the play, a practice that will deepen the conversation. End by asking the students how their understanding of the idea or theme under investigation has been changed or developed by the acts of social media translation they have collectively engineered.

REFLECTIONS

This exercise is both fun and revelatory, as students discover together the delights of applying their interpretive skills to social media as another mode of critical thinking. I created the exercise admittedly with a bit of trepidation since, unlike my students, I am not a particularly avid user of social media. I assumed that my students would be more comfortable explaining social media than interpreting Shakespeare, but I was pleasantly surprised with what I encountered. Students actually struggled a bit to explain their use of social media but were fairly adept at isolating, paraphrasing, and explaining how a passage in *Hamlet* crucially develops the theme of dissembling. In other words, they were better close readers of Shakespeare's difficult and unruly play than of their own tweets.

As I asked them to "analyze" their own *Hamlet* tweets, Instagrams, or other social media applications, many student groups could only partially explain why they made their interpretive decisions. For instance, one group chose the famous sequence in act 3, scene 3 in which Claudius, thinking he is alone, confesses his murder of King Hamlet and prays for guidance, while Hamlet contemplates killing Claudius as he prays. The students created a tweet in Hamlet's voice of Claudius's confession but then could not explain why they chose to write from Hamlet's perspective. Still, the group's inability to explain this decision allowed us to envision effective alternative translations. One group suggested that the tweet should focus only on Claudius's confession, should be in his voice, and should use key words—like "rank" and "guilt"—that embody his moral ambivalence and greed (or as one student put it, "how messed up Claudius is"). Another student suggested that the tweet could be from the audience and could warn Hamlet that Claudius has just confessed; she suggested that this warning could finally impel Hamlet "to act." The entire exchange revealed that students had developed the ability to interpret the text well enough not only to translate it but also to improve each other's translations.

As we progressed through the exercise, the students' questions to one another and their interpretations of others' translations tended to improve. For instance, in one moment, many students took particular pleasure in analyzing hash tags. In another, a lively debate broke out about whether or not

Hamlet would be a "tweeter" or "subtweeter" because he is so passive. And in yet another, students debated whether or not Facebook was an appropriate platform to communicate adequately all the verbal acrobatics and existential crises the play embodies. Their conclusion: it *is* an appropriate platform, because as one student asserted, everyone "dissembles on Facebook," which makes everyone a bit "like Hamlet."

. . . .

For more exercises that can be used to teach genres, try these:

Reverse Entropy (Discussions)
The Descriptive Word (Essentials)
The Six-Word Story (Stories)
Splicing (Stories)
Dramatic Scansion in Everyday Life (Plays)
Playing with Genre (Plays)
Director's Cut (Plays)
Moving Scenes (Plays)
What is "Literature"? (Canons)
Is This Book Literature? (Canons)
Literature Class Band (Canons)
Build-A-Canon (Canons)
Fill in the Blanks (Words)
Imitate This (Styles)
Making It Graphic (Pictures)
Reading without Reading (Objects)

CANONS

The exercises in this section pull back even further than the ones in "Genres," inviting students to think about literature as literature (what counts?), about the role of authors (how do they matter?), and even about syllabuses (why read *this* instead of *that*?). Many are icebreakers or first-day exercises, designed to get students thinking about some of the assumptions they may have brought to a course on literature in the first place. All the exercises encourage reflection on the larger questions that underlie discussions of literary canons: what belongs, what doesn't, and why?

Do we know a work of literature when we see it? The first two exercises ("What Is 'Literature'?" and "Is This Book Literature?") let students grapple with this question by literally handing them texts to inspect, compare, and debate. The next two exercises ("Putting a Face to a Name" and "Literature Class Band") turn from the matter of the text to the figure of the author. How does one's sense of an author—including his or her age, or gender, or reputation, or race—shape expectations about the status or value of the literary texts that author produces? The last three exercises ("Judge a Book by Its Cover," "The Blank Syllabus," and "Build-A-Canon") use your own course syllabuses to prompt discussions about the ways canons themselves are built and rebuilt, shaped and reshaped, by scholars and readers alike. After trying one or more of these activities, your students will likely never look at a syllabus, an author, or the text in their own hands the same way again.

What Is "Literature"?

Christopher R. Trogan

A first-day exercise that asks one of the most basic questions in a literature class.

Genre: *any*
Course Level: *introductory*
Student Difficulty: *easy*
Teacher Preparation: *medium*
Class Size: *any*
Semester Time: *first day*
Writing Component: *none*
Close Reading: *low*
Estimated Time: *45 to 50 minutes*

EXERCISE

In preparation for the first day of class, assemble a number of different "texts" from a range of printed media. Include traditional literary examples (select passages from novels, plays, or poetry, each on its own sheet of paper; try to include excerpts from both canonical and noncanonical texts), as well as nontraditional items, such as an advertisement, an informational brochure, a train schedule, a musical score, or a photograph. If you wish, the traditional examples may be from your own syllabus, but they do not need to be.

In class, put your students into small groups and distribute one example to each group. If you have a small class, you can give each group more than one example. Ask each group to decide whether its item is a work of literature, and why. While all students must contribute to the discussion, one student in each group must take notes and another student must report to the class. Announce a set amount of time (ten to fifteen minutes is usually sufficient) to arrive at a response and a rationale.

Once the groups are ready, reconvene the class and collect the examples. Project each example in the front of the room as the student reporter offers the group's position, analysis, and defense. If you don't have an overhead projector or screen, you can ask each group to hold up the example or pass it around the room. For each example, establish a dialogue between yourself, the group, and the rest of the class: What criteria did the group use to determine whether its example is a work of literature? Does the rest of the class agree with these criteria and with the group's position?

After you have moved through each of the examples (you can consider timing them: a few minutes each), extrapolate to larger questions: Are the criteria used to define "literature" static or fluid? If the former, who defines these criteria, and what are they? If the latter, can't anything potentially count as "literature"? Where, and how, do you draw the lines? What are the implications of all this for someone taking a "literature" course?

REFLECTIONS

This exercise works very well on the first day of class. Students do not expect to be confronted with such a question—one they often assume is predefined but quickly discover is much more open and complicated. However, the nature of the exercise allows them to explore the topic lightheartedly and build a sense of teamwork. They quickly get to know each other's personalities by the way each student responds to the question (aesthetically "conservative" students are likely to argue against the photograph or train schedule as literature, while more aesthetically "liberal" students are likely to argue for it), so it also works well as an icebreaker exercise. Indeed, I always include a photograph—in which I am pictured—as one of the examples. During group discussion, I choose this example last and use it to move into an informal introduction of myself to the class. They realize that their professor is a person, too!

"What is 'Literature'?" is particularly suited to introductory classes, and works with syllabuses that include primarily canonical texts, noncanonical texts, or a mixture of both. Including excerpts from both canonical and noncanonical texts in the examples you give out can help students think about gradations of "literary" status even among the works they decide count as "literature." I typically begin the exercise by stating, "This is a literature class, but what is 'literature'?" This helps students realize that unlike the definitions of many other disciplines (psychology, accounting, medicine, law), the very definition and discipline of "literature" is up for discussion. This recognition is eye-opening and empowering: students understand that they have the power to question the status and value of everything they will read during the semester and that this questioning is crucial to any literature course. In short, it prepares and excites them for the challenges to come.

For example, in one class I distributed a musical score of Beethoven's Fifth Symphony, a Nike sneaker advertisement, Wordsworth's "Lines Composed a Few Miles above Tintern Abbey," Jamaica Kincaid's "Girl," the first paragraph of Kafka's "The Metamorphosis," a comic book, a train schedule, and a photograph taken at my recent family reunion. I asked each group to argue whether their example was "literature," based on specific criteria that they were to develop. The arguments that the groups offered were based on interesting criteria: whether the example contained "language," whether it was "fictional" but also expressed something "true," and whether there was something "aesthetic" or "artistic" about it. One group even noted that their example was a work of literature because it was "intertextual." These arguments also led naturally to discussions of what these terms mean.

I found that the line between "literature" and "not literature" was most difficult to draw when the example involved something informational or utilitarian or when the example contained no words (for example, the visual or musical examples). In this particular experiment, the students ultimately deemed all the texts "literature" except for the family reunion photograph and the train schedule. What was most important, of course, was the process, which left students with an appreciation not only for the immense difficulty of defining what literature is but also for the valuable questions about truth, fiction, and art that such an endeavor provides.

. . . .

Is This Book Literature?

Lydia G. Fash

A hands-on exercise that encourages students to consider the label "literature."

Genre: *fiction*
Course Level: *any*
Student Difficulty: *easy*
Teacher Preparation: *medium*
Class Size: *any*
Semester Time: *early or late*
Writing Component: *none*
Close Reading: *low*
Estimated Time: *variable, 20 to 45 minutes*

EXERCISE

This exercise invites students to think about how their reactions to an unfamiliar text are often framed, if not predicted, by cultural assumptions about what constitutes "literature." "Is This Book Literature?" works best in classes that include at least one noncanonical text or a text from a stereotypically "lesser" literary genre (such as domestic or sentimental fiction). Classes with book lists that include a range of different book types—from, say, mass-market or trade paperbacks to Norton Critical Editions—are also good candidates for this exercise, which can be done with one text or several.

From the syllabus, select a book that most students likely do not know well and would not immediately characterize as "high" literature—again, a noncanonical text or "minor" text will work best—and tell them to bring their copy to class. Divide the students into small groups and ask them to examine the physical artifact before them. What do they notice about this book? Is there a preface? What are the margins like? What is the font like? What does the cover look like? Who published the book? Is there a bibliography, footnotes, or endnotes? Does it contain images? Ask each group to draw conclusions about the book's value and status from these observations. How much do they think the book costs? Is it "scholarly"? Is it "literature"? If so, is it part of the "literary canon"? Why or why not? How do they know?

After five or ten minutes, reconvene as a whole and ask the groups to share their conclusions. A few additional questions may help deepen the conversation: Is the text necessarily "literature" because it has been assigned? Can students actually judge the book before they have read it? Is the idea of "literature" internal (determined by "literary" language) or external to the book (determined by a publisher who calls something a "classic")? What was the publisher's motivation in designing the physical codex that is in front of the students? Who does the publisher think will be reading the text? In other words, is there a presumed consumer (and is that consumer identified with a particular class, race, gender, religion, and/or nationality?)? Do all the students agree on the book's status? Is it "literature," in other words, or something else?

Once the class has reached a consensus about these matters, or agreed to disagree, you might move into a discussion of the role that social and critical forces (book reviews, literary prizes, literature classes, and so forth), rather than purely aesthetic ones, play in labeling a book as "literature." Clarify with students what role the term "literature" and the idea of literary worth will play in your class. (Terry Eagleton's "What is Literature?" in *Literary Theory: An Introduction* can be a useful resource here.) You might also examine the process of canonization itself, particularly if the book you have chosen hails from a "lesser" genre but can now be considered part of the canon. Texts like Catharine Maria Sedgwick's *Hope Leslie*, Harriet Wilson's *Our Nig*, and Harriet Beecher Stowe's *Uncle Tom's Cabin*, for example, come to mind. The full exercise, which usually takes forty-five minutes or so, can also be conducted in as little as twenty minutes, simply by reducing the number of texts or questions you try to tackle.

REFLECTIONS

Using the physical artifact of the book as an entrée, this exercise encourages students to consider how literary worth is created and communicated and how related cultural assumptions affect our readerly perceptions. "Is This Book Literature?" works particularly well at the start of the semester, but it can also be successful later in the term, especially if students have begun to let cultural judgments about a text's worth impact their readings, or if you would like a way to introduce a text less common in the classroom or less familiar to students.

This exercise can also set up a productive discussion of how canons and values can shift: Stowe's book, after all, though long dismissed by critics, sold more copies in the nineteenth century than any other American novel. Alternately, the assignment might offer a means to consider contemporary value-making structures like literary prizes and book clubs. For example, while the logo of Oprah's Book Club and the corresponding questions at the end of the book might help a text sell in the mass market, it probably does not make students feel the book is "literature."

In my own class, a first-year seminar, I have asked students to do this exercise at the beginning of the term with a Dover Thrift Edition of Sarah Orne Jewett's *The Country of the Pointed Firs*. The thin book, which has small margins, rough yellow paper, and a very brief introductory note, did not scream "literature." Still, the students quickly noticed that the back of the Dover Thrift Edition labeled *Country of the Pointed Firs* both a "classic" and a "fictional masterpiece." Since the text on the physical book claimed literary importance and yet students had never heard of Jewett, discussion turned to the definition of "literature." At first, students contended that "literature" was something that both had stood the test of time and was defined by literary language. (Students guessed that our book, originally published in 1896, fit both requirements.) During subsequent conversation, however, we challenged these initial conclusions: couldn't something written yesterday be "literature," and isn't it possible to have "literature" celebrated (as in the case of Hemingway, for example) for its straightforward language?

Students also wanted to rely on the pronoun "we," an imaginary group that finds a book "good" because, the students said, "we" can "relate to" it. When pressed, one student realized that her "we" was, most precisely, a particular type of person fortunate enough to be attending a small liberal arts college. The idea that the assumed reader—or book purchaser—belongs to a specific race, class, or gender helped us to think about how and why the traditional canon of nineteenth-century U.S. authors is dominated by middle- or upper-class white men. Though Willa Cather, as the back of our Dover Thrift Edition says, fully expected Jewett to achieve permanent recognition, Jewett owes the increased attention she currently receives to feminist efforts to expand the canon. After our fruitful discussion, students left the class both interested in reading Jewett and more aware of the social and critical forces that label a work "literature."

For a variation on this exercise, instead of asking students to bring in a single book, bring all the books on your syllabus to class and distribute one to each group. For their individual text, let each group decide the answer to the question, Is this book "literature"? Then let groups make a case to the class for or against their volume. Or consider combining this exercise with another in this section, "Judge a Book by Its Cover," which focuses specifically on book jackets. Or follow up with "How to Read a Bookstore" (in the "Genres" section), which invites students to investigate how the book is marketed online or in bookstores. Books labeled "classics" have a different feel from those labeled "best sellers" in either venue. The purpose of "Is This Book Literature?" is to ask why this is so and to debate, as professional literary critics often do, whether or how the distinction is meaningful.

. . . .

Putting a Face to a Name

Elizabeth Leane

An icebreaker that encourages reflection on the figure of the author.

Genre: *any*
Course Level: *introductory*
Student Difficulty: *easy*
Teacher Preparation: *medium*
Class Size: *small to medium*
Semester Time: *first day*
Writing Component: *none*
Close Reading: *none*
Estimated Time: *variable, 20 to 40 minutes*

EXERCISE

Find online images—artworks or photographs—of well-known writers. These may be writers whose work is to be studied in class; who are identified with the period, nation, or movement being studied; or simply whose names students will likely recognize. The number of images should be half the number of students in the class. Print out the images, ideally in color, without any identifying labels. On separate pieces of paper, print out in large type the names of the authors. Depending on what is being studied in your class, you might want to include authors whose images are likely to provoke discussion for several different reasons: because they are particularly iconic (Shakespeare); because they question assumptions students make about identity based on names (George Eliot); because the image reveals well-known contextual associations (a group portrait of the Brontë sisters); because the work of the author in question was or is particularly closely tied to his or her visual image (Byron or Oscar Wilde); or, conversely, because the author is famously private or reclusive (Emily Dickinson, Thomas Pynchon, or J. D. Salinger).

On the first day of class, distribute images and names randomly. Ask the students to find the person holding the name they think belongs to their author's image, or vice versa, and to introduce themselves. If you have an odd number of students, you can either make this a feature (for example, the label "Percy and Mary Shelley" could be matched up with separate images of the authors) or simply hold an image or name yourself and wait to be approached. Ask each pair to spend a few moments discussing with each other why they think they are the right match of author and image. It should take no more than ten minutes to complete this matchmaking portion of the exercise.

Then ask each pair to introduce one another to the class and, together, to explain why they think the name and image match. When all pairs are done, identify any mismatches and ask the class as a whole to suggest solutions. The class can then discuss what they have learned in the process, particularly through the mismatches. Why were some images easy to connect with names and others not? What factors did students use in making their identification? All told, this exercise can take as little as twenty minutes or as long as forty minutes, depending on class size.

REFLECTIONS

This exercise works best for classes focusing on canonical literature. It is intended as an icebreaker activity on the first day of the semester and is most suitable for classes that cover not just the literary text but the literary author as well.

As an icebreaker, the exercise is effective because the students usually require several encounters before they find their matching image or name. The pairs themselves have a sense of joint achievement (if correct) or joint merriment (if wildly incorrect). In this sense, it is vital that you create a relaxed, lighthearted atmosphere in which mistakes are expected and do not reflect negatively on the students. I have found that a good way to do this is to confess to a mistaken assumption I have made in the past about an author based only on his or her name—the more embarrassing, the better.

"Putting a Face to a Name" requires that students reflect on the construction of authorial identity and the role of celebrity in literary culture. In thinking about the factors that led to their pairing, students usually point to clues such as their own cultural capital (they will probably recognize images of Shakespeare); automatic connections they make between the author's person (gender, dress, pose), their name, and their work (a seemingly demure mobcapped Jane Austen); or historical context, including the medium (photograph or painting, the style of a period).

By carefully selecting images, the instructor can nudge the class toward a particular issue. A good example comes from a recent class in an introductory literature unit that I regularly teach as part of a team. One of the images provided was Cecil Beaton's 1956 photograph of T. S. Eliot, in which three slightly different exposures are superimposed. The students did not automatically identify Eliot, but once the match between image and name had been made, they were intrigued by what the multiple exposures might signify. Those who had already read the assigned text, "The Love Song of J. Alfred Prufrock," tentatively pointed to the sense of an incoherent, fragmented self the poem evokes, which piqued the other students' interest. This led to discussion of the use of poetic personae and the extent to which a poetic voice can be identified with the author. The students also raised the question of age, pointing out that in the photograph provided, Eliot is an elderly man, although some of his best-known poems, including "Prufrock," were written when he was in his twenties and thirties.

This exercise, then, can stimulate discussion of how particular authorial images come to be circulated and perpetuated and how such portraits relate to the reception of an author's work. You can ask questions that encourage students to go beyond face value in their understanding of literary celebrity: for example, whether reclusiveness is a refusal to create an authorial image or merely another means of doing so. For classes focusing on a particular period, movement, or national context, you can lead discussion toward the assumptions students bring to the class, how they have been formed, and how they might be questioned. Depending on the level at which the class is working and the time available, you may like to introduce the notions of the "intentional fallacy" and the "death of the author" and to explain why they do not make the figure of the author redundant in analysis of literary texts and cultures. You could distinguish between the author as the assumed source of meaning in a text and the author as an important paratextual and epitextual consideration (while avoiding these technical terms). In my experience, the conflation of these things is a common source of confusion for beginning students.

Because this is an icebreaker at an introductory level, however, you should not try too hard to direct the class toward a particular end. The exercise should be generative of questions rather than answers and above all should be fun, allowing students to relax and shed inhibitions about the texts and authors they will encounter in their studies.

. . . .

Literature Class Band

Claire Cothren

A first-day exercise that encourages students to think critically about literary canonization.

Genre: *any*
Course Level: *introductory*
Student Difficulty: *easy*
Teacher Preparation: *medium*
Class Size: *any*
Semester Time: *first day*
Writing Component: *none*
Close Reading: *none*
Estimated Time: *45 minutes*

EXERCISE

On the first day of class, show students the iconic cover art for the Beatles' album *Sgt. Pepper's Lonely Hearts Club Band*, which pictures the band members in front of a collage of more than fifty other artists, actors, athletes, philosophers, celebrities, and various historical figures. (Copies of the album sleeve can be found in many places online, including the Beatles' official website, http://thebeatles.com.)

Explain that the collage features images of individuals the band members liked and admired—figures they would enjoy having in attendance at one of their concerts. After identifying a few of these individuals and commenting briefly on their various credentials, ask the students to imagine that they have the opportunity to create a "literature class band." They should consider whose work they would most like to study in a literature class and then select a dozen or more of these figures for inclusion on a class "album cover."

Allow students five to ten minutes to discuss their ideas in small groups. Encourage them to share their favorite authors or works, and then reconvene the groups to solicit nominations. (For a class size that is medium or large, consider asking groups to agree on just one author to nominate, with backup candidates at the ready if another group chooses the same author.) If the classroom is equipped with an instructor's computer and access to the Internet, you can easily create, on the spot, a makeshift album cover by copying and pasting to a Word document images of the authors whom students identify. (Alternatively, you can ask a tech-savvy student or two to do the job.) If the classroom is not equipped in this way, you or the students can simply list the authors on the board.

After displaying the names (and, if possible, images) of at least a dozen literary figures, ask students to talk about the "album" they've created. Questions to consider: Are these figures ones you are likely to encounter in a traditional literature classroom? Why (or why not)? Do they represent "true" literature? "Great" literature? Who gets to decide? Also: What do these figures have in common (nationality, gender, genre, race, time period)? After a closer look, do any figures seem to be missing or underrepresented? Why might their omission be considered problematic? Do literary figures have to be poets, playwrights, or novelists, or can they include other kinds of writers? This entire exercise takes roughly forty-five minutes, though you can adjust the timing by limiting or expanding the number of authors included on your album cover.

REFLECTIONS

"Literature Class Band" is a fun first-day activity that allows students to get to know each other by discussing their favorite literary figures. While many enjoy discovering that they share an interest in certain authors, they find even more compelling the ensuing class discussion about how to define literature.

Sgt. Pepper is a useful starting point for this discussion because once students observe the relative diversity of the figures on the Beatles' album (Bob Dylan, Shirley Temple, Sonny Liston, James Joyce), they also tend to think about their literary preferences in more inclusive terms. From there, students can begin to consider questions of literary canonization—whether, for example, the work of young adult fiction writers, rappers, or graphic novelists is (or should be) studied alongside the work of novelists, playwrights, and poets. The visual component of the exercise is particularly important because it helps students identify canonical trends or aporias (like the predominance of men), not only on the *Sgt. Pepper* cover but also (often) in their own nominees, as well as in the literary canons from which many class syllabuses typically draw.

When I used this exercise in an introduction to literature course, students were quick to nominate "classic" Western novelists and playwrights for their band, including Shakespeare, Fitzgerald, Hawthorne, Poe, Hemingway, Faulkner, Steinbeck, Dickens, and Austen. They also offered up a few of their favorite contemporary authors—J. K. Rowling, Stephenie Meyer, and Suzanne Collins. However, it was with some hesitation that they ventured to list "alternative" choices such as speechwriters (Martin Luther King Jr.), lyricists (Kanye West), or screenwriters (Quentin Tarantino). A discussion of why the class felt more reluctant to name some band members than others not only helped students to reach conclusions about which texts are already widely canonized in the West but also encouraged them to think critically about trends in genre, style, and periodization. In examining the "album cover" that we created, students further noted the overwhelming representation of white British and American men. We were then able to discuss what factors contributed to this canonical trend as well as the need and potential for change.

Although I have had great success with this exercise in general literature surveys, it could also work well in genre courses (classes devoted to the gothic, science fiction, mystery, detective fiction, or romance) and in contemporary fiction survey courses, where canons have yet to solidify.

· ·

Judge a Book by Its Cover

J. Michelle Coghlan

A first-day exercise that encourages students to consider the visual cues of literary canons.

Genre: *fiction*
Course Level: *any*
Student Difficulty: *easy*
Teacher Preparation: *medium*
Class Size: *any*
Semester Time: *first day*
Writing Component: *none*
Close Reading: *none to low*
Estimated Time: *35 to 40 minutes*

EXERCISE

Choose two or three books (they may be popular or canonical) and cart into class as many different editions of them as you can. (A suitcase to carry them all makes a nice stage prop.) Any book with a range of covers will do, though books with long, diverse, or controversial publication histories work best: James Fenimore Cooper's *The Last of the Mohicans*, Herman Melville's *Moby-Dick*, or Vladimir Nabokov's *Lolita*. Should it prove useful to you, many books have critical works dedicated to their publication history (for example, Cathy Davidson's "The Life and Times of *Charlotte Temple*: The Biography of a Book" examines dozens of editions of Susanna Rowson's best-selling seduction novel). The exercise itself, however, does not require such scholarly apparatus; it can be conducted simply by relying on available editions in your library.

Divide the class into small groups, distribute different editions of each book to each group, and ask the students to do what they have always been told not to do: judge a book by its cover. If you are not able to bring physical copies of the different editions themselves, you can instead bring photocopies of the individual covers, whose images can usually be found online. Color copies work best, especially for paperback editions. Place one cover on each page and then distribute to the different groups.

After you distribute the books, provide students with a list of guiding questions: What kind of image, typeface, or layout has the publisher chosen for each cover? What does the cover seem to say about the kind of story this book tells? Does the edition dive right into the tale or does it include a scholarly introduction or preface? Taken as a whole, what kind of audience does this book seem designed for, and how do you know? If you have brought physical copies of the books, encourage students to look at the back covers and tables of contents too. This group portion of the exercise takes roughly fifteen minutes.

Next, reconvene the class as a whole and allow another fifteen to twenty minutes for groups to share their findings. What was the most interesting thing they discovered? What surprised them the most? Which of the editions scream "canon" and which keep readers guessing? Be sure to leave yourself enough time at the end to make a few salient general comments—about books, readers, canons, and commerce.

REFLECTIONS

I like to do this exercise on the first day of the semester, introducing as many books on the syllabus as possible. Not only is it a nice icebreaker for students to get to know each other, but it also gets them excited about all the texts they will soon be reading. The purpose of the exercise is to encourage students to consider the ways that literary texts change over time, shaped by forces of reception and canonization. The history of book covers can reveal much about shifting literary contexts. Trends in scholarship or the marketplace can even give old texts new life.

When I tried this exercise in a course on American best sellers, students quickly observed that Raymond Chandler's 1940 hard-boiled detective novel *Farewell, My Lovely* takes on a different aura when we encounter the Vintage reprint edition emblazoned with a single white manicured hand with red polished nails, and wrapped in the signature pink and purple shades of chick lit. Others marveled at the unexpected disparity between an image of a languid hunter perched atop a tree in the highbrow 1914 clothbound edition of Edgar Rice Burroughs's *Tarzan* and the big-haired beefcake swinging from vines above a beleaguered (and barely dressed) damsel in distress from the late 1980s Ballantine version they had been assigned. Still others dissected the scholarly apparatus included in the Penguin edition of Louisa May Alcott's *Little Women*, an element they noted had been conspicuously absent from the other paperbacks on our syllabus.

There were many questions generated during our discussion: Can such wildly different-looking texts even be called the same book? Could the stature or "street cred" of *any* given text be diminished or reinforced by the way it is packaged for its imagined readers? Does every book cover ultimately work to calibrate the demands or expectations we might have of the book inside it, whether we realize it or not? These queries set the stage for the way that we later encountered (and reconsidered) every other best seller on our syllabus. But the most tangible takeaway of this exercise was that our course was grounded from the outset in my students' newfound insight that book covers might color the way we approach a given text and that those cultural cues have changed over the life of a novel. In other words, this exercise did not just open new avenues for approaching familiar texts: it also shed light on the wider cultural context that had shaped each book's ever-shifting material form. It turns out that sometimes you really can judge a book by its cover.

. . . .

The Blank Syllabus

Chris Walsh

A do-it-yourself exercise that invites students to complete your syllabus by selecting some of the course readings.

Genre: *any*
Course Level: *any*
Student Difficulty: *moderate*
Teacher Preparation: *medium*

Class Size: *small to medium*
Semester Time: *early*
Writing Component: *before class*
Close Reading: *none*
Estimated Time: *30 to 45 minutes*

EXERCISE

Begin by circulating an incomplete copy of your course syllabus to the class. I call it "the blank syllabus," but of course it is not entirely so. Certain things have to be on there: contact information, office hours, a course description, and many of the course readings. What is left blank are the assigned readings for some of the class sessions, like so:

October 25

_____ & _____

October 27

_____ & _____

Tell students that, for their first assignment of the course, they are invited to fill in these blanks with texts not already assigned from the course anthology. (Having a course anthology greatly simplifies the selection process, but it is not in fact essential. You can also have students simply go online and do a little sleuthing.) Send them away with the following instruction:

> With your course anthology in hand, choose a reading not already on the syllabus and prepare a short presentation (no more than two minutes) that advocates for including your selection as required reading for the class. What made you choose this piece? What does it teach us about the author, about history, about life?

In a small class, sometimes every student's selection can be added to the syllabus; in that case, you might also have each student write a short paper (roughly two pages) that explains the reason for adding his or her chosen text. Invite students to make presentations based on these papers when their readings come up on the schedule.

For a medium-sized class, assign students to work outside class in small groups. Ask them first to decide which text to advocate for and then to prepare a brief presentation to persuade their classmates to vote for their selection. More detailed instructions for the group version of this exercise can be helpful. Here is a sample presentation prompt from an American literature survey course:

> In our next class meeting, your group will have eight minutes to advocate for a selection of your own choosing (one *not* already listed on the syllabus) from the *Norton Anthology of American Literature*, volume B. Your

presentation should both entertain and persuade. Recite a favorite quotation or two, or act out a scene. Strive to pique our curiosity. Why should we read this piece? What genre is it? Who wrote it and why? What is its historical context? How does the piece connect to themes discussed in class or in the *Norton* editors' introduction? What makes the piece enjoyable and enlightening? You don't have to answer all of these questions, but your presentation should tell us about both the substance and style of the selection and about why you think it's worth our time.

When class reconvenes, let each group present its nominee in turn. Write these nominations on the board but intervene as little as possible, reserving judgment and letting the students take the lead. Keep careful track of time so that each group has the opportunity to make its case—and, ideally, to answer questions from the other groups. Then take a vote, by hand or by ballot, to declare the winning nominations. Be prepared for more than one round of voting, as well as for more conversation between rounds. Actual classroom presentation and discussion time for this exercise generally take between thirty and forty-five minutes, depending on the size of the class and the intensity of the debate.

Follow up as soon as you can by circulating the now-completed syllabus. If possible, include students' names next to their selections, to give them both full credit and a heads-up since they will help initiate the discussion of the text that day. ("Tess and Calla, remind us why you thought it would be a good idea to read 'Rip Van Winkle.'") A revised schedule might look something like this:

October 25

Irving, "Rip Van Winkle" (B: 29–41; Tess and Calla)
Bryant, "Thanatopsis" (B: 123–124; Jenn and Oscar)

October 27

Poe, "The Raven" (B: 637–640; CeCe and Malcolm)
Poe, "The Cask of Amontillado" (B: 714–719; Evan and Lee)

REFLECTIONS

The blanks on the syllabus at first shock students. Isn't it the *teacher's* job to tell them what to read? But they quickly get into the spirit of the exercise. Looking for a selection, they read independently and actively, browsing possible texts in a way they never would if the teacher had chosen all the readings. Making the case that the whole class should read their selection, they connect with their peers not just socially but intellectually, reporting enthusiastically about what they have found. Reading their selections as a class and knowing that they have shaped the course in significant ways, they engage in discussions with each other and with their teacher with an increased sense of responsibility for their own education.

This exercise does present some challenges. Teachers typically lament not being able to choose *more* readings for their classes, and the blank syllabus means choosing *fewer*. What about "coverage"? And what if students choose badly—only the short or easy or familiar stuff—or material that you know nothing about or that strikes you as unteachable? While the exercise may lead to some healthy questioning of these concerns (What *about* coverage? Who knew that poem was so good?), they are legitimate. Addressing them becomes easier when you remember the various kinds of trust that the exercise both requires and fosters: in your students' willingness and ability to take on their responsibility; in your own skills as an able guide who knows the lay of the land, if not every nook and cranny of it; in literature's power to connect to students before a teacher's intervention (ideally the teacher's intervention deepens the connections). Using a course anthology also means you trust its editors to have excluded clunkers.

I have used this approach in classes without anthologies, though. A few years ago, in the third week of a seminar on the contemporary American novel, for example, students made short presentations for their candidate novels, and we voted to read one (*Everything Is Illuminated* by Jonathan Safran Foer) for the final class meeting. The students loved it. My only regret is that I didn't leave room for another student-selected novel or two.

How many readings to have the students select is of course up to you. You might start on a smaller scale, reserving just one week for students to design. The more I do this activity, the more blanks I leave. In my experience, the blank syllabus has been the difference between teaching a survey and leading an expedition, between reading a map and actually exploring the territory.

· ·

Build-A-Canon

Adrienne Brown

A review exercise that asks students to think like literary historians.

Genre: *any*
Course Level: *any*
Student Difficulty: *moderate*
Teacher Preparation: *low to medium*

Class Size: *small to medium*
Semester Time: *midterm, last day, exam review*
Writing Component: *in class*
Close Reading: *none to low*
Estimated Time: *45 to 50 minutes*

EXERCISE

Start class with a brief (five-to-ten-minute) group conversation about the concept of the canon. Did your students have any "canon wars" in their respective high schools? Use their own experience as a jumping-off point for defining on the board the concept of the canon and its stakes. What are the different ways they might use the word *canon* today? Since this exercise works best at key review moments—either at midterm, on the last day, or for an exam review—you might also remind the class of the different stylistic canons they have already moved through (or ask them to identity those canons themselves). If your class hasn't explicitly discussed the concept of a canon before, you can simply offer a few examples of some of the ways critics have grouped literature into discrete canons in the past (early modern, Romantic, Victorian, and so on).

Next, divide the class into small groups of three to five students each. Ask the groups to take their reading for that day's class, pair it with a text from earlier on the syllabus, and discuss the utility of thinking of these two texts as together forming part of a canon. (If you are looking for more coverage, you can assign each group a different text for comparison.) Give each group a list of characteristics they might use to justify their pairing of texts as a canon. Prepare this list the night before, and include ten to twelve different elements that their texts might have in common, which could range from the broadly defined (form of narration, temporality, setting, genre) to more specific themes previously discussed in class. Some of the elements I have included, for example, are character agency, humor, inscrutability, economy and the circulation of objects, the place of the individual, the relationship between generations, the role of the Other, faith, the place of history, the local versus the global, and the construction of social categories like race, gender, class, and sexuality.

Direct the groups not only to identify the common characteristics their chosen texts share—tell them to focus on three to five—but also to discuss the kinds of broader knowledge they can glean from treating their texts as part of a canon. What thematic claims, for example, can they make about their canon based on these two texts? In what ways might the two texts *fail* to make sense as a larger group? Finally, have students come up with a name for their particular canon.

After roughly fifteen minutes, give each group at least four to five minutes to present its findings to the class and to entertain comments. Encourage the other groups to ask questions, posing a few yourself, if necessary, to model this engagement. You might ask whether a canon would have held together had the group focused on different elements. Or ask the class after each presentation to pick one additional element from the list to think about together, and see if the class's findings complement or complicate the group's decision about whether the texts form a canon. Conclude the conversation by asking the class whether constructing a canon strikes them as a useful idea or an antiquated one, and why.

REFLECTIONS

In addition to working well as a midterm review or an end-of-semester wrap-up exercise, "Build-A-Canon" is handy for helping students approach a particularly challenging text, since it allows them to produce knowledge about that text obliquely. Since the exercise begins with the basic elements of a compare/contrast assignment, students of all levels can say a lot right off the bat. This exercise also gives students practice in moving from the nitty-gritty work of close reading to the production of larger stakes and claims in a short amount of time, making this exercise particularly useful to do around the time a paper is due.

The pedagogical aim behind this exercise is to empower students to inhabit the position of the literary historian by making active choices about the shape and dissemination of knowledge. Students can have a tendency to think about previous claims for and groupings of literature as untouchable pronouncements handed down from on high. Having students enact the labor behind the production of such assertions can make the work of analyzing literature more approachable while also making students more comfortable questioning previous critical paradigms.

I first used this exercise while teaching a discussion section on contemporary fiction, itself an indeterminate field that could mark either an emerging literary period or a distinct thematic canon. In our wrap-up discussion, students imagined the possible futures for the status of contemporary fiction as a canon and how the last thirty years of literature may be taught once it is no longer "contemporary." Some students were a little bashful about coming up with a name for their canon, but the groups that did really sold it.

Students were also quite interested to talk about their own experiences of the canon. Many recalled books being banned or causing controversy in their own high schools. Twain's *Adventures of Huckleberry Finn* frequently recurs in students' accounts, allowing us to talk about the multiple valences of the term "canon" as it references both value-based gatekeeping and period-specific coherence. I ask them what the canon of American literature would look like both with and without *Huck Finn*—most students are familiar enough with the book to hazard generative answers. Engaging their personal experience can help students understand how decisions about what we read shapes how we read. In the end, the exercise encouraged them to stop thinking about themselves as passive consumers of texts (and lectures!) and to imagine themselves as stewards of texts.

I also recently adapted this exercise for a class on suburban literature, in which I asked students to reproduce another disciplinary apparatus of the field: the anthology. Groups were charged with curating a chapter of an anthology on suburban literature around a theme of their choosing. They picked the readings they would include, a mix of selections from the syllabus and outside texts, and came up with a representative illustration and a pitch to the class as to why their chapter was necessary to the anthology. The invented chapters were excellent—including "A Woman's Place Is in the Home: Suburban Constructions of Motherhood," "Sex and the Suburbs," "Anthologizing Changing Suburban Marginality," and "Stories of the Self: The Poetry of the Suburbs"—and incorporated a broad range of materials, from the poems of Gwendolyn Brooks and Anne Sexton, to songs by Arcade Fire and Ben Folds, to films and television shows with suburban themes, such as *The Graduate* and *The Cosby Show*. For each item, the students also provided brief annotations explaining why their chosen materials should go into the anthology and what role they play in telling us something about suburban representations as a genre and the suburbs as a place.

I've also done this as a final assignment, asking students to write an introduction for their anthology as well as headnotes situating each work within the edition's larger aims. A good model for writing the headnotes is the *Norton Anthology*, though I recommend setting a word limit (no more than four hundred words) on these headnotes to keep things manageable. This capstone writing exercise is not easy, but it is a nice break from the more standard forms of essay writing to which the students are accustomed.

• •

For more exercises that can be used to teach canons, try these:

How to Read a Bookstore (Genres)
Updating a Classic (Genres)
Mixtape Maker (Genres)
Social Media Meets Classic Literature (Genres)
Reading without Reading (Objects)
Making Manuscripts (Objects)

WORDS

Of all the words at a writer's disposal, why did an author choose this word? Often literature's smallest part can offer students the biggest key for unlocking and inhabiting a text. The exercises in this section focus on the importance of words as the fundamental building blocks of literature. Emphasizing diction and grammar, denotation and connotation, repetition and singularity, these classroom lessons ask students to pause and take stock of individual words in all their nuance and complexity.

Dictionaries play a starring role in this section. The first three exercises ("Keywords," "Vocabulary Bites," and "Le Mot Juste") all incorporate the usage of a dictionary or thesaurus as tools for understanding both the histories and the afterlives of words. The next three exercises ("Word Clouds," "Aphorisms," and "Fill in the Blanks") further bring out the *diction* in *dictionary*, sharpening students' awareness of the look, sound, and significance of words. The final word exercise ("The Fascination of What's Difficult") reminds students that every word constitutes a specific grammatical part that contours and textures a larger linguistic whole. Invoking word play, word clusters, and word etymologies, along with neologisms, synonyms, and homonyms, word exercises teach students how to have fun with language.

Keywords

Susan J. Wolfson

An exercise that sharpens attention to words and their development across a piece of writing.

Genre: *any*
Course Level: *any*
Student Difficulty: *easy or moderate*
Teacher Preparation: *low*
Class Size: *small to medium*
Semester Time: *any*
Writing Component: *before class, optional after class*
Close Reading: *high*
Estimated Time: *30 to 50 minutes*

EXERCISE

Words have careers worth following.

Before class meets, give students this fun assignment:

From our readings, choose a word ripe for following. As you select your keyword, consider these questions: What kind of career can you describe for your word as you track each appearance? Does its usage change or deepen in each subsequent context, in its turns and returns? How might your keyword focus the text's larger issues and themes, or even the process of literary representation? As you follow your keyword (and, if you like, any of its close cognates) across the text, consult the *Oxford English Dictionary* (*OED*), or any dictionary that can help, to investigate the word's nuanced meaning, its etymological history, its related verbal forms, and its historical usages. With this history of your keyword in mind, return to the text and ask yourself why the author selected this word and not another. What precise ideas or values does the word convey? Does it vary, repeat, return? Why and to what effect? Before we meet next, write a paragraph or two about what you've discovered. What questions occurred as you followed the career of your keyword? What larger historical or cultural or linguistic sites does your word inhabit? And what specific thematic or conceptual issues does it evoke in the text? Bring a copy of your paragraph to class, and we'll share our keywords.

When class reconvenes, ask each student for his or her keyword, writing these on the board. Ask students if they can see any patterns or if any words stand out as especially surprising or intriguing. Where does this word occur and recur? Does it occur in more than one grammatical form (noun, verb, adjective, adverb)? What textual sites does a word inhabit? How does its career evoke, and concentrate your attention on, thematic or conceptual issues? Invite students to discuss their keywords and their locations in more detail.

When everyone has presented his or her word (consider two to three minutes per student), you can develop the exercise in any number of ways: by focusing a rereading with attention to these words, by talking about the importance of the history of words, or by setting up a writing assignment that will build on the keyword exercise.

REFLECTIONS

"Keywords" is an enjoyable way to teach students the value of careful reading, rereading, reflection, and synthesis that are foundational to lively critical analysis. It's also a great exercise for shy or inexperienced students because its first steps are collection and investigation, with a report of findings. This exercise is so effective for close reading that I often use it more than once in a single course ("Have I got a word for you today!" one student exclaimed. "I've just found my new favorite word," another announced.)

You may know Raymond Williams's *Keywords: A Vocabulary of Culture and Society*, a lexicon and brief discussion of some of the significant and binding words in social thought. Williams's keywords are big-concept: *culture, society, ideology, art, nature*. While these major "keywords" can be exciting, I tell students that words in a more minor key can also have surprising and revealing careers, turning up unexpected pay dirt. The venture gets students involved in the fun and value of reading carefully—and seeing how this attention can be the foundation of a critical project. If you're teaching a text populated with big-concept words, such as *Paradise Lost*, advise students to resist the lure of *rise, fall, lost, sin*, and *justice* and encourage them to focus their curiosities on the unexpected. Taking this advice to heart, one of my students wondered about the event of "dreadful" in Adam's era of innocence (Adam, having heard of "Death," thinks it "Some dreadful thing, no doubt"). Tracking the word, she discovered that personified Death had a "dreadful dart" and that Eden's gate (in Adam and Eve's last vision of Eden) is guarded from their return by angels with "dreadful Faces." Another student was intrigued by "undelighted" in the first view Satan has of the Paradise he's determined to ruin: "the Fiend / Saw undelighted all delight." She discovered through her keyword search not only that *undelighted* is used only here in *Paradise Lost* but also that the *OED* lists this instance as the first usage, leading her to appreciate Milton's linguistic strategy of characterizing Satan by pained exclusions.

Before sending students off on this assignment, I model the exercise for them. I begin my courses on Romanticism with William Blake's *Songs of Innocence and of Experience*, seemingly simple poems with complex psychological and sociological vectors. Using a dictionary or the *OED*, I show students how Blake mobilizes "Innocence" (a negation: *in-noxious*; without harm) and "Experience" (*ex:* from + trial "peril") as states of consciousness, mindful of the double play of Milton's *Paradise Lost* (all paradises are paradises lost). I then draw attention to words present in both *Innocence* and *Experience* (such as "weep" and "wander"), and we assess their different force. For instance: *wander* (in Latin it's *errare,* closely related to "error") has a path of peril in *Experience*. But I ask, Is this so in *Innocence*? Is this life without peril? without perils recognized? with perils projected from the minds of "experienced" readers?

What I like best about this keyword exercise is its versatility. It can be used with one text or with multiple texts across the semester (students might follow the evolving career of a single keyword across the course readings). It can be combined with posting exercises, with paper assignments, or with group work (consider placing students in small groups to work together on a keyword or constellation of words). And it can be used to teach students how to use literature databases available in most libraries.

For advanced classes, students may investigate LION (Literature Online database) to research the afterlife of a keyword in the writer's other works or in the works of his or her contemporaries or successors. You can search not only by word but also by author, genre, title, and time range. (Google Books, which has many of the same search features, is another viable option.) These exercises inspire lively meetings in which we all teach and learn from each other. Not only do students begin to produce an inventory for their essays in my courses, but also they find it valuable for other classes and other disciplines, such as political science and history—sharpening their attention to the way words do not just deliver information but form and shape information. "Keywords" is an especially adaptable and productive learning tool.

Vocabulary Bites

Danielle Wood

An exercise for teaching students the joys of being a logophile.

Genre: *any*
Course Level: *any*
Student Difficulty: *easy*
Teacher Preparation: *medium*
Class Size: *any*
Semester Time: *early*
Writing Component: *none*
Close Reading: *high*
Estimated Time: *15 to 25 minutes*

EXERCISE

In the 1994 movie *Reality Bites*, the heroine Lelaina (Winona Ryder) is stopped in her tracks when a potential employer challenges her to give an on-the-spot definition of the word *irony*. "I know it when I see it," protests a flailing Lelaina, who soon after is shown up by her pal Troy (Ethan Hawke) and his effortless definition of the term. Regardless of whether we are satisfied by Troy's explanation ("It's when the actual meaning is the complete opposite from the literal meaning"), the scene gives us pause to consider how often we read, and use, words that we may not be able accurately to define.

For this exercise, you will need to make copies of two to three pages of text. Any genre will do, provided the work features complex vocabulary. Consider using Renaissance drama (Shakespeare's *The Winter's Tale* or Jonson's *The Alchemist*) or seventeenth- and eighteenth-century poetry (Milton's *Paradise Lost* or Pope's *The Rape of the Lock*), though even modern and contemporary fiction works well (I have used works by such logophiles as Angela Carter and Virginia Woolf). Take the copies to class along with your favorite dictionary or technological device that enables access to a quality online resource. The *Oxford English Dictionary* (*OED*) is always handy, and if you are teaching a work from an early period, you might consider introducing students to older dictionaries like Samuel Johnson's 1775 *A Dictionary of the English Language* or, for American texts, Noah Webster's 1828 *American Dictionary of the English Language* (or subsequent editions).

Give each student the handout, with instructions to read it slowly and carefully and to underline any words for which they could not, if challenged, provide a dictionary-style definition. (You can do this exercise in groups as well.) Readers frequently make educated guesses, often very good ones, about the meanings of words they don't precisely know. Make it clear that the point of the exercise is to isolate those very words: the ones you might gloss over or make quick assumptions about. From experience, I have learned that it's important for me to take a copy of the text myself and do the exercise alongside the students, stressing to them that I have chosen a passage that sends *me* to the dictionary.

Once everyone has finished (allow five to ten minutes, depending on the length and complexity of the passage), ask students to call out the words they underlined, and write them on a blackboard or whiteboard, taking care to reinforce a sense of collaboration ("Yes, I underlined that one too" or "Did anyone else underline that word?"). Now give students another five to ten minutes to look up the identified words in their print or Web dictionary. You can divide up the words and assign each student a different word, or if you are using groups, you can divvy them up by word clusters (for example, nouns to one group, verbs to another).

Then have students or groups report back to share their discoveries. Where appropriate, you can instruct students to look not only at the words the class has underlined but also at the words that neighbor them in the dictionary—are there any interesting or useful connections to be drawn?

REFLECTIONS

"Vocabulary Bites" is a great exercise to conduct in the earliest weeks of the semester. I have used it to pose an ongoing challenge. "For this semester," I suggest, "try not to ignore any words you can't define. Whether you are reading the newspaper, a novel, or a menu, read with a dictionary alongside you, or jot down challenging words and look them up later." Students inevitably prefer to use the Web for looking up definitions, so you might also recommend, in addition to the *OED*, reputable online dictionaries like *OneLook Dictionary Search* or *YourDictionary*, both of which collate word definitions from hundreds of other dictionaries. I always make time in subsequent classes for students to share their new word discoveries, making sure I have a few of my own.

I have used this exercise with many genres (poetry, drama, fiction, nonfiction) and with many texts, including Charlotte Brontë's *Jane Eyre*, Angela Carter's *The Bloody Chamber*, and Virginia Woolf's *Orlando*. In my classroom this dictionary exercise has provided the opportunity to define gorgeous words like *lachrymose*, *eldritch*, *lacustrine*, *tmesis*, and *tortuous* (which many students read, at first, as the more familiar word *torturous*). It has encouraged recognition of the way word usage can change over time (think of *decimate* and *enormity*). And it has enabled discussion of the strange and delightful quirks of the English language, in which the word *last* can be both "final" and the foot-shaped mold for a shoe.

While comparing J. M. Barrie's *Peter Pan* and Disney's *Peter Pan* in a page-to-screen unit, students and I turned to our dictionaries to decode Barrie's description of the fairy, Tinker Bell, as "slightly inclined to *embonpoint*." While some of the dictionaries played the definition of *embonpoint* quite straight ("exaggerated plumpness, stoutness"), the *OED* ventured to say that it meant "plumpness" in a "complimentary or euphemistic sense," while yet other dictionaries associated *embonpoint* with such words as "voluptuousness" and indicated that it might refer specifically to a woman's bosom. Not only did this research enable us to observe that Disney's animators had perhaps been led by the particular word *embonpoint* to interpret Tinker Bell's form as curvaceous (rather than simply chubby), we were also given an unexpected case study in what might be gleaned from looking up the same word in multiple dictionaries.

I have found that this exercise can be particularly inspirational for aspiring writers in the room, since it highlights how words are the beginning, middle, and end of the craft. (As Richard Rhodes says: "Words are the model, words are the tools, words are the boards, words are the nails.") The principle behind the exercise is a simple one. It poses, and answers, the question any serious student of literature needs to ask: why this particular word and no other?

. . . .

Le Mot Juste

Manuel Herrero-Puertas

An exercise that teaches diction by having students rewrite a pivotal word or phrase.

Genre: *any*
Course Level: *introductory*
Student Difficulty: *moderate*
Teacher Preparation: *medium*
Class Size: *any*
Semester Time: *early*
Writing Component: *in class*
Close Reading: *high*
Estimated Time: *25 to 30 minutes*

EXERCISE

For this diction exercise students will need access to a good dictionary; the *Oxford English Dictionary* (*OED*) is ideal, but other dictionaries, as well as thesauruses, are also fine. You can cart into class a handful of dictionaries, you can set up an in-class computer with online access to the *OED*, or you can simply invite students to use their laptops, iPads, or even smart phones.

Begin by dividing the class into groups of two to four students. Distribute to each group a handout with the same poem or paragraph of prose. When preparing the handout, cross out an especially significant word or phrase (don't delete the word, just cross it out so that the word is still visible). Inform students that each group will have to find a substitute for this crossed-out bit. But here's the rub: their mission is not merely to find a substitut word but to choose one that alters the overall meaning of the passage as little as possible.

Here are some examples of significant words and phrases from American literature that make excellent candidates for this type of word exercise:

- "But I reckon I got to ~~light out~~ for the territory ahead of the rest" (Mark Twain, *Huckleberry Finn*)
- "I become a ~~transparent eye-ball~~. I am nothing. I ~~see~~ all" (Ralph Waldo Emerson, *Nature*)
- "If you ~~surrender~~ to the air, you could *ride* it" (Toni Morrison, *Song of Solomon*)
- "pallidly neat, pitiably respectable, incurably ~~forlorn~~!" (Herman Melville, "Bartleby, the Scrivener")
- "Split the ~~lark~~ and you'll find the music" (Emily Dickinson)

During the first stage of the exercise (allow roughly fifteen minutes), groups work by themselves with your occasional assistance. Since the goal is to find a word or expression that best matches the crossed-out original, group members begin by brainstorming possible substitutes. Remind them that they need to consider both the meaning of the crossed-out word per se and the larger meanings and associations that the word instills in the longer passage and in the work as a whole. As they consult various library or online sources—which may include, for example, a thesaurus on synonyms and antonyms—be sure to encourage each group to investigate the etymologies of the words they are replacing. (If students are new to the *OED*, you may need to preface the exercise with a short tutorial.)

After they agree on one substitute word or phrase, give students five or so minutes to prepare a two-minute presentation justifying their choice. Invite a spokesperson for each group to present and write their word choices on the board. Once the round of presentations is over, briefly let students argue for which candidate words they like the most and why; let them know that they are no longer allowed to advocate for their own group selection. Then put the final decision to a vote. Close off the exercise by discussing with the class the winning substitute and its relation to the original: Why is this new word or phrase an optimal choice? In what ways does it respect the author's original? Are there ways in which it departs from the original? Why do you think the author settled on the original exact word or phrase out of so many possible choices?

REFLECTIONS

"Le Mot Juste" is a simple and elegant way to teach the creative possibilities of literary diction. It performs many tasks at once (which is why it's a good exercise to schedule relatively early in the semester): it models good reading habits like using the dictionary; it increases students' awareness of the nuances of literary language; it highlights the connotative and denotative weight of particular words or expressions; and it focuses attention on the relation between sound and sense. For students new to literary research, it can be adapted to teach students the different ways to use the *OED* or the importance of synonyms and antonyms. But whether you pitch it as an exercise on diction, dictionary usage, or both, the overall point of this exercise is to introduce students to the richness, variety, and history of words.

"Le Mot Juste" works wonders with famous lines from canonical texts. Students may have read or heard famous literary lines before, but have they truly understood them? In my Classic American Literature class, many students already knew that Huck Finn "lights out" for the territories in the end, but they were excited to learn from the *OED* that in the 1880s "to light out" meant both "to decamp" and "to attack." This new information led to a lively debate on whether Huck's final reckoning was evasive, invasive, or perhaps both. For some of my students, Huck Finn was innocently "leaving" for the territory; for others, the novel ends with Huck blindly embracing the ideology of Manifest Destiny and setting out "to conquer" the West. These opposite interpretations raised for us important questions regarding Huck's character development and Twain's critique of the national character: Can one really shed "*sivilization*"? Why does Huck presuppose that the "territory" isn't already populated? In the end, is Huck discarding American values or, by pushing the western frontier, is he embodying them to the core?

Words matter. This is the lesson that students seem to take away from "Le Mot Juste." Gustave Flaubert, who would spend days and weeks looking for the right word to fit in the right place, coined this phrase. As I often remind my students, he was not doing so out of narcissistic perfectionism but out of the conviction that, to borrow an architectural metaphor, words function as the keystones and pillars that define the shape and meaning of an entire edifice. In my teaching practice, I have found "Le Mot Juste" an engaging way of illustrating this principle.

. . . .

Word Clouds

Lisa Fletcher and Joanna Richardson

A collaborative exercise for finding the key words in a novel.

Genre: *fiction*
Course Level: *any*
Student Difficulty: *easy*
Teacher Preparation: *low*
Class Size: *any*
Semester Time: *any*
Writing Component: *none*
Close Reading: *high*
Estimated Time: *variable, 15 to 60 minutes*

EXERCISE

This exercise involves all students working together to identify repeated words in a novel and to sort them into clusters or "word clouds." It works best with a novel that is strikingly repetitive. We have had particular success using it to teach novels like William Faulkner's *As I Lay Dying* and Kazuo Ishiguro's *Never Let Me Go*, both of which employ narrators with limited vocabularies. This exercise also works very well when teaching novels with strong imagery or symbolism communicated through associated words, as in Emily Brontë's *Wuthering Heights*.

Arrange the classroom so that all students can see the blackboard or whiteboard, and ask for two volunteers who will be writing on the board throughout the class (they will each need a marker or chalk as well as an eraser). With smaller groups, invite students to gather around the board.

Ask the class which words are repeated in this novel. We find the exercise works best on the spot, as a way not merely to test recall but more importantly to encourage diving back into the text. As students call out words to be written on the board, encourage your two volunteers to work together to group particular words, creating multiple semantic clusters or "word clouds." Prompt them to be creative: if a particular word seems especially important, they might write it in big letters. Clouds that seem to be connected in some way can be linked with lines or arrows, or you might offer different colored markers for highlighting and linking.

The board will fill with sets or columns of words and may begin to appear messy or chaotic. When this happens, ask the students how they might rearrange the word clouds to find the patterns in the text. Are there any words that seem to be in the wrong cloud? Are some words so significant that they belong in more than one cloud or should even stand alone? Have any words that are not repeated multiple times in the novel made it onto the board? (Our classes have found this with "clones," a word that only appears once in Ishiguro's *Never Let Me Go*. This exercise led students to argue that the novel is not so much a story about cloning as it is a parable about contemporary society.)

While you may need to contribute a word or two to jump-start a new cloud or to help students see connections, try to avoid preempting the students' discoveries during this exercise. We have learned through experience that the exercise works best when the teacher is not in charge of the board, especially when he or she knows the novel very well. Not only are the students with the markers energized by their role, but also the class as a whole becomes less dependent on the instructor.

REFLECTIONS

This deceptively simple activity is one of our favorite methods for inspiring students to pay attention to the importance of diction in novels. The exercise is quite flexible and can be introduced at almost any point in a lesson plan. And it can also be employed for almost any duration, introduced as a short fifteen-to-twenty-minute pace changer or extended into an entire fifty-to-sixty-minute class. The goal either way is the same: "Word Clouds" creates a big-picture view of a novel by focusing on the text's smallest parts—its individual words.

For example, when we had students look for word repetition in Faulkner's *As I Lay Dying*, they immediately thought of "box" and "coffin." But as the exercise progressed and students identified more and more repeated words, they observed how frequently Faulkner uses the words "wood," "wooden," and related terms, like "logs," "sticks," "planks," "lumber," and "tree." As students continued to look closely at the novel, they noticed the connection between this list of words and still others: "pale wood," "pale wooden eyes," "wooden-faced," "wooden-backed." Eventually, by linking words and word clouds, they began to see how key words define each character in Faulkner's novel and, moreover, how the same word cloud often links family members.

Case in point: Faulkner describes Jewel as "motionless, lean, wooden-backed, as though carved squatting out of the lean wood" and his mother Addie as a "bundle of rotten sticks."

To cap off the class, we like to step back and pose some summarizing or clarifying questions. We often ask, What does the work we've done on the board tell us about this novel? Or, If someone were to walk into our classroom right now and look at this board, what could they guess about the novel we've been reading? Could they identify its genre, or work out its themes? At the end of this class, our students are always reluctant to clean the board, and they frequently snap photographs. In the end, not only do they leave the room with a better understanding of the language of this particular novel and its deeper meaning, but also they realize that they can use this technique for studying any work of fiction.

. . . .

Aphorisms

Keri Walsh

Aphorisms can be tough nuts to crack. Here's one way.

Genre: *any*
Course Level: *any*
Student Difficulty: *moderate*
Teacher Preparation: *medium*
Class Size: *any*
Semester Time: *any*
Writing Component: *in class*
Close Reading: *medium*
Estimated Time: *variable, from 45 to 80 minutes*

EXERCISE

"All art is quite useless." "A little learning is a dangerous thing." "Living well is the best revenge." Aphorisms attract attention with their sense of completeness and self-containment. But the brevity that makes aphorisms so delicious can also make them difficult to talk about. Their epigrammatic quality can seem to send the signal "Case closed. There's nothing to discuss here, folks." This word exercise gives students a chance to get beyond the crisp authority of the aphorism and to open up the many debates that are condensed within its short and glossy form.

Aphorisms can be found almost anywhere—in essays, poems, novels, manifestos, and theoretical texts. The exercise will be most successful if you have a set of at least ten different aphoristic statements that belong to some kind of a group (they are part of the same poem, are by the same author, or were published in the same book). If they are especially dispersed, you will probably want to type up your chosen aphorisms on a handout.

First, ask students to select one of the aphorisms from the collection. The exercise works best when students choose the aphorism that interests them the most, so avoid assigning the aphorisms randomly. It's not a problem if more than one student selects any given statement or if some of the statements aren't covered at all. Simply encourage students to choose a line that attracts or moves them. It might be a sentiment that they innately disagree with, or one that makes them laugh, or one that engages with a subject they care about. Or it might be one that strikes them as paradoxical or mysterious in a way they'd like to investigate further.

Instruct students to write out their aphorism at the top of the page. Then ask them to write freely about that aphorism for ten minutes. Tell them that they can write about it in relation to anything they like and that they should not feel constrained to relate it back to the larger text at hand or to material that has been covered in the class. This is an exercise geared at opening up the broadest possibilities for interpreting the line students have selected. They can write about their aphorism in relation to anything that comes to mind: their walk to class that morning, a painting they saw once, a book they're reading in another class. I recommend that you also participate in the exercise by selecting an aphorism and writing for ten minutes yourself. This keeps you connected to what the students are doing, and if you feel comfortable doing so, you can bring your own responses into the discussion.

Once the writing period has elapsed, open up the discussion by asking for a volunteer to tell the class which aphorism he or she picked and where the freewriting led. Usually discussion begins easily at this point, but if it doesn't, you can share your own response first. One good way to handle the flow is to ask, after a student speaks, "Did anyone else write about this same aphorism? Would you like to chime in?" If you have a class of more than about twenty students, you can break into smaller groups to discuss the responses and then ask students to report back to the whole group. Discussion can last between thirty minutes and an hour, depending on the energy of the class.

As the conversation nears conclusion, ask students to reflect on how these aphorisms relate to the meaning of the larger text they appear in, if there is one. You might also ask students to think about the aphorism form itself. What are its particular strengths as a genre? In what situations might you want to write an aphorism? What kinds of thoughts can—and can't—be accommodated in an aphorism? Usually students discover a number of generic affinities: with poetry (for its condensation, its precise use of language), with philosophy (for its use of logical-sounding assertions and authoritative tone), and with comic writing (for the way aphorisms play with logic and language to subvert readerly expectations).

REFLECTIONS

"Aphorisms" can be used to teach formal literary features like voice or style, but it works especially well as a word exercise. I often end the discussion by asking students to circle what they consider to be the single most important word in their aphorism and explain why. Alternatively, this can be done at the start of the exercise as a writing prompt for students: ask them to select a single word and then jot down how the word conveys the meaning or effect of the aphorism as a whole. Because of their brevity and intensity, aphorisms make it easier for students to explore language at the level of individual words. As a group, students can tease out the large payoff of small words or phrases, relating each aphorism to the next to find patterns, see contradictions, and create a bigger picture.

The exercise works well for generating discussion of actual aphorisms, such as those found in the works of Cicero ("A room without books is like a body without a soul"), Michel de Montaigne ("The most universal quality is diversity"), or Alexander Pope ("To err is human; to forgive, divine"). But it works equally well for approaching poems, novels, or other texts that have aphoristic qualities: Gertrude Stein's *Tender Buttons* ("Any space is not quiet it is so likely to be shiny"), Polonius's speech to Laertes in *Hamlet* ("Neither a borrower nor a lender be"), T. S. Eliot's *The Waste Land* ("Thinking of the key, each confirms a prison"), or Yeats's "Sailing to Byzantium" ("That is no country for old men"). It can also productively focus discussion of theoretical or manifesto-like texts—Walter Benjamin's "On the Concept of History" ("The true picture of the past whizzes by") or Mina Loy's *Feminist Manifesto* ("Leave off looking to men to find out what you are not")—not to mention comic one-liners by authors like Dorothy Parker ("Brevity is the soul of lingerie") or Woody Allen ("I am at two with nature"). It works for proverbs, maxims, laws, or any collection of short statements.

I use this exercise whenever I teach Oscar Wilde's *The Picture of Dorian Gray*. The exercise provides a useful way to open up some of the big questions that the novel's famous preface raises about the relationship between art and life. Wilde's preface turns some fairly entrenched critical values on their heads, and this exercise helps students start thinking along with Wilde about the nature of personal, intellectual, and aesthetic experiences.

For instance, one of my students chose from this preface the statement "Those who go beneath the surface do so at their peril." Initially, this aphorism seems to rebuff everything students have been taught about the value of literary interpretation. How can they avoid going "beneath the surface"? And what kind of "perils" is Wilde talking about? The student who selected this aphorism wondered whether Wilde's own writing was not already dangerous on the surface. Aren't Wilde's aphorisms in general, the student challenged, "his most potent, influential weapon?" Inspired by this particular aphorism, we concluded the exercise by considering the kind of creative and quick-footed reading practices an aphoristic writer like Wilde requires, before we returned to a consideration of the larger process of interpretation itself and the active critical awareness it demands.

When we reach the end of our study of *The Picture of Dorian Gray*, I ask students to revisit the "Aphorisms" exercise and think about whether Wilde's novel did in fact seem to honor the values asserted in the preface. Usually they conclude that Wilde's *Dorian Gray* is in some ways a more traditional moral parable than the preface led them to believe it would be. This realization leads to a discussion about why Wilde might have appended the preface in the first place, and to a sense of its complex relationship to the novel and to Wilde's life and public career.

. . . .

Fill in the Blanks

Megan Quinn

An exercise in word choice inspired by the popular word game Mad Libs.

Genre: *any*
Course Level: *introductory*
Student Difficulty: *easy*
Teacher Preparation: *medium*
Class Size: *any*
Semester Time: *any*
Writing Component: *in class*
Close Reading: *high*
Estimated Time: *25 to 30 minutes*

EXERCISE

Find a passage from a text on your syllabus that is particularly rich in the conventions of its genre or the stylistic tells of its author, such as a passage of horror in a Gothic novel or a bit of Wordsworthian blank verse with lots of characteristic imagery. (Nearly any passage students have read for homework will do, since they are not likely to have committed the lines to memory.) Type out the passage (around 150 to no more than 200 words) in 14-point font with double-spacing. Should you choose a longer passage to break up consecutively among the students' groups, divide it into sections roughly equal in length (and no more than 200 words each) and type them out in separate documents.

Next, delete roughly fifteen words per passage (or section of a passage) and replace them with numbered blanks. For deletion, choose a range of words that highlight the author's language choice, sentence structure, and literary style. The idea is to give students an opportunity to explore the author's word usages across nouns, verbs, adverbs, and adjectives. Then, on the reverse side of the document, make a numbered list with descriptions of the types of words required in the corresponding numbered blanks in the passage; each entry in the list should also have a blank for the students to fill in. These descriptions may be as general as "singular noun" and "present tense verb." Or, to draw out the author's tics and the students' amusement, try more specific instructions; for instance, for an author heavily concerned with sensory experience, try "adjective to do with the senses."

Introduce the activity with irony—acknowledge that sitting in class doing an exercise inspired by Mad Libs may feel silly, but explain that the iconic middle-school pastime relies on our sense of incongruity, and thus our sense of convention, so drawing and filling in blanks in a text can help us think about sophisticated issues of word choice, sentence structure, style, and generic conventions. Divide students into groups of three or four and distribute to each group one handout, list side up. Instruct the students not to turn the sheet over until they are done with the list. Give them a set amount of time to fill in the blanks on their handout, first the list and then the corresponding blanks in the passage (depending on the standard length of each section, this could take anywhere from five to fifteen minutes).

Instruct students to try to select only words the author might use, but be sure to let them know that the tone or content need not be serious. Tell them, for example, to pick the most "Faulknerian" or "Wordsworthian" words they can think of, but not necessarily to limit themselves to imitation; they may feel free to reach into parody. Students should be encouraged to have fun with this exercise, imagining themselves as, say, a group of Jane Austen's peers playing history's very first edition of Mad Libs. When the groups have finished and the laughter has subsided (students tend to have a ball with this exercise), reconvene the class and invite one member of each group to read out their revised passage. If you choose to divide one long passage into shorter sections, stage this class reading in the correct order of the full original passage.

Then circulate the original passage on a new handout in regular, single-spaced type and ask for a volunteer to read it aloud, encouraging the students to circle or underline what interests them. ("Fill in the Blanks" can thus be the perfect prelude to the more serious "The Blow Up," the first exercise in "Essentials.") Ask the students which of their versions seemed to come closest to capturing the style of the original. Did anyone get some of the words exactly right, and could more than a good memory account for this? Are there any words, phrases, images, sentence structures, or plot elements that the author tends to repeat? Do the small words (conjunctions, prepositions, pronouns, interjections) form predictable or significant patterns of their own? Are there word forms (lengths, tenses, compound forms) or parts of speech that show up more than others? How do those repeated elements affect our understanding and experience of the work?

End by circling back to the students' filled-in blanks: When were their versions of the passage funny—was it when they subverted the author's style the most obviously, or when they came closest to it? Why or how might that be?

REFLECTIONS

Why draw blanks for your students? Because it removes the text from its familiar and perhaps intimidating context, giving students space to see it in a new and productively playful light. "Fill in the Blanks" also offers an accessible way for students to explore the particularly difficult concepts of word choice, sentence structure, genre, and style. Selecting words to fill in blanks is a concrete way of experiencing how genre and style conventions affect individual word choice: students may not know how to define "genre" or "style," but they know when a word, perhaps comically, does or does not fit the blank in a text. This is a great stress-reliever exercise that also happens to have a high intellectual return. Students find the exercise highly engaging; as one student said while reading aloud her group's filled-in passage and lighting on a particularly great word choice, "Oh, that's good."

For a class on William Faulkner and Henry James, I blanked out a range of stylistic and thematic tics in a passage from Faulkner's *Absalom, Absalom!*: the frequently used word "wistaria"; sequences of two or more verbs, adjectives, or adverbs separated by "and"; adjectives to do with the senses; compound nouns and adjectives with and without hyphens; and the season. One group of students, responding to the request for a "singular noun (plant)," immediately got "wistaria." For the "adjectives to do with the senses," another student commented, "There's so many of those." And for the season, still another remarked, "It's always summer."

In the students' readings of their passages, absurdly Faulknerian elements got big laughs, from strings of verbs separated by "and" to the compound adjective "Cassandralike," chosen by one group to form the (incorrect but very Faulknerian) phrase "sleeping Cassandralike hand." Immediately after the readings, I asked the students if they would have thought their passages were unaltered Faulkner if they'd heard them out of context. The answer was a resounding yes, an implicit recognition that Faulkner's style is already almost a parody of itself. Comparing the groups' choice of verbs, students discussed Faulkner's preference for "simple" verbs. And when asked to describe the differences between Faulkner and James, they remarked on Faulkner's concern with "seeing and touching and feeling" versus the "stuffy" James with a prose style more "exclusively adjectives with verbs." My question about what makes a plant Faulknerian elicited a list of "something with a very heady scent," "something that lingers," something that is "overflowing" and "disorderly," and something that "goes along with senses and passions"—a description that might well describe Faulkner's lush style itself.

As playful as this word exercise may be, it is also striking for its versatility; it is as useful at the introductory level as at the advanced. The passage you select need not be from the syllabus; indeed, "Fill in the Blanks" can be a successful icebreaker activity on the first day of class. Consider giving students passages from three or more authors you'll be covering over the course of the semester as a way to start off your course with an immediate focus on words and styles. Or keep "Fill in the Blanks" in mind for an advanced literature class covering authors known for their especially idiosyncratic, identifiable, or inspirational writing styles (James Joyce, Charles Dickens, Gertrude Stein, Toni Morrison).

Whatever you choose to do, be sure to ask students how they might have designed the exercise. When I asked for student feedback from the Faulkner and James class, they suggested versions of the exercise in which students would be asked to choose Faulknerian words for blanks in a passage of James and vice versa. As one student said, since Faulkner operates more on a "prose level" whereas James works more on a "plot level," an exercise featuring James could ask students to fill in plot elements. There are many variations on this word exercise, which might even include asking students to pick a passage and design their own version of "Fill in the Blanks." One of the most exciting things about the exercise is precisely its ability to inspire creativity.

The Fascination
of What's Difficult

Adam Potkay

A grammar exercise that navigates the syntactical and lexical fullness of early poetry.

Genre: *poetry, especially early Renaissance through Romantic*
Course Level: *any*
Student Difficulty: *moderate or hard*
Teacher Preparation: *medium to high*
Class Size: *small to medium*
Semester Time: *early*
Writing Component: *optional*
Close Reading: *high*
Estimated Time: *45 to 50 minutes*

EXERCISE

Choose a short piece of verse—a sonnet or a section of a longer poem, say—and prepare a handout with a set of six to eight grammatical, lexical, and explicative questions. (Students will need access to the *Oxford English Dictionary* [*OED*], and ideally Samuel Johnson's 1775 *A Dictionary of the English Language*.) Almost any early poem will do; I have had great success using this exercise on poems as various as Shakespeare's sonnets, Milton's *Lycidas*, Pope's *The Rape of the Lock*, and Shelley's *Mont Blanc*. The questions on your handout should encourage students to identify parts of speech, look up the meaning of words, and explicate grammatically complex phrases—that is, to translate them into plain English.

How does this work? Consider the opening quatrain of Shakespeare's Sonnet 73:

That time of year thou mayst in me behold
When yellow leaves, or none, or few, do hang
Upon those boughs which shake against the cold,
Bare ruined choirs, where late the sweet birds sang.

A syntactic question I have asked is, What is the object of *behold*? A dictionary question is, What are the appropriate *OED* definitions of *choirs* and *late*? And an explicative question is, What do lines 3 and 4 translate to in plain

English?—a question that requires, or fosters, understanding the grammatical apposition of "boughs" and "choirs."

Begin class by taking as much time as you need to review basic grammatical terms, including *noun, pronoun, verb, subject, object,* and *antecedent*. (Students usually require such review because, for example, they may know what a pronoun is but don't understand that the antecedent is the noun the pronoun stands for.) A quick review might take anywhere from five to ten minutes. Then assign students to small groups in class and circulate your handout, asking each group to work their way through the questions in sequence. If you have six to eight questions, allow roughly fifteen to twenty minutes for the group work. And be sure to circulate among the groups to speed things along if some of the students get stuck.

Leave time at the end of class (at least twenty minutes if possible) for students to report on what they learned about the poem. Invite them to share the difficult phrase or line that fascinated them the most and explain how they arrived at their paraphrase. Ask them for their thoughts on why grammar might be an important part of close reading a text. What did they learn from this grammar exercise that they might have missed otherwise? How did a deeper knowledge of the poem's parts of speech and syntactical intricacies shape the meaning of the poem?

REFLECTIONS

Designed to facilitate the close reading of English or other European poetry, especially from the early Renaissance through Romanticism, "The Fascination of What's Difficult" (a title borrowed from W. B. Yeats) teaches students how grammar can often be the key to unlocking the meaning of a poem. For a student of literature, it might seem that nothing is less sexy, or more difficult, than grammar. But one cannot really understand a poem without understanding its grammar. And the grammar of early modern poets often challenges ready understanding, sometimes by imitating the Latin poets that early modern writers knew and loved, as in Pope's wonderfully compressed lines "Diana Cynthus, Ceres Hybla loves" and "Beaus banish Beaus, and Coaches Coaches drive."

But even when a poet's syntax seems more straightforwardly English, it can still reward a closer look. Take this quatrain from John Donne's lyric "A Valediction: Forbidding Mourning":

Dull sublunary lovers' love
(Whose soul is sense) cannot admit
Absence, because it doth remove
Those things that elemented it.

While some anthologies provide a dictionary definition of "sublunary" (the *Norton Anthology*, for example, defines the word as "beneath the moon, therefore earthly, sensual, and subject to change"), the passage raises more questions than any editor could or should address. For example, my students were at first puzzled by the antecedent of "it" both in the stanza's third line and in its fourth line, but by breaking down the stanza into its parts of speech, they were able to land on the correct antecedents (respectively, "absence" and "love"). Words I invited students to look up in the *OED* were "sense" in "(Whose soul is sense) cannot admit" and "elemented" in "Those things that elemented it," which lead students to offer paraphrases like "lovers whose essence or only reality is sense bound" and "love that is fundamentally constituted by physical contact." My students came to appreciate that they were grappling, in a way they otherwise wouldn't, with what the poem means, or how it generates meaning.

This word exercise trains students to attend not just to the meaning of individual words but also, and no less importantly, to their grammatical and lexical relation to one another. Words never carry meaning in isolation, which is why any close reader needs to keep an eye on a poet's precise grammatical and syntactical choices. I have found that taking the time to teach the grammar of early poetry not only produces in students a fascination for what's difficult but also helps them to discuss poetry *as* poetry—a genre deeply invested not just in words but in their interplay.

· ·

For more exercises that can be used to teach words, try these:

Parts of Speech (Poems)
Be Pedantic (Poems)
Close Listening (Poems)
Adaptation (Plays)
Soliloquy (Plays)
First Things First (Styles)
One-Sentence Pastiche (Styles)
Convolution (Styles)

STYLES

If the preceding exercises focus on words in all their weighted particularity, the exercises in this section place words in their dynamic relation to one another. How words are collected and combined, paced and punctuated, sounded and sequenced all add up to what we call "style." What makes a style distinctive? How does style convey meaning? Why do authorial styles change? Exercises on tone, voice, and diction attune students to the subtleties of literary style, from the grand style to the plain style and all the innumerable writing styles in between.

Where and when does style matter most? The opening exercises in this section locate style variously at a text's beginning ("First Things First"), middle ("Dramatic Echoes"), and end ("The Forgers' Circle"). Classifying, comparing, describing, and even performing literary styles teach students to attend to the formal and oratorical complexities of sentence structure and syntax. Imitation emerges as an especially popular method for offering students an inside view into what it means to be a literary stylist. The three imitation exercises included here ("One-Sentence Pastiche," "Imitate This," and "Convolution") invite students first to imitate a line, then a paragraph, and finally an entire poem. This section comes to a full stop on one of style's least discussed but most important elements: punctuation ("Punctuation Matters").

First Things First

Naomi Milthorpe

A dynamic group exercise using famous first lines to encourage close reading.

Genre: *fiction*
Course Level: *introductory*
Student Difficulty: *easy*
Teacher Preparation: *medium*
Class Size: *any*
Semester Time: *first day*
Writing Component: *none*
Close Reading: *high*
Estimated Time: *15 minutes*

EXERCISE

It's the first class of the semester. Maybe it's the first literature class your students have ever taken. Either way, you want to make sure that they begin the year with close reading at the front of their minds. Using famous first sentences, this exercise is designed to stimulate detailed attention to a text's form and content, and especially its style.

Choose a selection of striking first sentences from novels and list them on a single sheet of paper. The handout is for students to use and take away at the end of the class, so allow plenty of writing space around each sentence. Three to five sentences are ideal to keep the class engaged for the duration of the exercise. Be prepared either to project this same sheet on an overhead or PowerPoint or to copy it on a whiteboard or blackboard; choose a method that will also let you mark up the sentences for everyone to see.

Begin the class by outlining the idea that thinking critically about literature is not simply a matter of understanding story and character but also of paying attention to how language makes meaning. Emphasize to students that this exercise isn't a test of their knowledge or a tool for working out the plot of the novel. Ask the students, with your brief introduction in mind, to take a few minutes to examine each sentence. Encourage them to use their sheets to make note of the things that stand out, that seem strange, that confuse them—anything at all. Then, beginning with one sentence, initiate a full-group discussion. (If you have time, you can also separate students into groups or have them work in pairs before reconvening as a group.) Start simply: ask them about aspects of prose style and narrative form first, before introducing questions about content and generic markers.

Possible questions can include the following: What sort of words does the sentence use? What do you notice about punctuation and syntax? What is the sentence's tone? Can we tell anything about the novel's setting (its time or place), characters, theme, or other narrative elements? Does the sentence seem to be written in a particular genre?

As the students offer answers and ideas, annotate the sentences as you project them (encourage students to do the same on their sheets). Keep the discussion fast paced to prompt students to think on their feet and trust their instincts. This exercise need not take more than fifteen minutes, though the more examples you provide, the more intensive the exercise.

REFLECTIONS

"First Things First" works best as a short, sharp introduction to close reading and as a way to get new students talking and working together as a group. It has worked well in my courses to get past the initial class silence and really focus on skills development and critical thinking from the first moment the students enter the classroom. Providing the printed sentences on a sheet encourages close textual work, while using an overhead or PowerPoint fosters group cohesion.

In the past, I have used this exercise in introductory courses and always chosen sentences from novels that are not on the required reading list, in order to separate discussion of form from the baggage of plot or character analysis. But this exercise could also work in a more specialized or advanced course, using sentences from the genre or historical period you'll be examining.

Some novels with good discussable first sentences include Toni Morrison's *Beloved* ("124 was spiteful"), Mark Twain's *Adventures of Huckleberry Finn* ("You don't know about me without you have read a book by the name of 'The Adventures of Tom Sawyer,' but that ain't no matter"), F. Scott Fitzgerald's *The Great Gatsby* ("In my younger and more vulnerable years my father gave me some advice that I've been turning over in my mind ever since"), and of course Charles Dickens's *A Tale of Two Cities* ("It was the best of times, it was the worst of times"). For its pithy imperative tone, I especially like to use Herman Melville's *Moby-Dick* ("Call me Ishmael"). And who can resist, for its pleasurable blurring of the axiomatic and the ironic, Jane Austen's *Pride and Prejudice* ("It is a truth universally acknowledged, that a single man in possession of a good fortune must be in want of a wife")?

Canonical texts are especially suitable candidates for inclusion on your handout. For example, I always include *Pride and Prejudice* up front on my list, since some students may know the novel or film adaptation and feel more confident in their readings, but be sure to ask them to try to forget about Lizzie and Darcy for a minute and think instead about tone, irony, and language. George Orwell's opening sentence in *Nineteen Eighty-Four* ("It was a bright cold day in April, and the clocks were striking thirteen") prompts immediate reflections about style. Students tend to notice that the sentence is fairly unobtrusive ("bland" is the word they often use), but they also note that the two halves of the sentence seem symmetrical, as if the second part mirrors the first. Particularly attentive students will usually counter that the second half of the sentence has a few too many syllables—something seems "off" in Orwell's rhythm (you can ask students to consider whether this is a fault in the writing, or a clue about lack of balance within the narrative). Students usually also offer ideas about time (April and springtime, yes, but more important, how clocks striking thirteen is weird).

By the end of the class, your students should leave with greater confidence in their first impressions and with more experience in reading closely to gain critical distance. They will also leave with a sheet of paper covered in annotations, a good model for the kind of marginalia skills we expect of close readers. Finally, the exercise provides a handy reference point for the rest of the semester; whenever you want to turn to detailed close-reading exercises on passages or lines of text, you can remind your students of the importance of "First Things First."

. . . .

Dramatic Echoes

Hollis Robbins

A playful exercise in understanding literary style through dramatic interpretation.

Genre: *drama*
Course Level: *any*
Student Difficulty: *easy*
Teacher Preparation: *low*
Class Size: *any*
Semester Time: *midterm*
Writing Component: *none*
Close Reading: *medium to high*
Estimated Time: *variable, from 20 to 60 minutes*

EXERCISE

This exercise helps students understand literary style by first translating the written word into dramatic performance. "Dramatic Echoes" works best with plays, particularly those driven by language, and especially with scenes that draw humor from miscommunication and/or overt misdirection or that involve ambiguity and evasion. Shakespeare's plays provide many such scenes, but similar excerpts from almost any drama will be effective. The opening scene from Tom Stoppard's *Arcadia* works wonderfully well, for example, as does the opening scene (or really any scene) from David Mamet's *American Buffalo*, or almost any scene from Lillian Hellman's *The Little Foxes*.

To begin, select a relatively short dramatic scene featuring two or three characters and ask for two different groups of students to play the parts. Give the two groups (as well as the rest of the class) five or more minutes to scan the scene, taking care to indicate where it should end. While the students are preparing, clear an area large enough to enable both groups, with texts in hand, to act out the scene. When the students are ready, explain to the volunteer actors that their performances will "echo" each other, line by line. In other words, after a character from the first group delivers a line to his or her fellow actors, the same character from the *second* group will deliver the same line to *his or her* fellow actors. Every line will be repeated in this fashion until the end of the scene.

Initially this repetition exercise may be met with mirth. After only a few exchanges, however, both the actors and the watching students will understand the "play" that the repetition of each line allows—with language, with pacing, with emphasis—and will shift their attention to the stylistic choices each actor makes.

At the conclusion of the performance (which is generally met with applause), ask the students to comment on the scene and the exercise. You can prompt them with specific questions, though students will generally have a great deal to say and to ask. What choices did the actors make in translating the written style on the page to the oral style of the stage? How did the act of repetition affect (or accentuate) those choices? Is there a right way to say a particular line? Do certain lines lend themselves to multiple interpretations? How does the acted scene help illuminate the play's own literary style? Give the actors and the audience equal time to comment on what was learned by the repetition. If a group asks to perform the scene again without an echo, say yes. Because the whole exercise can take as little as twenty to thirty minutes (depending on the length of the scene you have selected), you may also find you have time to repeat the lesson with a new cast of students eager to give it a try.

REFLECTIONS

While "Dramatic Echoes" is suitable for drama courses at all levels, it is particularly effective for introductory classes and for students with mixed levels of performance experience. It works best midway through the semester, after students have become accustomed to reading aloud but may still be struggling with the analysis of literary style and with the project of reading passages whose meanings can be elusive or opaque.

At once simple and complex, the exercise is disarming. Nonactors who volunteer to perform in one of the groups will appreciate the extra time between lines as well as the atmosphere of "play," which suggests there is no right or wrong way to deliver a line. Students with acting experience will likewise appreciate the extra time to ham up a line or "outdo" the other student playing the same part. Students who may not initially have understood the scene will appreciate hearing each line twice. Everyone will remember this exercise and the acted scene more thoroughly than other scenes in the play. Most important, by converting the written word into spoken performance and then repeating each line, often with a new reading, "Dramatic Echoes" not only amplifies the specific choices that help define a writer's style but also helps students think concretely about what goes into making those choices.

In my own classroom, I have successfully used an excerpt from *King Lear,* act 4, scene 6, featuring Edgar leading the blind Gloucester to the edge of what he thinks is a tall cliff. The exercise opens with a pair of Gloucesters asking, "When shall we come to the top of that same hill?" During the exercise a few years ago, one Gloucester (who seems never to have acted before) said lines such as "Methinks thy voice is alter'd; and thou speak'st / In better phrase and matter than thou didst" flatly and straightforwardly (though correctly), while the second Gloucester delivered the same lines in a vaudevillian style, to suggest overt suspicion. The first Edgar used the extra time to formulate his responses to both readings, choosing generally to respond to the second, more vaudevillian Gloucester far more than the first. The second Edgar then parried by responding flatly to *his* Gloucester, eliciting laughter from the students watching, the merriment provoked by a recognition that Shakespeare's lines allow such play.

I have had similar success with *Hamlet,* act 5, scene 2, where the entrance of the fey courtier Osric, with his line "Your lordship is right welcome back to Denmark," breaks the tension after the news of Rosencrantz and Guildenstern's deaths. Often the two actors playing Osric do not quite understand at first how to comport themselves while the two Hamlets speak about him in his presence to Horatio. They also don't quite know how "campy" to play him. The repetition of Osric's flowery diction, however, whether the actors play it up or not, helps the students recognize the courtier's inflated sense of self and provokes conversation after the exercise, not only about Shakespeare's intentions in scripting the scene (Is Osric meant to be a complete fool? Does he understand the gravity of the wager he was sent to announce?), but also about the playwright's use of language to convey character and diffuse tension simultaneously.

Through repetition, "Dramatic Echoes" encourages students to focus on the contingent, ironic, and sometimes absurd aspects of a written text that is meant to be performed and whose performance in turn sheds light on the style of the literary work itself.

The Forgers' Circle

Cody Walker

A creative style exercise that focuses on poetic closure.

Genre: *poetry*
Course Level: *any*
Student Difficulty: *moderate*
Teacher Preparation: *medium*
Class Size: *small to medium*
Semester Time: *any*
Writing Component: *in class*
Close Reading: *medium to high*
Estimated Time: *50 to 60 minutes*

EXERCISE

Select a poem that students are not likely to know, and distribute it to the class with the last two or three lines missing. Provide a bit of context for the poem (if necessary), and discuss with the students the poem's form, rhythm, tone, imagery, and diction. Then ask the students to complete (or forge) the ending on their own, noting that they should not write their name on the sheet provided but instead write their forgery anonymously. These attempts should adopt the theme and style of the poem so closely that they might be mistaken for the original ending. Tell the students that you're going to play along as well (though in fact, unbeknownst to the class, you'll simply be transcribing the poem's actual ending onto your sheet). Give the students up to twenty minutes to complete the assignment.

Next, collect all the forgeries, rearrange their order, and redistribute them at random. Make sure to include your "forgery" (with the proper ending) in the pile, and to receive a sheet yourself when they are redistributed. Give the students a minute or two to read and think about the forgery in front of them. Now invite the students, one by one, to read the forged ending out loud and then tell the class what they like best about it. You can model the process by going first, reading the student forgery in front of you and noting perhaps how a particular word in the forged ending echoes another in the poem or how the rhyme snaps the poem shut.

When all the forgeries have been read aloud, reveal the ruse. Tell your students that the original has been in the mix all along and ask them to vote for the entry they think is the original. (They will have already been warned not to Google the poem in class. That skews the competition and ruins the fun.) After the votes are counted, but before the results are revealed, ask the students to offer a bit of testimony. How did they go about completing their forgeries? What specific elements of the poem (imagery, tone, music) did they work hardest to capture? And how did these considerations affect how they voted?

Finally, reveal the results. Did students vote for the original or a forgery? (For contemporary free verse poems, don't be surprised if a forgery wins the day.) You might even award a small prize to the student whose entry receives the most votes; if the original ending wins the contest, the prize should go to the student whose entry finishes second.

Amidst the fun and congratulations, a serious conversation should ensue: What did the class learn about the poem, and the poet, under consideration? How does impersonating, say, Marianne Moore, or John Berryman, or Yusef Komunyakaa, help us to better understand their particular style, or, more broadly, the craft and artistry of poetry? And what might the exercise teach us about poetic closure? Do we prefer a conclusion that "clicks," as William Butler Yeats once wrote, "like a closing box," or do we favor a more elliptical ending?

REFLECTIONS

"The Forgers' Circle" masquerades as a creative writing assignment, but it's really an exercise in critical close reading. Does the poem's structure rely on formal patterns, such as rhyme and meter? If so, the student will need to recognize and reproduce such patterns. Do sonic effects like alliteration, consonance, and assonance make themselves felt? Is the poem loud—in its language, its imagery—or is it quiet? The successful forger will account for such tendencies as he or she becomes, for a stanza or so, Gerard Manley Hopkins or Emily Dickinson.

In my classes, we often talk about the gestures that poets make: Walt Whitman's wide-armed welcome, Robert Frost's wry shrug. These gestures, of course, don't descend from the heavens; they result from a number of stylistic choices that poets make—of syntax, of punctuation, of diction. Forging the endings to poems forces students to consider such choices. In introductory classes, poems no longer seem like mysterious artifacts; they become engines of great power that can be taken apart and rebuilt. (William Carlos Williams's definition of a poem—a "machine made of words"— proves useful here.) In more advanced classes, students who are themselves novice poets often discover strategies that they can use in their own writing. Forging a poem by Sylvia Plath may encourage them to reach for bolder metaphors; forging a poem by Ogden Nash may inspire them to use rhyme for comic effect.

Not long ago, in a British poetry course, I asked my students to forge W. H. Auden's "August 1968," an eight-line poem written in the shadow of the Soviet invasion of Czechoslovakia. Omitting the poem's final two lines, I passed around copies of the poem:

> The Ogre does what ogres can,
> Deeds quite impossible for Man,
> But one prize is beyond his reach,
> The Ogre cannot master Speech:
> About a subjugated plain,
> Among its desperate and slain,
> [two more lines].

We discussed the poem's meter (fairly regular iambic tetrameter), its rhyme scheme (loudly chiming couplets), and its tone (somewhat light, but with a dark backdrop). The students then forged the final lines. The winning student entry—"The Ogre struts among the dead, / But all his glories go unsaid"—impressed us with its sonic echoes (the hard *g* sound in "Ogre," "glories," and "go"; the short *u* sound in "struts," "among," and "unsaid"), its metrical deftness, and its resonant final rhyme. Auden's actual ending—"The Ogre stalks with hands on hips, / While drivel gushes from his lips"—took the silver medal.

I've seen "The Forgers' Circle" brighten countless classrooms; students often single it out as their favorite activity of the semester. The exercise has several benefits for students: it can introduce them to the style of a new poet; it can help them think more deeply about stylistic choices; and it can show them how style itself is a form of play (as Frost once wrote, riffing on a line from *Hamlet*, "Play's the thing"). Not least, "The Forgers' Circle" can provide a shot of confidence to the student who walks out of class having bested Auden, Gwendolyn Brooks, Elizabeth Bishop, or even the Bard himself.

One-Sentence Pastiche

Alicia Christoff

A classic pastiche exercise on a very small scale.

Genre: *fiction*
Course Level: *any*
Student Difficulty: *easy or moderate*
Teacher Preparation: *low*
Class Size: *small to medium*
Semester Time: *midterm, late, last day*
Writing Component: *in class*
Close Reading: *low*
Estimated Time: *30 minutes*

EXERCISE

Taking a famous line from a novel or short story and rewriting it in the style of another author gets students thinking about fiction in new ways—and it usually gets them laughing too. All this one-sentence pastiche exercise requires is that students have read fiction by a handful of different authors. In advance of your class, select a single sentence from the novel or short story the class has read most recently. Choose a line that you feel is particularly representative of the work or of the author's style—a line that screams, for instance, "Jane Austen" or "Marcel Proust."

Begin the in-class exercise by showing students the line in print and reading it aloud so that they can register both the sound and the look of it. (If you like, you can also put the line on a handout so that students can have it in front of them while they work.) Next, it's time to get creative. Ask them to rewrite the same sentence in the style of another author you have read in the course. Tell them which author to imitate, but otherwise give them complete artistic liberty: the main goal is to embody, as completely as possible, the voice of the alternate author. Encourage students to err on the side of exaggeration or loving mockery if they are feeling unsure—whatever it takes to write like Austen or Proust! Give students a good five minutes or more to carefully craft and construct their new sentence, using the model sentence as a jumping-off point. Then ask students to share what they have written with the class as a whole.

Reading their sentences aloud to each other generates both laughs and nods of recognition. (For a fun variation that puts multiple authors in play, let students decide which writer from the syllabus to imitate; when each student reads his or her sentence aloud, let the other students guess whose style is being imitated.) Ask students to reflect on the process of imitation itself. Focusing on individual examples helps students get at the formal choices that make each writer distinct (What did you have to do to alter the sentence? Did you have to add or eliminate clauses? change from first- to third-person? introduce dialogue?) and to compare the styles of different writers (Do they use different types of metaphors? How long are their sentences?). This exercise can also work well as an invigorating review before an exam or as a way to wrap up a semester.

REFLECTIONS

"One-Sentence Pastiche" takes abstract reflection and brings it right into the student's hand. It is amazing to see what students intuitively pick up about an author's style that they may not be able to articulate except in the way it flows from their pens—especially when the pressure is kept low in the spirit of lighthearted pastiche. Moreover, analyzing each other's sentences, down to punctuation and word choice, helps students get a lived sense of what it means to close read fiction and to identify what makes a given author distinct. Discussion quickly comes to center on important topics like voice, point of view, metaphor, diction, word choice, sound, rhythm, pace, plotting, and sentence structure. Perhaps most important, comparison of several different rewrites will help students really "get" the inseparability of form and content.

In a nineteenth-century British fiction course, I had my students rewrite a sentence from George Eliot's *Middlemarch* describing Dorothea's breakthrough: "It was as if some hard icy pressure had melted, and her consciousness had room to expand; her past was come back to her with larger interpretation." One student delighted us with her rewrite à la Brontë: "I felt as though the clouds were clearing; the warmth of the sun melting the numbness that hindered me from returning to my past." The change here is not only a shift from third to first person but also a shift in metaphor, which reminded and got us talking about how important weather is in the novel *Jane Eyre*.

Another student wrote a Dickensian version of the same sentence that had us all cracking up: "She felt her consciousness expand, the hard, icy pressure inside her melting, settling back with a sigh like a satiated glutton at someone else's feast, loosening his belt in utter fulfillment, even his spirit at ease upon consideration of the fact that what now fortified his stomach was drawn out of the pocket of another man." This student's "satiated glutton" (and the poor man whose pocket he was stealing from) got us talking about Dickens's extreme characters and what they allow him to portray. As the sentence switched modes, though, one student noticed that there was suddenly no more room for "her" revelation. Which led us to ask, In Dickens's novels, can characters change in the same way they change in Eliot's?

By rewriting a single sentence, students learn that style is not immaterial. Not only is it made up of a string of specific, concrete choices, but it is also more consequential than it may at first appear. As students discover, stylistic choices dictate not only *how* things are said but also *what* can be said in the first place.

Imitate This

Lindsay Reckson

A creative style exercise that models close reading and encourages playful writing.

Genre: *fiction or poetry*
Course Level: *any*
Student Difficulty: *moderate*
Teacher Preparation: *low*
Class Size: *small to medium*
Semester Time: *any*
Writing Component: *before class*
Close Reading: *medium to high*
Estimated Time: *30 to 50 minutes*

EXERCISE

Choose a text on the syllabus that students perceive as dense, difficult, or intimidating. For this exercise I often prefer contemporary fictional works with experimental voices and styles: Junot Díaz's *The Brief Wondrous Life of Oscar Wao*, or Lydia Davis's collected short stories. Modernist and postmodernist poems and novels also make good candidates: Gertrude Stein's *Tender Buttons*, Thomas Pynchon's *The Crying of Lot 49*, or Gabriel García Márquez's *One Hundred Years of Solitude*.

In advance of classroom discussion, ask students to write a one-page creative imitation: a short piece of writing in the style of the text you'll be discussing. Ask them to begin by noticing the formal qualities of the work: What does it look like on the page? Who is speaking, and what characterizes his or her voice? Is the tone light or serious? How does the text incorporate allusion, ambiguity, imagery? Does it use rhetorical figures (metaphor, metonymy, chiasmus)? If you're working with poetry, ask students to also notice how the poem uses sound (rhyme, euphony, consonance, alliteration) and rhythm (meter, repetition, caesura, line breaks).

Length restrictions are helpful; ask students to write no more than twenty lines of poetry or a few double-spaced paragraphs of prose. Assure students that the content of their imitation need not match the text they are reading (in fact, they may well wish to explore the humor of the mismatch). Their goal is not to reproduce the text exactly but to borrow its comportment, or the details of how it communicates.

As part of this assignment, next ask students to write a paragraph analyzing their creative work. What kind of formal or linguistic techniques did they try to imitate? Where do they see examples of these in the text? And how do these techniques affect the way we read and experience the text? Remind students to type and bring both their imitation and their analysis paragraph to class.

When class convenes, ask students to read their work aloud, either to the class as a whole (in a small class) or in groups of two or three (in a medium class). Be sure to have them bring copies of their imitation for everyone to read along. Invite those listening to try to pinpoint which stylistic technique the student writer was imitating and to find examples of it in the text. For each imitation, and only after other students have weighed in, invite authors to reveal how they approached their imitation: What stylistic features were they trying to capture? What difficulties did they encounter? What, if any, interpretive claims do they see emerging from their imitation? Allow roughly thirty minutes for this portion of the exercise in a small class where everyone speaks, and approximately five to ten minutes if you organize the class into pairs or small groups.

To conclude, allot fifteen to twenty minutes for the class as a whole to reflect on the exercise. Invite them to answer some larger questions about style, genre, or literature: What does style "do"? How does it construct the very specific world of the text? How does that world in turn invite, engage, agitate, or compel us as readers? And what are the stakes of imitation, when "style" is so often recognized as the mark of newness and originality? Ask students to submit their imitations and analysis paragraphs at the end of class, so you can return them soon after with appreciative comments and brief feedback on their analysis.

REFLECTIONS

Imitation breeds intimacy. By giving students the chance to creatively inhabit a text, this exercise encourages them to think carefully about the details of literary style and to begin to grasp the connection between form and content. It also gives students an entry into texts that might otherwise seem disorienting or overwhelming. A close-reading exercise in disguise, creative imitation enables students of all levels to recognize and analyze elements like voice, perspective, figurative language, and sentence structure. For this reason, the exercise works particularly well as a precursor to more formal writing assignments. By isolating and reproducing the formal characteristics of a text in a low-stakes and creative atmosphere, students begin to think *with* the text, rather than simply about it. They gain critical purchase on how literary meaning gets made and learn how to marshal close observation to support their claims.

Part of the appeal of "Imitate This" is that the results are unpredictable and often thrilling. When I asked my students to imitate Wallace Stevens's "Thirteen Ways of Looking at a Blackbird," for example, I expected them to reproduce the poem's precise imagery and gnomic style, its inflections and innuendoes. I did not expect "Thirteen Ways of Looking at Thirteen Ways of Looking at a Blackbird," a particularly inventive student imitation that transformed the act of reading and analyzing Stevens into a dynamic, multidimensional, even self-estranging process: "Among thirteen snowy stanzas / The only moving thing, / Was my eye reading about blackbirds." This particular imitation allowed the student and his classmates to collectively register the difficulty of reading modernist poetry even as they began to grasp the irreverent work of "making it new." Asking the class to reflect together on the process of imitating helped in turn to spark a discussion on modernist and postmodernist practices of appropriation, borrowing, and remixing.

The assignment can and should be tailored closely to the reading. For example, if you are teaching a novel with multiple narrators (Faulkner's *As I Lay Dying* or Toni Morrison's *Beloved*) you might ask students to narrate an event (real or fictional) from two or more perspectives. Or for a text that plays with questions of translation and authority (Jonathan Safran Foer's *Everything Is Illuminated*), consider asking students to translate a short selection from a familiar text (say, the school's honor code) into the voice of one of the novel's characters. Inviting students in a contemporary fiction class to imitate one of the works on the syllabus might produce a range of clever stylistic appropriations: for David Foster Wallace's *Infinite Jest*, a student may write just a few sentences, each with an extensive footnote; for Zadie Smith's *On Beauty*, a one-sided e-mail conversation; and for Jennifer Egan's *A Visit from the Goon Squad*, a PowerPoint presentation. Some of these imitations will be playful, others quite earnest. But in every case, I find students take seriously the opportunity to express themselves creatively, learning in the process how to recognize specific stylistic devices and the ways they shape the meaning of a text.

Students frequently surprise themselves and each other with the imitations they produce, and sharing their creative work goes a long way toward building camaraderie and encouraging experimentation in the classroom. Those who balk at traditional writing assignments often see this exercise as an opportunity to shine; others have the chance to push themselves beyond their comfort zone. Without the immediate pressure of analyzing, say, Wallace Stevens, students laugh and talk and begin to understand what constitutes literary style as such. Reflecting on their creative choices, they learn to think critically about their own reading and writing practices. And they return to the text with a more intimate sense of how and why it does what it does.

. . . .

Convolution

Jeff Dolven

An advanced, and crafty, imitation exercise for teaching style.

Genre: *poetry*
Course Level: *advanced*
Student Difficulty: *hard*
Teacher Preparation: *medium*
Class Size: *small*
Semester Time: *early*
Writing Component: *before class*
Close Reading: *medium*
Estimated Time: *50 to 60 minutes*

EXERCISE

Give students the following assignment:

Write an essay about a short lyric poem on our reading list, using only the words of your lyric. You need not use all the words, but your essay should have the exact same word count as the original poem. This means you can drop words, repeat words, or even couple and uncouple words to make new ones. You may also adjust things like verb tense or pronouns to keep your essay grammatical, though grammar may well take a back seat to creative wordplay.

Provide an example of your own, or use the Shakespeare model below, so students have an idea of what a stylistic convolution might look like. Sonnets work well for this exercise: They are short enough to fit the assignment and long enough to provide a wealth of vocabulary. Their characteristic autonomy also suits the closed world of the constraint. Try it, for example, with sonnets by William Wordsworth ("It is a beauteous evening"), Christina Rossetti ("Remember"), John Berryman (Sonnet 25), or Claude McKay ("If We Must Die").

Ask students to bring their miniessays to class, with both the original and their convolution on a single sheet of paper. Shuffle the student essays and pass them around. Alternatively, you can prepare a handout of all the student essays in advance and simply circulate them in class, assigning each student an essay not their own. Give each student at least five minutes to read silently the paper in front of them and to take quick notes on immediate impressions.

Next, invite students to read the essay in front of them aloud and to say what they learned about the original from reading its convoluted imitation. Now that everyone is free to use other words, they can paraphrase the essay, pointing out what words, phrases, sounds, or syntax stand out most to them. Reading aloud takes only a minute or so, but allow an additional four to five minutes for other students to respond to and comment on each piece. At this point the author will most likely chime in and explain his or her rationale for making certain creative choices.

Conclude the exercise by asking students what they learned about style from the practice of imitation. When they usually talk about poetry, what words do they lean on? What happens when they have to let go of their favorites and use only what the poem gives them? What is gained, and what is lost? What is the difference, anyway, between art and exercise, between poetry and criticism?

REFLECTIONS

Imitation is a powerful, and underused, mode of understanding: the constraints make for something like a deep-sea dive into a poem, from which students will surface with lots to say. For more advanced classes (this is an exacting exercise, best suited for majors), "Convolution" is an especially effective way to teach the classic components of style. More challenging than a straightforward style imitation, this exercise falls somewhere between commenting on and rewriting the text under study. Its power is to immerse students in the poem's climate of diction, to strip them of their customary language of response, and to make them work within the model's own linguistic universe. It sacrifices the objectivity of the professional critic for the complicity of the creative imitator.

I have found that "Convolution" is an especially useful exercise for teaching Shakespeare's habit of revolving and recirculating his words. Here is his Sonnet 30 (116 words long), followed by a sample convolution of the same length:

> When to the sessions of sweet silent thought
> I summon up remembrance of things past,
> I sigh the lack of many a thing I sought
> And with old woes new wail my dear time's waste:
> Then can I drown an eye, unused to flow,
> For precious friends hid in death's dateless night,
> And weep afresh love's long since cancelled woe,
> And moan th'expense of many a vanished sight:
> Then can I grieve at grievances foregone,
> And heavily from woe to woe tell o'er
> The sad account of fore-bemoanèd moan,
> Which I new pay as if not paid before.
> But if the while I think on you, dear friend,
> All losses are restored and sorrows end.

If "sought" is the past of "sigh," then "summon" is "moan," afresh: "sigh" and "summon" are the new woes which restore old grievances. Restore, but not end or cancel. The *I* expends old woes as new, "as if not paid afore," as if the *I* can grieve datelessly. For the *I* cannot remember before loss, cannot remember un-grief. The thing the *I* remembers, and the thing the *I* accounts lost, is weeping. If all loss is paid with grieving, if all accounts are cancelled with moans, the *I* loses lack—grief, woe, and moan all vanish—and lack is precious, for lack is the past. (Remember, the *I* sought things, but things hid then, too.)

An essay made of Shakespeare's raw material has to reckon with the sonnet's obsessive repetition of its words, words like "woe" and "moan" that the lines cannot let go of. This particular imitation captures how the chain of woes leads back only to another woe—never, as one might expect, or hope, to some original happiness. The speaker knows no other object of nostalgia than his or her own sorrow. I have seen students again and again led to such unforeseen epiphanies by imitation, often through the mere act of confining themselves to a sonnet's claustrophobic diction. The exercise leads to an interpretation, but only by way of an experience.

The constraints for an advanced style exercise like this could be even tighter: you might insist on using every one of the sonnet's words (only rearranging them) or only the poem's given grammatical forms (instead of freely conjugating, nominalizing, or pluralizing, as here, with a couple of adventitious homonyms along the way). There are liberties to take, too: I learned recently that one student of mine has used his miniessay as text for a choral composition. But the exercise is plenty challenging as it is, for it cannot be done without getting all the language in mind at once and without thinking in the poem's own terms. "Convolution"—imitation with a twist—is often the best way to discover the importance of poetic diction, by learning a poem's language from the inside out.

Punctuation Matters

Anne-Marie Womack

An exercise in close reading an oft-neglected element of style: punctuation.

Genre: *any*
Course Level: *any*
Student Difficulty: *moderate*
Teacher Preparation: *medium*
Class Size: *small to medium*
Semester Time: *any*
Writing Component: *in class, optional after class*
Close Reading: *high*
Estimated Time: *40 to 50 minutes*

EXERCISE

Before class, choose a few short literary texts that use punctuation in dramatic and deliberate ways and reproduce them on a handout. Short poems by Langston Hughes, Emily Dickinson, E. E. Cummings, and Percy Bysshe Shelley all work well. On this same handout, include a selection of nonliterary texts whose distinctive punctuation provides a range of additional examples for students to work with. These other texts can include (1) strikingly punctuated book titles, such as Brad Listi's *Attention. Deficit. Disorder.* or Damián Baca's *Mestiz@ Scripts, Digital Migrations, and the Territories of Writing*; (2) comparative sentences, such as "A woman without her man is nothing" versus "A woman: without her, man is nothing"; or (3) even phone texts with emoticons, which let students analyze how they use contemporary punctuation to signal emotion. As you select examples, keep in mind that the goal of this exercise is to draw students' attention to the effects of punctuation in shaping style, helping them to apply close-reading skills to grammar and to incorporate punctuation into a more nuanced reading of texts. If you like, instead of a handout you can project the texts in class on a PowerPoint slide or upload them to your course website.

Provide students with the compiled list. Working in groups of three to four, invite students to interpret the meaning of a particular passage or line by studying its punctuation, the most overlooked element of style. Encourage them to focus first on what they already know implicitly, asking, What does the significant punctuation usually tell us in any sentence? What actions or meanings does the punctuation commonly signal? Then, direct them to apply that knowledge to the text at hand: How does that knowledge create meaning in your specific passage or line?

Stagger students' starting points (have group A start with one text, group B with another, etc.) to ensure that each example will have people prepared for discussion. If you have many groups, you can assign more than one group to the same text. As you circulate among the groups, remind students to keep their attention focused on specific marks of punctuation, especially if you find them primarily summarizing the texts. Students need to be taught that punctuation does more than adorn words; it tells us *how* to read words.

After the allotted group time (I recommend fifteen minutes or so), reconvene the students as a full class and review each example. Draw attention to their readings and interpretations (especially conflicting ones) by recording them on the board. As the examples begin to build, start to compare and contrast writing styles. This portion of the exercise might take five minutes per example. In the remaining minutes of class, or as a brief homework assignment, consider asking students to compose a short paragraph in which they choose one of the discussed examples, introduce the key quotation, and analyze how the author's particular punctuation choices shape meaning. This writing component provides practice for tying explicit evidence to deeply analyzed interpretations of a text.

REFLECTIONS

This exercise helps students analyze all the stylistic devices available to writers, not just diction and form alone. Students can produce complex readings as they consider the figurative meanings of punctuation and the responses audiences may have to a single period, comma, dash, question mark, colon, semicolon, ellipsis, exclamation mark, or parenthesis.

When reconvening the full class for discussion, I find it can be helpful to begin with the nonfiction title *Attention. Deficit. Disorder.*, before launching into a literary text. This interesting and efficient starter example helps students understand how an author might use periods to slow down the reader or, in combination with the words themselves, create an incongruous tone. Some of my students perceive irony and humor in this title, while others see a type of therapeutic slowing down for a disorder characterized by frantic speed—a debate that ultimately demonstrates how even standardized and rule-driven grammar can create multiple meanings and interpretations. When we then segued into an analysis of Langston Hughes's "Let America Be America Again," students were primed to attend to the nuances of punctuation and immediately zeroed in on the poet's strategic use of parentheses. Often a device of subordination—or as my students put it, "something that is not the main point"—parentheses in this poem typographically dramatize how the voices of minorities have been subordinated in America.

These close analyses can also invite discussions on textual variants, those differing versions of a text that exist because of authorial revisions, editorial changes, or errors in typesetting. Famous examples include those in the many versions of the Bible (variants in Matthew 5:27–32, for instance, muddle whether divorce or remarriage constitutes adultery) or in the American canon (Walt Whitman's poem in the 1856 edition of *Leaves of Grass* titled "Poem of Walt Whitman, an American" became "Walt Whitman" by 1860 and finally "Song of Myself" in 1881). In an example from the British canon, Shelley's "Ozymandias" appears in two versions: one in which the line "Stand in the desert . . . Near them, on the sand" appears with ellipsis and one in which it does not. The ellipsis dividing the line creates space in a space-conscious form, literalizes distance in a description of physical distance, and evokes time passage in a poem on the same theme. This version also makes the line a visual representation of the preceding "Two vast and trunkless legs of stone." All of these effects come together to forge a substantially stronger meaning through a single ellipsis.

By investigating seemingly small punctuation choices, students learn that grammar, while working on us almost automatically, is a provocative site for constructing meaning. I have used this exercise to teach a range of literary and critical skills: intertextuality, signaled by quotation marks around quotes; gendered language, signaled by punctuated hybrid words like *(wo) men* and *s/he*; and equality or ranking, signaled by commas in lists. I have also witnessed lively classroom debates over the necessity of the Oxford comma, that optional comma before the conjunction at the end of a list. Students on both sides of the issue can research how their position clears up certain sentence ambiguities while remaining vulnerable to others. Common Internet examples demonstrate especially humorous problems in paternal heritage: "I'd like to thank my father, Elvis, and Marilyn Monroe" or "To my parents, Ayn Rand and God." At the end of this exercise, students will be able to think more critically about punctuation in all its various roles: creating meaning, controlling tempo, and conveying emotion. They will learn, in short, that "punctuation matters."

. . . .

For more exercises that can be used to teach styles, try these:

Read, Reread, Close Read (Discussions)
The Blow Up (Essentials)
The One-Liner (Essentials)
The Six-Word Story (Stories)
Splicing (Stories)
First Paragraphs (Stories)
Alternate Endings (Stories)
Form and Content (Poems)
Dramatic Monologue (Poems)
We've Got the Beat (Plays)
Adaptation (Plays)
Moving Scenes (Plays)
Is This Book Literature? (Canons)
Literature Class Band (Canons)
Keywords (Words)
Vocabulary Bites (Words)
Aphorisms (Words)
Fill in the Blanks (Words)

PICTURES

Literary texts often function visually, whether through the careful description of objects or scenes, through allusions that call up powerful images, or through the very medium of graphic representation itself. The exercises in this section use creative visualization to capture, map, and depict literary imagery, setting, and action, while also training students in the techniques of "close viewing." This turn to the visual can give students unexpected insights into literary description, narrative perspective, and characterization, while also helping them uncover shapes and patterns they may only have dimly glimpsed before.

Tap into your class's latent creativity with one of the first three exercises ("Draw Me a Picture," "Island Mapping," and "Reverse Ekphrasis"), which invite students to put pencil to paper and draw. (No actual artistic experience is required.) Or shift the creative medium to photography, using the next exercise ("Novel Portraits") to offer a lesson in visual literacy by challenging students to construct a portrait gallery of literary characters. Or use the last set of exercises to prioritize the viewing and interpreting of visual images themselves, whether you want to show students how to read graphic novels ("Close Reading Comics"), help them convert narrative texts into visual narratives ("Making It Graphic"), or ask them to collect and present images that extend or contextualize the allusions they find in their texts ("Digital Literacy"). Is a picture worth a thousand words? In this section, every word, it seems, demands its own picture.

Draw Me a Picture

William A. Gleason and Amelia Worsley

burdy

A creative exercise that helps students think about the stakes of literary imagery.

> Genre: *fiction or poetry*
> Course Level: *introductory or intermediate*
> Student Difficulty: *easy*
> Teacher Preparation: *low*
> Class Size: *small to medium*
> Semester Time: *any*
> Writing Component: *none*
> Close Reading: *medium to high*
> Estimated Time: *40 to 50 minutes*

EXERCISE

Choose a descriptive passage from a poem, short story, or novel. The passage could describe a setting, object, or person. It might do so straightforwardly, or it might proceed by way of metaphor. The main point is to find a passage where visualization seems to matter. This exercise can work, with varied effects, on descriptive passages from any period—from Charles Dickens's *Bleak House* to Virginia Woolf's *Mrs. Dalloway*, from Ezra Pound's "In a Station of the Metro" to Rita Dove's *Thomas and Beulah*.

As you guide the class to the passage, hand out blank sheets of 8.5 × 11–inch paper and (if you have them) pencils to each student. (Eraserless mini-pencils are perfect: they allow students to draw without the compulsion to "correct" as they go.)

Ask one student to read the passage aloud to the class. Then ask every student to sketch his or her own picture of what they understand these lines to represent, encouraging them to refer back to the passage as they draw. Give students five to ten minutes to complete their drawings. When everyone is finished, ask the students to pass their drawings to the person on their right. Tell them to look over the drawing they've just received—and then, after a few moments of looking, to pass *that* drawing to the right as well. The aim is to have students pass them quickly (after ten to fifteen seconds of looking, tops) so that students can register how different the drawings are without necessarily studying each one intently. Continue looking and passing until each student receives his or her original drawing back. If your class is not seated in a circle, you can have them pass in serpentine fashion by rows, with the last person in the last row passing to the first person in the first row. For the passing portion of the exercise, allow three to five minutes for a small class and five to seven minutes for a medium class.

Allocate another thirty minutes to discussing the sketches. Ask the students to reflect on what they've just done, both in the act of drawing the picture and in the experience of seeing the other students' drawings. Questions you might ask: What was it like to draw this? Was it difficult to convey this language in the form of pictures? Why or why not? How many times did you need to read the passage before you decided where to start drawing? Did you start from the beginning of the passage, or somewhere else? How does the language of the passage guide you through the scene? What problems did you encounter as you progressed? Did you hesitate about what any of the lines you read meant to your picture? How did you understand your perspective in relation to that of the speaker of the passage?

Be sure to ask students questions about the effects of seeing the other drawings: How did they differ from each other? Did seeing the other drawings change your mind about your sense of what the passage is trying to help readers visualize, or help you to see something you hadn't seen before? Did you understand yourself to be depicting the same thing as other readers? Does the description support different perspectives? Do you think a line drawing in pencil is the best way to represent this scene, or would other artistic approaches or tools make it easier?

Finally, turn the conversation back to the text as a whole: How do the language and perspective of these particular lines shape or reflect larger concerns of this poem, story, or novel? How might our discussion change your reaction to other passages you remember visualizing as you read?

REFLECTIONS

At a basic level, "Draw Me a Picture" encourages students to read the text more closely than they might otherwise and to realize where the text is ambiguous. But this exercise also works wonderfully to open a discussion about the ways in which literary imagery and the experiences it produces are both like and unlike pictorial representation. The eye moves differently over a page than over a painting; we ask our imaginations to work in different ways under different circumstances.

The goal of the exercise is not to decide which drawing is the "right" one but to help students reflect on how and why different readers visualize descriptions differently. It focuses on how the language of the passage—its diction, structure, and perspective—helps to create the picture each student sees. Disagreement about these inferences can be productive, as it highlights the multiple resonances of descriptive language. Discussions like this also help students to see where they may have been using their own imaginations to "fill in the gaps," and such insight underscores how the knowledge and experience each student brings to the text might change it.

Although some students may feel silly about drawing a picture—or sheepish about their artistic abilities—we find that these reactions pass quickly and that students take this unusual classroom activity quite seriously. (Some may even ask for more time to put finishing touches on rather elaborate sketches.) The first thing most students notice is how different their sketch is from everyone else's. This is typically true even with the most seemingly straightforward passages; as a result, the class becomes eager to figure out why.

We most recently tried this exercise with the first fifty lines of Ben Jonson's seventeenth-century country house poem "To Penshurst" in a course on literature and environment. Despite the seemingly straightforward graphic nature of these lines, in which the speaker describes the house and its setting, the students' drawings differed dramatically. Prominent aspects of one student's sketch were barely emphasized in another's. ("Oh, there are horses in the poem!" exclaimed one student as the completed drawings were being passed around.) Some students imagined the "ancient pile" as a thatched cottage, others as a larger structure. Some placed the house at the center of the scene; others pictured it in the distance, preferring to foreground the features of the landscape that surround the house. Several students commented that they had to read the poem several times before beginning, since the poem proceeds by negative definition, telling them at the outset what *not* to draw rather than what *to* draw.

Questions of perspective, point of view, framing, scale, and textual chronology became more important as our discussion proceeded. Some students chose a bird's-eye view, while others imagined that, like a landscape painter, they were embodied in the scene, though all at different levels and perspectives. The poem encompasses radical changes in perspective that a landscape painting is less able to achieve. A few students had therefore chosen to represent this seventeenth-century poem using more "modern" visual techniques. One student told the class that she made the "purpled pheasant with the speckled side" much larger than the horses because the magnified pheasant demanded to be drawn in more detail. A simple question about the difference between a landscape painter's perspective and the implicit point of view of the speaker or narrator of "To Penshurst" led to a spirited discussion about the different kinds of descriptions we can expect from disembodied versus embodied speakers. As the students considered the role of Jonson's language in guiding the reader's attention, they came to argue for the importance of the passage's proto-cinematic quality: the description starts with the house but then zooms out and back in—at one moment looking from a seemingly distant, aerial view; at another, providing a close-up of the oddly artificial "painted partridge." The snapshot students had drawn was a static representation of a kinetic experience. On reflection, the poem seemed far less linear than it had first appeared.

This is just one example of where "Draw Me a Picture" might lead, though questions of perspective, embodiment, and temporality are important to many descriptive passages. Different descriptions encourage different practices of mental visualization. Two dimensions are sometimes not enough. Descriptive language from different periods produces the necessity for different drawing techniques: for this reason, this exercise can be a useful one at the beginning and end of a survey course.

. . . .

Island Mapping

Matthew T. Lynch

A collaborative mapping exercise that helps students analyze literary islands.

Genre: *fiction or drama*
Course Level: *introductory or intermediate*
Student Difficulty: *moderate*
Teacher Preparation: *low*
Class Size: *small to medium*
Semester Time: *early*
Writing Component: *none*
Close Reading: *medium*
Estimated Time: *30 to 40 minutes*

EXERCISE

Islands have long attracted the interest of writers, whether as the setting for a specific episode (the Jackson Island sequence in Mark Twain's *The Adventures of Tom Sawyer*, or Lilliput in Jonathan Swift's *Gulliver's Travels*) or as the site for an entire work. They appear in a wide range of genres and periods, from Shakespeare's *The Tempest*, to Daniel DeFoe's *Robinson Crusoe*, to Lucy Maud Montgomery's *Anne of Green Gables*. Whether based on actual or imagined places, islands provide dynamic literary settings because they are self-contained and tend to represent a world apart. From the Age of Discovery to the present, textual islands have often functioned as the tabulae rasae of new beginnings and new possibilities, or simply as a space detached from "civilization."

Choose a text with an island setting and guide students to a description of the island in the text. Ask them to take out a piece of paper and a pen or pencil, read the description silently to themselves, and then draw a map of the island. When they are finished (this should take about five to ten minutes), ask them to describe their images to you as you draw a composite map of the island, using either the board or an overhead projector. (As an alternative, you can designate one of the students as the official "sketch artist.")

Let students debate the "correct" configuration of the island, and ask them to support their claims using specific evidence from the text. Stop when the class reaches a consensus. If the class cannot reach a consensus, help them return to the descriptive passages for a closer look. If no consensus can be reached even after your intervention, ask students why the description of the island might be ambiguous and what this ambiguity might suggest about possible themes.

If the island is one that other critics or artists have tried to draw before— there are several hypothetical maps of Lilliput or Utopia, for example—you can conclude the exercise by circulating or projecting these maps for the students to compare to the composite drawing they have created. Whose drawing is most accurate? Why? Here again, ask students to support their claims by finding specific evidence from the text. (This version of the exercise empowers students by giving authority to their original readings and allows them to challenge readings done by experts.) All told, the exercise takes roughly thirty to forty minutes.

REFLECTIONS

"Island Mapping" is an active exercise that brings the written word alive, encourages close and careful reading, and works with any genre or period. As students debate the "correct" depiction of the island under discussion, they discover which of their visual claims can and cannot be supported by textual evidence. In the process, they usually discover something new about the function of the island in the larger text as well.

In my classes on utopian and dystopian literature, for example, I use this exercise to help students engage with Thomas More's *Utopia*, particularly Raphael Hythloday's description of the island in Book II. While my students quickly agree that the island resembles the shape of a crescent moon, they can't decide which way to orient it, as Hythloday never indicates the direction to which the bay points. Particularly perceptive students also notice that if Utopia's circumference is five hundred miles, its diameter cannot be two hundred miles. The island itself is thus mathematically impossible. (One of my students even devised a formula to determine whether the size and distribution of Utopia's towns allowed them to fit on the island!)

This exercise therefore helps students recognize that while More's Utopia may be a "good place," it is also quite literally "nowhere," suggesting that "the best state of the commonwealth" can never exist in its complete form. These cartographic complications also compel students to question Hythloday's reliability, allowing them to engage critically with the discussion about an ideal society in which he participates and which is so central to the text as a whole. "Island Mapping" thus immerses students in precisely the conversation More wanted his readers to have: how do we create and maintain a more perfect society?

Other variations of this exercise could include drawing houses (the House of the Seven Gables, Gatsby's house, Northanger Abbey, or the House of Usher), ships (the *Pequod* or Odysseus's ship), or interior spaces (the "red-room" in *Jane Eyre*, the yellow wallpaper in Charlotte Perkins Gilman's short story, or a personalized Room 101 from *Nineteen Eighty-Four*). What is important is to engage students' imaginations and visual skills to help them transform the settings of texts into dynamic spaces of interpretation, analysis, discussion, and possibility.

· ·

Reverse Ekphrasis

Emily Hyde

A creative exercise in transposing media.

Genre: *fiction or poetry*
Course Level: *any*
Student Difficulty: *easy or moderate*
Teacher Preparation: *low*
Class Size: *small*
Semester Time: *any*
Writing Component: *in class or after class*
Close Reading: *medium*
Estimated Time: *30 to 35 minutes (version 1), 55 to 65 minutes (version 2)*

EXERCISE

Ekphrasis is the literary description of a work of art; it is a rhetorical device in which the verbal tries to overcome the visual. I offer here two versions of an ekphrasis exercise, only one of which requires you to teach the term. Both make use of the strange potency of transforming one medium into another.

The first version, "Drawing Time," works particularly well with fiction or epic poetry, preferably a text with a complicated narrative scheme. Good candidates include *Beowulf* (because of the two battles separated by fifty years), Joseph Conrad's *The Secret Agent* (which operates via "sudden holes in space and time"), and Arundhati Roy's *The God of Small Things* (with its disjunctive, nonlinear structure). The second version of this exercise, "The Artist's Statement," works well with texts that include ekphrastic objects, such as Keats's "Ode on a Grecian Urn" or W. H. Auden's "Musée des Beaux Arts," or texts that include artists at work, like Lily Briscoe in Virginia Woolf's *To the Lighthouse*.

For version one, "Drawing Time," begin by asking your students to draw how time works in your novel or poem. Can the narrative action be captured visually? This group exercise can be done in two ways. Invite students to make individual drawings on paper, and then have them compare drawings with the person next to them. Or have students work in groups of two or three and draw on the board together. Getting students up in front of the classroom is often the best approach, since it allows them to "teach" their drawing to the rest of the class. Allow ten minutes or so for the creative portion of the exercise and at least twenty minutes for class presentations and general conversation to follow.

Before they begin drawing, encourage students to brainstorm possibilities: maps, graphs, charts, diagrams, shapes, logos, or forms of visual representation specific to your text. A word of caution: at the start of the exercise, be sure to intercept the student who thinks he or she must write down every plot point—often in comic strip form—and who will certainly run out of time. This is an exercise not in bookkeeping but in capturing language visually (though certain novels might be provocatively reduced to ledgers or logbooks).

The second and longer version of this exercise, "The Artist's Statement," can be applied directly to an ekphrastic object. Take some time to prepare the students by teaching the term "ekphrasis," which, at its most basic level, connotes description. Etymologically, the word means "to speak out," and this gives a sense of the rhetorical valence of the term. An ekphrastic object is one that has been given voice by the poet or writer. It will be important to stress the antagonism generated by ekphrasis—I often like to conclude with a line attributed to singer and songwriter Elvis Costello: "Writing about music is like dancing about architecture. It's a really stupid thing to want to do."

Instruct students to describe the ekphrastic object at one more remove, in even more impoverished language. Ask them to imagine that Keats's Grecian urn or Lily Briscoe's painting is being displayed in an art gallery, and the students have been selected to write the artist's statement that will accompany the object. The artist's statement is a genre that includes technical specifications about the work of art as well as descriptions of the artist's process and goals. Today, it is often written by the artist in order to introduce and explicate the work of art, and if an artist appears in your novel or poem, you may invite students to write in that character's voice.

There are many resources online, pitched to artists, for writing these statements, or you can prepare an in-class handout with some models. Prompts may include the following: What is the title of this work of art and what are its materials and provenance? How do you begin an artwork? How do you know it's done? What are your goals and aspirations as you work? How do you make decisions? What do you want the public to take away from this work of art? How does your art relate to the art of your contemporaries? Defining "ekphrasis" and briefly studying some model artist statements takes roughly twenty minutes of class time.

The students can write their artist statements either in class or out of class; for in-class writing, allow students fifteen minutes or more. Stress to the students that the brevity of these statements (less than two hundred words) should breed creativity. The artist statements can be shared in one of two ways: I have collected them on the course website for students to browse and compare, and I have also asked students to read out their statements in class. Encourage the rest of the class to pose questions to the student who is presenting, such as, What made you focus on that particular color? or Why do you think the artist had that particular goal in mind?

When all the statements have been shared (this takes between twenty to thirty minutes), ask students to reflect on the constraints of the exercise and the difficulties of ekphrasis itself. What is lost when we move between media? What is gained? What is our readerly experience of the transformation? There are no right answers to these questions, and they will inevitably lead back to close readings of the work of literature itself.

REFLECTIONS

Both versions of "Reverse Ekphrasis" have their benefits. The first approach can provide a creative way to conclude classwork on a long novel or poem. It works well even with nonmajors and with freshmen because it lets them respond to a work of literature outside the traditional forms of written argument and verbal discussion. Students with talents in drawing, architectural modeling, and data visualization can also teach their English-major classmates to look beyond plot details to larger shapes and patterns. The second approach focuses students' attention more closely on the literariness of ekphrasis by asking them to produce yet another description of the work of art. This second version also can easily double as a creative and a critical writing assignment. You may discover that certain students are better writers when speaking through a persona, and you may be able to help them translate some of the confidence of that voice into their argumentative writing.

In both versions, the way you set up the exercise will vary case by case, depending on the text. Teaching *Beowulf*, I received X-marks-the-spot type maps of Beowulf's adventures as well as a stunningly simple graph of "Monster Density" versus "Price of Gold." For Conrad's *The Secret Agent*, I watched as a group of students argued about where to place the bomb blast on a graph. They finally settled on making it the zero value on the x axis since the explosion never actually occurs in the novel. They then had to debate how to represent the forensic investigation of the blast, and where to place one character's reimagining of the scene. I have found that in general students do tend to gravitate toward graphs as their drawing method of choice. They love to debate about the x axis and the y axis and to figure out what sort of line, shape, or color might best convey a particular narrative arc.

For "The Artist's Statement," the story that you set up for your students will also vary depending on the ekphrastic object at hand. In *To the Lighthouse*, Lily Briscoe is sure her painting will be hung in attics or rolled up and stuffed under a sofa. So I asked my students to picture Lily, ten years after the novel's close, as a well-known painter preparing for a retrospective exhibit and writing a statement to accompany the painting that was recently retrieved from the Ramsays' attic. One student produced the following title and description: "Lily Briscoe, *Elegy for a Moment*. Medium: Canvas, Oil Paint, Time."

In both versions of this exercise, students are confronted with questions about medium, difference, and constraint. Their creative responses require the ability to close read across media, but discussion will naturally move back toward the literary and its representational strengths and weaknesses. By inviting students to cross borders and to articulate the difficulties they encounter on the borderline, these exercises broaden students' understanding of what literature can do and what they can do with literature.

Novel Portraits

Susan Jaret McKinstry

An interdisciplinary exercise in which students develop interpretive skills by creating photographic portraits.

Genre: *fiction*
Course Level: *any*
Student Difficulty: *moderate*
Teacher Preparation: *medium*
Class Size: *any*
Semester Time: *midterm to last day*
Writing Component: *after class*
Close Reading: *low*
Estimated Time: *1 hour*

EXERCISE

This collaborative exercise takes approximately two weeks to pull off, though just one hour of actual class time as it concludes. Most of the work done is outside class (taking each team about four hours), with e-mails to the instructor during the process and an in-class exhibition and critique at the end. The exhibit works particularly well if students have chosen different novels and characters, so the exercise should come later in the term. Novels stuffed with eccentric and colorful characters make particularly good candidates for this exercise: books by Charles Dickens, George Eliot, Herman Melville, Emile Zola, Marcel Proust, Zora Neale Hurston, Gabriel García Márquez. But in truth any novels with strong character descriptions will do.

Divide the students into project teams (ideally three to four students per team) to create a photographic portrait of a character from a novel. First, have each team meet outside class to select a brief, compelling textual "portrait" of a character from any of the texts they have read in the course: a description, dialogue, or event that brings that character to life. I prime students for this part of the exercise by regularly assigning this simple but effective reading prompt and small-group discussion starter: Come to class with the passage you think best describes Character X. Then, ask each team to create a *visual* portrait of that character by selecting a sitter, costume, props, setting, and pose, photographing it, and printing the final portrait (on regular 8.5 × 11–inch paper on a good printer) in color, sepia tones, or black and white.

Because the result might be an accurate historical re-creation of the novel's period or might diverge dramatically—the teams are free to take whatever approach they wish—next ask each team to write a concise exhibit label (approximately 150 words) that explains their portrait as an illustration/interpretation of the novel's character. This is an essential part of the exercise: the labels turn the project from playful to meaningful by asking the group to articulate their intellectual and aesthetic decisions, link the textual evidence to the visual work, and speak to an audience beyond the course.

I provide precise instructions, format, and examples for the label:

Cite the lines from the novel that you selected to define the character (including author and date). Then write a concise interpretation of the portrait. What do you want the gallery viewer to notice? What artistic choices did you make? What should the viewer see in the photo, and what does it mean? What do you want the viewer to understand about the portrait, about the character, and about the novel? Include a brief description of the process of creating your photograph.

Ask each team to send you a final draft of the label for editing; this assures a good, consistent result and a more professional-looking exhibit. Or if you prefer, you can have the student teams do this last round of editing themselves.

Finally, have the class curate an exhibition of their portraits and labels, displaying them in the classroom, a hallway, or a small gallery. (The ideal number of objects in the exhibition, given the limits of space and time, can help determine the number of teams.) The exhibit can be very simple and temporary, lasting one class period and requiring only tape or some other method to attach the work to the walls, or it can be more formal if time and space allow. If the exhibit can be public, ask the class to select an exhibition title (we briefly brainstorm suggestions) and write an introductory placard. I usually volunteer to contribute this placard, which comes directly out of the explicit goals of the course and exercise (it is quite fun to write).

The project then culminates in a "gallery opening" and portrait critique during class (either public, with students inviting friends, or private, only for the class itself). First let everyone explore the gallery, quietly examining the portraits and labels. Then gather the students for a public critique, on the model of a studio art class: as each team stands by its work, have the rest of the class discuss each portrait and label, pointing out compelling visual details and asking the team questions about their process and product. Since the students all know the novels, the conversation can focus on how the team has translated that shared text into a visual object: what they highlighted and how they used visual tools to illustrate the selected quotation from the novel and create the character's portrait.

REFLECTIONS

"Novel Portraits" highlights questions of genre, history, and technology as students develop their textual and visual interpretive skills. It helps students recognize how writers create characters in rich, complex ways far beyond visual descriptions. It encourages close reading and collaborative debate, since each team has to select an illustrative passage from the novel and then decide how to bring that character to life in a different medium. I use this exercise with students in a midlevel Victorian novel class, although "Novel Portraits" would effectively highlight characterization and culture in novels from any literary tradition or historical period.

Creating the portrait provides a lesson in visual literacy, as the students make visual choices based on their interpretative goals. They can use their own camera or phone, so the project allows for a wide range of artistic and literary backgrounds, building on students' familiarity with visual technologies including websites, smart phones, and social media. Students love this element of the project, and they are very comfortable with the concept of image as a form of characterization. I ask them to think about film ads or Facebook profile pictures, and I show them a few Victorian portraits because I want them to consider how images can work as historic markers. I was able to collaborate on the exercise once with a studio art professor teaching photography, and once with a cinema and media studies professor teaching digital portraiture (all three of us are planning our next collaboration). Through the exercise, the students share their disciplinary knowledge (the literature students know the novel; the art students know their medium) to design and create an aesthetic and interpretive product they could not have made alone: an ideal collaboration.

The exhibition provides a valuable opportunity to publicize students' interdisciplinary collaborative work. Since each team makes deliberate choices in their portraits, the exhibition and critique foster conversations about literary, artistic, and social conventions, changing technologies, and interpretive strategies. Students with diverse academic backgrounds will point out differing elements of others' portraits, such as lighting and composition, symbolic meaning, literary allusions, or historical elements, and learn from one another's comments and questions.

I introduce this exercise at the halfway point in the Victorian course, when students have read George Eliot's *Middlemarch*, Charlotte Brontë's *Jane Eyre*, Emily Bronte's *Wuthering Heights*, and George Du Maurier's *Trilby*, which results in a wonderful variety of portraits. In the most recent class, two teams created memorable portraits from *Middlemarch*. One, titled *The Best Part of Myself*, depicted Mary Garth in "pensive solitude" in her garden, surrounded by the effects of the influence of her parents, whom she had once called the "best part" of herself. To render Mary's somber pensiveness, the students took the picture outside in natural lighting and then converted it to sepia, with a heightened contrast and lower saturation. The second portrait, *A Young Widow's Unveiling*, depicted the moment in the novel when Celia Brooke removes her sister's widow's cap—a brief aside in the text but represented by the students as "a dramatized and transitional moment in Dorothea's character." As they noted in their label, "Ultimately the onlooker is asked to consider whether Dorothea's eventual characterization as a fully realized woman and wife is a natural progression into womanhood or else a loss of idealism, and the striking black-and-white contrast underscores the moral ambiguity of this moment, as does Dorothea's expression of innocence and fear."

I have assigned versions of "Novel Portraits" five times, in collaboration with studio art photography classes using only Victorian-era photography techniques, with advanced digital students using all the current digital tools, and in my Victorian class alone, and the results always amaze us.

· ·

Close Reading Comics

David M. Ball

An exercise that introduces students to the medium-specific principles, and hidden challenges, of close reading comics.

Genre: *graphic narrative, comics*
Course Level: *any, especially introductory*
Student Difficulty: *easy*
Teacher Preparation: *low*
Class Size: *any*
Semester Time: *early (for courses on graphic narrative) or any (for other courses)*
Writing Component: *none*
Close Reading: *medium to high*
Estimated Time: *40 to 45 minutes*

EXERCISE

As the first assigned graphic narrative for a course exclusively devoted to comics, or as an introduction to studying comics in a thematic course, ask students to read with care a single, relatively discrete multipanel composition before coming to class. This primary text can be almost anything, from a four-panel *Peanuts* strip or Golden Age superhero story to single or multiple pages from one of the more widely taught contemporary cartoonists such as Art Spiegelman, Alison Bechdel, or Chris Ware.

At the beginning of class, first ask the students to outline the basic story being told. Tell them to focus only on plot—what happens—not on the visual aspects of the text. Record their responses on the top half of the board until you have an agreed-upon outline of the story. (In a larger class, you can divide the students into small groups to perform these and subsequent tasks.)

After ten to fifteen minutes of this student-directed exposition, ask the class to return to the text and describe what they *see* on the page, not in the context of the story they've just put together, but as a visible artifact. Focusing this way works against students' conventional impulse to read comics quickly and pictographically and facilitates instead a conversation that might be termed "close viewing," one that attends to questions of line, color, and composition that will be largely unfamiliar to English majors and more recognizable to those with experience in art history or film studies classes. (This turn may thus invite contributions from students with different disciplinary expertise.)

As students respond, record their observations on the bottom half of the board, offering follow-up questions to help them think spatially and visually: If this comic or narrative were a map, what would the biggest words on that map be? How are the observations on the comic's content ratified or complicated by attention to its form? In what ways is this enforced division between plot and presentation undone by the simultaneity of reading and seeing in comics? Much of the medium-specific information that might have gone unnoticed in the opening conversation about narrative now begins to become visible to students.

With these two trajectories of interpretation in place, the class is now primed to see connections between form and content, a technique of close reading that will already be in place for literature majors but one made productively unfamiliar amidst the imperative to *see* as well as *read* when analyzing comics. Highlighting these aspects of the text under discussion will help students to see comics not simply as a series of generic conventions—the all-too-common expectations of talking animals, superheroes, and the like—but as a medium capable of as wide a range of creative expression as other artistic modes.

Particularly engaging for these initial conversations are open questions that put into doubt the early assurances of plot summary and complicate students' desire to "solve" the text: In what ways do formal decisions of the text correspond to, or conflict with, the larger movements and themes of the work? How do images function pictographically and the lettering of words function visually in the text, and how do the two interact meaning-fully in the panels under discussion? How do gutters (the spaces between the panels) function for the reader, and how do we account for the passage of time both within and between the panels on display? In terms of telling stories, what abilities do comics have that aren't available to authors and artists in other mediums? These are just a few of the more general questions you can ask to point students toward methodological and medium-specific concerns in a course either incorporating or devoted exclusively to graphic narrative.

This process could also be effectively reversed, isolating a single panel of a conventional four-panel newspaper strip to focus on matters of composition and line, and then uncovering subsequent panels to relate more familiar notions in the literature classroom of syntax and narrative. However you execute the exercise, allow approximately forty to forty-five minutes to cover all the bases.

REFLECTIONS

Comics offer the college-level literature instructor an opportunity to en-courage critical thinking about a medium that students believe they know intimately but that they have most likely never considered in formal terms. As such, comics have become increasingly prevalent on syllabuses, concur-rent with a remarkably generative rise in the publication and reception of graphic narratives everywhere from literary prize committees to *New York Times* best-seller lists. Studying comics in the context of a close-reading ex-ercise enables students to try their hand at multimodal, verbal-visual texts while formulating a working vocabulary for describing the relationship be-tween comics' form and meaning. It also builds upon the strengths of litera-ture instructors and majors, while opening up classes to multidisciplinary modes of inquiry that acknowledge the medium-specific demands of analyz-ing comics.

Such a classroom exercise could draw upon any rich primary text as subject matter, but I have had the greatest success using Chris Ware's *Thanksgiving*. Originally published as a set of four serial covers and an online supplement for the November 27, 2006, issue of the *New Yorker*, *Thanksgiving* offers a nar-rative of the former and current residents of a single brownstone apartment. (At the time of this writing, high-quality images of *Thanksgiving* are avail-able at http://acmenoveltyarchive.org/gallery/index.php?dir=556.) Telling a metafictional story of alienation and loss on what is regarded as a day typically reserved for community and family togetherness, *Thanksgiving* encourages the reader to make connections that the characters themselves can't perceive, leading to an awareness of the otherwise invisible histories contained in both architectural spaces and human memories.

Ware's text works well for this exercise because it so nicely models the focus on sequentiality in many of the most foundational definitions of comics, such as the provocative and accessible introduction to Scott McCloud's *Understanding Comics*. My students are often eager to solve the "puzzle" of these serial covers, pointing out, for example, that the illuminated fourth-floor window in the first cover is the scene depicted in the bottom half of the second cover, which itself represents the same apartment during the childhood of the protagonist and its current inhabitants. Ware's work is also conspicuously difficult, a useful lesson for the possibilities present in the work of close reading (and an instructive example before the add/drop course deadline for students who might be inclined to see a college course on comics as an opportunity to avoid rigorous thinking).

I frequently follow this close-reading exercise with an assignment on terminology, providing introductory glossaries from literary, art historical, and film studies textbooks and asking students to compose definitions of key terms borrowed from these contiguous disciplines with examples drawn from *Thanksgiving* or an anthology of contemporary comics. An extremely useful one-page guide to such terminology is available in Jessica Abel and Matt Madden's *Drawing Words and Writing Pictures*.

As comics become increasingly visible in literary anthologies and on syllabuses in literature departments, established and beginning professors alike have a valuable opportunity to use visual-verbal texts both to enliven the practice of close reading in their courses and to challenge the conventional assumptions we bring to the practice of textual analysis. "Close Reading Comics" embodies one way to begin these conversations among our students and with each other.

· ·

Making It Graphic

Bridgitte Barclay

A visual exercise that helps students think—graphically—about narrative.

Genre: *fiction*
Course Level: *introductory or intermediate*
Student Difficulty: *easy*
Teacher Preparation: *low*
Class Size: *small to medium*

Semester Time: *any*
Writing Component: *in class*
Close Reading: *medium*
Estimated Time: *50 minutes*

EXERCISE

Choose a portion or aspect of a novel or short story that you feel would benefit from particularly close attention. At the beginning of class, guide students to the relevant passage or pages (or, if you are asking them to work with the whole text, simply ask them to take out their books) and give them five to seven minutes to reflect, in writing, on the topic you have identified. It can help to give students a few brief prompts as they prepare to write. Tell them to mark down any specific examples they feel best demonstrate the topic at hand.

Next, arrange students into groups of three to five and ask each student to share with the others in the group what he or she has written. Give students approximately ten minutes for this portion of the exercise; the goal is for each group to come to a consensus on the topic and to select the most pertinent examples.

Now give each group this challenge: convert their ideas into a brief graphic narrative. Each group should use at least five frames to convey their ideas and will need to discuss how, and why, to draw the frames in a particular way. (Provide sheets of blank paper for this portion of the exercise.) Groups will also need to write a short paragraph describing the rationale behind their frames, in order to articulate the specific decisions they made in converting their ideas into graphic form. Give each group roughly fifteen to twenty minutes for this portion of the exercise.

If your class has not already studied graphic narrative in the course, you might consider providing a ten-minute minilesson on the form; Scott McCloud's *Understanding Comics* works exceptionally well for this purpose. Borrowing from McCloud, I focus on four key aspects of graphic narratives: how graphic images use amplification through simplification (how a character's most unique or prominent feature is represented visually); the interplay of pictures and words within a frame (how an image is immediate and words are perceived); framing itself (what is in the frame and what we are meant to perceive outside of it); and closure (the act of connecting frame to frame and the active role that a reader takes in this process). If you have already covered the graphic novel form in class, ask students to pull out their notes from those days.

If you are using this exercise to explore characterization, it may help to show students some of Kate Beaton's literary comics from *Hark! A Vagrant* (online or in book form). She has a strip, for instance, that characterizes Heathcliff from Emily Brontë's *Wuthering Heights* in comparison to Mr. Rochester from Charlotte Brontë's *Jane Eyre*; this is a great example for showing students how images, and the choice of characteristics they emphasize, help graphically depict a character.

When all the groups are finished drawing and writing, have them present their narratives to the rest of the class, one by one, either by passing the frames around (and reading the paragraphs aloud) or by using a document projector. Encourage discussion by letting the groups pose questions to each other as they present. At the end of the exercise, discuss as a class how they have taken part in narrative by choosing what to frame and how to make images out of words.

REFLECTIONS

The goals of "Making It Graphic" are to encourage students to read closely and to think carefully about narrative form. Their focalization, depiction of characters, choice of what to represent, and gaps between frames require determining exactly what is important to the text and what needs to be emphasized. The performance of this exercise is thus fundamentally an act of critical interpretation: students have to think about not only what strikes them as important but also *why* it is important and what it proves.

I have used this exercise to discuss many different kinds of narrative matters, including plot and genre in Edgar Allan Poe's *The Narrative of Arthur Gordon Pym* and frame stories and characterization in John Connolly's *The Book of Lost Things*. For example, in my class on contemporary global literature, I use the exercise to help students think about the character development of David, the young protagonist in *The Book of Lost Things*. I ask the students to consider how David is introduced, how he relates to others in the text, what plot points enable (or fail to enable) his growth, and how he has (or has not) changed by the end of the text. In creating their frame series, the students then often choose an early scene featuring David's flaws or limitations for their opening frame, a few of the most important plot conflicts involving David's failures or successes for their middle frames, and an image (or images) of David by the novel's end (or the point we are up to in the text) for their final frame or two.

Students respond positively to this exercise, learning from and enjoying the task of choosing and articulating important conflicts in character development or, in the case of a static character, noticing how the character does not change in the midst of major plot points. Thinking through how to translate from a written medium to a visual one, and deciding what character traits and scenes are important enough to depict, both engage students' critical-thinking skills and function as prewriting for more in-depth close reading or character analysis.

. . . .

Digital Literacy

Ron Thomas

A PowerPoint exercise that combines textual analysis with Web research.

Genre: *any, especially fiction*
Course Level: *advanced*
Student Difficulty: *moderate*
Teacher Preparation: *low*
Class Size: *small*
Semester Time: *all semester*
Writing Component: *before class, in class*
Close Reading: *low*
Estimated Time: *20 minutes (per presentation)*

EXERCISE

This exercise invites students to create a brief PowerPoint presentation on a text, combining traditional literary analysis with research from the Web. It can work with any author, text, or genre, though it works especially well with historical fiction. It is intended as a semester-long classroom activity (ideal for seminars) with two or three students presenting their PowerPoint each week.

Begin on the first day of class by explaining the assignment and having each student sign up to present on one of the texts on the syllabus. Plan on modeling the assignment yourself in the next class meeting, so students will have a clear idea of what their PowerPoint presentations should look like. Offer them the following core guidelines:

Locate a dozen allusions—to persons, places, things, or events— throughout the text. Then create a brief PowerPoint presentation (about sixteen slides) that connects these allusions to their broader cultural, historical, or natural context. Surf the Web for images and information that clarify or contextualize the allusions you have chosen to highlight for us. Most of your PowerPoint slides should contain an image, a few facts about the image, and the quotation(s) from the text that occasioned your gloss in the first place.

You may organize your slides however you wish: chronologically (art history in Wendy Wasserstein's *The Heidi Chronicles*), thematically (religion in Marilynne Robinson's *Gilead*), or topically (popular culture in Ana Castillo's *The Guardians*). Be creative: a slide might feature a list of characters, a narrative chronology, a map, a historical photograph, a book cover or movie poster, the lyrics of a song, or a type of animal or tree. It's fine to depart from the text and incorporate a few slides that relate to the writer's life, but most of your slides will link specific allusions inside the text to the cultural contexts outside it that give them meaning. The operative slide format here is "allusion plus image." Brief audio or video files are allowed.

Give every slide a title to help orient your audience. Your PowerPoint slide sequence should begin with a title page (the author and title of your book, and the topic of your presentation). Then provide a picture of the author (with any pertinent information), and finally a table of contents for your presentation. The rest of the presentation should consist of twelve more slides, with each slide glossing a different textual allusion. Your last slide could say, "The End," or "Finis," or "That's All Folks!" On this slide you may also wish to restate a theme, pose a question or two for the group, or link to other books the class has read. Then come to class prepared to share the discoveries of your PowerPoint presentation!

Allot roughly twenty minutes in total for each presentation (one presentation a day is ideal, though more are possible in a seminar). This period should include comments and questions from the group. If you see a really good slide during a presentation, you might say so. At the end of every presentation, lead the class in applause, and be sure to ask if anyone wishes to comment on the just-concluded presentation: its format or its illumination of the book.

You can always gather more information anonymously by surveying the class early (What was your initial response to this exercise, your response to the model, to the final instructions, and to the first few student presentations?) or late (What did or didn't you like about the exercise, what did you learn about the texts studied, about yourself as reader/researcher/presenter, and about the creativity of your peers?). Don't forget to ask each presenter to submit the PowerPoint to you electronically (or in printed form if you prefer); it is helpful to have a copy in hand for purposes of grading and providing more feedback.

REFLECTIONS

What I like most about this digital exercise is how engaged students become with literature when presenting it through a more visual and interactive medium. The exercise not only empowers student presenters to control their own meaning-making (their own discovery of knowledge), it also enables student listeners to empathize more readily with other students' responses to texts. Through the PowerPoint presentations, students can sharpen their cross-cultural awareness, learning as much (if not more) from their classmates' gendered or multicultural perspectives as they might from just your own. With this exercise I have found that each slide becomes a teachable moment involving student, classmates, and instructor and that (surprisingly) no two presentations are ever the same.

Some students may be a bit anxious when they receive the assignment, less because of having weak computer skills than having to make an in-class presentation. Invariably though, they awaken to the creativity of the process and really seem to enjoy bringing black-and-white texts to colorful digital life. Since I began regularly using this classroom technique in my American literature classes, I have found that students read (and eventually write) better while also developing a deeper appreciation for the writer's own aesthetic skills. Course evaluations further indicate that the students' genuine admiration for the work of their peers greatly inspires their own unique interpretive efforts.

In my contemporary American novel course this fall, I presented a model PowerPoint on Julie Otsuka's *When the Emperor Was Divine*. Aside from appreciating the usefulness of my model, students came away with a greater sense of the historical reality of the author's fiction, due in part to slides I'd made of lunch lines at Tanforan, of General MacArthur returning to the Philippines, and of Hirohito's Humanity Declaration. One student's later presentation on the theme of religion in Marilynne Robinson's *Home* prompted another student to declare, "I'm going to write my research paper on that topic." Presentations on Jennifer Egan's *A Visit from the Goon Squad* elicited several different responses: "So there really is a Mab? [Mahubay Gardens, San Francisco]," "Two years before Woodstock? [Monterey Pop]," "What's a slide guitar? [Scotty's instrument]," and "Can a presidential election [in this case, Bill Clinton's first] really change how a person views the world?" After presentations on Toni Morrison's *Home*, my students now know what a CIB (combat infantry badge) medal is, and they know all about the AME (African Methodist Episcopal) church. Following a slide on "Eugenics," they discussed with some interest Cee's newfound self-respect, and they had no problems seeing the sweet bay tree as a metaphor for Frank's inscription, "Here Stands a Man."

Practicing digital literacy in the classroom encourages careful, active reading. The exercise need not take too much of students' time, though students usually throw themselves into it. Whether they are researching and preparing their PowerPoint, presenting it before class, or evaluating one another's performance, students tend to do very well, perhaps because they are generally more digitally (if not culturally) literate than we are. Computers are redefining literacy, and digitization is transforming storytelling itself. "Digital Literacy" capitalizes on this cultural and pedagogical revolution.

· ·

For more exercises that can be used to teach pictures, try these:

Mapmaker (Stories)
Diagram This (Stories)
Set Design (Plays)
Director's Cut (Plays)
Putting a Face to a Name (Canons)
Literature Class Band (Canons)
Judge a Book by Its Cover (Canons)
Poetry Broadside Gallery (Objects)
Online Commonplace Book (Objects)

OBJECTS

The material history of (and within) books can be rich terrain for literary analysis. The exercises in this final section treat books as objects to be touched, produced, and reassembled or as archives *of* objects to be excavated for the contextual stories they tell. Several activities reach back into the collateral history of texts as artifacts, resurrecting such lost aesthetic forms as the broadside, commonplace book, and hand-stitched quire. Others invite students to research the material stories of forgotten objects, bringing what they learn back to the text to show how even small details can produce big epiphanies.

What can we learn by objectifying books? The first exercise ("Reading without Reading") asks students to "read" books without actually looking at them, relying on the sense of touch to speculate about a book's quality, genre, or content. The next three activities turn existing texts into new objects, either by recasting a poem as a broadside ("Poetry Broadside Gallery"), reformatting and reassembling passages into medieval manuscripts ("Making Manuscripts"), or collecting, sharing, and responding to textual excerpts in a digital version of the old-fashioned commonplace book ("Online Commonplace Book"). Finally, the last three exercises turn students into detectives, curators, and prop hands, asking them to investigate the peculiar histories of textual objects ("Object Lesson" and "The Things Inside Books") or to think hard about the ways in which dramatic objects are handled—or might be handled—on the literary stage ("Chekhov's Gun").

Reading without Reading

Seth Studer

A tactile exercise that helps students think critically about the material composition of books.

> Genre: *any*
> Course Level: *any*
> Student Difficulty: *easy*
> Teacher Preparation: *medium*
> Class Size: *small to medium*
> Semester Time: *early*
> Writing Component: *none*
> Close Reading: *none*
> Estimated Time: *40 to 50 minutes*

EXERCISE

Choose twenty books from your home or office. When you select these books, disregard their content; rely instead on their physical properties. Include a variety of shapes, sizes, textures, bindings, and paper quality. To maximize the physical diversity of your collection, combine traditionally assigned literary texts with nonliterary texts (such as phone books or cookbooks).

Bring the books to class, but make sure your students cannot see them. Break the class into groups of three or four, selecting one student per group to serve as the silent "librarian." Ask the other students to close their eyes. Distribute the books among the groups (no fewer than three books per group). Ask each "blind" student to pick up, feel, and describe aloud one of the books you have distributed. Instruct them to analyze each book's physical components and speculate about its genre, style, content, quality, value, and cost. They should, in short, "read" the book without reading it.

Instruct the librarians to transcribe what their group members say and to list these statements in two columns: one for descriptive statements about the book's tactile or other sensory qualities (some students smell the books) and the other for evaluative or speculative statements that assess the book's other attributes (genre, value, etc.).

While your students examine the books, write some keywords on the board: *size, shape, texture, paper weight.* After ten minutes, assign new librarians, ask the other students to close their eyes, and rotate the books. Repeat the exercise. (If desired, repeat it a third time.)

After the final round, all the students will open their eyes and observe the books they've been assessing. They will typically talk among themselves, eagerly looking around to identify a particular book that felt strange in their hands. Reconvene as a class. Ask each librarian to read a few of the statements they recorded. As they read, use the keywords on the board to categorize the students' statements and evaluations. Now discuss the results: Did the physical components of a book provoke particular evaluations of that book? If so, how and why? In what ways does a book's material composition impact its reception?

REFLECTIONS

This exercise develops students' understanding and appreciation of literature as a material object. I developed the exercise for an advanced English course that examined the circulation of literary texts. To focus students' attention on how a book's material properties may subtly shape the reading experience, I asked students to "read" several books with their hands, without knowledge of the titles or content. For many students it was their first experience analyzing a literary object *without* grappling with literary language. Leaving close reading to the side, this exercise elicits fruitful discussions about a book's status as object and commodity, and about how features as seemingly inconsequential as the weight, bulk, or even smell of a book might shape readerly assumptions or critical interpretations.

I encourage my students to understand each aspect of a book's design—binding, trim size, texture, the quality of the paper—as economic and cultural decisions made by publishers, on the same level as decisions made by authors. These decisions are loaded with meaning, and our postexercise discussions typically focus on how and why, for instance, a mass-market paperback sends different cultural signals than a trade paperback does, all content aside. Additionally, an instructor may use this exercise to supplement discussions of e-readers and the digitization of literature. What is gained or lost when a small device, capable of holding thousands of books, essentially flattens the physical diversity that students encounter in this exercise?

When writing keywords on the board, you might borrow vocabulary from the publishing industry: *trim size* (page size of trade or mass-market books), *cover material* (cloth or paper), *page cut* (cut edge or deckle edge). These terms offer students precise language with which to think about the physical properties of books as well as the choices available to publishers.

Here are some of the types of books I have used in this exercise: a Penguin Classics paperback; a Vintage trade paperback; a glossy "For Dummies" textbook; an oversized graphic novel; a Dover edition with thin pages; a cloth-bound translation of Homer with deckle-edged pages and a fabric bookmark sewn into the binding; a book of recipes bound in a sturdy, three-ringed binder; a squat sci-fi paperback; an introduction to sociology textbook; a *Where's Waldo* book; a coffee-table book; a miniature book; and a fifty-year-old Book of Common Prayer.

The above list combines books familiar to English majors with books they do not typically encounter in literature courses. Including too many familiar books risks a discussion that will veer toward literary analysis. Including too many unfamiliar books, however, severs the connection between the exercise and the students' broader study of literature. A balance of familiar and unfamiliar books has worked well for me: it helps students recognize how a book's physicality influences their experience and interpretation of its content. They may have read *Lolita* three times, or they may have never encountered a miniature book before, but they begin interpreting both based on how the books feel in their hands.

I find it useful to include a book or two from the course syllabus (for example, a trade paperback of *Song of Solomon* in my contemporary American literature course) to serve as a nexus between the exercise and the course material. I have also used clothbound, hardcover editions of *Harry Potter* (after removing the dust jacket, as students can often identify it); students are typically surprised after "the big reveal," when they compare their analysis of the clothbound tome with their feelings toward the series. When the book is merely an object, students associate its binding and size with serious adult fiction or new editions of canonical literature. When they discover it is *Harry Potter*, they speculate about how its physical form may have collaborated with J. K. Rowling's writing to shape their childhood impressions of the story's depth, gravity, and adventure. A former student once told me, in mock frustration, that she could no longer touch a book without thinking of this exercise. The work of literary analysis begins before the pages open.

. . . .

Poetry Broadside Gallery

Chelsea Jennings

A visual spin on literary interpretation that offers a thought-provoking review of course content.

Genre: *poetry*
Course Level: *introductory or intermediate*
Student Difficulty: *moderate*

Teacher Preparation: *low*
Class Size: *small to medium*
Semester Time: *midterm to last day*
Writing Component: *before class*
Close Reading: *low*
Estimated Time: *40 to 50 minutes*

EXERCISE

Prepare students for this creative adaptation exercise by defining *broadside*: a single unfolded sheet of paper printed on one side to be hung on a wall or post; an ephemeral, low-cost form of street literature. Show students some examples of poetry broadsides. Many examples can be found online, and James Sullivan's *On the Walls and in the Streets: American Poetry Broadsides from the 1960s* can serve as a resource for the history of broadsides and their recent use. In your discussion of broadsides, guide students toward the understanding that broadsides do not merely illustrate a poem's content; they also interpret the poem's mood, ideas, and formal strategies through typography, layout, color, and image. If time permits, poems printed as broadsides can be integrated into the reading for the course, and students can practice analyzing how the visual aspects of broadsides impact interpretation.

Next, give students at least a week to complete a version of the following assignment:

> Choose a poem our class has covered and create a broadside that offers a complex and visually compelling interpretation of this poem. To create your broadside, you are welcome to use any methods, digital or analog, that suit your purpose. Feel free to draw on our class discussions as inspiration. When you're done, write a brief artist's statement (three hundred to five hundred words) that explains which aspects of the poem your broadside explores or emphasizes. Bring a hard copy of both your broadside and your printed artist's statement to class on the day the assignment is due.

For the class period when student broadsides are due, arrange the classroom so that students can walk through the space and view the broadsides with artists' statements alongside. If possible, have students tape the broadsides and statements to the wall with a low-tack tape (such as drafting tape) to simulate the broadside's origin as an ephemeral public posting; otherwise, the texts can be laid out on desks. If space allows, place a blank sheet of paper next to each student's broadside so that classmates can respond with observations, compliments, and questions.

Once students have had time to view all the broadsides (allot ten minutes for a small class, fifteen minutes for a medium class), reconvene for a full-class discussion. Leave at least twenty-five to thirty minutes for students to talk about the exercise and what they learned. Questions you might ask include the following: What strategies worked well in your classmates' broadsides? Where in the broadsides did you see important class themes or topics emerge? How did your reading of a particular poem change when you read it in this form? What did you learn by creating your own broadside? In smaller classes, you might ask students to print copies of their broadside for the entire class, so at the end of the session each student walks away with a collection of poetry broadsides.

REFLECTIONS

"Poetry Broadside Gallery" works particularly well as a catalyst for midterm or end-of-term review of what students have learned—either to brainstorm for a paper, prepare for an exam, or simply wrap up a unit or course. In addition to offering an engaging way to review course material, this activity helps students in introductory courses grasp that a poem does not have one "correct" reading—particularly when two students create very different broadsides for the same poem. It also allows students to translate their close reading of a poem into writing by way of the visual, which can be very helpful for those students (particularly nonmajors in introductory courses) who may be better able to convey the complexity of their understanding of a poem through a broadside and artist's statement than through academic writing.

I have used this exercise in a general literature course as well as a twentieth-century American poetry course and have found it amenable to a wide variety of poems, although length is a major limiting factor, since longer poems need to be excerpted to fit on a single sheet of paper. I have focused on nineteenth- and twentieth-century poems, but given the broadside's long and fascinating history, this exercise could be easily adapted to earlier poems, many of which first appeared as broadsides.

"Poetry Broadside Gallery" works especially well when students can respond to the poem in light of a broader context, such as the poem's composition, publication, or reception history; the historical period; the author's other works; or a course theme. For instance, after our course Reading Literary Forms covered some of William Blake's illuminated books, one student created a response to "The Tyger" that depicted a creator figure modeled on Urizen—made by overlaying cut-up pages from our edition of Blake—whose oversized hands held a small copy of one of the tigers Blake used to illustrate "The Tyger." This response was especially compelling in its ability to situate its reading of a single poem in relation to Blake's literary-visual oeuvre. Another memorable broadside layered several transparent copies of

Emily Dickinson's "Publication—is the Auction / Of the Mind of Man" at different angles so that the poem was only partly legible. The student's artist statement then addressed the poem's commentary on publication in light of the history of Dickinson's manuscripts and our larger discussions of legibility, visuality, and the space of the page.

Although it would be possible to assign a broadside and artist's statement without a gallery walk, students tend to put more energy into the assignment if they know it will have an audience beyond the instructor. I have found that the activity of interacting with classmates' broadsides is at least as valuable to students as creating their own, since it prompts them to reflect on the assigned poems in a new light. Upon seeing course texts and class discussions represented visually and filling the room, students in my courses have expressed surprise, excitement, and pride at how much they have learned.

. . . .

Making Manuscripts

Ann Hubert

A hands-on experience that invites students to produce and perform texts.

Genre: *any, especially early modern*
Course Level: *any*
Student Difficulty: *easy*
Teacher Preparation: *low*
Class Size: *small*
Semester Time: *midterm to last day*
Writing Component: *in class*
Close Reading: *none*
Estimated Time: *variable, 50 to 70 minutes*

EXERCISE

Ask students to pick their favorite passage from any text you have read so far (roughly a paragraph works best) and to bring it to the next class meeting. The night before class, prepare a set of faux manuscript pages—enough to give one to each student—by immersing unlined sheets of paper in water for a few seconds and then letting them dry out overnight. You will also need a number of small pieces of string.

When class starts, give each student one of these toughened pieces of paper and tell them that they will be making medieval manuscripts. In front of the class, demonstrate with your own sheet how to make the paper into a quire by folding it in half, how to rule the quire by drawing evenly spaced lines on it, and how to prick the quire by using your pen/pencil to punch three evenly spaced holes near the crease. (Fold the paper to resemble a greeting card, with the crease on the left-hand side, and line all four sides, from the crease to the edge.) Instruct the students to make their own quires and to copy their favorite passage onto it, moving sequentially through the quire pages and using as much space as needed to copy the passage. This part of the exercise takes approximately ten minutes.

When the students are done making their quires, put them into small groups (groups of four students is especially ideal). Pass out the string and have them "stitch" their quires together by tying pieces of string through the holes. Note that when the quires are stitched together, they should be placed one on top of the other so that each quire remains a separate entity and its pages do not intermingle with the other quires. Then have each group read out loud to the class the manuscript they have constructed. After each reading, discuss what emerges from the manuscript. What common interest binds it together? For the reading and discussion, allow seven to eight minutes per manuscript (four groups, for example, takes roughly thirty minutes).

Then ask one student from each group to remove his or her quire and to go to a different group. Have each group read out loud the new manuscript they have created. Discuss how the new text alters the previous understanding of the manuscript. Reading out loud a second time may take more class time than you have, so you can also ask groups to quickly peruse the new piece of their manuscript for five minutes and simply report their findings back to the class. Conclude by asking students what they learned from the exercise.

REFLECTIONS

This exercise illustrates the performativity of the medieval manuscript, from its genesis out of raw materials, to its binding, to its custom of being read aloud, and finally to its deconstruction and reconstruction with the subtraction and addition of texts. Through this hands-on engagement with and experience of medieval textual culture, students are able to recreate both the physical labor of book production and the oral-aural reading experience of manuscripts. Both of these processes differ vastly from our modern encounter with texts; as a result, this activity allows students to confront the alterity of medieval texts in a familiar and less intimidating manner.

Take advantage of the ease with which students are able to arrange and rearrange the quires within their manuscripts to encourage discussions about the rationale behind manuscript collation, how compiling texts in certain orders highlights different themes, and what varying textual com-binations might communicate about the owners of medieval manuscripts. When I used this exercise late in the semester, a manuscript emerged in one group with selections about a werewolf from Marie de France's *Bisclavret*, the dragon from *Beowulf*, the Prioress's dog from *The Canterbury Tales*, and Yvain's lion from Chrétien de Troyes's *Yvain*. The students immediately identified the common theme of animals in their manuscript and went on to conjecture that the owner of such a manuscript might have an interest in natural science, superstition, or human-animal relationships.

When this manuscript was deconstructed, the text about Yvain's lion was replaced by a selection about Chaucer's Pardoner, in which three men bury gold. This addition made the group reevaluate the emphasis on animals to consider how each animal represented wealth: in *Bisclavret* because the werewolf serves a king, in *Beowulf* because the dragon guards a hoard of trea-sure, and for Chaucer's Prioress because her dog is a symbol of her worldly possessions. The students were surprised to discover how such diverse texts were actually in dialogue with each other, and in more than one way at that. In fact, thematic similarities arose from the manuscript combinations that may not have come to light otherwise.

While I have used this exercise only in a medieval literature classroom, it could be implemented for later period courses too. In the Renaissance, for instance, manuscript culture still existed, and the binding of printed books at a purchaser's discretion was a common occurrence. Even as late as the eighteenth and early nineteenth centuries, before books were routinely sold already bound, some book purchasers chose to combine multiple texts into one volume according to their interests. This exercise can also be modified to mimic text selection for anthologies or the formation of literary canons.

. . . .

Online Commonplace Book

Lisa Gordis

A semester-long exercise that invites student to collect, share, and respond to passages from literary texts.

Genre: *any*
Course Level: *any*
Student Difficulty: *easy*

Teacher Preparation: *low to medium*
Class Size: *small*
Semester Time: *all semester*
Writing Component: *before class, after class*
Close Reading: *medium to high*
Estimated Time: *full class*

EXERCISE

This exercise updates the genre of the commonplace book for the digital age. Throughout the semester, students select passages to store in online commonplace books, use the entries in those books to shape class discussion, and ultimately produce physical versions of their books that not only record but also reflect on the process itself.

For each class meeting, ask each student to choose one passage (one to twenty lines) from the assigned reading and copy it into a word-processing file. Explain that each commonplace book entry should include a few sentences about why the passage was selected and what questions it raises about the assigned text or about the course material more broadly. Instruct the students to add each new commonplace book entry to the same file. Over the course of the semester, these collections of entries will constitute the students' personal commonplace books.

In addition to their personal commonplace books, the students also create a communal commonplace book. Before each class, ask students to post on the course website or blog their entries for that session, including both the passages they have selected and their comments about those passages. It's useful to have students tag or categorize their entries by text title (whatever works you are teaching that week, for example) so that participants can click on a title and review all the posts for that text. Be sure to have students post their communal entries early enough—I've found that 8 p.m. the night before class works well. You can also invite students to respond online to their classmates' posts. You may want to situate this element of the exercise in terms of the eighteenth-century practice of circulating commonplace books. If you're teaching American literature, you may want to compare the circulation of texts within the course website or blog with scribal publication of texts in antebellum reading circles.

At the beginning of each class session, give students two minutes or so to jot down the specific issues or passages that they most want to address in discussion. Then go around the room and ask students to share their lists of items. Often these issues are rooted in the students' own entries, although many students will also connect their postings to broader issues and to other students' ideas. As you go around the room, ask the students to help you group the various topics, thinking about which fit well together and what sequence might make sense. If you like, do this grouping on the board. Then use the class-generated sequence to structure discussion for the rest of the class meeting. (Before class, you can also do a preliminary grouping of the entries yourself, to look for patterns the students might not yet see.)

As the students add posts to their personal commonplace books, tell them that they may at any time choose to reorganize their list of passages, grouping them by theme as they see connections emerge or keeping the entries in chronological order. At the end of the semester, ask students to hand in printed versions of their commonplace books. You may ask students to reflect on whether they chose to reorganize their entries and why, what patterns they saw emerging in the course texts or in the selections they chose, what the experience of commonplacing was like, and/or how the printed forms of the commonplace books differ from the individual digital commonplace books and the communal online commonplace book. This final exercise encourages students to make connections across texts and to synthesize course material while helping them to anchor their thinking in specific examples.

REFLECTIONS

This exercise has multiple benefits. In addition to producing a physical record of the reading and reflection the students have done all semester, the communal postings anchor class discussion, help the class trace themes and questions across course texts, and assist students in developing paper topics. Because each student arrives in class with at least one passage he or she would like to discuss, the resulting conversations are lively, engaged, and grounded in the texts.

Students often post more than the minimum requirement. Some students post multiple passages and compare them, and many students post several paragraphs of discussion rather than just a few sentences. I have also found the agenda-setting model for opening class discussion more collaborative and less formal than putting student pairs in charge of moderating class sessions. The method also ensures that all students speak in the first five or so minutes of class, which makes it easier for them to keep talking.

I first developed this exercise for a course on colonial American women as readers and writers. Because the syllabus for that course included the Revolutionary-era commonplace book of Milcah Martha Moore, students considered the commonplace book assignment in a specific historical context. In the exercise presented here, the commonplace book functions as a method for promoting critical thinking and writing across the semester, though it can still be helpful to offer students some historical or cultural background on the genre itself when you introduce the assignment.

One technical decision you'll need to make is where to house the communal commonplace book. I am currently using a password-protected WordPress blog on my university's system as the platform for this exercise and have found that it works well. I have also used a wiki, which allows students to keep their entries on a single page and to reorganize them easily on the site but which adds extra steps for students to see each other's postings (and which therefore leads them to read each other's postings less regularly).

My commonplace book exercise is text focused, though you may also invite students to post links and images. (One colleague has used Pinterest as the platform for an image-oriented version of this exercise.) Even without this explicit invitation, I have had some students post material beyond the required text-based work. At the end of the term, one student handed in a beautiful printed and bound commonplace book that included photographs she had taken, poetry she had written in response to the passages she had posted, and an opening address to the reader in the style of an eighteenth-century preface. A student who worked with the Barnard Library zine prepared an elaborate textual collage using torn paper and unusual fonts in order to emphasize the circulation of textual fragments. Yet another student printed out an unadorned version of her commonplace book but purchased a beautiful notebook and went on to keep a handwritten commonplace book for the next several years. Whatever version of the exercise you use, feel free to encourage students to personalize their books to reflect their engagement with the course material.

Object Lesson

Janine Barchas

A show-and-tell exercise that provides historical context for close reading.

Genre: *any*
Course Level: *any*
Student Difficulty: *moderate*
Teacher Preparation: *low*
Class Size: *small to medium*
Semester Time: *midterm, last day, or all semester*
Writing Component: *before class*
Close Reading: *medium*
Estimated Time: *variable, from 10 minutes to full class*

EXERCISE

Ask students to select an object or thing mentioned in a literary work that, if better understood, might shed interpretive light on the historical context or meaning of the passage in which the object appears. Then tell them to research, illustrate, and possibly even make the object, bringing it to class for show-and-tell.

For the purposes of this exercise, define "object" as broadly as possible. In addition to individual physical objects mentioned in the text, tell students they are welcome to select professions, places, activities, or systems— anything that strikes them as potentially worth pulling out of the text for a closer look. The same goes for the "making" of their objects. Some might construct a physical replica; others might prefer to draw their object or prepare a PowerPoint or Prezi slide show. If the object can be performed (as in a song or a dance or a joke), let them perform it; if it can be prepared (as in a type of food), let them prepare and then share it. Some students may opt to research a historical object rigorously, rather than recreate it. The point of the exercise is for students to learn as much as they can about their object and then share that knowledge with the class, essentially creating a historical or visual footnote for something in the text.

There are several ways and times to do these unconventional student presentations. You can assign one or two students to each upcoming book on the syllabus, so they know in advance which week they should be selecting, researching, and sharing their object. This method spreads the presentations across the semester and makes for a more leisurely pace. Or, since the exercise does require a fair amount of student preparation, it can also work well when it's assigned at the beginning of a unit and students present all at once at the end. For example, you can devote either midterm week or the last day of class to the object lessons and simply put a strict time limit on each show-and-tell. If you have a medium-sized class, the exercise also works well as a group activity, with clusters of students coordinating research efforts on related objects (or the same object in different texts) from various perspectives. Although the group method delays the presentations, your own awareness of student research topics allows you to defer in class discussion to their growing expertise ("John, you're currently researching X in Swift; can you help us make sense of this mention of another X in Sterne?"). Such casual references to ongoing research build up a sense of scholarly community.

On a day when everyone presents an object, give each student or group three to four minutes to instruct the class. If student presentations are staggered throughout the semester, you can expand the presentation time to five or even ten minutes. After each presentation, prompt the rest of the class to reflect on how this newfound knowledge impacts their understanding of a given moment in a text.

REFLECTIONS

"Object Lesson" can be a nice gear-shifting activity. It lets students draw on creative talents that they don't have the opportunity to show in papers or in the verbal sparring of discussion. This assignment not only co-opts those talents for the literature classroom but also demonstrates concretely that an understanding of literature is enriched by knowledge of a work's historical and cultural context. "Object Lesson" invites students to become experts in something (it can be a very small thing) and to share that expertise with the class. Research of this sort can often be less intimidating than the task of finding scholarly criticism on a literary topic. In addition, because the exercise allows students to demonstrate or apply talents in other areas, it tends to build camaraderie and mutual respect. In my experience, the assignment combats intellectual myopia by showing the value of student interests in other disciplines (architecture, dance, art, music, medicine, fashion). A few students have even generously gifted me their objects, which in later courses I can produce during discussion of a specific passage in which they are mentioned.

For example, in my eighteenth-century British novel survey, a few students opted to combine sewing skills with word sleuthing in the *Oxford English Dictionary* (my university has an electronic subscription, which I link to the class Blackboard/Canvas online site, allowing most "object lessons" to start there). These students made a *Pamela*-style "shift" and also a "hussy"—that is, a needle case termed a "housewife." Both objects shed light upon wordplay in Samuel Richardson's novel, revealing how the heroine's clandestine activity of hiding manuscripts in her undergarments enacts a pun on her "shift" and how Mr. B's seemingly callous nickname (he calls Pamela a "hussy" several times) appears differently in light of its contemporary usage as an abbreviation of "housewife." Along with other references to needlework in the novel, the term "hussy" may hint at the couple's future domesticity and marriage.

Other students baked from eighteenth-century recipes and shared their dishes with the class while explaining the social context or economic significance of specific recipes. Some students researched (rather than made) historical objects, locations, or professions, sharing their newfound knowledge about things like the eighteenth-century postal service, medical tools, styles of carriages, and architecture through handouts or image-laden PowerPoint presentations. A few daring students performed period music (I recall a memorable hymn on guitar) or sang historical ballads. Some taught the class to play period games, prompting a discussion one year of why the card game Ombre features in Alexander Pope's *Rape of the Lock*; in another class, we mused about the choice of Speculation as an activity for the characters in Jane Austen's *Mansfield Park*. In both sessions, very little prompting was needed for the students to conclude that the rules of these well-known Georgian games mapped onto the motivations of fictional characters.

Internet resources, and not just Google Image, have made the data-gathering aspect of humanities research much easier. Even antiques in far-flung museums or collections, previously made visible only through the lens of a professor's slide carousel, are now accessible to students via their own laptops. Museums all over the globe provide searchable image databases of wide-ranging collections that respond well to keyword searches (for British and Commonwealth objects, for example, try the Victoria and Albert Museum, British Museum Collections Online, and the Royal Museums Greenwich). Not just traditional works of art but objects from watches to weapons to shoes to ceramics can be found in such databases in a few clicks, along with accurate historical information about their function or construction. In addition, free architectural tools like SketchUp (http://sketchup.com), a downloadable program that enables the quick-and-dirty modeling of architectural objects, allows students to visualize from scratch everything from Palladian architecture to the ha-ha. Scholars, too, are turning to these same electronic tool kits to reconstruct whole spaces and events from the past. My own 2013 website, What Jane Saw (http://whatjanesaw.org), for example, reconstructs as an e-gallery an art exhibition attended by Jane Austen in 1813. Free to anyone teaching aspects of the so-called "long eighteenth century," What Jane Saw is essentially a scholarly extension of the "object lesson."

The object approach, made easier by the Internet, has in recent decades been embraced by a number of subfields in the humanities—even in print. The 1990s saw a spate of published histories about objects (pencil, potato, cod, guns, germs, and steel) that renovated the object histories so popular in the 1750s, when novels narrated by lapdogs, coins, playing cards, or other inanimate objects came into vogue. Since then, "thing theory" has attempted to crystalize a vocabulary that focuses on the role of stuff in shaping both a sense of ourselves as unique individuals as well as, conversely, our shared humanity. Most recently, books in history and biography such as *A History of the World in 100 Objects* (2011) and *The Real Jane Austen: A Life in Small Things* (2013) appropriate long-standing curatorial strategies by replacing habits of mere attendant illustration (pictures in medias res) with the type of evocative starting object that launches a new chapter or narrative thread. In this manner objects are structuring even publications in word-based disciplines such as history and literature. All of this curatorial fervor in the humanities suggests that our new pedagogical imperative is to show our students not merely how to find information about objects and things but how to "curate" a meaningful selection and place it in historical, literary, and critical context.

The Things Inside Books

Karen Sánchez-Eppler

A Web-based exercise in historical research that turns students into material culture detectives.

Genre: *any*
Course Level: *any*
Student Difficulty: *moderate*
Teacher Preparation: *low*
Class Size: *any*
Semester Time: *any or all semester*
Writing Component: *optional*
Close Reading: *medium*
Estimated Time: *variable, from 10 minutes to full class*

EXERCISE

Divide the class into pairs or small groups. Ask each pair or group to pick an object described in the literary work they are currently studying and, using online databases or other Internet resources, to learn everything they can about the history of their chosen item. (Historical newspaper archives work well for this exercise, but industrial histories and the like can also be valuable.) We professional readers call this approach a "material culture analysis," but for nonmajors a phrase like historicizing "the things in books" conveys the point just as well. Ask them, How and where was this item produced, distributed, advertised, sold? What did it cost, who made it, and who profited? Who was the intended audience, and who actually used this thing? Encourage students to look for relevant period images, advertisements, or other mentions of their item—anything that might help them visualize the object itself.

A day or two before class, have each pair or group mount on a class website the materials they have found, by posting relevant links or images. Looking at the articles and advertisements together can be both helpful and entertaining, and visual images of the objects are immensely revealing, so this is an important step in advance of the class meeting.

When class reconvenes, invite a pair or a group to share their findings briefly with the rest of the class, using the links and images they have posted; five minutes for each pair works well. Then ask the class as a whole to discuss how knowing this information matters for the specific scene, character, moment of plot, or narrative strategies involving the item. Keep inviting additional groups to present on their objects, and repeat the process, moving once again from the "what did we find" of the presentations to the "why does this matter" of the interpretive close readings. Depending on how many days your class will devote to the literary work at hand (and the number of groups you have), you can spread these presentations out over more than one class period in order to give every group a turn.

As an optional exercise after class, you can ask students to write a short paper (two to three pages are adequate) that elaborates further on how their material culture research illuminates some aspect of the literary text. This follow-up writing exercise offers them a chance to think more deeply about how their findings matter. It can also be a preparatory assignment to a longer paper using historical tools for literary analysis later in the term.

REFLECTIONS

"The Things Inside Books" works particularly well with realist texts from the eighteenth century onward, but it can be adapted to any text from any period. It stresses both the "close" in close reading—how much meaning little details of texts can actually carry—and the rich rewards of online historical research and attention to material and cultural contexts.

Of all the activities I have done with students, this not apparently very literary exercise is surprisingly the one that has most regularly made me see and think about a text in a different way. It is also an occasion for harnessing the new resources of Internet databases to enable even beginning undergraduates to make real discoveries. (Indeed, this exercise works especially well with first- and second-year undergraduates.)

While the process of finding information is now far easier than ever before, the process of figuring out how and why this information matters remains a difficult skill. This exercise thus also offers a good opportunity to alert students to best practices in Internet research, teaching them how to evaluate the sites where they find their information and guiding them to the most useful resources in the field the class is studying. When you present this exercise, it is also useful to stress the importance of researching the history of the "thing" in terms both of the place and period represented in the literary work and of the place and period in which the literature was itself produced.

This assignment is about material epiphanies, and they often happen. Many years ago a group of my students found period photographs and newspaper descriptions of the American eagle over the Salem Custom House door. In his "Custom House Introductory" to *The Scarlet Letter*, Hawthorne's account of this "enormous specimen" had generally been taken by critics and teachers as a first occasion to talk about allegory, so it was a wonderful shock to learn with and from my students that the apparent excesses of this passage should also be considered instances of realism. This realization has now become something of a critical commonplace, but I like to think that my students got there first.

In another class students researched the tortoiseshell hairpins left on the dresser in the boardinghouse room where Lily Bart dies in Edith Wharton's *The House of Mirth*. These hairpins are obviously a poignant detail: the small, intimate props of beautification. But it turns out that a process for staining bone to produce cheap replicas of this rare material had been newly developed at the turn of the century, and New York newspapers and magazines of 1905 are full of ads and articles fretting about tortoiseshell authenticity. Surely Edith Wharton, and her initial readers, knew that the hairpins lying on Lily's dresser were themselves instances of the anxiety about appearance and true value that so haunt this novel and its heroine, but it is an insight that without such research would be lost on contemporary readers.

As an Americanist I use this exercise to introduce students to an array of digital resources relevant to American literary history; similar resources are likely available for other fields. Some of the newspaper and magazine databases I invite students to use require institutional subscriptions (such as Readex's America's Historical Newspapers and ProQuest's American Periodicals Series Online), but many other resources are freely available, including the Library of Congress's Chronicling America archive (http://chroniclingamerica .loc.gov) and Cornell University's Making of America project (http://moa .library.cornell.edu). The National Museum of American History (http:// americanhistory.si.edu/collections) has a fine searchable database of many of the objects in their collection, as does the Smithsonian (http://collec- tions.si.edu/search). And the Library of Congress's American Memory site (http://memory.loc.gov) includes an advertising section that students find especially useful. There are also a number of websites that help students assess what objects cost in real terms: I frequently use Measuring Worth (http:// measuringworth.com/uscompare) and the Economic History Association's calculator How Much is That? (http://eh.net/hmit). For particular texts, more specific digital archives and databases may prove valuable; ask your research librarian to help identify the resources that might work best for your class.

Some college and university museums also have rich collections of decorative arts, although these items are not always put on display. If your institution has such a collection, a variation on this exercise is to arrange a session at the museum for the class to see period objects in person. For example, when I have done this activity with *The House of Mirth*, I have asked our college museum to bring into their study room a selection of vases, lamps, tea sets, cigarette lighters, and society portraits. Students invariably report how transformative it is to see actual objects, not just descriptions or images. But this obviously takes a fair amount of time to organize, and it requires that the right things are available to be viewed. The exercise works perfectly well without this enhancement if it isn't an easy fit for specific literary texts or local collections.

One more variation on this exercise: instead of having every group present on a single text, I have sometimes spread the activity across the semester, asking a different pair or group to provide an excavation of a "thing inside the book" for each text we read. (I allow roughly ten minutes for the presentations.) Spreading this assignment out over the length of a course illuminates how the material world differs across time and place, highlighting industrial and consumerist changes in modes of production and distribution. With this variation, a survey on American literature takes us from Anne Bradstreet's "trunk" and "chest" to Gatsby's "beautiful shirts." In addition to tracking how different periods produce very different sorts of fetish objects, the exercise reveals shifts in representational strategies, helping students to appreciate the different ways—symbolic, sentimental, metaphoric, ironic, iconic—that authors use "things" in their books. Whether focused on a single text or deployed across the length of a course, this exercise demonstrates the interpretive rewards of paying attention to the material culture inside books while honing Web-based historical research skills to boot.

· ·

Chekhov's Gun

Keri Walsh

An exercise that reveals how every prop tells a story.

Genre: *drama*
Course Level: *any*
Student Difficulty: *moderate*
Teacher Preparation: *low*
Class Size: *small to medium*
Semester Time: *any*
Writing Component: *before class or in class*
Close Reading: *medium to high*
Estimated Time: *45 to 65 minutes*

EXERCISE

"Chekhov's Gun" begins as a short writing assignment (a paragraph or two) to be completed outside of class time. It can also be done as an in-class writing prompt if you have at least twenty minutes of class time to give students for writing. The exercise should be done only once students have read the entire play, and they should have a copy of the play in front of them. Here is the prompt:

> Chekhov said that "One must never place a loaded rifle on the stage if it isn't going to go off. It's wrong to make promises you don't mean to keep." This is a point not just about foreshadowing but also about the need for each object on the stage to be meaningful. Choose one object that appears on the stage in the work we are studying and trace it throughout the play. What do you think this object is doing in the play?

When you meet for class to discuss the prompt, you can start conversation by going around the room and asking each student to name the object they wrote about. List all of the mentioned objects on the board (or ask a student to take on that job) and begin a discussion by asking students what they each noticed about their particular object. If several students wrote about the same object, you might want to start the discussion there and then move on to the less frequently mentioned objects.

There are many questions that might focus your discussion. The following list moves from the object itself to characterization, staging, plot, and theme:

- How specific is the playwright's description of the object in the stage directions?
- Does any character describe the object to another character or to the audience? How do they describe it?
- How do you picture the object looking? (For instance, what color is it, or how big is it?)
- How much scope does the playwright leave for the director, actors, and set designer to interpret this object?
- How does the object transform from its first to its last appearance?
- Is the object used for the purposes of characterization? (For instance, a cane might be used for characterization if it is always carried by a particular character.)
- Is any particular character associated with the object? Or does it change hands? What is significant about these exchanges?
- Is the object intended to be handled by the actors onstage, or is it part of the set that they do not touch?
- Can you foresee any particular logistical challenges for the actors in interacting with the object? (For instance, balls that must be juggled, a violin that must be played, a plate that must be broken on cue?)
- Is there a moment (or moments) in the play when the plot actually depends on this object? (For instance, when letters or tokens are used for recognition between characters?)

- Does the object work in accordance with Chekhov's imperative that all objects onstage must be meaningful and placed onstage for a reason, or do some of the objects not seem to have a particular theatrical purpose? Are some objects red herrings? In the language of Chekhov, does the playwright "make promises" with the object, and are these promises kept or broken?
- How does the presence of the object reinforce or transform the themes of the play?
- How would the play have been different without this object?
- What do you think this object is doing in the play? Why did the playwright choose to include it?

To push students further, ask them to think of several different ways an object might be used on stage. For instance, instead of just carrying his sword in a traditional way, could Richard III use it as a crutch (as Mark Rylance used it when he played Richard in a Globe Theatre production)? Would such a use of his sword be comic, or would it evoke sympathy? Or both? Why? Challenge your students to think of as many ways as possible that the object might be used on stage. If the object they chose is not touched by any of the characters, ask why not. Perhaps it's a piano that no one plays— why? Push students to see how the objects help to create the meanings of the play. The entire discussion portion of the exercise might take thirty-five to forty minutes, depending on the number of different objects the students selected.

If there is time, conclude by taking ten minutes or so to show brief clips from recorded performances or films, to give a sense of how particular directors and actors have made use of certain significant objects. For example, if you have done this exercise with *Hamlet*, you might plan to discuss the moment at which the stage direction indicates that Hamlet "Takes the skull" from the gravedigger. Then you might show clips from two film versions of *Hamlet*: in the Kenneth Branagh version (1996), the gravedigger gently hands Yorick's skull to Hamlet, but in the Zeffirelli production (1990), the gravedigger *throws* it. Ask students to discuss the ramifications of this choice. How does it change the scene? Students often find it very exciting to see scenes they have read and discussed brought to life in a variety of ways that they may or may not have anticipated. They might notice that sometimes the actors blatantly disobey or transform a playwright's directions in relation to an object, but more often they maneuver creatively within the given instructions. Seeing performances also helps students notice how playwrights leave room for theater makers to become the dramatists' cocreators, allowing the actors to make important decisions about how to interact with objects on stage.

REFLECTIONS

One of the challenges in teaching dramatic texts is showing students how the theater uses physical objects, not just words, to create its meanings. This exercise explores how objects that appear in the stage directions of a play— objects that might be overlooked on the page—can become extraordinarily important on the stage. In dramatic performances the stage tends to be full of everyday objects whose symbolic value may not be immediately apparent. "Chekhov's Gun" helps students to appreciate the way in which realist play-wrights embed objects onstage to support and develop the themes of their plays.

This exercise can be done with plays from almost any period or genre, as long as they have at least five significant objects to discuss. For instance, in *Hamlet* there are Ophelia's book and coffin, the arras behind which Polonius hides, Yorick's skull, the swords with which Hamlet and Laertes fence, and the wine goblet from which Gertrude drinks. The exercise works best with realist plays of the nineteenth and twentieth centuries: Chekhov's *Uncle Vanya*, Tennessee Williams's *A Streetcar Named Desire*, Lorraine Hansberry's *A Raisin in the Sun*. I recommend introducing this exercise first with a realist play and then returning to the exercise later in the semester, if students encounter different kinds of plays. Then ask them how objects are used differently in nonrealist dramatic styles (such as Samuel Beckett's *Waiting for Godot*).

I often use this exercise with Ibsen's *A Doll's House*. There is a wide range of objects to write about in this play, including Nora's macaroons, her taran-tella costume and tambourine, the household letter box, and the cigar that Rank requests from Torvald. Students tend to make their most interesting discoveries about subtler elements of the set that even some critics overlook but that play an important role in the development of the play's themes. For instance, one student noticed that there is a round table off to one side at the beginning of the play. At one point, Nora hides under it when play-ing hide-and-seek with her children. But as the student observed, the table takes on a much different resonance by the play's end, when it moves to the center of the room and serves as a marker of the new equality between Nora and Torvald, who have their first honest conversation as a married couple seated around it.

Another student wrote about the Christmas tree in *A Doll's House*. She observed that the play begins as Nora returns from shopping: behind her is a porter delivering her family's Christmas tree. The student's response com-pared this festive entrance to the stage direction given at the beginning of the second act: "The Christmas Tree is in the corner by the piano, stripped of its ornaments and with burnt-down candle-ends on its disheveled branches." This student's decision to focus on the Christmas tree led to an interesting class discussion about an important element of the play that we hadn't discussed before: that it is set during the holiday season, a time of greater-than-usual pressure to keep up appearances. Also, by noting that the tree is stripped of its ornaments by the beginning of the second act, students came to the conclusion that Ibsen seemed to be using the tree to prepare the audience for Nora's own process of removing her ornaments when she changes out of her tarantella costume and into everyday dress at the end of the play.

A final note about the title of the exercise: the violence of Chekhov's governing metaphor need not be ignored. Chekhov's injunction that a gun onstage *must* be fired has led to interesting conversations about what constitutes a dramatic event, and why violence seems to be a privileged locus of action. My own students have suggested that Chekhov might have overlooked other things that could be done with the rifle, such as burying it, removing the bullets, or exchanging it for food. One student pointed out that Chekhov didn't say that the rifle had to be used to hurt or kill, just that it had to "go off." Perhaps it could be used to fire a warning shot that saves lives. Such debates can be very productive. If you are doing the exercise with a play by Chekhov (which I recommend), students may notice that Chekhov's own sense of action, and of objects, is considerably subtler and more complex than his advice about the rifle suggests.

This conversation about the governing metaphor of the exercise is also interesting if applied to plays in which a gun does play a central role in the dramatic action, such as Ibsen's *Hedda Gabler*. One student suggested that the presence of a gun onstage actually creates a temptation or demand for violence and that it would be better if Chekhov had constructed his example using a different object. This conversation can open the door to a critique of particular genres, such as tragedy, melodrama, and realism. In the context of a modern drama course, it can also be helpful in building a bridge to playwrights and theorists whose works critique traditional Western dramatic standards (such as Bertolt Brecht or Augusto Boal). But no matter what the course or context, it is fruitful to think critically about Chekhov's governing example.

. . . .

For more exercises that can be used to teach objects, try these:

How to Read a Bookstore (Genres)
Mixtape Maker (Genres)
Is This Book Literature? (Canons)
Judge a Book by Its Cover (Canons)
Reverse Ekphrasis (Pictures)
Novel Portraits (Pictures)

About the Editors

. . . .

Diana Fuss received her PhD in English from Brown University and is Louis W. Fairchild Class of '24 Professor of English at Princeton University, where she has taught since 1988. Her undergraduate courses focus on nineteenth- and twentieth-century British and American literature, gender and sexuality, narrative and poetry, criticism and theory, and film and media. Formerly director of graduate studies, Fuss has conducted the graduate pedagogy and dissertation seminars, and she has served on the advisory council for the McGraw Center for Teaching and Learning. In 2001 Fuss received the President's Award for Distinguished Teaching.

William A. Gleason received his PhD in English from UCLA and is professor and chair of English at Princeton University, where he has taught since 1993. His undergraduate courses focus on nineteenth- and twentieth-century American literary history, children's literature, and the literature of place. He has also led the graduate pedagogy seminar. A Faculty Fellow in the McGraw Center for Teaching and Learning, he is affiliated with American Studies, Urban Studies, African American Studies, the Princeton Environmental Institute, and the Center for Digital Humanities. In 2006 Gleason received the President's Award for Distinguished Teaching.

Contributors

Veronica Alfano is a faculty fellow at the University of Oregon.

Heather Alumbaugh is associate professor of English at the College of Mount Saint Vincent.

Jacquelyn Ardam is an instructor in the Department of English at UCLA.

Arthur Bahr is associate professor of literature at MIT.

David M. Ball is associate professor of English at Dickinson College.

Chris Baratta is an adjunct professor at Binghamton University.

Janine Barchas is professor of English at the University of Texas at Austin.

Bridgitte Barclay is assistant professor of English at Aurora University.

Clark Barwick is an instructor in the Departments of English and American Studies at Indiana University–Bloomington.

Ellen M. Bayer is assistant professor of literature at University of Washington, Tacoma.

Katherine Bergren is assistant professor of English at Trinity College.

Abigail Burnham Bloom is an instructor at Hunter College, City University of New York.

Andrew Benjamin Bricker is a postdoctoral fellow at McGill University.

Adrienne Brown is assistant professor of English at the University of Chicago.

John Bugg is associate professor of English at Fordham University.

Erin G. Carlston is professor of English at the University of Auckland.

Kristen Case is assistant professor of English at the University of Maine, Farmington.

Miriam Chirico is associate professor of English at Eastern Connecticut State University.

Alicia Christoff is assistant professor of English at Amherst College.

J. Michelle Coghlan is a lecturer in American literature at the University of Manchester.

Andrew Cole is professor of English at Princeton University.

Joyce Coleman is professor of English at the University of Oklahoma.

Claire Cothren is an instructor at Texas A&M University.

Ralph Crane is professor of English at the University of Tasmania.

Jay Dickson is professor of English at Reed College.

Jill Dolan is professor of English at Princeton University.

Jeff Dolven is professor of English at Princeton University.

Lydia G. Fash teaches at Emerson College.

Lisa Fletcher is senior lecturer in English at the University of Tasmania.

Amber Foster is an instructor at Texas A&M University.

Renée Fox is assistant professor of English at UC Santa Cruz.

Joseph Fruscione is a freelance writer and editor who taught at the university level for fifteen years.

Diana Fuss is professor of English at Princeton University.

Rosemary Gaby is senior lecturer in English at the University of Tasmania.

Melissa J. Ganz is assistant professor of English at Marquette University.

Patricia M. García is a lecturer in English at the University of Texas at Austin.

Sophie Gee is associate professor of English at Princeton University.

William A. Gleason is professor of English at Princeton University.

Lisa Gordis is professor of English at Barnard College.

Kenyon Gradert is an instructor at Washington University in St. Louis.

Simon Grote is assistant professor of history at Wellesley College.

Megan Lynne Hamilton is an English teacher at Kohelet Yeshiva High School.

Kerry Hasler-Brooks is assistant professor of English at Messiah College.

Manuel Herrero-Puertas is an instructor at the University of Wisconsin, Madison.

Benjamin Hilb is a lecturer in Literatures in English at the University of the West Indies, Mona.

Ann Hubert is an instructor at the University of Illinois, Urbana-Champaign.

Emily Hyde is assistant professor of English at Rowan University.

Susan Jaret McKinstry is professor of English at Carleton College.

Chelsea Jennings is a lecturer in the School of Interdisciplinary Arts and Sciences at the University of Washington, Bothell.

Douglas A. Jones Jr. is assistant professor of English at Rutgers University, New Brunswick.

Daniel Jump is an instructor at Yale University.

Sean Keilen is associate professor of English and provost at UC Santa Cruz.

Maureen Meharg Kentoff is a lecturer in American literature and culture at The George Washington University.

Michael Komorowski is a lecturer in English at Yale University.

Joel B. Lande is assistant professor of German at Princeton University.

Elizabeth Leane is associate professor of English at the University of Tasmania.

Wendy Lee is assistant professor of English at New York University.

Andrew Logemann is associate professor of English at Gordon College.

Matthew T. Lynch is an instructor at Indiana University–Bloomington.

Meredith Martin is associate professor of English at Princeton University.

Naomi Milthorpe is a lecturer in English at the University of Tasmania.

Jennifer Minnen is an instructor at Princeton University.

Melina Moe is an instructor at Yale University.

Patrick Thomas Morgan is an instructor at Duke University.

Guinevere Narraway is a lecturer at the University of Tasmania.

Stephen M. Park is assistant professor of English at the University of Texas–Rio Grande Valley.

Adam Potkay is professor of English at the College of William and Mary.

Megan Quinn is an instructor at Princeton University.

Lindsay Reckson is assistant professor of English at Haverford College.

Pamela Regis is professor of English at McDaniel College.

Joanna Richardson is associate lecturer in English at the University of Tasmania.

Hollis Robbins is professor of humanities at the Peabody Institute of the Johns Hopkins University.

Erwin Rosinberg is a lecturer in English at Emory University.

Vanessa L. Ryan is assistant professor of English and associate dean of the Graduate School at Brown University.

Nick Salvato is associate professor of performing and media arts at Cornell University.

Karen Sánchez-Eppler is professor of English at Amherst College.

Roy Scranton is an instructor at Princeton University.

Sunny Stalter-Pace is assistant professor of English at Auburn University.

Hannah Stark is a lecturer in English at the University of Tasmania.

Kimberly J. Stern is assistant professor of English at the University of North Carolina at Chapel Hill.

Kathryn Bond Stockton is distinguished professor of English and associate vice president for equity and diversity at the University of Utah.

Seth Studer is an instructor at Tufts University.

Ron Thomas is professor of English at Baylor University.

Christy Tidwell is assistant professor of humanities at the South Dakota School of Mines & Technology.

Christopher R. Trogan is a lecturer in English at Baruch College of the City University of New York.

Jennifer Waldron is associate professor of English at the University of Pittsburgh.

Cody Walker is lecturer IV at the University of Michigan.

Chris Walsh is associate director of the CAS Writing Program at Boston University.

Keri Walsh is assistant professor of English at Fordham University.

Benjamin Widiss is assistant professor of English at Hamilton College.

Johanna Winant is visiting assistant professor in English at College of the Holy Cross.

Stacy Wolf is professor of theater at Princeton University.

Susan J. Wolfson is professor of English at Princeton University.

Anne-Marie Womack is a postdoctoral fellow at Tulane University.

Danielle Wood is senior lecturer in English at the University of Tasmania.

Michael Wood is professor emeritus of English at Princeton University.

Amelia Worsley is assistant professor of English at Amherst College.

Benjamin Jude Wright is a visiting affiliate assistant professor of English at Loyola University.

Robert Yeates is an instructor at the University of Exeter.

Four Cross-Indexes to Help You Plan Ahead

EXERCISES THAT ARE (OR CAN BE) DESIGNED TO LAST THE FULL SEMESTER

It's Time We Talked (Discussions)
Digital Literacy (Pictures)
Online Commonplace Book (Objects)

Object Lesson (Objects)
The Things Inside Books (Objects)

EXERCISES THAT WORK PARTICULARLY WELL ON THE FIRST DAY OF CLASS

The Descriptive Word (Essentials)
Narrative Rounds (Stories)
First Paragraphs (Stories)
What is "Literature"? (Canons)

Putting a Face to a Name (Canons)
Literature Class Band (Canons)
Judge a Book by Its Cover (Canons)
First Things First (Styles)

EXERCISES THAT WORK PARTICULARLY WELL ON THE LAST DAY OF CLASS

The Descriptive Word (Essentials)
The Common Thread (Essentials)
Build-A-Canon (Canons)

One-Sentence Pastiche (Styles)
Object Lesson (Objects)

EXERCISES THAT REQUIRE OR RECOMMEND WRITING BEFORE CLASS

Put the Question (Discussions)
It's Time We Talked (Discussions)
The New Title (Essentials)
Let's Get Heretical (Poems)
Dramatic Monologue (Poems)
Be Pedantic (Poems)
Close Listening (Poems)
Playing with Genre (Plays)
Talk Show Host (Plays)
Staging the Scene (Plays)
Adaptation (Plays)
Soliloquy (Plays)

Moving Scenes (Plays)
Translating Sonnets (Genres)
Mixtape Maker (Genres)
The Blank Syllabus (Canons)
Keywords (Words)
Imitate This (Styles)
Convolution (Styles)
Digital Literacy (Pictures)
Poetry Broadside Gallery (Objects)
Online Commonplace Book (Objects)
Object Lesson (Objects)
Chekhov's Gun (Objects)

General Index

· ·